CLASSICS IN THEORY

General Editors

BROOKE A. HOLMES

MIRIAM LEONARD   TIM WHITMARSH

CLASSICS IN THEORY

Classics in Theory explores the new directions for classical scholarship opened up by critical theory. Inherently interdisciplinary, the series creates a forum for the exchange of ideas between classics, anthropology, modern literature, philosophy, psychoanalysis, politics, and other related fields. Invigorating and agenda-setting volumes analyse the cross-fertilizations between theory and classical scholarship and set out a vision for future work on the productive intersections between the ancient world and contemporary thought.

Narratology

Genevieve Liveley

OXFORD
UNIVERSITY PRESS

OXFORD
UNIVERSITY PRESS

Great Clarendon Street, Oxford, OX2 6DP,
United Kingdom

Oxford University Press is a department of the University of Oxford.
It furthers the University's objective of excellence in research, scholarship,
and education by publishing worldwide. Oxford is a registered trade mark of
Oxford University Press in the UK and in certain other countries

Published in the United States of America by Oxford University Press
198 Madison Avenue, New York, NY 10016, United States of America

British Library Cataloguing in Publication Data
Data available

Library of Congress Control Number: 2018957733

ISBN 978-0-19-968770-1

Printed and bound in Great Britain by
Clays Ltd, Elcograf S.p.A.

For Tulip

■ ACKNOWLEDGEMENTS

I gratefully acknowledge permission from Jim Phelan to reproduce a short extract from his 2007 essay 'Rhetoric/Ethics', published in David Herman (ed.), *The Cambridge Companion to Narrative*, Cambridge: Cambridge University Press, pp. 203–16.

I am also grateful to the University of Bristol's Institute for Advanced Studies for funding a period of research leave in 2013/14 which allowed a substantial portion of the book to be completed. Thanks too to Bristol's Faculty of Arts Research Fund and its School of Humanities for supporting a Visiting Fellowship at the University of Ohio's Project Narrative Institute in the summer of 2015. This book owes much to the insights of the 'Ohio School'—to Jim Phelan, Angus Fletcher, Sean O'Sullivan, and the participants of the 2015 Project Narrative Summer School, especially Rae Muhlstock and Greta Matzner-Gore. I am also indebted to Leon Golden for discussing his landmark translation of the *Poetics* with me and to Tim Whitmarsh for his generous readings of the draft manuscript. Thank you.

My grateful thanks are also owed to a number of my colleagues at Bristol: Ruth Coates for advice on translating various Russian texts; Lyndsay Coo for steering me away from too many misreadings of the Greek; Emma Hammond and Natalie Swain for also appreciating the Russian formalists (and much more besides); and Rob Crowe for his gimlet eye.

Finally, my thanks to Alex Wardrop, and to Lynette and Alex Hibbert for being so delightful. And, above all, to Richard and Tulip Huxtable—for everything.

▨ CONTENTS

1 Introduction

> *The story goes: In the beginning there was Aristotle who theorized*
> *"plot", then there came the novelists who theorized their own plots,*
> *then after some false starts (Propp, Benjamin, Bakhtin) narrative*
> *theory really took off with narratology (the structuralist-led "science*
> *of narrative"). However, like the dinosaurs, narratologists died out*
> *and were replaced by more mobile, covert forms of narrative theory*
> *within a "post-structuralist" diaspora. Narrative theory lives on,*
> *embedded in the work and tropes of post-structuralism.*
>
> Martin McQuillan, 'Aporias of writing: Narrative and
> subjectivity' (2000: xi)

In the beginning there was Aristotle...That's how one version of the
story goes, anyway.[1] Other tales and other tellers remind us that before
there was Aristotle there was Plato. And after Aristotle there came
Horace (and 'Longinus', and Dionysius of Halicarnassus, and Quintilian,
and Demetrius). Later, while the Anglo-American novelists were busy
plotting, the revolutionary Russian formalists were busy separating
fabula from *syuzhet*, discourse time from story time, and 'free' from
'bound' motifs, in their endeavours to develop a formalist 'science' of
literary poetics. What's more, before there were French structuralists
there were Chicago neo-Aristotelians, also inviting us to see narratology as a 'science' and pointing to 'grammatical structure' as the key to
understanding the formal mechanics and dynamics of story as discourse, as a purposive communication act.[2] And while the meteor
strike of poststructuralism may have wiped out most of the heavier
beasts of structuralism, the adaptive neo-Aristotelians have not merely
survived but thrived in the ensuing narratological 'rhetorocene' era.

---

[1] As Mezei 1996: 2 trenchantly observes: 'The his/story of narratology, like any story,
rather depends on who the narrator is.' Herman 1999 locates the origins of narratology with
the 'classical' structuralist project of the 1960s and documents the evolution of narrative
theory only back thus far. Fludernik 2005a (following Fehn, Hoesterey, and Tatat 1992)
acknowledges a prestructuralist 'archaic' period of narratology that begins with Henry
James, Percy Lubbock, and E. M. Forster.

[2] Crane 1953: 168–9: 'Before we can understand a poem as an artistic structure we must
understand it as a grammatical structure.'

Their interdisciplinary Aristotelian DNA has also helped them to live happily alongside newer postclassical narratological species.[3]

In their 2002 mapping of the evolution of these various new narratologies, Ansgar and Vera Nünning drew up a shortlist of topics warranting further future investigation, including among them an appeal for more research into the history of narratology.[4] So far, that call has been answered with new studies into the Russian formalists, the Prague school, and the German tradition of *Erzähltheorie*.[5] This book aims to extend the history of narratology beyond these early twentieth-century precursors to 'classical' structuralist narratology by going back further still—into the ancient world and to the earliest 'classical' origins of narrative theory.

The reception history that it tells offers some remarkable plot twists. We unmask Plato as an unreliable narrator and theorist, noting the absence of anything like a 'Platonic' theory of narrative in his *Ion* and *Republic*. We uncover Aristotle not only distinguishing between plot and story, but anticipating the Russian formalists' interest in story motifs, Barthes's interest in narrative nuclei, and Chatman's in story kernels. We also get a rare glimpse of Aristotle himself putting narrative theory into practice in the role of storyteller in his fragmentary work *On Poets*. In Horace's *Ars Poetica* we find a rhetorically conceived poetics and a sophisticated reader-response-based narratology evincing a keen interest in audience affect and cognition. And amongst the ancient scholia critics and commentators we come across untimely appreciation for such modern narratological concepts as variant, deviant, and embedded focalization, and for sundry forms of anachrony (including 'repeating' and 'completing' analepsis). These ancient theorists and critics turn out to have a specialist narratological lexicon as rich (and as vexing) as anything dreamt up by their modern counterparts too.

Those modern counterparts have no less fascinating stories of their own to tell regarding the ancient world of narrative theory. In many of these stories, Plato and Aristotle are characterized—mythologized even—as figures of ancient authority and atemporal wisdom. Their intuitions as narratologists *avant la lettre* provide credibility and philosophical integrity to the new 'science' of narratology—not only in its

---

[3] For a survey of the latest neo-narratologies see the range of entries in Hühn et al. 2014. Cf. also Fludernik 2005a, Prince 1995, Nünning and Nünning 2002, and Onega and Landa 1996: 12–35.

[4] Nünning 2003: 239–75. Cf. Nünning and Nünning 2002.

[5] On the Russian formalists see Schmid 2009a; on the Prague school see Schmid 2009b; on the German narratological tradition see Cornils and Schernus 2003, and Fludernik and Margolin 2004.

formalist and structuralist first phases but in some of the latest 'postclassical' neo-narratologies too.[6] In the storytelling mode that characterizes most narratological discourse (ancient and modern) Plato and Aristotle are figured in various aetiologies as pioneers, as patrons, as ancestors, as donors—sometimes of nothing more than a magical name with which to conjure. They are accordingly cast in traditional plots in which the maturity of any new narratological hero is proved by leaving these father figures dead at a convenient crossroads. As Russian formalist and literary historian Yury Tynyanov, reflecting on the place of formalism within the literary-critical tradition, suggested in 1921:[7]

When one speaks of "literary tradition" or "succession"...usually one implies a certain kind of direct line uniting the younger and older representatives of a known literary branch. Yet the matter is much more complicated. There is no continuing line; there is rather a departure, a pushing away from the known point—a struggle...Any literary succession is first of all a struggle, a destruction of old values and a reconstruction of old elements.

We are familiar with the Bloomian notion that poets are supposed to fight against their literary predecessors in an Oedipal struggle to make their own mark, but Tynyanov reminds us that literary critics and theorists may do the same.[8] Indeed, Tynyanov himself is here struggling to make space for his own ideas by pushing against those of fellow formalist Viktor Shklovsky—especially Shklovsky's theory of 'defamiliarization' (*ostranenie*), the process by which poets (and theorists and critics) are supposed to innovate within and against the constraints of literary tradition. Actually, Tynyanov and Shklovsky have very similar views on this and on poetics more broadly; they clearly descend from the same lineage and belong to the same formalist family. But Tynyanov seeks to 'push away' from this familiarity, not least of all by overemphasizing his own innovation and difference—even if that departure from tradition itself leads to a kind of return through 'a reconstruction of old elements'.

In the reception history of narratological poetics these familial and Oedipal patterns tend to recur, with Plato and Aristotle all too frequently embraced and then subsequently pushed away and pushed against—even though the attempted 'destruction of old values' may end up facilitating their reconstruction. As David Richter puts it: 'Like the novel, literary

---

[6] Cf. Ryan 1999.

[7] Tynyanov 1921 quoted in Eichenbaum 1965: 134.

[8] See Bloom 1973 and on Bloomian models in the classical reception tradition see especially Martindale 1993.

criticism is an institutional form, whose continuities may be sought in a tradition of common assumptions and problems, and whose evolutionary change is the history of experimental innovations seeking new forms of inquiry and new modes of explanation.'[9]

Framing these local familial plots of cross-generational inheritance and innovation, larger narratological aetiologies and genealogies have tended to place Plato and/or Aristotle at the base of a great (partheno-genic) family tree. Higher up, significant boughs are seen to branch off in various directions (Russian formalism, neo-Aristotelianism, structuralism), each with their own bifurcating offshoots (Prague formalism, rhetorical-narratological poetics, poststructuralism). In these genealogically con-ceived narratives, less emphasis is placed upon conflict or resistance and more upon continuity or resemblance.[10] David Herman offers us one such genealogy, emphasizing the fact that the structuralists were rather less 'revolutionary' than their 1966 manifesto proclaimed, and that their project represented less of a hostile bifurcation than a sympathetic convergence of pre-existing critical theories and traditions.[11] Indeed, the (Foucauldian) genealogical metaphor that Herman uses in his account of the structuralist reception of ideas first mooted by German morphologists, Russian formalists, New Critics, and neo-Aristotelians is explicitly (re)configured in this narrative as part of a plot:[12]

to uncover forgotten interconnections; reestablish obscured or unacknowledged lines of descent; expose relationships between institutions, belief-systems, dis-courses, or modes of analysis that might otherwise be taken to be wholly distinct and unrelated... to situate recent theories of narrative in a complex lineage, a network of historical and conceptual affiliations, and thereby underscore how those theories constitute less a singular continuous tradition of research than a cluster of developments marked by family resemblances.

As such genealogical models suggest, these plots are readily incorporated into an even larger 'grand narrative'—structured along the lines of a

---

[9] Richter 1982: 48.
[10] By a common focus, for example, upon literary discourse *qua* discourse, as speech act, enunciation, rhetorical communication, or variants thereon. Cf. Onega and Landa 1996: 26, who see the Russian formalists, New Critics, the Chicago school, and the structuralists as akin in forwarding 'theories of enunciation'.
[11] Herman 2005: 20.
[12] Herman 2005: 20–1. Cf. Herman 2005: 31 citing Hill 1998: 1: 'History, according to genealogists, is not teleological... They cannot identify a goal of a historical process, and then go on to show how it gradually emerged from its embryonic beginnings. Rather, they chart the processes that, by contingent confluence, produce a contemporary result. Hence the metaphor: no individual is the goal of a family history. Rather, a family is a vast fabric of relationships, and any one individual represents only one among many confluences of past lines of descent.'

(phylogenetic) evolutionary tree—which sees the history of a 'species' of literary theory and criticism like narratology in terms of its quasi-Darwinian evolution.[13]

It is precisely according to the pattern of this grandest of narratives that we find the transformation of 'narratology' into 'narrative theory' plotted in Martin McQuillan's version of narratology's history in this chapter's epigraph. In keeping with Darwin's own careful attention to evolutionary culs-de-sac and *aporiae*, McQuillan even includes some of the 'false starts' that emerge in this appropriately ateleological story of the 'origin of the species' before describing how the literary-critical equivalent of natural selection processes brought about the extinction of the structuralist dinosaurs, remnants of their DNA surviving in more adaptable poststructuralist species.[14]

Although both Herman and McQuillan carefully avoid plotting these histories of narratology as teleological, their respective genealogical and evolutionary patterning necessarily imposes a narrative sequence upon them. They choose different beginnings, but move through similar middles towards identical ends: both stories covertly privilege the developments of the latest postclassical or poststructuralist phase of narrative theory with its rich interdisciplinary plurality and *narratologies*. And they are not alone. Monica Fludernik, eschewing an explicitly genealogical or evolutionary plot structure for her 2005 history of narratology, bases it instead upon an analogously organic model of human biology. One of her classically troped plots for this history narrates 'The rise and fall of narratology' from its structuralist birth in the 1960s, through its maturation in the 1980s, followed by its terminal decline and death in the 1990s; a second plot describes 'The rise and rise of narrative *theory*' from its structuralist 'adolescence' through its ongoing growth and maturity in a poststructuralist phase, and its flourishing 'diversification of narrative theories' in the twenty-first century.[15] Whether genealogical, evolutionary, or both, teleological narrative structures imposing organically conceived beginnings, middles, and ends upon these narratological histories are hard to avoid, it seems.

[13] For an alternative mapping of narratology's genealogy see Darby 2001, who emphasizes difference and schism rather than continuity and evolution, positing a fundamental split between the Germanic tradition of *Erzähltheorie* and the broad American-French structuralist/poststructuralist tradition. On the cognitively delimiting narrative dynamics of such Darwinian models see Abbott 2003.

[14] McQuillan 2000: xi. De Jong 2014: 11 also uses this DNA metaphor. Cf. Morson 1999: 292–3, for whom Darwin's '*Origin of Species* stresses the messiness, historicity, and timeliness (not timelessness) of things . . . [and] imagines a world of constant small adjustments accumulating without plan, of adaptations tripping over earlier adaptations.'

[15] Fludernik 2005a: 36–7.

Yet literary histories, like other stories, are not neatly structured with the clearly defined beginnings, middles, and ends that Aristotle prescribed for plots in his *Poetics*. Indeed, the monstrous literary chimera that Horace describes in his *Ars poetica* might offer a better model to illustrate the shape of narratology's strange history, in its fusion of incongruous yet congruous parts joining together to make up a whole. Thus, the story this book sets out to tell about narratology recognizes the impossibility of turning a reception history of narrative poetics spanning more than two thousand years into a perfect plot. It attempts instead to tell a good story.

Narratology and its theorists, ancient and modern, have at least equipped us well to recognize and describe the operations and phenomena associated with such a telling.[16] Just as any storytelling involves making choices, selecting some characters and events at the expense of others, offering detailed descriptions and analyses of some features and elliptically passing over others, lingering over some moments and speeding through the rest, so the reception history offered here presents a particular focalized and emplotted narrative. Its emphasis is upon the destruction of old values and the reconstruction of old elements. The German morphologists, the Prague Circle, the Tel Aviv school, and key figures such as Mikhail Bakhtin, Jonathan Culler, Käte Hamburger, and Paul Ricoeur receive less attention than they deserve. Nor does this reception history tell the full story of narratology and genre, or of narratology and historiography—both rich and complex narratives in their own right.

And just as any narrative involves, in Jim Phelan's useful formulation, 'somebody telling somebody else on some occasion and for some purposes that something happened', the story I tell here has a particular 'somebody' in mind as its intended audience.[17] In fact, I have two somebodies: classicists and narratologists.[18]

---

[16] Some narratologists engage playfully with this idea: Herman, in the introduction to his own genealogical 'overview', first selects key moments or chapters in the history of narratology on which to 'focus' and then 'zoom[s] out to reveal the broader contexts' (2005: 20). De Jong 2014 offers a 'birds-eye view of the history of narratology' (3–6).

[17] Phelan 2015: 146.

[18] Because of this double focus, Greek and Latin has been kept to a minimum but ancient terms are used contextually throughout, while narratological terminology is similarly glossed and variants explained. All translations are my own unless otherwise indicated. Readings and translations of Plato's *Republic* are based on Slings 2003; Plato's *Ion* and *Phaedrus* on Burnet 1903; Aristotle's *Poetics* on Halliwell 1999; Aristotle's *On Poets* on Janko 2011; Aristotle's *Homeric Problems* on Rose 1886; Horace's *Ars poetica* on Rudd 1989; the Greek scholia on Erbse 1969–88 and van Thiel 2000; Servius on Thilo and Hagen 2011. On narratology's notorious terminological complexity see Toolan 1988: 9–11.

In the last thirty years the tools and terms of narratology have been taken up eagerly by classicists and have inspired many productive readings of a broad range of texts, from epic to elegy, ancient historiography to the ancient novel.[19] Massimo Fusillo's Genettean readings have revolutionized the study of the ancient novel. Irene de Jong has used Bal's narratological methodology to demonstrate how complex subjectivities and embedded focalization characterize Homeric narrative. John Winkler has put Barthes to expert use in his narratological readings of Apuleius. Stephen Wheeler has used Genette's theory of 'narrative levels' to expose new dimensions to the embedded tales-within-tales of Ovid's *Metamorphoses*. The fruitful merging of narratology with psychoanalytically informed theories of reading and reader response (inspired by Peter Brooks's influential work) has opened up further avenues leading to new narratological approaches to textual analysis—particularly in Latin literature: David Quint's landmark study, *Epic and Empire*, and Duncan Kennedy's characteristically nuanced readings of Latin love elegy have both used Brooks's model to release fresh insights into Latin poetry.[20] Although, as Mieke Bal appropriately warns, narratology is not 'some kind of machine into which one inserts a text at one end and expects an adequate description to roll out at the other', classicists have been relatively quick to test the potential of this new system of textual analysis, welcoming not only its taxonomies and technical vocabularies but the interpretative insights it can help to yield.[21]

For a much longer period of time narratologists have looked to the classics for equivalent insights. Successive waves in the modern history of narratology have seen each new generation of narratologists developing their own stories about how narratives and narrativity works, based upon the basic plots and precepts established in antiquity by Plato and Aristotle.[22]

---

[19] Cf. Fowler 2001: 68: 'Narratology...is an approach which has been taken up and adapted even by classicists relatively hostile to theory: terms like "prolepsis", "intradiegetic", and "focalization" are now as familiar to classical scholars as such non-jargon terms as "syllepsis", "propemptikon", or "prosopopoia".'

[20] See de Jong 2014 for an extremely useful overview (with bibliographies) of narratologically informed close readings of ancient Greek epic, historiography, and drama. On the ancient novel see Fusillo 1985, Winkler 1985, and Whitmarsh 2011; on the narrativity of Greek hymns see Faulkner and Hodkinson 2015. On Roman epic see especially Wheeler 1999 and 2000, Fowler 2000, Barchiesi 2001 and 1994, Rosati 2002, and Nikolopoulos 2004; on didactic see Gale 2004; on Roman historiography see Pausch 2011, Pelling 2009, Hardie 2009, and the essays collected in Liotsakis and Farrington 2016; on elegy see Liveley and Salzman-Mitchell 2008; and on lyric see Lowrie 1997.

[21] Bal 1997: 3–4.

[22] To avoid the unnecessarily complex spectrum of terminologies suggested by some in this field, I use the terms narratology and narrative theory as broadly interchangeable—and

This book sets out to examine the ways in which those ancient theories of narrative have been (re)shaped in and by these narratological stories. Following a broadly chronolinear narrative of reception, so as to better identify patterns of cause and effect or appropriation and resistance (whilst remaining vigilant for *post hoc ergo propter hoc* syllogisms) each chapter selects a key moment in the history of narratology on which to focus, zooming in from an overview of significant phases to look at core theories and texts. Its aim is not to argue that modern narratologies simply present 'old wine in new wineskins', but rather to stress the diachronic affinities shared between ancient and modern stories about storytelling. It seeks to highlight the distinctive contribution that classical poetics has made to modern narratology, at the same time recognizing that narratologists bring particular expertise to bear upon ancient literary theory and that their reception and readings can offer valuable insights into the interpretation of these notoriously difficult texts.

Its 'final cause' and overarching thesis, though, is the argument that a more joined-up appreciation of the familial, genealogical, phylogenetic relationships so widely argued to exist between ancient and modern theories of narrative helps us to better understand both species. For every literary theory and history both shapes and is shaped by its canon. As Geoffrey Hartman observed:[23] 'To take the metaphysical poets as one's base or touchstone and to extend their "poetics" toward modern poetry and then all poetry, will produce a very different result from working from Cervantes toward Pyncheon, or from Hölderlin toward Heidegger.' Aristotle's decision to take tragedy as his touchstone and to extend its poetics to explain all other kinds of (mimetic) poetry will have produced a very different result than if he had chosen Aristophanes' absurdist comedy or Sappho's lyric poetry instead.[24] Twentieth-century 'classical' narratology would have produced a very different set of results if it had chosen Roman rhetoric or Hellenistic poetics as its starting point. In choosing Plato and Aristotle—alongside Homer and the broader canon of classics—as among their foundational touchstones, modern narratology is similarly moulded by these parts of its canon, its own structures patterned by those exhibited in these objects of study.

---

do not reserve 'narratology' to describe only the 'structuralist' phase of narratological history. Cf. Nünning 2003 and Fludernik 2005a.

[23] Hartman 1980: 299, cited in Rabinowitz 1987: 10. This point is also well made by feminist narratologists: see Chapter 10.3.

[24] Cf. Richardson 2015: 95–8 on 'unnatural narrative' and ostensibly 'plotless' comedy in the ancient world (especially Aristophanes and Lucian).

We find a prime example of this in the ubiquitous presence of binary paradigms throughout this reception history. Beginning (in this plot) with Plato's Socrates' distinction between *logos* and *lexis* (the subject and style, or content and form of narrative discourse), and catalysed by Aristotle's direct response to the binary distinction apparently drawn between *diegesis* and *mimesis* in Plato's *Republic*, analogous binary oppositions come to dominate modern narratives about narrative.[25] Aristotle and Plato lead the treatment and taxonomy of narrative discourse in terms of its *muthos* and *logos*, plot and story, *syuzhet* and *fabula*, *histoire* and *discours* by subsequent generations of modern narratologists. Variations on Aristotle's Neoplatonic (or neo-Socratic) binarism form the bedrock of narrative theory from Russian formalism to poststructuralism.[26] And this pervasive binarism in narrative theory is only significantly challenged by the deconstructive neo-narratologies of recent years. Postclassical narratologies show that concepts of plot and story, based upon clear distinctions between the tale and its telling, are not always viable or reliable. Brian Richardson's theory of 'unnatural' narrativity, in particular, reminds us that there is nothing universal, transhistorical, or 'natural' about the dynamics of story and plot, of *lexis* and *logos*, *mimesis* and *diegesis*—or about any of the binaries shaping the theories and models of narrative that have dominated Western poetics since Plato.[27] By interrogating ancient and modern narratologies through the mutually imbricating dynamics of their reception, then, I hope that we may arrive at a better understanding of both.

[25] See Lloyd 1984 on the prevalence of such binary structures in Greek thought.

[26] For Fludernik 2005a: 38 the (Saussurean) foundation and legacy of structuralist narratology is 'the structure of binary opposition'. Cf. Gibson 1996.

[27] See especially Lowe 2000. Cf. Richardson 2002: 48–9 and Fludernik 1996: 333–7. On the radically different priorities and poetics of ancient Eastern narratologies, see Hogan and Pandit 2005.

2 Ancient narrative theory before Aristotle—Plato

> Socrates: I seem to be a ridiculous and obscure teacher, someone unable to express himself clearly.
>
> Plato, *Republic* 3.392d

2.1 *Arche*

Given the great many fictions, myths, and misreadings perpetuated about Plato's role in the history of narratology, a twenty-first-century Socrates might be justified in seeking to bar narratologists and literary theorists as well as poets and storytellers from his ideal city. At one extreme, Plato is simply overlooked, overshadowed by Aristotle's star billing in the role of the 'ultimate historical ancestor of narratology'.[1] At the other, Plato is credited with the recognition and anticipation of several of the foundational concepts of narratology: the first to identify the basics of genre theory, the first to recognize the implications of 'showing' versus 'telling', and the first to distinguish the mediating role of the narrator.[2] Drawing a direct connection between some of the earliest and the latest narratological conversations, Ioana Schaeffer and Jean Marie Vultur even identify Plato's concerns regarding the psychological dangers of *mimesis* as initiating contemporary narratological debates upon the effects of 'immersion' in virtual reality and interactive digital storyworlds.[3] The true story of Plato's role as narratology's founding father, however, is more mixed than any of these accounts allow.

---

[1] Cobley 2012: 348. Cf. McQuillan 2000.

[2] Margolin 2014: 647 argues for all of these as Platonic innovations. Kearns 2005: 201 and Pyrhönen 2007: 110 also trace the origins of genre theory back to Plato. Chatman 1978: 32 and 146 sees Plato's distinction between *mimesis* and *diegesis* as a distinction between showing and telling, and concludes from this Plato's invention of the narrator role ('insofar as there is telling, there must be a teller, a narrating voice'). Barthes 1966 and Fludernik 2005b: 559 see in Plato the first theory of speech representation. Cohn 1978: 78 credits the first allusion to 'interior language, inner speech, endophasy' to Plato.

[3] See Schaeffer and Vultur 2005: 238.

The impetus for the readings and representations of Plato as proto-narratological pioneer comes largely from the discussion of *diegesis* in Book 3 of the *Republic* 3.392c–398b, where Plato's character Socrates infamously observes (*Republic* 3.392d) that storytellers employ:

either simple narration (*haple diegesis*), or narration through imitation (*dia mimeseos*), or a mix of the two (*di' amphoteron*).

He goes on to illustrate this key formula by rewriting a well-known passage of mixed *diegesis* (*diegesis di' amphoteron*) from Homer's *Iliad* as simple narration (*haple diegesis*), transforming its 'mimetic' parts (*diegesis dia mimeseos*)—that is, its character speech—into narrated summary (*Republic* 3.392e–393d).[4] In turn, we find the summary of Socrates' tripartite typology of narrative itself subsequently being rewritten and transformed in modern narratological theory and scholarship.

H. Porter Abbott in his 2002 *Cambridge Introduction to Narrative* offers a fairly representative (mis)reading of Socrates' observations on the relationship between *mimesis* and *diegesis* as outlined in the *Republic*:[5]

According to Plato, *mimesis* is one of the two major ways to convey a narrative, the other being *diegesis* or the representation of an action by telling. By this distinction, plays are mimetic, epic poems are diegetic.

Here (and in numerous like readings) we see the *Republic*'s ideas about *mimesis* and *diegesis* being mapped on to modern narratological models of 'showing' and 'telling'—categories which play no part in the ancient discussion itself.[6] Yet there is not, as we will see, any neat diametric distinction between two narrative modes of *diegesis* and *mimesis*, between narration and dialogue, or between 'telling' and 'showing' to be found anywhere in Plato's writings.[7]

---

[4] Discussed more fully below, section 2.3.

[5] Porter Abbott 2002: 237. See also 2002: 75 where he defines *diegesis* as the term 'which Plato originally used to refer to the telling, rather than the acting, of stories'; and 2002: 231 where *diegesis*, he argues, 'goes back to Plato's distinction between two ways of presenting a story: as *mimesis* (acted) or as *diegesis* (told)'. Cf. Herman and Vervaeck 2005: 14, for whom '*Mimesis* evokes reality by staging it... [while] *Diegesis* summarizes events and conversations'. They direct their readers not to Plato but to Rimmon-Kenan (1983: 106–8) for confirmation of this interpretation of the *Republic* (2005: 181 n. 6). See Fludernik 1993: 27 for a more considered approach and a reminder that 'the dichotomy of *diegesis* vs *mimesis* tends to conflate... the grammatical issue of indirect vs direct discourse with the epic vs dramatic generic distinction a la Plato'.

[6] Cf. Chatman 1978: 32, Fludernik 2009: 64, Genette 1980: 164 and 1988: 17–18, Kirby 1991: 118.

[7] See de Jong 2005a: 19: 'It has become customary in narratological scholarship to equate Lubbock's famous opposition of "showing vs telling" with Plato's *mimesis* vs *diegesis*.' Cf. Prince 2003: 20.

While it may be true that Plato's *Ion* (written *c*.390 BCE) and Book 3 of the *Republic* (written *c*.375 BCE) both demonstrate proto-narratological concerns with the subject (*logos*) and style (*lexis*) or content and form of narrative discourse, alongside concerns with narrative affect and ethics, there is no systematic theory of narrative per se in either dialogue.[8] Nor is the incidental treatment of narrative that we do find in these dialogues consistent with Plato's own practice or the treatment of stories elsewhere in his writings.[9] Indeed, there is no such thing as a 'Platonic' theory of narrative.[10]

2.2 **Plato's *Ion***

In an early dialogue questioning the art or *techne* of poetry Plato offers an outline of the approach to stories and storytelling that we will subsequently encounter in the *Republic*, anticipating in particular some of the views about narrative *logos* and *lexis*, audience and affect that we see explored there.[11] In the *Ion*, Socrates makes the point that all poets essentially deal with the same core story content and material (*Ion* 531c–532a): Homer, Hesiod, and all the other poets, he says, tell stories about the same things—war, human society, the interactions of men, and of gods, their experiences in heaven and in the underworld, the lives of gods and heroes. But Ion insists that Homer does not treat this material in the same way as the other poets; he does not make the same kind of poetry out of the raw story stuff from which all these storytellers draw. The implication here is that in the poetic reworking of traditional story

[8] See Halliwell 2009: 41: '[T]here is no fully integrated theory of narrative, let alone anything we can call "Plato's theory" of narrative, to be found at *Republic* 3.392c–8b.'

[9] One of the many problems of Plato's supposed theory of narrative concerns its contradictory relation to his actual narrative *praxis*. Plato frequently has Socrates deploy myths and stories in his dialogues, among them: traditional *muthoi* such as the myth of Gyges (*Republic* 359d–360b), the myth of Phaethon (*Timaeus* 22c 7), the Amazons (*Laws* 804e 4); and *muthoi* apparently of Plato's own invention such as the myth of Er (*Republic* 621b 8), the myth of Theuth (*Phaedrus* 274c–275e), and the myth of Atlantis (*Timaeus* 26e 4). On Plato's use of myths and narrative see Brisson 1998 and Partenie 2009.

[10] Not all readings of Plato fall so wide of the mark: Rabinowitz 2005: 29 and Schneider 2005: 484 see in Plato's *Republic* and *Ion* an early narratological concern with audiences and reader response; Phelan 2014: 534–5, Korthals-Altes 2005: 142, and Booth 1961: 385 see an anticipation of narrative ethics: 'In *Ion* . . . Plato contends that poetry has inherent deficiencies in the ethics of the telling that can lead to deficiencies in the ethics of the told' (Phelan 2014: 535).

[11] As Fowler notes (2001: 65), to describe an ancient text or reading as 'anticipating' a later response is to highlight the omnipresence of plots and plotting in our own discourse and scholarly storytelling.

material (as distinct from invented stories) there exist two narrative levels: (1) the invariable stuff of story, held in common by all poets (*logos*); and (2) its variable treatment in individual stories told by particular poets (*lexis*). Plato's *Ion*, it seems, recognizes that there exists a distinction between basic story material and its emplotted treatment— but does not find this distinction between content and form particularly interesting.

For Socrates' principal concern in the *Ion* is not with form and composition but with the effects and affects of narrative. Looking forward to the ethical critique of poetry that we find in the *Republic*, in the *Ion*, too, Plato's Socrates articulates the view that poetry and narrative is ethically compromised and compromising because of the psychological and emotional impact upon its audiences. An important part of his understanding of the cognitive processes associated with storytelling in general involves the assumption that narrative is processed emotionally rather than intellectually. This potentially leads its agents and audiences to eschew logic and reason—as evidenced by the ways in which a particularly affective narrative and its performance can cause both narrator and audience to experience strong emotions, as if they were themselves suffering or witnessing the events being represented. As Socrates' storytelling interlocutor Ion reveals (*Ion* 535c–e):[12]

Ion: Whenever I tell of sad/pitiable things, my eyes fill with tears; and whenever I tell of fearful or terrible things, my hair bristles with terror, and my heart leaps...Each time I look down upon the audience from up on the stage I see them crying and looking fearful in sympathetic amazement with my telling.

For Plato's Socrates, such a reaction is not only irrational and illogical but psychologically and ethically dangerous. Socrates argues that, for a man to feel terror or pity when in perfect safety and surrounded by friendly faces, he must be 'out of his right mind' (*Ion* 535d). Socrates famously likens the irresistible power of poetry to draw men into this irrational state to the magnetic powers of a lodestone, to which poet, rhapsode, and audience successively surrender their reason—effectively and affectively 'magnetized' like the links in an iron chain (*Ion* 535e–356b). Although the point isn't fully developed here, Socrates' objection to the affectivity of storytelling is not limited to the risk of poet, rhapsode, and audience member potentially being not 'in his or her own mind'

---

[12] Cf. *Ion* 535b, where Socrates lists some examples of especially thrilling narratives (all of which are taken from his favourite poet, Homer): 'the lay of Odysseus [*Odyssey* 22]... Achilles attacking Hector [*Iliad* 22.312–66], or some part of the sad story of Andromache [*Iliad* 6.370–502 and 22.437–515], or of Hecuba [*Iliad* 22.430–6 and 24.747–59], or of Priam [*Iliad* 22.408–28 and 24.144–717]'.

(*emphron*: *Ion* 535b) but extends also to the risk of being in the mind of someone else—that is, to the psychological identification and empathy with other, especially undesirable, characters. The anxiety seems to stem from a wider principle (found throughout Plato's writings) concerning the ethical merits of unity and simplicity in social interaction, employment, and discourse, and in the concomitant ethical drawbacks aligned with multiplicity and plurality.[13] Socrates' criticism of Ion that he is 'a perfect Proteus in taking on every kind of shape' (*Ion* 541e) in adopting several different characters, viewpoints, and voices in his performances illustrates this principle well. Ion's identification with and impersonation of a full cast of characters (including slaves and women) compromises his own identity, *and* puts his audience at similar risk.

However, the form in which this key criticism is presented to us somewhat undermines its authority. For Plato, just like Ion, is also 'a perfect Proteus' (*Ion* 541e) in adopting several different characters, viewpoints, and voices in his philosophical dialogues. Here he not only plays the role of his philosophical hero Socrates but also the potentially compromising role of that Protean performer Ion. Just as Ion has memorized the words of Homer and aims faithfully to reproduce them in his performances, Plato has—or so he invites us to (dis)believe—memorized the words of Socrates and aims faithfully to reproduce them in *his* performances. What is more, in the *Symposium* (215b–216a), Alcibiades describes Socrates and his words as possessing just the same kind of 'magnetism' and irresistible force of attraction that Ion's poetry is supposed to have—and with the same kind of effects upon his audience too.

We should be wary of taking Plato's criticisms of poetry and poets at face value, then, and proceed cautiously when setting out to establish the principles on which he grounds his 'proto-narratology' both in the *Ion* and the *Republic*.

2.3 **Plato's** *Republic*

In many respects, the *Ion* serves as a prequel to Plato's more expansive—and more influential—treatment of narrative in Book 3 of his *Republic*, although Socrates does not pick up or expand upon his suggestion in the *Ion* that there exists an art or *techne* of poetry (*Ion* 532c). Instead,

---

[13] See Too 1998: 66–9 for a discussion of Socrates' 'privileging of simplicity and uniformity' in all things, including music, poetry, and speech.

continuing a discussion in Book 2 of the *Republic* concerning the legitimate and illegitimate content of stories, the key discussion of narrative in Book 3 opens with Socrates drawing a distinction between *logos* (the subject of discourse, or *what* is said) and *lexis* (the style of discourse, or *how* it is said) so as to better understand 'both the matter (*logos*) and the manner (*lexis*) of speech' (*Republic* 3.392c). As in the *Ion*, Plato assigns to his Socrates an a priori intuition that there are at least two fundamental tiers to narrative discourse—that is, a distinction between content and form.

He describes that narrative form as *diegesis*, observing that that 'all mythology and poetry is a narration (*diegesis*) of events, either past, present, or to come' (*Republic* 3.392d).[14] This clarification that *diegesis* basically comprises a form of temporally plotted discourse provides us with an important gloss on the term *diegesis* as it will be used as a technical term throughout Book 3 of the *Republic*.[15] Here, crucially, *diegesis* does not refer to a type or mode of narration but to narrative discourse broadly conceived.[16] This fundamental point is re-confirmed when Socrates makes his oft-cited observation (*Republic* 3.392d) that storytellers may employ 'either simple narration (*haple diegesis*), or narration through imitation (*dia mimeseos*), or a mix of the two (*di' amphoteron*)'. This tripartite subdivision distinguishes between two main forms of narrative (*diegesis*): 'plain', 'unmixed', or 'simple' (*haple diegesis*); and 'mimetic' or 'through imitation' (*diegesis dia mimeseos*). Socrates also allows for a third, hybrid form of narrative, blending or interchanging the two primary forms of *diegesis*: 'mixed', 'compound', or 'through both forms' (*diegesis di' amphoteron*).

Socrates' typology does not straightforwardly contrast *diegesis* with *mimesis*, then, but instead outlines three variant types of *diegesis* (narrative), qualified with descriptive modifiers: 'simple', 'mimetic', and 'mixed'. These qualifiers are fundamental to a proper appreciation of Socrates' ensuing account of the relative styles and merits of 'simple' narrative (*haple diegesis*) and 'mimetic' narrative (*diegesis dia mimeseos*) but they have too often been overlooked in the narratological reception

[14] Despite his own frequent use of 'philosophical' myths and narratives, Plato's use of the term *muthos* or *muthologos* typically carries pejorative undertones: a *muthos* is a myth, story, fable, or narrative *fiction*, a mimetic product which more or less closely re-presents an external truth, a falsehood by definition.
[15] See Halliwell 2009: 18.
[16] Halliwell 2009: 18 n. 6 refers to this as 'the genus *diegesis*': 'Modern narratological usage of "*diegesis*" etc. has, of course, several variants, complicated by the French distinction between "diégèse" and "diégésis"... But it remains an error to use "diegesis" *tout court* for one species rather than the genus when paraphrasing R. 392c–4c.'

of *Republic* 3—that is, studies which read and summarize *Republic* 3 straightforwardly as an embryonic theory of narrative.[17] To say that Socrates distinguishes simply between *mimesis* (imitation) and *diegesis* (narration) is to tell only part of the story.

Socrates' interlocutor Adeimantus admits that he does not fully understand these subtle distinctions between the three different types of narrative (an acknowledgement that these nuances may be tricky but that they matter) and Socrates offers a detailed illustration to help clarify things. The example he presents is drawn from the 'mixed' or 'compound' form of narrative (*diegesis di' amphoteron*) that is Homeric epic. The illustration, citing *Iliad* 1.12–42, is worth examining in detail (*Republic* 3.392e–393d):

Socrates: You know the beginning of the *Iliad*, in which the poet says that when Chryses begged Agamemnon to release his daughter, and Agamemnon grew angry with him, Chryses, his mission having failed, cursed the Achaians in his prayers to the god... Then you know that in the lines, 'And he begged all the Greeks, but especially the two sons of Atreus, the leaders of the men', there the poet is speaking in his own person (*legei te autos*); he never leads us to think that he is anyone else (*hos allos tis*) but himself. But in what follows he speaks as if he were Chryses and does all that he can to make us think that the speaker here is not Homer but the aged priest himself. And in this way he has composed nearly all of his narrative (*diegesis*) concerning the events that happened at Troy and Ithaca, and all of the sufferings of Odysseus... And a narrative (*diegesis*) it remains both in the speeches which the poet recites from time to time and in the intermediate passages... But when he speaks as someone else we say that he makes his own voice, as far as possible, just like that of the person he announces is about to speak... And speaking or acting just like someone else is an imitation (*mimeisthai*)... In such a case as this, then, it seems Homer and the other poets produce their narration (*diegesis*) through imitation (*mimesis*)... But if a poet does not at any point conceal his identity, then his poetry (*poiesis*) and narration (*diegesis*) happen without imitation (*mimeseos*).

What emerges from this illustration is: (1) that *diegesis* describes narrative in its broad rather than particular form; and (2) that underpinning Socrates' distinction between simple narrative and mimetic narrative is a second-level differentiation between narrative voice, depending upon whether the narrator speaks purely and simply in his own voice (*haple diegesis*) or whether he imitates and dramatizes the voice of a character and speaks as if he were that character (*diegesis dia mimeseos*). The mixed kind (*diegesis di' amphoteron*) involves alternation between these two

---

[17] Genette 1980: 162 also suggests 'pure' as a translation for *haple*. Cf. Chatman 1978: 312, Fludernik 2009: 64, Genette 1980: 164 and 1988: 17–18, Kirby 1991: 118.

modes with a poet-narrator periodically incorporating first-person direct speech into a predominantly third-person narrative, as Homer does in the narrative of Chryses' failed petition to Agamemnon (*Iliad* 1.12–26)—a passage that Socrates subsequently reproduces in the mode of *haple diegesis* to show what Homer might have said had he opted to appear and speak only 'as himself' throughout his epic.

Within this typology, Homeric epic is presented as the prime example of mixed narrative (*diegesis di' amphoteron*); tragedy and comedy typify the wholly mimetic type of narrative (*dia mimeseos*) found in drama; and the dithyramb—lyric poetry such as that composed by Pindar and Bacchylides, traditionally narrating mythical tales with virtually no dialogue—illustrates Socrates' preferred type of simple narrative (*haple diegesis*), in which 'the poet himself narrates' (*apangelias autou tou poietou*).[18]

However, this preference needs to be understood in the wider context framing Socrates' discussion of *lexis* and *logos* in *Republic* 3: his supposed theory of narrative has been developed not as its own objective, but as an instrument with which he can explain the impact of storytelling upon the citizens of an ideal republic. His principal concerns, therefore, are not with narratives but with ethics. Socrates' tripartite taxonomy of narrative, it emerges, overlays a wider debate concerning the ethical merits of unity and simplicity in social action, employment, and discourse—set in contrast to the ethical drawbacks aligned with multiplicity and plurality.[19] So, simple narrative (*haple diegesis*) is ethically privileged because of its plainness, simplicity, and purity of form; because it offers one voice and one viewpoint expressed through the mouthpiece of a single narrator speaking as himself. Mimetic narrative (*diegesis dia mimeseos*) is ethically problematic because it represents the opposite to this plain simplicity: the dramatic poet who employs such a narrative mode mimics and impersonates other characters, adopting multiple voices and viewpoints while hiding his own.[20] The third, mixed form of narrative, interchanging between the simple and the mimetic modes (*diegesis di' amphoteron*), is doubly compromised—and compromising—incorporating as it does the

[18] It is worth noting that Socrates uses the word *apangelia* (report, narrative, description) in place of *diegesis* to describe the particular type of 'narrative' discourse associated with dithyrambic lyric here (*Republic* 3.394c).
[19] It thus reiterates the same ethical considerations concerning narrative and narration seen in the *Ion* and discussed above (section 2.2).
[20] As Halliwell 2009: 24 n. 17 observes, 'Part of the force of ἁπλῆ, "plain" or "single", in the nomenclature of the typology depends precisely on a contrast with the "double" (διπλοῦς) or "multiple" (πολλαπλοῦς) voices of *mimesis*.' Ferrari 1989: 117 further suggests that *mimesis* in the *Republic* means 'imitates *many* things' (emphasis added).

mixed modes with the multiple voices and views of its characters interspersed with that of its narrator. Although Plato's Socrates intuitively recognizes in this discussion of voices and viewpoints that the mixed mode of *diegesis* necessarily incorporates a mixture of different physical, psychological, and ethical perspectives and positions, the narrative practicalities and implications of this 'focalization' hold no interest. Plato's Socrates is not concerned with how or why a single narrative might present multiple different points of view, but simply with the ways in which this multiplicity is received and emotionally processed by an audience.[21]

Socrates takes some pains to justify his concerns regarding the ethical dangers of the mimetic mode, of the psychological vulnerabilities inherent in identifying with multiple characters and points of view that are not one's own. Stories, either narrated in mimetic or mixed diegetic mode, expose author, storyteller, and audience to a kind of psychological multiplicity. This risks their potential identification with and imitation of characters and characteristics which are not their own, thereby destabilizing the desired unity and integrity of their personhood. It also risks their identification with and imitation of characters and discourses which are corrupting or debasing, thereby exposing them to bad role models and bad habits, threatening their own moral fibre and ethical disposition. Socrates offers a detailed catalogue of the many and varied characters which pose such dangers: women arguing with their husbands, defying the gods, boasting, behaving immodestly; women in trouble, pain, or lamentation, in illness, in love, or in childbirth; slaves (female or male); men who are bad, who are cowards, ruffians, boors, drunks, or who are mad (*Republic* 3.395d–396a).[22] It is, Socrates maintains, the job of the dramatic or epic poet to imitate all of these characters—and many more besides (*Republic* 3.397a–b, 3.395e–396a). The 'mimetic' poet is required to imitate 'anything and everything'—the good, the bad, the ugly, and everything in between (*Republic* 3.397a). He therefore exposes himself and his audiences to all the ethical dangers attending such multiplicity and variety, putting himself, those who read and perform his poetry, and those who hear or see it, into ethical danger.

Two key considerations emerge from this. First, Socrates shows in his catalogue of ethically compromising characters that his understanding of

---

[21] On point of view see Bal 1997, Booth 1961, Chatman 1990, de Jong 1987, Friedman 1955, Genette 1980, James 1972, Lanser 1981, Lubbock 2014, Niederhoff 2014, and Stanzel 1984.

[22] In Book 5 of the *Republic* (449b–457b) Socrates will suggest that both women and men can serve as the guardians of his ideal state, but here in Book 3 the *mimesis* of women is represented as a particular concern. As Too points out (1998: 67): 'Clearly the male citizen is the privileged model of identity' in Socrates' vision.

the term *mimesis* here equates more closely to what we might describe as 'identification' and 'replication' rather than 'imitation' or 'showing'.[23] What is more, he indicates through extensive illustration and explication that *mimesis* in this sense—that is, as a mode of *diegesis*—is to be understood as a specific and technical term only partially connected to the much broader realm of meaning attached to the term *mimesis* as it is used elsewhere in the *Republic* and elsewhere in the Platonic dialogues.[24] Indeed, at the end of the *Republic* Socrates takes up the idea of '*mimesis* as a whole' (*Republic* 10.595c)—that is, as encompassing all artistic, literary, and dramatic *representation*. This move reconfirms the status of *mimesis* in *Republic* 3 as a technical term with a narrower range of meaning, and reminds us that Socrates' specialist narratological type '*diegesis dia mimeseos*' is not determined by broader discussions of *mimesis* in the *Republic*.

Second, Socrates demonstrates his particular concerns about the impact that *diegesis dia mimeseos* will have upon its audiences; he is concerned implicitly with its reception. In this context he acknowledges the potential value of some mimetic narrative when it leads to a better understanding of positive role models to be followed or to the recognition of a bad role model to be avoided (*Republic* 3.395c–396a). Mimetic narrative is perfectly fine for the moderate man (as the guardians of Socrates' republic will be) if: (1) the *mimesis* undertaken is of a good character acting well; it is less than ideal but still acceptable if (2) the good character is not acting well; and it is even acceptable—in moderation—to 'imitate' or speak as a bad character if (3) he is being good; or if (4) he is being bad but the *mimesis* is itself not serious but playful (*Republic* 3.396c–e).[25] Selective *mimesis*, it seems, can produce an ethically beneficial and didactically useful impact, and narratives employing *diegesis dia mimeseos* in either whole or in part can play a positive role in the education of the ideal republic's guardians. Socrates is not arguing, then, for a total ban on all narrative, all poetry, or even all mimetic narrative, as is sometimes supposed: his selective prescription against *mimesis* in Book 3 of the *Republic* contains too many holes to be holistic.

Rather than any straightforward prescription against *mimesis*, therefore, Socrates offers us a set of conditional guidelines, predicated on ethical and educational values, with which to grade the merits of narratives employing some element of *diegesis dia mimeseos*. Instead of a fixed

---

[23] Ferrari 1989: 116 suggests that '"emulation" would be closer to the mark'.
[24] On which see Halliwell 2002: 37–147.
[25] On *paidia* as a mode of quasi-satirical *mimesis* see Ferrari 1989: 119.

taxonomy of narrative discourse, we are presented with a contingent hierarchy of narrative form, with each place in the scale determined by its perceived ethical characteristics and cognitive effects. At the top of this typological ladder we find simple *diegesis*, and below that mixed *diegesis*. Lower down we encounter the best kinds of *mimesis* dealing exclusively with good characters doing good things, and so on, down the scale, to mimetic narrative dealing exclusively, and seriously, with bad characters doing bad things.

This scale of more or less ethically acceptable forms of *mimesis* offers us a more nuanced way to assess the ethical value of different kinds of narrative—although Socrates is silent on the specifics of which particular ancient works might map onto this scale.[26] This ethical dimension further explains why Socrates' preferred narrative style allows a mix of 'imitation and simple narration [in which there is] a small portion of imitation in a long discourse' (*Republic* 3.396e). And it also helps to explain why Socrates subsequently describes the 'mixed style', blending plain *diegesis* with *mimesis*, as particularly 'sweet' (*Republic* 3.397d): like other sweets, this kind of narrative is something of an unhealthy treat that is especially popular with children and the ignorant general public— among them, Socrates' present interlocutor Adeimantus who, it emerges, has a personal penchant for mimetic drama (3.397d).

2.4 *Teleute*

Adeimantus' preference for the sweetness of mimetic *diegesis* reminds us that Plato himself never speaks directly 'as himself' anywhere in his dialogues. It is impossible to ignore the fact that the discourse of the *Republic* (although, strictly speaking, a representation of dialectic rather than of narrative discourse) incorporates a number of features which should invite censure under the terms of Socrates' narratology. The dialogue that makes up the *Republic* is composed of the very 'mimetic' discourse of which Socrates explicitly disapproves. Plato's characters converse in a quasi-dramatic style through which the voice of the dialogue's author (Plato) is subsumed and throughout which he speaks 'as if he were someone else' (*hos allos tis ho legon*), as if he were Socrates or Adeimantus: we even encounter the character Socrates speaking as

---

[26] The only concrete example he offers in this section is (once again) Homeric epic: 3.396e.

if he were Homer, in an imitation-within-an-imitation (*Republic* 3.393e–394a).[27] And, in direct contrast to Socrates' approved style of narrative discourse (that containing only a minimal amount of mimetic dialogue and selectively imitating the speech of good men), the mimetic discourse of the *Republic* directly imitates a great many characters, both good and bad.[28]

In fact, we might include all of Plato's dialogues within the category of mimetic *diegesis* (*diegesis dia mimeseos*). That includes all those such as the *Republic*, *Symposium*, *Charmides*, *Lysis*, or *Protagoras*, which are set within some kind of framing narrative in which a first-person narrator sets out faithfully to report a philosophical conversation he has witnessed or recorded, in addition to those such as the *Gorgias*, *Phaedrus*, *Crito*, *Euthyphro*, *Sophist*, or *Meno* in which the dialogue is immediately dramatic and unmediated by any such introductory frame.[29] Applying Socrates' narratological taxonomy to the wider Platonic corpus (while noting—crucially—that this taxonomy is nowhere else in Plato's work articulated in these same terms) it is clear that the mimetic form dominates Platonic dialogue. Even in those dialogues such as the *Gorgias* and *Phaedrus* which include some internal narration or simple *diegesis* (reporting historic events or myths), Plato never appears or speaks 'as himself' but hides his own voice underneath that of other speakers.[30]

Aristotle makes substantially the same observation in his own dialogue *On Poets* (fragment 15) and in the *Poetics* (1.1447b 11). Here he lumps together under the category of 'unclassified' *mimesis* the mimes of Xenarchus and Sophron, and 'the dialogues of Socrates'. Since Socrates infamously wrote no dialogues of his own, this would include Plato's dialogues. Indeed, Aristotle's pairing of Sophron and Socrates seems particularly provocative in this context, given the tradition which credited Sophron's comic sketches as a direct influence upon Plato in his

---

[27] See also Blondell 2002: 238 and Lowe 2000: 94–5, who points out: 'Characterization and the motivation of speech are explored with considerable dexterity, including a naturalistic attention to verbal idiosyncrasy and detail: Plato's dialogues are the closest attempt before New Comedy to capture the cadences of everyday Attic conversation.'

[28] On the enduring question of why Plato adopts the dramatic dialogue form as the vehicle for his philosophy see Gill 1996 and 2002, and McCabe 1994.

[29] See Morgan 2004 for a discussion of the different narrative forms of (and in) Platonic dialogue.

[30] See Blondell 2002: 91 for the view that 'even his "reported" dialogues include large amounts of direct *mimesis* of speakers of many different kinds'. In the ancient reception of Plato's works we also see critics and readers classifying the dialogues according to his own 'Socratic' model of simple, mimetic, and mixed *diegesis*. Cf. Diogenes Laertius 3.50. See also Nünlist 2009b: 94–115.

decision to adopt the dialogic form for his philosophical writings.[31] Nevertheless, Aristotle not only labels Plato's dialogues as forms of literary *mimesis*, but calls them 'Socratic dialogues' (*Sokratikous logous*). He clearly sees a distinction between the voice and viewpoint that belongs to the author of these mimetic works (Plato), and the voice and viewpoint of their principal character-narrator (Socrates). Aristotle distinguishes carefully between what Plato says and what Plato's Socrates says—attributing the prescriptions voiced in the *Republic* to 'Socrates' rather than to Plato.

Following Aristotle's lead, we should be wary, then, of assigning any theory of narrative voiced in the dramatic dialogue that is the *Republic* directly to Plato himself. We will not find a 'Platonic' theory of narrative either in Plato's *Ion* or the *Republic*. We will not find an uncomplicated 'Platonic' relationship between *diegesis* and *mimesis* there either. Taken as an embryonic phase in the history of narrative theory, Plato's 'Socratic dialogues' offer something of a false start—an evolutionary prequel, perhaps, rather than an introduction proper to narratology's story.[32]

[31] See Haslam 1972.
[32] The description of early evolutionary phases in narrative terms as 'prequels' is gaining currency in scientific discourse: see Society of Vertebrate Paleontology (2014).

3 Aristotle

> Socrates: I invite any champions of poetry—not poets themselves, but lovers of poetry—to offer a prose defence on its behalf, to show that poetry is not only a source of pleasure but also of benefit to the state and to the wellbeing of mankind.
>
> Plato, *Republic* 10.607d

3.1 *Arche*

Incomplete, contradictory, abstruse, and sometimes simply garbled, the disjointed set of lecture notes that comprise Aristotle's esoteric treatise *Poetics* (*Peri poietikes*) represents the first attempt at a systematic theoretical mapping of Western poetics—and remains one of the most influential.[1] Several of the concepts discussed in the *Poetics*, written sometime in the 330s BCE, still play an important role in twenty-first-century narrative theory and many more narratological features and functions are implicitly assumed or hinted at as Aristotle's theory of poetry unfolds. Tzvetan Todorov's appropriately unsettling image captures the incongruity of this well:[2]

Aristotle's *Poetics*, twenty-five hundred years old, is at once the first work entirely devoted to "literary theory" (quotation marks are indispensable here to forestall anachronism) and one of the most important in the canon. The simultaneous presence of these two features is not without paradox: it is as if a man with an already greying moustache were to emerge from his mother's womb.

---

[1] Heath 1996: vii suggests that 'what is presented as a single continuous text may in fact juxtapose different stages in the development of Aristotle's thinking'. See Hardison and Golden 1968: 55–62 for a useful overview of the text's status as incomplete 'lecture notes' (compiled by Aristotle or a student) or as an esoteric work (composed for a closed circle of academicians). Translations of the *Poetics* necessarily smooth out the bumpy textual problems presented by the Greek and give the illusion of a much more coherent discourse than the messy version of the original that we have inherited. Whalley's somewhat eccentric 1997 presentation captures some of the original's inchoate qualities but is a challenging read as a result. The problematic Greek text has also resulted in a great diversity of different translations and interpretations—several of which flatly contradict each other. The studies collected in Rorty 1996 give a good sense of the range of very different readings authorized by this challenging text.

[2] Todorov 1981: xxiii.

Aristotle is frequently posited as the founder of modern narratology, and the *Poetics* is widely cited as narratology's first, foundational work of narrative theory and criticism. The 2005 *Routledge Encyclopaedia of Narrative Theory* discusses Aristotle's influence upon nearly forty narratological features, ranging from actants and audiences, *katharsis* and character, ethics and episodes, to core concepts such as plot.[3] Irene de Jong even debates 'whether Aristotle may be credited with the invention of the notion of the narrator as an agent who is to be distinguished from the historical author, one of the basic principles of modern narratology'.[4]

Above all, though, Aristotle is lauded for his recognition of plot (*muthos*) as the organizing principle that configures the stuff of story (*praxis*) into narrative discourse (*lexis*). His intuition that narrative functions on different levels and that there is an important distinction to be drawn between the tale and its telling is widely regarded as the first principle of narratological analysis. For Christoph Meister, Aristotle's discussion of plot introduces a core concept that remains essential—and essentially Aristotelian—to our basic grasp of narrative and its dynamics:[5]

> Aristotle's *Poetics* presented a ... criterion that has remained fundamental for the understanding of narrative: the distinction between the totality of events taking place in a depicted world and the *de facto* narrated plot or *muthos*. He pointed out that the latter is always a construct presenting a subset of events, chosen and arranged according to aesthetic considerations.

Aristotle's recognition of the primacy of plot as the organizing principle that configures the stuff of story—the recognition that there is a difference between what subsequent generations would identify as *fabula* and *syuzhet*, *discours* and *histoire*, story and plot—is the key that opens up a text for narratological analysis. Only once this distinction between the tale and its telling is established can we appreciate the finer details of narrativity. As Peter Brooks puts it:[6]

---

[3] Herman, Jahn, and Ryan 2005: *s.vv.* Kearns 2005: 201 traces the origins of genre theory back to Aristotle; Rabinowitz 2005: 29 and Prince 2014: 398 see in Aristotle's *Poetics* an early instantiation of concern for the role of the reader and narratee; Schneider 2005: 484 sees in Aristotle's concept of *katharsis* the origins of reader-response theory. Chatman 1978: 111, Herman 2007: 13, Jannidis 2014: 19–20, and Rimmon-Kenan 1983: 34 all see Propp's model of folktale character functions and Greimas's actants resembling Aristotle's theory of character.

[4] De Jong 2005a: 20. See Morrison 2007 on the narrator in Greek poetry.

[5] Meister 2014: 627.

[6] Brooks 1984: 4–5. Chatman 1978: 18–21 similarly sees Aristotle as setting a 'precedent' for later narratologists to follow. See also Chatman 1978: 92 where, amidst his critique of the formalist and structuralist story grammars prescribed by Propp and Todorov, he observes that 'this is what Aristotle was also doing ... he must have intuited the structure before formulating its rules'.

one must in good logic argue that plot is somehow prior to those elements most discussed by most critics, since it is the very organizing line, the thread of design, that makes narrative possible because finite and comprehensible. Aristotle, of course, recognized the logical priority of plot, and a recent critical tradition, starting with the Russian Formalists and coming up to the French and American "narratologists", has revived a quasi-Aristotelian sense of plot.

It would not be too wide of the mark to characterize that ongoing critical tradition and the evolving enterprise of contemporary Western narrative theory as still responding to Aristotle's provocations, first formulated some two and a half millennia ago, concerning the form and function of *muthos*.[7] Brooks's own definition of plot as a 'series of events' clearly echoes Aristotle's definition of plot as the 'arrangement of incidents' (*sunthesin ton pragmaton*: *Poetics* 6.1450a 3–4); as does Ronald Crane's description of plot as 'a particular temporal synthesis effected by the writer of the elements of action, character, and thought'.[8]

Of course, Aristotle's influential literary critical theories of narrative did not emerge fully formed and moustachioed *ex nihilo* but were influenced by a variety of wider foundational sources—and they retain some distinct qualities of those earlier narrative theories.[9] The success of Aristophanes' literary-critical comedy *Frogs* demonstrates the pre-existing and popular understanding in fifth-century BCE Athens of poets as 'makers' of a material form which could be weighed, measured, and assessed according to various metrics.[10] Aristotle was also, for a while, a member of Plato's Academy and would have encountered Plato's theories about the ethical and psychological deficiencies of poetry there. In the long reception history of narrative theory, then, Aristotle's *Poetics* is already a work that offers us a response to a pre-existing (proto)narratological tradition.

3.2 **Aristotle and Plato**

In the *Republic* (10.607d), Socrates had issued a challenge to those who love poetry 'to offer a prose defence on its behalf', and in his

[7] See Lowe 2000 on Aristotle's contribution to 'the invention of western narrative'.

[8] Brooks 1984: 12 and Crane 1952: 620 and 618. Ryan 1991: 120 also echoes Aristotle in her view that 'Plots originate in knots.'

[9] See Halliwell's discussion of the intellectual context for the *Poetics* 1998: 1–41. Heath 1996, Else 1957, and Ledbetter 2003 also offer accessible overviews.

[10] See, for example, the scene in which the poetry of Aeschylus and Euripides is weighed like cheese and then evaluated using tape measures, yard sticks, and set squares (*Frogs* 799–83). The Greek conception of a poet or *poietes* (ποιητής) as a 'maker' and a poem as something 'made' (ποίημα, *poiema*) underpins this gag.

Poetics Aristotle takes up that invitation. Plato's Socrates outlined a psychological model of narrative, concerned principally with the negative pedagogical and psychological impact of storytelling. Aristotle shares that interest in the reception of different kinds of narratives. But his theory of poetry aims to demonstrate that the effect and affect of narrative discourse is positive and pleasurable rather than harmful. To this end he develops a broadly rhetorical model of narrative, exploring the communication and cognition processes associated with storytelling, observing the ways in which narrative and other kinds of *mimesis* help us to learn, and mapping the ways and means a narrative can and should be arranged so as to produce pleasurable affects upon its audience. Thus, the focus and *telos* of Aristotle's defence and theory of poetry is directed towards poetry's final cause, upon product, pedagogy, and pleasure as they impact positively upon audiences and readers—from a stance that simultaneously declares its relation to and difference from that of Plato's Socrates, in 'a destruction of old values and a reconstruction of old elements'.[11]

Aristotle signals the direction in which his reception of Socrates' narrative poetics is going to take in his opening statement of 'first principles' (*Poetics* 1.1447a 13–18):

First... epic and tragic poetry, along with comedy, dithyramb, and most music sung to the reed pipe and lyre, are all, on the whole, kinds of *mimesis*. But they differ from each other in three ways: by representing in different *media*, by representing different *objects*, or by representing in different *modes*.

For Plato's Socrates, all forms of poetry were varieties of *diegesis*—the umbrella category of 'narrative' under which different types of poetry were subcategorized according to their dominant style of presentation (Plato, *Republic* 3.392d). For Aristotle, the opposite is the case: *mimesis* is the umbrella category, the genus to which all the poetic arts belong, and of which epic and tragedy are the principal species. It is important here that we notice Aristotle's concept of *mimesis* overlaps with but is not precisely the same as Socrates'. *Mimesis* in Book 3 of the *Republic* specifically referred to imitative and dramatic impersonation. *Mimesis*

---

[11] Tynyanov 1921 quoted in Eichenbaum 1965: 134. For illuminating discussions of the politics and principles of pleasure in Aristotle's *Poetics* see Belfiore 1992 and Too 1998: 82–114. Hardison and Golden 1968: 116 offers a misleading interpretation in declaring that Aristotle has no interest in poetry's final cause or its impact upon audiences and readers: Hardison claims in his commentary that 'the *Poetics* is... concerned with the nature of tragedy, not the response of the audience'. Heath 2009: 9 offers a more cogent insight into Aristotle's understanding of narrative cognition, observing that 'Aristotle seems deliberately to link the pleasure we get from imitations to reasoned inference'.

in the *Poetics* refers to a much broader and more systematic concept of 'representation' (its most apt translation).[12] It is a highly provocative term of reference for Aristotle to select as his dominant category of organization here. It not only subsumes Plato's *diegesis* within its reach, but also overtly challenges the ethical foundation of Socrates' tripartite typology of narrative styles. In the terms of this typology, Plato's Socrates set out a socially and ethically defensible spectrum of poetry, with mimetic tragedy and comedy at one end and diegetic Homeric epic at the other. Socrates expressly identified his own ethical preference for simple or pure narrative (*haple diegesis*) containing little or no mimetic dialogue (although he ultimately allowed that a little bit of playful *mimesis*, if it represented good men experiencing good things, probably wasn't all that bad). But Aristotle indicates that his own preferences lie at the opposite end of that spectrum—that is, with tragedy, and with the serious *mimesis* of serious men experiencing bad things in a straightforwardly dramatic representation with little or no narrative parts.

Further underlining this point of departure from Socrates, Aristotle's early definition of *mimesis* as the representation of people 'acting' or 'in action' (*Poetics* 2.1448a 1: *prattontas*) clearly echoes Plato's *Republic*, where *mimesis* was defined as an imitation which 'emulates people acting (*prattontas*) obligatory or voluntary actions and as a result of that action (*praxis*) believing they have done well or badly—and in all of this either sorrowing or rejoicing' (*Republic* 10.603c). Aristotle uses the logic of this basic premise to nuance and so undermine Socrates' blanket condemnation of all mimetic poetry on ethical grounds. Aristotle sets out to prove that objecting to *mimesis* is facile: there are many different kinds of actions that are open to mimetic representation—some of which are bad, some of which are good. Furthermore, there may be psychological and pedagogical benefits in safely experiencing pain and pleasure, in 'sorrowing or rejoicing' in sympathy with characters in a story.

Having established the outline of this 'first principle' and the notion that *mimesis* operates in different media (*Poetics* 1.1447a 18–27: visual, musical, linguistic, choreographical[13]), Aristotle goes on to argue his second principle that *mimesis* can be further subcategorized according

---

[12] Aristotle's thoughts on *mimesis* are the subject of a great many studies. See in particular Halliwell 2002, Golden 1992, and Woodruff 1992.

[13] Aristotle frequently draws analogies between *mimesis* in poetry and in painting: 1.1447a 18–27. Similar parallels are drawn by Plato's Socrates: *Republic* 373b, 377e, 596c. Aristotle also draws analogues with music and seems to borrow some phrases directly from Plato: references to 'rhythm, language and music' (*Poetics* 1.1447a 22) echo Plato's *Republic* 398d and 601a.

to its representation of different ethically coloured objects (*Poetics* 2.1448a 1–4):[14]

Since the practitioners of *mimesis* represent people in action (*prattontas*), and since these people must necessarily be good or bad (for character generally accords with these types, and it is goodness and badness that differentiates all character types), then they can represent people either as better than us, or as worse, or as just the same.

Aristotle can now use the ethical dispositions of characters (and their actions) mimetically represented in these various media as the grounds for a rudimentary theory of genre: classifying genres according to the mimetic objects which they represent allows him to conclude that 'comedy aims at representing men as worse, tragedy as better than in real life' (*Poetics* 2.1448a 18–19). This point further enables Aristotle to counter Socrates' claim that dramatic *mimesis* is ethically and socially dangerous across the board. What is more, it allows Aristotle to reinforce on ethical grounds one of the cornerstones of the *Poetics*—the argument (*contra* Plato's Socrates, who prefers Homeric epic), that it is tragedy that represents the pinnacle of poetic form.

For Plato's Socrates, the sort of mimetic discourse encountered in tragedy was deemed ethically compromised because of the polyphony of voice and viewpoint that it invites. Socrates praised Homer because his poetry supposedly contains only a little mimetic discourse or character speech and for the most part (or so he claimed) Homer 'speaks as himself' in simple narrative (*haple diegesis*). Aristotle, it seems, has this in sight when he defines his third type of *mimesis*: the mode. In line with Socrates' tripartite distinction between the simple, mimetic, and mixed modes of narrative (*Republic* 392d–394c), Aristotle describes his own tripartite typology—continuing to use *mimesis* rather than Plato's *diegesis* as his dominant category of organization (*Poetics* 3.1448a 18–23):[15]

There is a third difference: the mode in which these objects may be represented. In the same medium we can represent the same objects by combining narrative

---

[14] Here Aristotle is also drawing upon Plato's *Laws* (659c and 798d), where characters are similarly categorized according to whether they are ethically better or worse than us.

[15] There is no scholarly consensus on whether the text here should be translated as describing a tripartite or bipartite schema. Lucas 1968: 66–7 offers a useful overview of the key textual considerations in his commentary to 1448a 20–4 and retains Kessel's punctuation of the Greek text so as to suggest a bipartite model. Genette 1980: 393 similarly reads a bipartite model, distinguishing between narrating (telling) and performing (showing) the action and character parts. Janko 1987, Hardison and Golden 1968, and Butcher 1955 also see a bipartite arrangement. De Jong 1987: 247 expresses a 'slight preference' for the tripartite schema, a view shared with Rabel 2007: 10, Halliwell 1998: 128, Else 1957, myself, and many others.

with impersonation, as Homer does; or by speaking in our own voice without changing; or by impersonating all the characters as if they are living and moving.

Aristotle borrows Socrates' Homeric example to illustrate the first of these three mimetic modes, as well as the formulation used by Socrates to describe what happens in narrative discourse when the poet-narrator 'speaks as someone else' (cf. *Republic* 3.392e–393b). But whereas Socrates was concerned that the mimetic imitation of bad people doing bad things risks psychological exposure on the part of author, artist, and audience to all that badness, Aristotle takes the opposite view. Through *mimesis*, he claims (*Poetics* 4.1448b 1–8), we gain not only understanding but also cognitive pleasure.[16] And if the impact of any mimetic representation is ultimately pleasurable or educative, then it cannot in itself be a bad thing. To illustrate this point he offers two practical examples drawn from the visual arts, one emphasizing the particular pleasure that viewers experience in actively recognizing the subject of a portrait painting (*Poetics* 4.1448b 14–19), the other demonstrating that even when the object of *mimesis* is unpleasant, its affect may be the reverse (*Poetics* 4.1448b 9–12). In both of these cases it is the *mimesis* itself rather than the object imitated which causes the pleasurable response; it is the viewer's (re)cognition of the artful *mimesis* which produces the pleasure of understanding. Like Plato, Aristotle is interested in the psychological aspect of the mimetic arts in general, and the literary arts in particular, but approaching the question from the other side of the frame, as it were, his emphases and his conclusions are very different.

Alongside Aristotle's insistence that *mimesis* has a pleasurable and positive educational affect upon audiences, we encounter his theory of *katharsis*: the idea that poetry and drama somehow produce beneficial, quasi-homeopathic, emotions in their audiences.[17] When he first introduces this idea in the *Poetics* (6.1449b 28) he appears to assume that his audience will already be familiar with this term and offers no definition of what this difficult concept means. It is clear that Aristotle's ideas about the effects and affects of *katharsis* are not restricted to tragedy alone but extend theoretically to all poetic genres, both serious and unserious. Presumably, the promised but now lost second book of the *Poetics* offering a fuller treatment of comedy would have discussed *katharsis* as one of the proper pleasures pertaining to comic discourse, and it is

[16] Aristotle also discusses the pleasures and pedagogic values of poetry and other liberal arts in his *Politics* 8.1337b. In his *Metaphysics* (1036a 28 and 1059b 29) he describes how learning is linked to recognition and perception of the universal.

[17] For a detailed analysis of Aristotle's theory of *katharsis* see Halliwell 1998: 184–201 and 350–6. On Aristotle's view on rhetoric and emotion see Hyde and Smith 1993.

evident from the comparisons drawn between epic and tragedy in chapter 24 of the *Poetics* that Aristotle sees *katharsis* as an appropriate response to epic narratives too (*Poetics* 24.1459b 7–15).[18]

As far as this concept of *katharsis* impacts upon Aristotle's wider narratological theories, the most salient feature of this phenomenon is the focus its spotlight lends to the role of the audience and reader. Aristotle represents *katharsis* as the *telos* of poetry, the final product that is realized as the audience cognitively processes the plot to its end point (*Poetics* 6.1449b 23–8):

> Tragedy is the *mimesis* of an action that is serious, complete, and of a certain magnitude; in embellished language of distinct kinds in its separate parts; in the mode of drama (*dronton*), not of narrative (*ou di' apangelias*); and through pity (*eleou*) and fear (*phobou*) producing the purgation (*katharsis*) of these emotions.

Plato's Socrates feared that poetry would stir up its audiences' emotions; Aristotle hopes that it will. For Aristotle, that's precisely the point, the *telos* of poetry: that is what art is for. At *Republic* 3.387b–d and 10.606b–d Plato's Socrates argued that exposure to emotional content such as pity and fear renders audiences slaves to their own emotions. Aristotle's model of *katharsis*, in contrast, argues that such exposure somehow establishes emotional equilibrium.

Quite how this effect is produced is never made clear, but Aristotle does give some indication of the conditions that are necessary (if not fully sufficient) to bring it about. In fact, as the following chapters of the *Poetics* will go on to confirm, Aristotle's definition of tragedy here offers us an excellent *précis* of his wider working definition of narrative. So, we learn from Aristotle's reception of Plato's Socratic theory of poetry and its effects that, allowing for minor variations in the particular requirements of dramatic and narrative modes, poetry is essentially: (1) a mimetic form centring upon (2) an action which is (3) complete (having beginning, middle, and end—as we will be advised presently), and (4) of an appropriate length (of both story time and discourse time); (5) composed of 'embellished' or literary discourse (incorporating rhetorical figures and features including metaphor, metonymy, and metre); (6) presented predominantly in a mode either dramatic, narrative, or a mix of the two; in order (7) to arouse an appropriate emotional response in an audience.[19]

---

[18] On the 'lost' book of *Poetics* dealing with comedy see Janko 1984. *On Poets* offers some evidence of Aristotle's consideration of comic *katharsis* outside the *Poetics*, as does his *Politics* (especially 1341b 38–40, 1342b 37, and 1342a 17).

[19] Aristotle's description of tragedy as 'serious' (*spoudaios*) here would appear to form part of his direct response to Socrates' rejection of the 'serious' (*spoude*) treatment of

It is useful to bear this formulation in mind when attempting to make sense of the intricacies and contradictions of the *Poetics* and its narratology. As his definition of tragedy makes clear, Aristotle sees its narrative dynamics as broadly rhetorical: its aim is to elicit an emotional response in its readers, auditors, and viewers; its *telos* is to purposefully persuade an audience to feel certain things. And Aristotle's interest in the various technical components of a good, bad, or indifferent story (a dramatic or narrative plot's arrangement of action and incidents, story and discourse time, linguistic medium and mode) is focused upon and around the ways in which these elements synergistically succeed or fail to achieve that end.[20]

So, we find that Aristotle tends to prefer direct *mimesis* to indirect *mimesis* because of the greater emotional impact it can bring to an audience. Despite his obvious admiration for Homer (aptly described in the *Poetics* as the most dramatic of epic poets: 4.1448b 35–6; 24.1460a 9–11), Aristotle declares tragedy superior to epic precisely because of its mimetic and emotional immediacy. He recommends that a poet should work out a plot not only in word (*lexis*) but also in gesture (*schema*); performing or viewing the actions associated with an emotion makes the emotional content of a verbal narrative more affective (*Poetics* 17.1455a 22–31). He prefers certain kinds of plots (*muthoi*) because audiences find them easier to follow or derive greater pleasure from working them out. His views on character (*ethos*) and characterization are coloured by the degree to which audiences will find characters and their actions plausible and affective, or improbable and ridiculous. He recommends or criticizes various dramatic and narrative approaches to diction (*lexis*), thought (*dianoia*), spectacle (*opsis*), and musicality (*melopoeia*), in terms of their likely cognition and reception by an audience and their ultimate contribution to the affectivity of the work.[21] While these last four features and their affects are of less obvious relevance to a study of ancient and modern narratology (and Aristotle himself shows only limited interest in them), if we are to appreciate fully the theory of narrative that the

---

mimesis on ethical grounds (*Republic* 3.396d). There is also a Platonic (Socratic) quality to Aristotle's description of the tragic mode as *mimesis* literally 'acting' or 'doing' (*dronton*) and not 'through telling' or 'through narrating' (*di' apeggelias*)—a formulation that twists Socrates' definition of drama as '*diegesis dia* [through] *mimeseos*', and of epic as '*diegesis di'* [*through*] *amphoteron*' (*Republic* 3.392c–398b).

[20] As Belfiore 1992: 57 puts it: 'the final cause (*telos* or *ergon*) of tragedy is the functioning of the plot to produce pleasure and *katharsis* by means of pity and fear'.

[21] In this light it is clear why Aristotle's broadly 'rhetorical' theory of narrative and poetics would come to hold such appeal for the Russian formalists, the Chicago school, and the rhetorical narratologists of the Ohio school.

Poetics sketches out, we must recognize this pervasive focus upon audience cognition and response that ties together the organization and presentation of this theory.

3.3 *Muthos*

Aristotle signals that plot or *muthos* is going to be the primary focus of his theory of poetry in the opening lines of the *Poetics*, where he declares his intention to investigate 'the construction of plots' (*Poetics* 1.1447a 9: *sunistasthai tous muthous*).[22] For Aristotle, the *muthos*—defined as the *mimesis* of action (*praxis*) and the arrangement (*sunthesis*) of incidents (*pragmata*) (*Poetics* 6.1450a 2–4)—is the *alpha* and *omega* of poetry. He declares that: 'the incidents and the *muthos* are the end goal (*telos*) of tragedy, and the end is the most important thing of all' (*Poetics* 6.1450a 22–3); that 'the *muthos* is the first principle (*arche*) and the soul (*psuche*) of tragedy' (*Poetics* 6.1450a 38); and that 'the structure of the incidents (*sustasin ton pragmaton*) is the first (*proton*) and most important (*megiston*) part of tragedy' (*Poetics* 7.1450b 21–2). Aristotle abstracts the real (or mythical) world actions and incidents that literary discourse represents from their literary re-presentation. He positions those real or mythical world actions and incidents as the raw material which the poet transforms into a mimetic work of art, the 'soul' of which is its *muthos*.[23] From this conceptual position, Aristotle is able to make a series of important analytical and inductive observations about dramatic and narrative poetry in general, and about a selection of tragic and epic poems in particular.

First, he can identify *muthos* as something artificially constructed; the organization of invented or pre-existing story stuff (the *logos*—which Lucas defines as 'the raw material or argument for a plot') into plot (*Poetics* 1.1447a 8–9).[24] That story stuff may comprise the raw material

---

[22] On Aristotle's use of *muthos* and its cognates in and outside the *Poetics* see Halliwell 1998: 57 n. 16. On the problems of mapping modern narratological terms onto Aristotle's *muthos* see Downing 1984, Belfiore 2000, and Pier 2003: 73–97.

[23] Else 1957: 242 argues that Aristotle sees *muthos* as the soul of a poem in the same way that he sees the soul as the essence of a man, taking this as a clue to how Aristotle conceives of the chronological priority of plot: 'For Aristotle the plot precedes the poem, but it too is essentially "made" by the poet, even if he is using traditional material.' In the same way, the subject matter of the poem and plot pre-exists the action which the plot rearranges.

[24] Lucas 1968: 91. On the various uses to which Aristotle puts *logos* in the *Poetics* see also Janko 1987: 222–3. Cf. *Poetics* 5.1449b 7, 9.1451b 8–9, and 17.1455b 1. The terms Aristotle uses in association with *muthos* (*sunistasthai, sunistanai, suntithemi, suntithenai*) clearly

of real world actions and events as well as the stuff of myth and history, which most ancient poets reconfigured and embellished in their dramatic and epic narratives. Indeed, the distinction that Aristotle will subsequently signal between stories (*logoi*) and plots (*muthoi*)—between traditional or invented story material (the Trojan War, say) and its particular emplotment in a narrative or dramatic form (Homer's *Iliad*)—carries particular significance and analytical value in a literary culture in which the retelling of familiar stories rather than the invention of new ones was the norm.[25] The ancient poet typically demonstrated his artistry less in his invention than in his plotting—that is, in his adaptation of familiar myths; his selection and suppression of details; his manipulation of temporal sequence and point of view; his arrangement of incidents. And it is on these grounds that Aristotle will to go on to define a poet as a 'maker' not of verses or stories but of plots (*Poetics* 9.1451b 27–30).

Aristotle is then able to drill down into the component features of *muthos*, particularly those which work to achieve an emotional impact upon an audience, such as transformations (*peripeteia*) and recognitions (*anagnorisis*) (*Poetics* 6.1450a 31–4).[26] These transformations (or reversals) and recognitions should be at once surprising and foreseeable, and so play pleasurably upon audience cognition and anticipation.[27] As Kermode puts it, *peripeteia* is 'a falsification of expectation, so that the end comes as expected, but not in the manner expected'.[28] In maintaining that 'tragedy's most potent means of emotional effect are components of plot' (*Poetics* 6.1450a 32–4), Aristotle can even argue that 'a plot should be structured so that, even without seeing it performed, the person who hears the events that occur experiences pity (*eleos*) and fear (*phobos*) at what happens—as one would feel hearing the plot of the *Oedipus*' (*Poetics* 14.1453b 3–6). Those feelings of pity and fear appear to be linked mimetically in some way to the recognition of an empathetic 'fellow feeling' (*philanthropos*) on the part of the audience (*Poetics* 13.1453a 1–3).[29]

---

and consistently convey a notion of the active construction, organization, and arrangement of raw story material—the processes which achieve a satisfactory *sunthesis* of incidents and events. Cf. *Poetics* 13.1453a 19.

[25] *Poetics* 17.1455a 34, 17.1455b 17, 24.1460a 27.

[26] Aristotle's *Rhetoric* (1.11.23–4) also identifies such 'transformations' or 'reversals' as powerfully affective features, inciting wonder or excitement in an audience.

[27] Halliwell 1998: 208 captures this paradox perfectly in his formulation: 'action is confronted by its own unintended outcome'.

[28] Kermode 1967: 53.

[29] Carey 1988 sees the *philanthropos* as an effect of the plot upon the audience.

Next, Aristotle can establish the requisite qualities and patterns that make a plot well constructed. For Aristotle, the most important of these are: (1) wholeness, that is having appropriate points of beginning, middle, and end (*Poetics* 7.1450b 25–34); (2) appropriate size (in terms of both discourse and story) to maximize audience appreciation (*Poetics* 7.1450b 34–1451a 15); (3) coherence, meaning a size and arrangement which allows for clear perception and retention in the memory (*eumnemoneutos*) of the audience or reader (*Poetics* 7.1451a 4–10); (4) unity (*Poetics* 8.1451a 15–35); (5) and a probable (*eikos*) or necessary (*anangkaios*) sequence of events (*Poetics* 9.1451a 37). He can therefore establish the qualities that conversely distinguish a poorly constructed plot, namely those which he describes as 'episodic' (*epeisodios*), in which actions, events, and episodes follow each other without unity, that is without coherent arrangement or continuity, probability or necessity (*Poetics* 10.1451b 32–5).[30]

He can also identify different types of *muthos*: a *muthos* will be either simple or complex according to the simplicity or complexity of the action (*praxis*) which it re-presents (*Poetics* 10.1452a 11–17).[31] Furthermore, a *muthos* can be either single (*haplous*) or double (*diplous*), according to whether it plots along a single or dual plane (*Poetics* 13.1453a 12–16); that is, whether it focuses on the fortunes of a single character, or follows also the fortunes of his enemies. The plot of the *Odyssey*, for instance, is both complex (involving numerous recognitions) and double.[32]

Underpinning each of Aristotle's theories concerning the composition of a successful plot is the idea that a properly configured *muthos* should be able to impact emotionally upon its audience and deliver to them the appropriate pleasure (*Poetics* 14.1453b 10–11) at its resolution. In order to do this it must be complex yet still intelligible: the effects (and affects) of reversals, recognitions, and resolutions depend upon the audience's ability to make cognitive connections between disparate parts of the plot.[33] As the English terms for these phenomena suggest (each with its backward-looking prefix), they require an audience to re-member, re-arrange, and re-compose the series of incidents and actions presented to them in the *muthos* into a coherent and pleasing pattern: the audience

---

[30] For two very different accounts of the importance of unity to Aristotle's theory of narrative see Heath 1989: 38–55 and Halliwell 2012.

[31] Aristotle's differentiation between single (*haple*) and double (*diple*) plots recalls Plato's distinction between simple (*haple*), mimetic, and mixed modes of narrative.

[32] Cf. *Poetics* 13.1453a 31–2 and 24.1459b 14–16.

[33] Lucas 1968: 113 notes that Aristotle's idea of a 'beautiful' (*kalon*) plot 'includes intelligibility'. Hardison and Golden 1968: 290 also refer to the Aristotelian 'imperative of intelligibility'.

no less than the poet is required to synthesize the component parts of a tragic or epic narrative.

To that end, the poet must first produce a certain kind of plot (*Poetics* 7.1450b 23–37):[34]

[A] tragedy is the *mimesis* of an action that is whole, complete, and of a certain size... A whole is something that has a beginning, middle, and end. A beginning is something that does not necessarily follow as a consequence of anything else but after which something else organically exists or happens. An end, contrariwise, is something that is inevitably or usually the organic result of something else but from which nothing else follows. A middle is that which follows something and something follows it. Well-constructed plots, therefore, should not begin and end randomly, but should follow the pattern described.

What may seem like an unhelpful statement of the obvious here is more apposite when we remember that the tragic and epic narratives of the ancient literary tradition were typically drawn from a familiar 'myth-kitty': as Aristotle himself points out, Homer's *Odyssey* might have taken as its starting point any number of well-known adventures in which its eponymous hero featured, but Homer intuitively knew how to select his material so as to craft a dynamic plot (*Poetics* 8.1451a 22–9). Homer is exemplary in selecting the first link in a causal sequence which will arouse the desire in his audience to learn of the con-sequence.[35]

Throughout Aristotle's account of plot unity it is the audience or reader from whose viewpoint this ideal wholeness is to be perceived. Although he declares that discussion of '[the audience's] powers of perception (*aisthesis*) are not part of this treatise' (*Poetics* 7.1451a 6–7), in practice he repeatedly turns to the cognitive processes by which an audience comprehends a plot. The perfect plot must represent a perfect unity in order to be perfectly coherent to its audience.[36] As the discussion of the appropriate magnitude of a plot makes clear, it is the cognitive apprehension of something—be it an object, an animal, a play, or a story—which determines whether that thing can be understood to possess beauty and unity. Taking the example of an animal which is too

[34] This definition of beginning, middle, and end echoes Plato's *Phaedrus* 264 b–c. Cf. Aristotle's observations on identifying integral and non-integral plot parts at *Poetics* 8.1451a 29–35; and his comparison of epic to an animal at 23.1459a 20.

[35] Cf. Booth 1961: 126: 'When we see a causal chain started, we demand... to see the result. Emma meddles, Tess is seduced, Huck runs away—and we demand certain consequences.' For Propp 1968, the beginning is marked by a lack; for Kafalenos 2006 by lack of equilibrium; for Phelan 1996 and 2007b by a lack of relational stability. The term 'myth-kitty' is Larkin's (1983: 69).

[36] Halliwell 1989: 156 n. 6 observes that 'Aristotle endows the term *praxis* with the new sense of a coherent set of events.'

minuscule to be perceived and an animal which is too gigantic to be seen whole (he suggests one a thousand miles long), Aristotle stresses the point that these things are not beautiful because they defy our ready comprehension. One can barely be seen and the other is so vast that 'those who contemplate it lose any sense of unity and wholeness' (*Poetics* 7.1450b 36–1451a 3). It is those who view and contemplate these creatures who are Aristotle's primary focus here, just as it is a tragedy's audience, and a narrative's readers, upon whom his theory of plot unity concentrates.

In the same way, the comprehension and memory of the audience and reader are foregrounded when Aristotle summarizes his position on plot magnitude (*Poetics* 7.1451a 5–15). The constraining factor imposing the appropriate limit of magnitude upon a plot is not measured in terms of narrative complexity, of the number or diversity of incidents and episodes, nor of the length of either discourse or story time involved—but rather in terms of human mind and memory. Aristotle is acutely aware that the cognitive processes associated with *muthos* require a co-making or co-poiesis involving both the poet and his audience.

A secondary imperative concerning unified plot structure and its cognitive processing by an audience emerges from this definition of plot magnitude: a plot should not simply arrange its incidents into a merely temporal sequential series of events, but connect them logically and causally 'according to probability or necessity'. Indeed, we find probability (*eikos*) and necessity (*anangke*) attached to several of Aristotle's conditions for the well-constructed *muthos*. He advises that key tragic plot devices such as transformation (*peripeteia*) and recognition (*anagnorisis*) should be perceived by an audience as both unexpected and inevitable (*Poetics* 10.1452a 18–21):[37]

they should develop from the structure of the plot, so that they follow on as the necessary or probable result of the preceding action. It makes all the difference whether a thing happens because of, or only after, its antecedent.

Aristotle has already made the point that the greatest affect is achieved when a plot's incidents appear 'contrary to expectation yet because of one another' (*Poetics* 10.1452a 4). Here he reiterates that it is not enough for events merely to follow each other in linear temporal (*post hoc*) sequence, but there must be a logical causal (*propter hoc*) connection between them, because (from the audience's perspective) this arrangement is more artistic, more wondrous (*thaumastos*), and more affective.

---

[37] Belfiore 1992: 111–31 offers an insightful study of Aristotle's views on necessity, probability, and plausibility. See also Currie 2013 on the unexpected.

In fact, he offers the intriguing suggestion that where there are no real or logical causal connections between two random or coincidental events (he gives the example of a toppled statue happening to crush a known murderer: *Poetics* 9.1452a 4–10), an audience will itself invent or supply some kind of causal connection (a kind of poetic justice in the case of the statue which so happened to be an image of the murderer's victim).[38] In this important observation Aristotle recognizes that an audience does not passively watch as a plot plays out its twists and tensions, reversals and recognitions, tightening towards its climax or *desis* and untying towards its denouement or *lusis*. He acknowledges that the audience itself actively and cognitively participates in that tying and untying— even to the extent of making apparently meaningful connections out of chance coincidence.[39]

Aristotle offers a fascinating glimpse of his own understanding of the cognitive processes by which this co-configuration of plot takes place. When he turns his attention from tragic to epic plots in the final chapters of the *Poetics* he expands upon his earlier discussion of wondrous (*thaumastos*) plots and irrational (*alogos*) incidents, observing that 'epic offers greater scope for the irrational (which is the chief element in what is wondrous), because we do not actually see the actors of the narrative' (*Poetics* 24.1460a 11–14). He suggests that to hear or to read about (and thus to imagine) Achilles chasing Hector around the walls of Troy (as narrated in Homer's *Iliad* 22.131–87) offers a very different cognitive experience to watching this improbable scene performed on a stage: the narrative experience is affective, the dramatic experience ridiculous.[40]

Aristotle further emphasizes the pleasurably affective impact of wondrous incidents in narrative by observing that all storytellers exaggerate—and do so specifically to give *pleasure* to their audiences (*Poetics* 24.1460a 16–18).[41] This leads to a discussion of the ways

---

[38] Rimmon-Kenan 1983: 17 nicely illustrates our tendency to infer causal connections even when only temporal connections are given, with an old 'joke': 'Milton wrote *Paradise Lost*, then his wife died, and then he wrote *Paradise Regained*.' For a different take on causality in Aristotle's account of the 'murder of Mitys' see Currie 2007.

[39] By extension, and with the audience again foremost in mind, Aristotle prescribes that characters (like the plots they perform) must behave in characteristically 'probable' ways, and proscribes extraneous, improbable, and supernatural plot resolutions (*Poetics* 15.1454a 33–1454b 7).

[40] As Heath 1996: lvii puts it: 'Keeping an irrationality out of sight of the audience makes it less salient, and so helps to keep intact the impression that everything is properly connected.' Cf. Phelan 2017: 34–6 on Aristotle's treatment of such 'probable impossibilities'.

[41] Plato (*Republic* 1371a 31) attributed the pleasure of such incidents to cognitive curiosity, the human desire for and pleasure in learning. Cf. Aristotle's own emphasis upon learning as a source of pleasure at *Poetics* 4.1448b 1–8.

in which the best storytellers successfully negotiate the Scylla and Charybdis of narrating stories which are, on the one hand, sufficiently wondrous (*thaumastos*) but are not excessively irrational (*alogos*) or unconvincing (*apithanos*), on the other. An audience's pleasure in witnessing exciting incidents can be marred and the wondrous lose its affect if pushed too far.[42] The secret to this successful negotiation lies in the effective telling of lies—in the manipulation of an audience's cognitive reasoning through syllogism and enthymeme, in order to represent the impossible as both probable and convincing (*Poetics* 24.1460a 18–29):[43]

> Homer has taught the other [poets] the proper way of telling lies/fictions, that is, by using syllogism (*paralogismos*)...What is convincing though impossible (*adunata*) is always preferable to what is possible (*dunata*) and unconvincing (*apithana*). Stories should not be made up of irrational (*alogos*) detail; so far as possible there should be nothing irrational, or, if there must be, it should lie outside the plot (*exo tou mutheumatos*).

What Homer does successfully and skilfully, according to Aristotle, is to direct his audience to draw false inferences. To adapt Aristotle's somewhat awkward illustration here, audiences are prone to processing narrative details using false logic, thus: (A) Odysseus was last seen wearing a purple cloak pinned with a golden brooch; (B) a stranger arrives in Ithaca reporting that he has seen a man wearing a purple cloak pinned with a golden brooch; (C) therefore the stranger has seen Odysseus. In Homer's account, the syllogism is not processed by the audience (the audience knows very well that the stranger is Odysseus himself) but by a character: Penelope (*Odyssey* 19.249–50). Aristotle's own logic seems to be that Homer (and his crafty internal character-narrator Odysseus) hides a bigger fiction—a wondrous, marvellous, exciting, or surprising incident (*thaumastos*), something improbable or impossible (*adunatos*)—by dressing it up in vivid, realistic detail (a figurative, narratological purple cloak pinned with a golden brooch). Alongside this important observation about narratees processing narratives, Aristotle also notices that audiences on the whole prefer, and experience greater pleasure and excitement from, those plots which present probable impossibilities

---

[42] In modern idiom, the equivalent of 'jumping the shark': a term arising from a 'wondrous' incident in the TV series *Happy Days* (in which a water-skiing Fonzie infamously does just that) which strained credibility and stretched audience patience too far, thereafter providing TV critics with a convenient (and quasi-Aristotelian) benchmark of the acceptable and unacceptable *thaumastos*.

[43] Aristotle discusses paralogism (or syllogism) in his *Sophistic Refutations* 5.167b 1–8 and *Rhetoric* 2.19 and 24. It is also worth noticing the logical and semantic incompatibility that Aristotle suggests here between stories (*logoi*) and irrational detail (*alogos*): both terms share the same lexical root.

ARISTOTLE **41**

over those which offer improbable possibilities.[44] Real life, the raw stuff of story, may be full of random coincidences and seemingly impossible or incredible incidents, but once this material is transformed into mimetic drama or narrative, audiences expect to find—and so look for—meaningful cause and effect, a synthesis of incidents arranged according to a series of probable or necessary connections.

3.4 *Katholou* and *idion*

As part of his detailed discussions of *muthos*, Aristotle considers those parts of a story that are essential and those that are inessential to its plot. Reverse-engineering the 'argument' or 'whole thing' (*katholou*) of two traditional stories from their familiar literary forms, Aristotle sets out all the significant story material, the core set of narrated situations and events, and orders them in their chronological sequence. His first summary looks at a tragic narrative, apparently based on Euripides' tragedy *Iphigenia in Tauris* (*Poetics* 17.1455b 3–12):[45]

We might look at the argument (*katholou*) of something like the Iphigeneia, thus: a certain girl was being sacrificed but disappeared in front of the eyes of those offering her up. She settled in a foreign land where the custom was to sacrifice strangers to their goddess, and eventually came to be the priestess overseeing this same ritual. Her brother happened to arrive (that a god directed him to go there, and to what end, lies outside of the plot (*exo tou muthou*)). He arrived, was seized, and was about to be sacrificed, when he made himself known ... saying, as was probable, that it had turned out to be not only his sister's fate to be sacrificed, but his too. And so he was saved.

Here the *katholou*, the argument or 'whole matter' of the Iphigenia story, is more expansive than the *muthos* of Euripides' tragedy. The plot of the play opens at Tauris with Iphigenia, a priestess of Artemis, standing before a bloodstained altar; her opening speech filling the backstory of her own sacrifice and disappearance, as well as giving background on the grisly Taurian custom of human sacrifice. Aristotle aptly begins his description of the *katholou* with those chronologically prior events, before reconstructing the rest of the story's key incidents in concise

---

[44] Lucas 1968: 230. Rationalizations in his own narratological terms of the impossible (*adunatos*) and illogical (*alogos*) incidents of Homeric epic are likely to have made up a significant part of Aristotle's lost *Homeric Problems*.
[45] Cf. Belfiore 1992.

chronolinear sequence—stressing both the causal and probable relationship between each significant incident as it occurs.

Aristotle's second summary deals with an epic narrative and complicates things by introducing two alternative terms with which to describe such a synopsis (*Poetics* 17.1455b 17–23):

> The *Odyssey's* story (*logos*) [or story of Odysseus] is not long: a certain man is away from home for several years, watched by Poseidon yet all alone. Back at home his possessions are being wasted by suitors and his son is being plotted against. But he arrives home, storm-tossed, and making himself recognized by only a few, attacks so as to save himself and destroy his enemies. That is the essential core (*idion touto*), while the rest is just episodes/digressions (*epeisodia*).

This summary follows the same basic re-ordered temporal-causal format as the general *katholou* of the Iphigenia story. It similarly focuses upon the initial conditions of the story (Odysseus' absence from home for many years, harried by Poseidon, separated from his men, and the resulting trouble at home); recognition (by a select few of his household); and resolution (in this case a double ending, in which Odysseus triumphs and his enemies are defeated).[46] But it leaves out a mass of events which Aristotle deems incidental and extraneous to the workings and *telos* of the plot. It does not seem to matter to Aristotle why or how Odysseus is away for many years, why or how he comes to be alone and watched by Poseidon. In keeping with his wider focus on ends rather than means, the consequences of these incidents are what matter most to Aristotle, and Odysseus' decade of adventures and misadventures are dismissed as mere episodes/digressions (*epeisodia*).

In this context, the essential *idion* of the *Odyssey* is reconstructed upon the same principles as the *katholou* of the Iphigenia story, where we see the same focus on the same narrative features, and a similar spotlight upon those actions and events which form the main storyline and action—excluding, in the Iphigenia story, the secondary 'subplot' involving Orestes' mission to recover a statue of Athena. Aristotle's tragic *katholou* and epic *idion*, then, both describe a clear narrative tier that is conceived as distinct from that of the *muthos*.[47]

The fact that Aristotle uses different key terms in reference to this narrative tier is significant here. The term *logos* is used throughout the *Poetics* in a wide array of both technical and non-technical applications,

---

[46] Aristotle refers to the double-plot structure of the *Odyssey* ('with opposite outcomes for good and bad characters') at *Poetics* 13.1453a 30–3.

[47] Meijering 1987: 226–30 offers a neat summary of the various uses to which the Greek scholia put the term *idion* and its cognates.

sometimes indicating a generalized sense of 'narrative discourse', sometimes 'the raw material or argument for a plot'—hence its received binary pairing with *muthos*.[48] In the context of Aristotle's summary of the *logos* or 'story' of the *Odyssey*, the second of these values is clearly implied: the narrative discourse of Homer's epic can hardly be described as 'not long' (as Aristotle claims: *Poetics* 17.1455b 17)—although its core narrative argument focusing upon the the forty-one days of Odysseus' return journey home to Ithaca *is* comparatively short.

In his *katholou* and *idion* of the stories of both Iphigenia and Odysseus, Aristotle is concerned with the nucleus of this basic story material, and that which is poetically configured into the plot of a tragic or epic narrative. Anticipating the Russian formalists' interest in story motifs, Barthes's interest in narrative nuclei, and Chatman's in story kernels, Aristotle reconstructs here the set of core 'motifs' (motif is defined by Prince as 'a minimal narrative unit at the syntactic level') that make up distinctive versions of two well-known myths.[49]

Although his undertaking is less ambitious than Propp's famous 'morphology' of the essential motifs of some one hundred traditional Russian fairytales, Aristotle undertakes something in a similar vein in his identification of the core motifs in the narratives of Iphigenia and Odysseus. For he indicates that his synopsis of the 'Iphigenia' is based on the plot of at least two separate stories, one by Euripides and another by a less well-known tragic or dithyrambic poet, Polyidus (*Poetics* 17.1455b 9–10). It is also possible that his reference to 'the story of the *Odyssey*' (*Poetics* 17.1455b 17) encompasses not only Homer's *Odyssey* but also 'the story of Odysseus' as retold by those other epic poets upon whose efforts at plotting Aristotle pours criticism elsewhere in the *Poetics*.

In this light we find a possible rationale as to why Aristotle elects to identify some parts of the *fabula* as inside and others as outside these plots. For the formalists, motifs 'can be logically essential to the narrative action and its causal-chronological coherence . . . or they can be logically inessential to it'.[50] Aristotle, it seems, has circumscribed a similar set of essential and non-essential motifs in these two stories and their familiar plots. His reconstruction of both stories in order to distinguish between their inessential (what the formalists would describe as 'free') and essential ('bound') motifs even anticipates Tomashevsky's recommendation that critics identify the core motifs of a narrative 'by retelling the story in

---

[48] See Lucas 1968: 91.
[49] See Tomashevsky 1965: 68, Reformatsky 1973: 197, Propp 1968: 14, Barthes 1966, Chatman 1978: 52, and Prince 2003 *s.vv.*
[50] Prince 2003: 55.

abridged form, then comparing the abridgement with the more fully developed narrative'.[51]

We may not agree with Aristotle's intuitions in differentiating essential from inessential, free from bound, but the operating principle of the theory and the methodology itself has validity. Thus, the specifics of Odysseus' adventures, the islands and peoples visited on his way home from Troy, are inessential to the plot of 'the story of Odysseus'—even though they represent some of the most colourful components of Homer's canonical (re)telling of this myth in the *Odyssey*. Another storyteller could change and rearrange all of these exciting incidents without impacting upon the essential narrative action or its causal-chronological sequence. Similarly, in the story of Iphigenia in Tauris, the details of how and why Orestes should turn up as a stranger in Tauris, the motivation and completion of his mission, are non-essential to the *muthos*—even though these incidents are arguably central to the religious dynamics of Euripides' tragedy (an important aspect of Greek tragedy that Aristotle consistently ignores). Another tragedian or poet could have Orestes arrive at Tauris on any number of missions, any of which would service the need to account for his coincidental reunion with his sister, and without impacting upon the main narrative action or its temporal-causal coherence.

In sketching out these two story summaries in *Poetics* 17, then, Aristotle is also sketching out the faint outlines of two revolutionary narratological principles—not only that of plot as a reworking of basic story material but also that of plot comprising essential and non-essential motifs. To pursue Todorov's uncanny image of Aristotle's narratology as a man with an already greying moustache emerging from his mother's womb, we notice that it is as if those moustaches are also already curled and waxed.

3.5 *Ethos*

Although Aristotle has fundamentally different views of character and characterization to those of most modern readers and critics, famously

---

[51] Tomashevsky 1965: 71. Cf. Prince 2003: 7: 'ARGUMENT: The summary of a narrative (usually consisting of the most important KERNELS making up that narrative). In Aristotelian terms, the set of events significantly involved in the ACTION of a play or epic. Some of these events may lie outside the PLOT proper of the epic or play: they may occur before its BEGINNING, for example. In other words, argument is a larger concept than plot: the murder of Laius is part of the argument of Oedipus Rex but not part of its plot.'

proposing that it would be possible to have a tragedy without character (*aneu ethon*) but not without plot (*Poetics* 6.1450a 23–4), his take on the 'incidental' role of character in both dramatic and narrative poetry is broadly aligned with that of Henry James, who famously asked:[52] 'What is character but the determination of incident? What is incident but the illustration of character?'

Aristotle too sees action and character as closely and dynamically interconnected: character (*ethos*) is configured by action (*praxis*). Indeed, one of the central tenets of Aristotle's theory of poetry is that mimetic art represents people 'in action' (*Poetics* 2.1448a 29). Agents are necessary in a narrative as agents act; but character is something extra, determined by the whys and the ways in which the agents act. The only character quality, if we can deem it as such, with which agents come pre-equipped is their innate nobility or baseness, that which determines their status as high (*spoudaios*) or low (*phaulos*). Like social status (say, whether one is born into an aristocratic family or born into slavery), these funda-mental characteristics appear to precede action and characterization proper.[53]

Otherwise, in the *Poetics*, as in his *Nicomachean Ethics*, Aristotle insists that character is the product of action: not only of actions actually or habitually performed, but of the purposeful decisions and choices taken about future actions—whether or not carried out.[54] In the *Poetics* we also find character defined as the colour that fills in the preliminary outline sketch afforded by the plot (*Poetics* 6.1450b 1–3), and as 'that which reveals moral choice' or *proairesis* (*Poetics* 6.1450b 7–9; cf. *Poetics* 15.1454a 15–21). Character actions and choices (which will be conveyed to an audience through character speech) will in turn demonstrate four key qualities: (1) *goodness* (characters should not be wholly unsympa-thetic); (2) *appropriateness* (women should behave like women, slaves like slaves); (3) *likeness* (characters should be both realistic, and 'like us'); and, finally, (4) *consistency* (characters should behave and speak according to the same principles of necessity and probability which govern a good plot).[55]

---

[52] James 1894: 392. For a contrary view see Fludernik 1996: 13: 'In my model there can...be narratives without plot, but there cannot be any narratives without a human (anthropomorphic) experiencer of some sort at some narrative level.'

[53] Cf. Hardison and Golden 1968: 82–3 for the view that nobility and baseness are not part of *ethos* at all.

[54] See in particular *Nicomachean Ethics* 6.13.

[55] Aristotle insists in the third book of the *Rhetoric* that different types of characters should speak differently and on different subjects, according to what is probable and appropriate to their type. He maintains that characters of each class, age, sex, and nation-ality will express themselves differently and that these nuances must be observed in the mimetic reproduction of their speech (*Rhetoric* 3.1408a 26–32).

Aristotle's observations upon both the subordination and contribution of *ethos* or character(ization) to plot inform his wider theories of poetics too. In neither of his plot summaries, for example, is character high-lighted: Iphigenia is identified merely as 'a certain girl', Odysseus 'a certain man'. Aristotle shows no concern with psychology, no interest in the concepts of hero or villain, nor, for that matter, in any of the archetypal actor functions or actants—helper, princess, or dispatcher—identified by twentieth-century narratology. Instead, he is primarily interested in character types, and in their social and familial relation-ships: in sisters and brothers (Iphigenia and Orestes), fathers and sons (Odysseus and Telemachus), friends and enemies.[56] In his discussion of narrative affect in the *Poetics* (14.1453b 14–21), Aristotle had empha-sized that there is nothing affective about enemies or 'neutrals' behaving with enmity towards one another. Therefore, if a plot is to move its audience with feelings of pity and fear, it must aim for a plot where there is enmity between friends and families (*philoi*). Indeed, it is on this basis that Aristotle contends there are only four basic plot patterns (*Poetics* 14.1453b 26–36), each one centring on some kind of conflict involving a social or familial relationship, with action or non-action and recognition before or after the (non)event driving each plot dynamic in a different direction—but in each case with the aim being to arouse emotions of pity and fear in the audience. In keeping with his emphases both upon affect and upon the synthesis of plot and character, Aristotle's classification of plot types is essentially predicated on the ways and degrees to which its character-agents achieve the final cause of their literary form—their emotional impact on an audience.

3.6 *Dianoia*

If Aristotle's treatment of *ethos* is slightly superficial in comparison to his treatment of *muthos*, his treatment of *dianoia* (character thought or intention) as the third component of tragedy is downright perfunctory. He simply directs his audience to his other work '*peri rhetorikes*'—his *Rhetoric* (*Poetics* 19.1456a 33–1456b 8).[57] In his brief discussions of

---

[56] As Belfiore 2000: 44 puts it: 'In each of [Aristotle's] four basic plot patterns, *philos* harms or is about to harm *philos*.' See also Belfiore 1992: 41–82.

[57] Both *Poetics* and *Rhetoric* share a common emphasis upon what the poet or speaker must do in order to produce the appropriate emotional responses in his audience: that is, *katharsis* in the case of poetry (*Poetics* 6.1449b 28) and persuasion in the case of rhetoric

dianoia there and elsewhere in the *Poetics,* Aristotle stresses the
rhetorical aspects of poetry, particularly as regards the convincing construction and presentation of character speech, so as to persuade an
audience to feel pity, fear, anger, and empathy (*Poetics* 6.1450b 4–12;
19.1456a 34–8; cf. *Rhetoric* 2). Such emotions are ideally elicited by
character action, but character speech is also an effective vehicle: in
line with Aristotle's general preference for dramatic over narrative
form, first-person character speech (impersonation within narrative) is
deemed more affective than third-person description, and direct impersonation through action (drama) is the most affective of all.[58] Thus,
when the direct mimetic demonstration of *ethos* through action is not
an option, then *dianoia*—the rhetorical expression of 'moral character' and intended action through character speech—offers an appropriate substitution.

The precepts outlined in Aristotle's *Rhetoric* help to reinforce the logic
of this—and to illustrate the synergies that Aristotle sees between drama,
narrative, and rhetoric. Indeed, throughout the *Poetics* Aristotle assumes
that an audience's understanding of a well-constructed plot is analogous
to their understanding of a well-presented argument.[59] Both the poet and
the orator aim to persuade their respective audiences by constructing an
intelligible and coherent discourse which appeals to their audiences'
emotions and expectations, and conforms to their presumptions about
what is logical, probable, and credible—manipulating where appropriate
their cognitive susceptibility to syllogism and enthymeme, to drawing
probable rather than true inferences.[60] Similarly, in the *Rhetoric* Aristotle
insists on the importance of structuring a speech like an epic poem,
offering a clearly defined beginning, middle, and end, and foreshadowing
in the *exordium* the work's key motifs, to help the audience focus their
attention appropriately. Drawing an analogy between epic, tragic, and
rhetorical beginnings, he advises (*Rhetoric* 3.14.6) that 'in speeches and
epic poems the *exordia* provide a foretaste of the theme, in order that
the audience may know beforehand what it is about, and that their

(*Rhetoric* 1.1355b 35–6a 20). On Aristotle's *Rhetoric* see Eggs 1984 and the essays collected
in Enos and Agnew 1998.

[58] This tallies with Aristotle's implicit suggestion in the *Poetics* that the greater the
degree of direct *mimesis*—the closer the audience can get to the action, as it were—the
more potent the affect.
[59] See Halliwell 1998: 100–103 on the affinities between poetry and rhetoric in the
Poetics, although he dismisses 'the common misconception that the stress of Aristotle's
tragic theory on pity and fear implies a rhetorical point of view'.
[60] In *Rhetoric* 2.19–24 Aristotle describes the ways that thought ought to be expressed in
speech form—including through enthymeme.

minds may not be kept in suspense'. Likewise, in a detailed discussion concerning the various emotions that an orator may seek to arouse in his auditors, Aristotle's *Rhetoric* also deals with audience cognition and anticipation, stressing the value of incidents and occurrences that are 'contrary to expectation' in arousing emotions of pity and fear.[61] Aristotle does not employ here the term *peripeteia*, but he clearly has something like a dramatic 'turning point' in mind. In his *Rhetoric*, then, Aristotle may be prescribing the best way to arouse pity and fear in the audience of a speech, but this rhetorical programme—with its emphasis upon the manipulation of *ethos* and *dianoia*—corresponds closely with that of his *Poetics* and discussions there of the best ways to arouse pity and fear in the audience of a tragedy. Aristotle's *Poetics*, it seems, offers us a partly 'rhetorical' theory of narrative.

3.7 **Diegetic** *mimesis*

Having initially proposed that all poetry is mimetic, Aristotle appears to perform an unhelpful *volte-face* on this position when, at the end of his treatise, he turns abruptly from 'tragedy and dramatic *mimesis*' to epic and 'diegetic *mimesis*' to offer us some final thoughts on narrative poetry (*Poetics* 23.1459a 14–17; cf. 24.1459b 33–6). Here epic is described for the first time in the *Poetics* as a mode of *diegesis* as Aristotle seeks to distinguish its generic form from that of tragedy. As his ensuing discussion makes muddily clear, all poetry is mimetic but some types of poetry are more mimetic than others.[62]

Praising Homer for his uniquely dramatic style of epic narration, Aristotle maintains that a good narrative plot should be constructed according to exactly the same principles already established for tragic plots (*Poetics* 23.1459a 16–24). With the obvious exceptions of music (*melopoeia*) and spectacle (*opsis*), epic and tragedy are composed of exactly the same principal parts: plot (*muthos*), character (*ethos*), thought (*dianoia*), and language (*lexis*). The core qualities and patterns that make a narrative plot well constructed (which here means to arrange in dramatic style—*sunistanai dramatikous*) thus mirror those already

---

[61] Book 2 of Aristotle's *Rhetoric* offers an extensive catalogue of the different emotions that an orator should understand and know how to perform and elicit in an audience, illustrated with examples drawn from tragedy and Homeric epic.

[62] In fact, Aristotle's exclusion of dithyrambic, lyric, and elegiac poetry from his discussion of ancient poetics already suggested this.

prescribed for dramatic plots: (1) unity, here understood specifically as a unified 'singleness' of action, rather than thematic, temporal, or character-based unity (cf. *Poetics* 8.1451a 15–35); (2) quasi-organic wholeness, having appropriate points of beginning, middle, and end (cf. *Poetics* 7.1450b 25–34); and (3) a formal coherence which allows it to deliver the 'proper pleasure' to its audiences.[63] The *telos* of narrative poetry is clearly signalled (just as it was for tragedy) as the production of an appropriate audience affect: narrative plots must be complete, in order to be coherent, and so pleasurable to an audience.

A narrative plot that is dramatic in its arrangement relies upon the same cognitive and affective devices as a tragic plot. It too should be structured around the actions of its characters, leading them—and the audience—through transformation (*peripeteia*), recognition (*anagnorisis*), and suffering (*pathos*), through to a satisfactory denouement (*lusis*). And although Aristotle does not explicitly remind us here that these devices work upon audience anticipation to effect a particular cognitive pleasure based upon experiencing and understanding a sequence of events that are at once surprising and foreseeable, the repeated emphasis upon epic's similarity to tragedy here makes these conditions clear: as in tragedy, epic's most potent means of affect are the components of its plot.[64]

Aristotle next turns from the similarities between tragedy and epic to their differences. Apart from the obvious distinction in metre, epic differs from tragedy most fundamentally in terms of its size—that is, its greater story and discourse time, its wider temporal and geographical range, and its more expansive cast of characters. In his discussion of tragic plots, Aristotle emphasized that the appropriate size of a tragic *muthos* was no more or less than that which allowed for clear perception and retention in the memory (*eumnemoneutos*) of the audience or reader (*Poetics* 7.1451a 4–10). He now makes the same point about epic narrative (*Poetics* 24.1459b 16–31): the ideal duration of an epic is one in which 'it should be possible for both the beginning and the end to be held in clear sight'.[65] And with an eye still towards affectivity, Aristotle claims that the wider temporal range available to epic allows greater scope for

---

[63] Aristotle's emphasis upon the particular form of pleasure induced by narrative picks up on Plato's reference to the same (*Republic* 10.607d). For modern narratological studies of such 'pleasure' see in particular Brooks 1984.

[64] Cf. *Poetics* 9.1451a 35–7 on the proper sequencing of events; and *Poetics* 10.1451b 32–5 on episodic plots.

[65] It is worth noting that Aristotle is assuming a traditional and performative model of reception for epic narrative, which would be narrated aloud by professional rhapsodes to an audience (hence his references to those 'listening' and 'hearing').

the development of variety and diversity 'for the benefit of the audience' (literally, 'the one listening', *ton akouonta*).

In these prescriptions about discourse and story length, Aristotle seems unconcerned with the physical and practical limitations imposed upon storytelling in the context of its ancient dramatic performance or recitation. His recommendations are rather concerned with the cognitive limitations of the audience. Aristotle apparently cares less about the length of time an audience must sit listening to or watching a narrative unfold, and more about the amount of story time an audience must grasp in order to cognitively process its plot. Aristotle's views on the ideal length and magnitude of a *muthos* refer then not only to the duration of the story's telling but to the timespan of the *fabula*—what Prince in his *Dictionary* defines as 'the set of narrated situations and events in their chronological sequence; the basic story material (as opposed to plot or *syuzhet*)'.[66]

However, having initially admired the narrative potential of epic and commended the opportunities for variation afforded by its length and scale, Aristotle apparently performs another U-turn here. Weighing up the relative merits of tragedy and epic he concludes that tragedy is better than epic because it is smaller in scale (*Poetics* 26.1462a 18–1462b 6). Now epic is judged inferior to tragedy, narrative deemed inferior to drama, because length and magnitude bring with them not only desirable storytelling opportunities pleasing to an audience, but also undesirable risks displeasing to it—above all, the risk of compromising the unity and intelligibility of the plot in telling a story that is too varied, too complicated, or too long. For, as we have seen, Aristotle is consistently and above all concerned with the impact of a story upon its audience. Narrative range and variety are important because of their positive affect upon the narratee, but only within appropriate bounds. Too much variety and too wide a range in the *fabula* compromise the unity and therefore the intelligibility of the plot. Hence Aristotle's 'Goldilocks' theory that the ideal narrative should be not too long and not too short, its plot not too varied and not too monotonous, neither too simple nor too complex, its action comfortably unified and 'singular' so as to achieve the ideal conditions for its reception.

---

[66] Prince 2003 *s.vv.* Belfiore 2001 has shown that we can better understand the treatment of time and temporality in the *Poetics* in the light of Aristotle's *Physics*. In his *Physics* Aristotle maintains that change and time can only be measured against each other: 'time is a measure of change' (*Physics* 4.10–14). Belfiore argues by extension that the 'limit of magnitude' in tragic plots is dependent upon the time required for its 'change of fortune' to unfold (44).

It is in this context that Aristotle's controversial comments on narrative time and temporality should be understood. Drawing a distinction between what is possible in dramatic versus narrative *mimesis*, Aristotle states that whereas it is technically impossible for the dramatic poet to show two or more separate scenes as unfolding onstage simultaneously, this is perfectly possible for the narrative poet (*Poetics* 24.1459b 22–7). Much has been made of Aristotle's apparent interest here in narrative order and temporal structure, but he actually has very little to say on this.[67] There is nothing here in reference to the sophisticated anachronies which are such common features in Homeric epic, nor to the prophecies and flashbacks so often found in tragic poetry—both of which are regularly commented upon by ancient scholia critics.[68] Instead, what really seems to interest Aristotle here is the potential benefit which the relative temporal freedom of narrative over drama, of epic over tragedy, has to offer audiences—and it remains a quirk within the modern reception of the *Poetics* that so many modern critics ignore Aristotle's views on this vexed issue of 'simultaneous narration' in Homeric epic.[69]

What is more, it is in the same context of narrative affect and impact that Aristotle's discussion of the proper use of the poet's own voice needs to be understood (*Poetics* 24.1460a 5–11):

Homer deserves praise for many things and especially for the fact that, alone of all poets, he understands the role of the poet's own voice. For the poet should speak as little as possible in his own voice, since this is not mimetic. The other poets play a part/act as themselves throughout their poems and only occasionally and briefly try *mimesis*, whereas Homer after a brief prelude/proem/preamble at once brings onstage a man or a woman or some other figure/character (*ethos*)—none of whom is lacking in character (*ethos*).

There are, in this analysis, three key elements to the mixed mode of *mimesis* that is Homeric epic: (1) the non-mimetic parts in which the poet speaks in his own voice (the first-person invocations to the Muses, and apostrophes); (2) the mimetic parts in which Homer speaks as one of

---

[67] Cf. Scodel 2008, de Jong 2001b: 589–91, Auerbach 1974: 3–23, Shklovsky 1990: 150, Zielinsky 1899–1901.

[68] As Lucas 1968: 223 notes: 'In the Messenger's speech two situations are amalgamated as they never can be in epic... The death of Neoptolemus is combined with the sorrow of Peleus, the passing of Oedipus with the conflicting emotions of his daughters.'

[69] As Nünlist 2009b: 69 n. 17 puts it: 'if modern scholars had given due weight to this passage, the bibliography on the alleged absence of simultaneous scenes in Homer might be shorter'. Ancient critics, probably following Aristarchus rather than Aristotle, are more nuanced in their approach to the question of simultaneity. See Nünlist 2009b: 69–71 for a selection of telling examples from the scholia.

his characters (character speech); and (3) the narrative parts in-between (third-person narrator speech).[70]

Homer's short introductory proems—in which we hear 'the voice of the poet himself' invoking the Muse—are evidently non-mimetic. Aristotle has previously suggested that if a poet narrates in his or her own voice then the work s/he produces is not mimetic: he denied poetic status to the proto-scientific works of Empedocles (despite the fact that he writes like Homer in hexameter verse: *Poetics* 1.1447b 17–19), and effectively excludes from his mimetic canon the works of ancient lyric, elegiac, and didactic poets who narrate their own personal experiences and emotions in their own first-person voice(s). To similarly deny mimetic status to those moments in which Homer briefly plays or speaks as himself (as, for example, in the opening line of the *Odyssey*, which begins 'Tell to *me*, Muse, of the man who…') is broadly consistent with such a view.[71] However, Aristotle praises Homer for speaking 'as little as possible in his own voice', for limiting the profile of his narratorial *persona*.

Comparisons with the epic poetry of Homer's near-contemporary Hesiod suggest that Aristotle may be right in singling out Homeric epic as distinctive in this regard. In stark contrast to Homer's low-profile identity as poet-narrator (achieved through his restricted use of the first-person voice and short proems), Hesiod constructs a highly visible storytelling *persona* for himself: the extended proem of the *Theogony* runs to 115 lines (8.9 per cent of the total poem), most of which are concerned with introducing Hesiod's narrative *persona* as a Boeotian poet-shepherd.[72]

For some critics, Aristotle makes an important ontological move here. In identifying parts of epic as non-mimetic, de Jong has suggested that Aristotle's theory stages an encounter between the poet speaking non-mimetically 'as poet', and mimetically either 'as character' or 'as narrator'. Thus, she suggests: 'it was Aristotle who made the first step

[70] On Homer ostensibly 'speaking as himself' see de Jong 2009: 93–9 and Block 1982.

[71] In his *Rhetoric* (3.14.6) Aristotle identifies the opening lines of the *Iliad* and *Odyssey* as equivalent to the introductory *exordia* of a speech, supporting this interpretation of the *Poetics* as presupposing a separation between proem and poem proper. Cf. Genette 1980: 37 n. 9 who, like Aristotle, regards Homer's proems as 'nonnarrative discourse'.

[72] Roughly 45 per cent of the lines of Homer's *Iliad* and 67 per cent of the *Odyssey* represent the direct speech of characters, whereas only thirty-four lines of the total 1,022 comprising Hesiod's *Theogony* (3.3 per cent) and only twelve lines out of the total 828 comprising the *Works and Days* (1.4 per cent) are in character speech. Debates both ancient and modern about what constitutes reported and direct speech renders these percentages 'guestimates'. On Hesiod's narrating *persona* see Griffin 1986.

in distinguishing between author (poet) and narrator'.[73] Robert Rabel advances de Jong's hypothesis to argue for the rhetorical 'representation' of a storyteller in Homeric epic, identified with the Muse(s), to which he refers throughout his own study as 'the Muse(s)-narrator'.[74] For Rabel, Aristotle's analysis suggests that Homer speaks (1) non-mimetically in *propria persona* in the brief proems that we find introducing the *Iliad* and *Odyssey*; (2) mimetically in the *personae* of his characters in the many direct speeches of the *Iliad* and *Odyssey*; and (3) mimetically in the *persona* of the 'the Muse(s)-narrator' in the remainder of his narrative.

The Homeric narrator whom we encounter in the *Iliad* and *Odyssey* may well be, as Scott Richardson describes him, 'a fictional character of sorts, a metacharacter, who plays his role not on the level of the story, but on the level of the discourse, the telling of the story'.[75] But this is not what Aristotle says or suggests anywhere in the *Poetics*. Despite the attention that Aristotle gives to *mimesis*, he never allows for the possibility that a poet-narrator might extend his *mimesis* of characters and actions to that of a narrating *persona* too. To have done so would have allowed him to defend all kinds of poetry against Socrates' criticisms in the *Republic* and to have challenged Socrates' willingness to accept some types of poetry but not others into his ideal state. It would also have brought lyric, didactic, and elegiac poetry within the compass of his own poetics. Aristotle might well have argued that every poetic 'voice' is always already mimetic: even the quasi-autobiographical voices found in ancient lyric and elegy belong to self-evidently and artificially mimetic poetic *personae*. No one speaks naturally in metre, after all. But he does not do this.

In the final analysis, any interest in narrators in the *Poetics* is overshadowed by Aristotle's principal interest in audiences. What matters most for Aristotle's reception-orientated model of poetics is the affect(s) of narrative *mimesis*. And we must turn elsewhere to gain an insight into

---

[73] De Jong 1987: 8. Her position later becomes more cautious. Cf. 2005b: 620: 'It is a matter of debate whether Aristotle may be credited with the invention of the notion of the narrator as an agent who is to be distinguished from the historical author, one of the basic principles of modern narratology. In chapter 24 of the *Poetics* he claims that poets should speak as little as possible themselves, and then continues to praise Homer, who "after a brief proem at once brings on stage a man or woman" ... [T]his could imply that for Aristotle the poet after the proem no longer speaks as himself but assumes a role or persona, that of narrator.' Ridgeway 1912: 235–41, Kitto 1966: 25, and Dupont-Roc and Lallot 1980: 380 offer similar readings.

[74] Rabel 2007.   [75] Richardson 1990: 2. See also Block 1982: 7.

how Aristotle might have understood the role of the storyteller. Indeed, we must look to a story in which Aristotle casts himself as narrator.

3.8 *Teleute*

Aristotle's esoteric *Poetics*, through a long reception process incorporating countless readings and misreadings, has profoundly influenced the shape of modern narratology. Yet there is little evidence to show that this treatise was influential to any significant degree in the ancient world.[76] Instead, the current evidence strongly suggests that Aristotle's poetic theories would have circulated in the third to first centuries BCE in two altogether very different vehicles: his major exoteric works *On Poets* and *Homeric Problems*.[77] There is, in fact, a reference to *On Poets* in chapter 15 of the *Poetics* (15.1454b 18), and general critical consensus that chapter 25 relates to a selection of material originally included in *Homeric Problems*.[78] These texts therefore offer us an ideal—and rare—opportunity to review Aristotle's theory of narrative in practice.

If the extant fragments of Aristotle's six-book exegetical commentary *Homeric Problems* (mostly preserved as quotations in secondary sources) are any guide, then this work is not our greatest literary loss from antiquity.[79] As the following quotation from the grammarian Athenaeus indicates, it appears to have been concerned with problems of consistency and probability—and primarily with responding to scholarly criticisms of Homer, explaining historical and antiquarian points of detail, and solving practical and moral problems presented by Homer's texts. Here the 'problem' appears to be the lack of extra-marital sex permitted

---

[76] On Aristotle's influence and reception in antiquity and beyond see especially Halliwell 1998: 286–323, Richardson 1980, Rostagni 1955: 188–237, and Brink 1963: 79–119.

[77] Janko 2011: 393–8 narrates the history of Aristotle's *On Poets* and *Poetics* and tells a persuasive story about why the former eclipsed the latter in antiquity. He also (2011: 358–9) offers a useful conjectural reconstruction of the complete argument of *On Poets*. See also Halliwell 1989: 149: 'The three books of *On Poets*, and the six or more books of *Homeric Problems* (presumably not in dialogue form), were in fact the two chief works in which Aristotle's ideas on poetry were disseminated in the ancient critical tradition; while the *Poetics*, originally produced for use within the philosophical school, never became at all readily available or widely known.'

[78] Cf. Kennedy 1989: 149, Else 1957: ix, Bouchard 2010, Halliwell 2002: 263–4.

[79] Halliwell 1989: 149–83 provides an accessible introduction to Aristotle's *Homeric Problems* and *On Poets*. See Carroll 2009 on potential links between Aristotle and the Homeric scholia.

to Menelaus in Homer's narrative (*Homeric Problems* F 144 Rose [Athenaeus 556d–e]):[80]

"We might be surprised," says Aristotle, "that nowhere in the *Iliad* does Homer have Menelaus go to bed with a concubine, [despite] having so many women ... it seems the Spartan does not want to shame his wife Helen, for whose sake he had put together the expedition to Troy. Agamemnon, meanwhile, is mocked by Thersites for having many women" ... "But it is improbable (*ouk eikos*)," says Aristotle, "that all his many women were for use, but were instead supposed to be a sign of prestige. In the same way, Agamemnon did not acquire a great volume of wine just so that he might get drunk."

This Homeric problem, according to Aristotle, is one principally relating to historical convention and its solution lies in understanding its 'probable' cause: that concubines in Homeric society likely signalled status rather than sex. This solution clearly corresponds with Aristotle's emphasis on probability throughout the *Poetics*. However, its easy dismissal of any psychological dimension to Homer's presentation of Menelaus' sexual fidelity to Helen demonstrates the narrowness of Aristotle's approach to Homer's narrative and to the complex characterizations often found therein. It also reminds us of the lesser significance (in comparison to plot) that Aristotle ascribes to character and characterization (*ethos*) across the *Poetics*, providing a glimpse, perhaps, of that theoretical stance put to practical application here.

Besides the fragments like this quoted in various Homeric scholia and commentaries, chapter 25 of the *Poetics* (25.1460b 37–1461b 25) appears to offer a condensed reworking and theoretically oriented digest of some of the key headlines of *Homeric Problems*, explicitly focusing as it does upon poetic and narrative 'problems' (*problemata*) and their 'solutions' (*luseis*). Without better knowledge of Aristotle's more expansive treatment of Homeric epic, however, *Poetics* 25 as it currently stands is riddled with puzzling ambiguities. Not least among these include the chapter's final summation pledging solutions to help solve problems with epic and tragic plots—among them, the impossible and unnatural, the irrational and illogical, the harmful and immoral, the contradictory, and the technically incorrect (*Poetics* 25.1461b 21–5). Debates on the nature and scope of these problems and their solutions remain vexed.

Aristotle's work *On Poets* is potentially more promising as an aid to negotiating some of the vagaries of the *Poetics* and in demonstrating Aristotle's theory of poetry in practice. Like the *Poetics*, Aristotle's

---

[80] On Aristotle's *Homeric Problems* and their relation to the *Poetics* see Bouchard 2010 and Huxley 1979.

dialogue reads in many places as a celebration and defence of poetry against the charges levelled against it by Plato's Socrates. Halliwell makes the case that *On Poets* may be read as 'an explicit, even polemical response to Plato', while Janko reads fragment 44 from the dialogue as an 'implicit reply to Plato's provocative condemnation of poetry as *mimesis*'.[81] Other fragments from his work *On Poets* similarly suggest Aristotle's resistance to Socrates' views on poetry in the *Republic*, including the observation that Plato's own writings represent the very mimetic mode that Socrates denounces. According to Aristotle (fragment 43a):[82]

[Plato] brought in very many further innovations, and introduced a form of dialogue by mixing it from poetry and prose, <representing> people asking questions, replying, and narrating.

The comparison that Aristotle draws between Plato's philosophical dialogues and Sophron's dramatic mimes in a separate fragment (44) suggests that we should regard the principal charge of fragment 43a above as relating to the mimetic form of Plato's writings: they mimetically reproduce and imitate characters in conversation 'asking questions, replying, and narrating'. Thus, Aristotle neatly exposes one of the central contradictions of Plato's proto-narratology in the *Republic*: its condemnation of mimetic forms of *diegesis* is itself formulated and delivered through that very mode.

In his work *On Poets*, Aristotle also appears to have been critical of Socrates' condemnation in the *Republic* of the affective powers of *diegesis dia mimeseos* in general and of the dramatic narratives of tragedy and comedy in particular. In a passage which clearly responds to Plato's *Republic* 10.606 a–b, Aristotle promotes his own theory of *katharsis* and argues that through the observation of others' emotions in both tragedy and comedy we learn to understand, release, and moderate our own emotions (fragment 55).[83] It is hardly surprising, then, that the fifth-century CE Neoplatonist philosopher Proclus, in his *Commentary on Plato's Republic* (fragment 56 in Janko's reconstruction of *On Poets*), refers to Aristotle's work *On Poets* as his 'dialogue *contra* Plato'.

But there was evidently much more to *On Poets* than an attempt to refute Plato and his Socrates. The studies by Rostagni, Laurenti, and,

---

[81] Janko 2011: 318–19 and Halliwell 1989: 150. Rostagni 1955: 263–77 and Ford 2004: 334 take different readings of Aristotle's resistance to Plato's Socrates but, as Janko 2011: 320 n. 2 suggests, the rejection of Plato's theory of poetry in *On Poets* might account for Plato's failure to appoint Aristotle as his successor as head of the Academy.

[82] Text and translation in Janko 2011: 442–3, reconstructed from Themistius' *Oration* 26 (*On Speaking*), 319A. See also Aristotle, *Poetics* 1.1447 b 9–13.

[83] On the verbal echo between these two passages see Janko 2011: 321.

most recently, Janko show that the three books of this dialogue originally comprised a sort of reflective history of poets and their poetry, a collection of anecdotes and stories about the lives of famous poets and the origins of the various literary genres in which they wrote.[84] It is not hard to imagine why such a work might have held more popular appeal than the set of lecture notes which then, as now, essentially comprises the *Poetics*. Amongst other stories and anecdotes, *On Poets* narrates Homer's biography (fragment 65), tells the story of how Susarion came to invent comedy (fragments 32–3), how tragedy subsequently evolved as a distinct genre (fragments 33b–42), and how philosophy evolved (fragments 43–4), with Plato himself credited with perfecting the dramatic fusion of verse and prose that characterizes his philosophical dialogues (fragment 43).[85] This diachronic sketch of literary history shares a broadly teleological emphasis with that outlined in the early chapters of the *Poetics*. In the *Poetics* Aristotle was principally concerned with the formal and final causes driving the evolution of poetry towards its perfect point (that is, Athenian tragedy). But in his work *On Poets*, as might be expected, there appears to be a greater focus on the efficient causes instigating the development of poetry from its primitive roots to its fifth-century BCE flourishing, and greater emphasis is accordingly placed upon the poets who make this happen.[86]

So, where Aristotle's *Poetics* was interested in Homer's plots, Aristotle's *On Poets* is interested in Homer's own life story. The account of Homer's early life (reconstructed by Janko with reference primarily to Pseudo-Plutarch, *On Homer* 1.3–4) is brief but offers us an excellent opportunity to appraise Aristotelian storytelling in the light of Aristotelian theories of story. According to Aristotle:[87]

On the island of Ios, at the time when Neleus, son of Codrus, was leading the Ionian migration, a local girl, having been impregnated by one of the divinities who dance with the Muses, and feeling ashamed of the episode because of the size of her belly, went to a place called Aegina. Some pirates who had disembarked there enslaved her and took her to Smyrna, which was at that time under Lydian

---

[84] Janko 2011, Laurenti 1984, Rostagni 1955: 255–322. See also Halliwell 1998: 1–2, 327.

[85] In Janko's reconstruction (fragment 43a), Aristotle also attributes to Plato the innovation of first fitting together the various discourses of ancient philosophy (natural science, ethics, mathematics, theology) and creating an organic unity ('a single living creature') from their parts.

[86] On the contribution of such diachronic studies of narrative to modern narratology see Fludernik 2003 and de Jong 2014.

[87] Translation adapted from Bassino 2014. Identified as fragment 65a in Janko 2011: 470–3. Cf. his commentary 527–8. On Pseudo-Plutarch's narrative *On Homer* see Keaney and Lamberton 1996, who date the essay to the last quarter of the second century CE, and Graziosi 2013: 79–82.

control. They sold her to the king of the Lydians, a friend of theirs named Maeon. He fell in love with her because of her beauty and married her. As she was whiling away the hours by the banks of the river Meles, it happened that her contractions started and she gave birth to Homer beside the river. Maeon accepted the child and raised him as his own, for the girl had died immediately after the delivery.[88] Not long afterwards, Maeon himself died. And because the Lydians were being colonized by the Aeolians and had decided to leave Smyrna, the leaders had made a proclamation that anyone who wished to join with/ follow them should go out of the city. Homer, although he was still young, said that he too wanted to *homerein* (i.e. to join with/follow); as a result of which he was called Homer (i.e. the Joiner/Follower) instead of Melesigenes (i.e. Born beside/Son of the river Meles).[89]

Of course, what we have here may represent a more or less verbatim quotation of Aristotle's own words from his dialogue *On Poets*, or merely Pseudo-Plutarch's own summary retelling of the story found there.[90] We do know from another ancient source (Diogenes Laertius' *Lives of the Philosophers*) that the third book of Aristotle's dialogue *On Poets* narrated a life of Homer—perhaps, as Janko suggests, to provide his readers with 'an entertaining "myth" at the end of the work'.[91] We know that much of the raw material for this 'myth' appears in both traditional and other fourth-century BCE biographies of Homer. And we know that Aristotle's *muthos* varied in significant ways from these other biographies, including that written by one of his contemporaries, Ephorus of Cyme—whose version is quoted as an alternative to Aristotle's story by Pseudo-Plutarch (*Life of Homer* 1.2).[92]

---

[88] Although the manuscripts supply the name 'Cretheis', I follow Janko 2011: 528 in seeing this as a later gloss.

[89] The story of Homer's life continues beyond this segment from Pseudo-Plutarch (1.4), a flashforward moving the narrative swiftly on from Homer's infancy to his maturity and death. There is no signal from Pseudo-Plutarch that his source has changed in 1.4, yet the style and tone of its telling is very different from the preceding 'Aristotelian' section. The narrative abruptly shifts into a different register, baldly linking together quotations of four short verses in the form of two prophetic oracles, a fisherman's riddle, and a funerary epigram—as found in Antipater of Thessalonica (or possibly of Sidon), the *Certamen*, and anonymous *Vita Homeri*. As Janko 2011: 527 concedes, 'Exactly how much of this passage is by Aristotle is not certain, as the author [sc. Pseudo-Plutarch] could have changed sources without saying so.' I adopt a more cautious approach than Janko's in assigning to Aristotle only segment 1.3 from Pseudo-Plutarch 1.1–5.

[90] On the formal features of the dialogue, including its likely speakers, see Janko 2011: 324–9. It seems probable that, unlike Plato who speaks through his character 'Socrates', Aristotle included himself as a 'character' in his dialogue(s).

[91] Janko 2011: 527. Cf. Graziosi 2002 and Rostagni 1955: 305–6.

[92] See Gigante 1996: 26 and Beecroft 2010: 73. It is noteworthy, given Aristotle's criticisms of annalistic history in the *Poetics*, that Ephorus appears to have been the first ancient historian to plot his material thematically rather than chronologically.

Approaching Aristotle's tale with due caution, we can nevertheless identify some of its narratologically significant 'Aristotelian' features. First, we notice that the author has selected an appropriately narrow focus—with clear beginning, middle, and end—for his plot (cf. *Poetics* 7.1450b 25–34). This is not the story of Homer's life, but the story of how 'Homer' came into being, how an ordinary Ionian kid named 'Melesigenes' (meaning 'son of Meles', or as Aristotle has it here, 'one born beside the river Meles') became the legendary 'Homer'. It is an origin story, an aetiology no less than a biography—a narrative prequel relating a kind of 'Homer: The Early Years' or 'Homer Begins'.[93] In keeping with the precepts outlined in the *Poetics*, Aristotle has not made the mistake of assuming that a plot will necessarily be unified and coherent if it is built around the life of an individual (*Poetics* 8.1451a 15–35). Following the example of Homer himself, whose *Odyssey* Aristotle praises for not attempting to include every incident in the hero's life, the action here is composite, coherent, and tightly plotted, dealing only with Homer's conception and childhood, and ending at the point of a new beginning.

Second, we notice that, although the central plot follows a broadly linear chronological sequence, it covers a couple of key incidents quasi-analeptically: we hear about the impregnation of an unnamed Ionian girl by a follower of the Muses, and about the decision to evacuate Smyrna, only after the event.[94] The plot begins (if not actually *in medias res*) by situating both story place ('on the island of Ios') and time ('at the time [of] ... the Ionian migration') within a turbulent zone of socio-political upheaval. Indeed, despite the mythological character of the raw story stuff on which this plot is based, the specificity of this opening immediately helps to establish the foundations of a storyworld which is not only realistically mimetic but—crucially—dramatic. Even the seemingly fantastical and exciting incidents—the supernatural character of Homer's father and the kidnap of his mother by pirates—are presented in a wholly plausible fashion, and are fully integral to the plot. Aristotle appears to be taking the dramatic-narrative style of Homer himself as his template for this brief narrative (cf. *Poetics* 4.1448b 34–5; 4.1448a 21–2; 24.1460a 5–11).[95]

---

[93] In this respect Aristotle anticipates the postmodern trend for film and novel 'prequels'.

[94] Although the fondness of classical Greek for past participle forms means that we should not overstate this anachrony.

[95] Pirates and kidnap feature as key narrative tropes in the ancient Greek novel, which emerges as a distinctive genre only in the middle of the first century CE. Aristotle's direct influence on this genre is unlikely, although—to paraphrase a very postmodern pirate, Captain Jack Sparrow—it's not impossible, just improbable (2003: *Pirates of the Caribbean: The Curse of the Black Pearl*).

The arrangement of the ensuing sequence of events is, moreover, patterned in broad accordance with Aristotle's prescription in the *Poetics* that the incidents and actions making up a plot should not be linked by mere temporal succession but motivated by probable (*eikos*) or necessary (*anangkaion*) causality (*Poetics* 9.1451a 35–7). In Forster's famously Aristotelian example: 'The king died and then the queen died' is only a story; 'The king died and then the queen died of grief' is a plot because here we encounter causation.[96] Here in Aristotle's narrative we find more nuanced examples of such causation: an unmarried girl leaves the relative safety of her home because she has been raped and made pregnant; unprotected, she is captured by pirates who sell her on to the Lydian king Maeon because he happens to be 'a friend of theirs'; Maeon falls in love with her because of her beauty; adopts her child as his own because she dies in childbirth; and 'not long afterwards' dies himself. No direct causality is attributed in this last case, but—as Aristotle notices in the *Poetics*—human susceptibility to drawing false inference and syllogism potentially supplies grief as the missing causal link here (as it does for Forster's 'story').

Driving this plausible *muthos* forward we see a cast of character actors also behaving in accordance with the Aristotelian principles of probable or necessary *ethos* (characterization): shame drives a girl, unmarried yet pregnant, to flee her home; love drives a king to marry this beautiful, pregnant, vulnerable girl; fear of invasion drives the Lydian leaders, in the absence of their king, to evacuate their city; and a young orphan, the dead king's adopted son, chooses to go with them, driven hard by necessity (cf. *Poetics* 15.1454a 32–6). What is more, necessity and probability drive Aristotle's selection of this cast of characters in the first place. In his *Poetics*, Aristotle warned (*Poetics* 14.1453b 21–5) that a storyteller 'cannot undo time-honoured plots . . . but he can be inventive as well as making use of traditional stories'. Here we see that precept put into practice as Aristotle inventively incorporates most of the traditional tales about Homer's birth even as he configures them into his own new plot. So, Homer's mother is raped by a *daimon* 'who dances with the Muses' to explain her baby's subsequent poetic genius; she ends up in Lydian Smyrna to account for the enduring tradition that placed Homer's birth there; she gives birth beside the river Meles to account for Homer's supposed 'real' name Melesigenes; and, after her death, her baby is adopted by King Maeon to explain Homer's ancient nickname,

---

[96] Forster 1927: 86.

Maonides. Significantly, the identity of Homer's 'real' father is left obscure, and Homer's mother is identified only as 'a certain girl' (*kore*).[97]

The central characters of Aristotle's story experience plenty of suffering (*pathos*: cf. *Poetics* 11.1452b 9), but no obviously dramatic transformation (*peripeteia*) or recognition (*anagnorisis*) in this short narrative. Nevertheless, the *telos* of the plot—the transformation of Melesigenes into Homer—which is at once both surprising and foreseeable, does play upon the audience's anticipation of such, and affects a distinctive cognitive pleasure through our recognition (and re-cognition) of how Homer came by his name.

Several etymological variants purporting to explain the source of Homer's name were popular throughout antiquity. One tradition, seeing in the name Homer the Greek word for 'hostage'—*homeros* (ὅμηρος)—simply claimed that Homer or his father had once been taken hostage.[98] More imaginatively, Pseudo-Plutarch, our source for Aristotle's narrative here, attributes one of the most enduring versions to Ephorus, who claimed (Pseudo-Plutarch 1.5.2):

His name was changed to Homer after he went blind; this is what the Cymaeans and the Ionians called the blind on account of their needing *homereuontes* (guides) [literally, people to follow].

The folk etymology underpinning this version of Homer's name relies upon the supposed need for the blind to 'follow' (*homerein*) a guide and (playfully?) casts Homer—who all other Western poets 'follow'—as himself originally a blind 'follower'. The same etymology may inform Aristotle's explanation that Homer receives his name when he declares his wish to 'follow' (*homerein*) the Lydian leaders in the evacuation of Smyrna.

However, Janko suggests a more persuasive and appropriately 'Aristotelian' etymology for Aristotle's narrative: the key verb here—*homereo* (ὁμηρέω), a compound based upon ὁμ- (together, with) and ἀραρίσκω (join, fit together)—means 'join together, meet with'.[99] This is certainly the sense in which it is used in Homer's *Odyssey* 16.468. So, when Aristotle has young Melesigenes wishing to 'follow' (*homerein*) the Lydian leaders, it is probable that he also means to 'join together with' (*homerein*) them. When we consider that, in the Greek lexicon, a poet is

---

[97] Recall Aristotle's identification of Iphigenia in *Poetics* 17.1455b 3.

[98] This tradition is preserved in Proclus, the *Certamen*, and several of the ancient *Lives of Homer*. See Graziosi 2002: 79–82.

[99] Janko 2011: 528. In *Theogony* 39, Hesiod also describes the role of the Muses as 'fitting things together (*homereuein*) with their song'.

a 'maker' (*poietes*) and a rhapsode (according to one etymological tradition) is 'one who stitches or strings songs together' (from the compound of ῥάπτω—one who stitches—and ᾠδή—songs), it is wholly apt that the future poet Homer should take his name from the act of 'joining together'.[100] And when we recall that, in Aristotle's *Poetics*, a poet is a maker of plots, one who literally 'fits together' incidents and events into well-arranged plots (*Poetics* 1.1447a 9: *sunistasthai tous muthous*), it is not only Aristotle's alternative etymology for Homer that seems the perfect fit. Aristotle's narrative *praxis* and his narrative theory join together pretty seamlessly too.

---

[100] On this etymology of 'rhapsode' see Pindar, *Nemean* 2.1–3.

4 Ancient narrative theory after Aristotle—Horace

> *The writings of Socrates will show you material, and words will easily follow when material is already provided.*
>
> Horace, *Ars poetica* 310–11

4.1 *Arche*

If we heed Aristotle's own warnings about drawing false inferences based on the fallacious logic of *post hoc ergo propter hoc* temporal-causal connections, then we should be cautious about making direct connections between the narrative theories of Aristotle and later theorists in antiquity.[1] As Richard Janko reminds us:[2] 'there is as yet no solid evidence that...anybody until later antiquity, knew the *Poetics*'. We should especially resist the assumption that ancient narrative theory after Aristotle necessarily responds to his *Poetics*. Yet, in several of the histories, genealogies, and backstories that contemporary narratologies trace for themselves, post-Aristotelian writers such as Horace are assumed to form part of a straightforwardly linear reception and refinement of the proto-narratological ideas first set out in the *Poetics*. Thus, it is principally into the role of Aristotle's legatee that most modern narratological encyclopaedias and handbooks tend to cast Horace and his *Ars poetica*—a verse epistle addressed to the Piso family, written sometime around 10 BCE.[3] Heta Pyrhönen's claim that 'Aristotle's precepts were reformulated and popularized by the Roman poet Horace in

---

[1] On Aristotle's influence and reception in antiquity and beyond see especially Halliwell 1998: 286–323, Richardson 1980, Rostagni 1955: 188–237, Brink 1963: 79–119, and Poulheria 1995 and 1997.

[2] Janko 2011: 397–8.

[3] Laird 2007 offers a good general introduction to the *Ars poetica*; Brink 1971 and Rudd 1989 offer more detailed commentaries; and Russell 1973 and 1981 remain useful surveys. See also Freudenberg 2002. Golden 2010 offers an excellent study of the reception of the *Ars poetica* from the sixteenth century to the twenty-first.

his *Ars poetica*' is fairly typical.[4] Patrick O'Neill in the *Routledge Encyclopedia of Narrative Theory* posits a similar relationship between the two, and extends the reach of Horace's supposed inheritance well into the twentieth century. In this reading, Aristotle is credited with first identifying the advantages of Homer's epic technique, and his successors—specifically Horace—with raising it 'to the status of a prescriptive structural principle'.[5]

However, the dynamics of this complicated reception pattern suggest otherwise. Renaissance readers saw Horace's accessible and authoritative *Ars poetica* as a straightforward reformulation of Aristotle's confusing and contradictory *Poetics* and so made retrospective sense of Aristotle's proto-narratological precepts in the light cast by Horace's. They did so despite the fact that Horace's poetics show zero concern with the cornerstones of Aristotle's *Poetics* (unsurprisingly, given that Horace is unlikely to have read the *Poetics*): there is nothing here on *mimesis*, *katharsis*, or *muthos*.[6] Nevertheless, using the latter work to fill in the gaps and *aporiai* in the earlier, Renaissance critics subsequently saw clear correspondences between the two theorists and their theories, thereby establishing an accepted heuristic fiction—passed on to modern narratologists through our own reception of that Renaissance scholarship—that Horace's *Ars poetica* represents a Roman reworking of Aristotle's *Poetics*: *post hoc ergo propter hoc*.[7]

4.2 Horace's 'Letter to the Pisones' or *Ars poetica*

Modern theorists and critics who insist upon seeing an Aristotelian influence on Horace's precepts have produced somewhat skewed readings

---

[4] Pyrhönen 2007: 110–11. Cf. Kearns 2005: 201–2.

[5] O'Neill 2005: 366–70.

[6] Horace's insistence that a *fabula* (story or play) should imitate reality (*Ars poetica* 338: *proxima veris*) or that a poet should look to real life for its models (*Ars poetica* 317–18: *respicere exemplar vitae morumque*) represents only the most superficial analogue to Aristotle's sophisticated concept of *mimesis*.

[7] A series of major commentaries and translations of the *Poetics* emerge in the sixteenth century, among them Robertello's *In librum Aristotelis de arte poetica explicationes* (1548), Minturno's *De poeta* (1559), Julius Caesar Scaliger's *Poetices libri septem* (1561), and Lodovico Castelvetro's *Poetica d'Aristotele vulgarizzata e sposta*. In England, however, it was not until the next century that the authority of the *Poetics* began to be taken seriously—largely as a result of commentaries upon Horace's *Ars poetica* arguing for a genealogical link between the two works. Lucas 1968: xxii–xxv offers a succinct summary of the transmission and translation of the *Poetics*. For a summary overview of the legacy of the *Poetics* see Habib 2005: 60–1.

of the *Ars poetica* as a result. Irene de Jong invites us to see Aristotle's ideas on narrative unity in the *Poetics* as forming a principal component of Horace's famous preference for beginning a story in the middle (*in medias res*), suggesting that:[8]

Two features are combined here: (1) an author should not treat everything but concentrate on a single action (cf. Aristotle, *Poetics* 8) and (2) he or she should start at the end (possibly including earlier phases of the fabula in the form of analepses or flashbacks).

Elsewhere, she refines this reading but still maintains that Horace is responding directly to the *Poetics*, claiming that, in the *Ars poetica*:[9]

[Horace] is adopting ideas of Aristotle, as set out in chapter 8 of his *Poetics*. Both Horace and Aristotle are therefore talking about the choice of the *fabula* (e.g. the ten years of Odysseus' return) out of the material (the life of Odysseus from his birth).

This isn't exactly what Horace himself has to say on the matter of starting a story *in medias res*. According to Horace, Homer's arrangement of the story in the *Iliad* represents a model of narrative organization because he opens his story in the thick of the action—*in medias res*—without an introductory exposition and without then retrospectively filling in the backstory with a completing analepsis (*Ars poetica* 147–50):[10]

> He does not trace the rise of the Trojan war from [Leda's] eggs:
> he always hurries straight to the action and into the middle of
>   things,
> just as if they were [already] known to the audience, and what
> he despairs of being able to polish in his writing/hand, he leaves
>   out.[11]

Horace says nothing about starting 'at the end' as de Jong suggests above (a reading which is hard to square with Horace's own *in medias res*

---

[8] De Jong 2005c: 242. Cf. Aristotle, *Poetics* 8.1451a 15–35 on the necessity of careful selection and arrangement of story material in order to construct a coherent and unified plot—with reference to Homer's *Odyssey* but without explicit discussion of the *in medias res* trope. *Poetics* 23.1459a 30–7 offers a closer parallel to Horace in its praise for Homer's decision not to narrate the beginning and end of the Trojan War in his *Iliad*, but to focus upon just one episode (sc. in the middle).

[9] De Jong 2007: 9 n. 20.   [10] Cf. Genette 1980: 51–4.

[11] Similar observations on Homer's emplotment of his story are made in the Homeric scholia (cf. schol. B *Il.* 2.494–877) and in Pseudo-Plutarch (2.162). The scholia note that after beginning *in medias res*, Homer then supplies any salient missing details from the backstory via flashbacks and digressions. Horace seems to claim (wrongly) that Homer simply leaves such details out.

formulation), although his reference to Homer's exemplary instincts in selecting some material from the Trojan myth-kitty and rejecting the rest certainly does indicate recognition of a distinction between what de Jong terms the *fabula* from the raw story material.[12]

Similarly interested in pressing the Aristotelian tenor of Horace's poetics, Robert Scholes and Robert Kellogg in their 1966 *Nature of Narrative* read Horace's commendation for beginning a story *in medias res* as a commentary upon the signal importance of Aristotelian narrative unity and singularity of plot:[13]

starting a story with a plunge *in medias res*, which came to be thought of as a typical "epic" device in Western literature, does not merely mean Homer—nor Horace who pointed out the device—starting in the middle and then filling in both ends of the hero's life ... The deeds of Achilles, or the life of Achilles, or even the death of Achilles are not the subject of this narrative. The plot of the *Iliad* focuses on one episode in the hero's life, just as his characterization focuses on one element of his psyche; and the subject is the same in both—anger.

Again, this isn't exactly what Horace himself has to say on the matter. He draws no explicit or inferential connection between singularity of action, unity of plot, or of character, as Scholes and Kellogg suggest. Rather, Horace praises Homer for the ways in which he ingeniously selects and structures his material from an already familiar story.

Indeed, if we resist the urge to read Horace through Aristotle, we notice that the emphasis in this key section of the *Ars poetica* is not upon plot unity—or any kind of unity—but upon the arrangement and sequential ordering of pre-existing story stuff, according to the principles that Roman rhetoric recognizes as 'disposition' or *dispositio*.[14] It is not an easy task to establish a reliable chronology of influence here but just as it is reasonable to assume Horace did not know Aristotle's *Poetics*, it is safe to assume that Horace would have known the *Rhetorica ad Herennium* (*Rhetoric for Herennius*)—the oldest extant Roman handbook on rhetoric—and Cicero's *De inventione* (*On rhetorical invention*). These

---

[12] In formalist and structuralist narratologies, this corresponds with the *syuzhet*.

[13] Scholes, Phelan, and Kellogg 2006 [the 1966 edition is revised and expanded with Phelan in 2006]: 209–10. Their reading of Horace is strongly coloured by Aristotle's points in *Poetics* 23.1459a 30–7.

[14] A point recognized by Prince 2003: *s.vv.* He defines the narratological concept of *in medias res* as: 'The method of starting a narrative (and, more specifically, an epic) with an important situation or event (rather than with the first situation or event in time). Homer opens the *Iliad in medias res* (in the midst of things) rather than *ab ovo* (with the account of Helen's birth, for example) ... Originally ... it referred to a principle of selection (Horace): the narrator starts with the situation pertinent to his or her account (and takes its constituents to be well-known).'

works both consider in detail the matter of *dispositio* (structure): the careful arrangement of individual words, sentences, and ideas—of both *verba* (words) and *res* (things or actions)—in order to achieve optimal impact and effect upon an audience (*Rhetorica ad Herennium* 316; *De inventione* 1.9). The art and the aim of *dispositio*, we are advised by these handbooks, is the judicious division of the whole so as to achieve the desired effect of either tension or completeness. Tension is achieved by arranging the division so as to focus principally on the beginning and end; completeness by focusing on the beginning (*initium*), the middle (*medium*), and the end (*finis*).[15] In this light, Horace's most famous precepts on narrative sequencing and structure would appear to owe more of a direct debt to Roman rhetoric than to Aristotelian poetics.

Indeed, Horace's related precepts on the reworking of traditional story stuff also looks to be informed by rhetorical rather than Aristotelian theories. In addition to his praise for Homer's careful arrangement of traditional story material at *Ars poetica* 147–50, Horace advises: 'A writer should either follow tradition, or invent internally consistent details' (*Ars poetica* 119–20: *aut famam sequere aut sibi convenientia finge,/scriptor*). And he repeatedly stresses the virtues of treating familiar material (*Ars poetica* 131: *publica materies*) rather than inventing new stuff, recommending 'poetry crafted from the familiar' (*Ars poetica* 240: *ex noto fictum carmen*).[16] Niall Rudd argues that Horace here 'means style, not content' on the basis that this poetic crafting is to be achieved through 'linkage and combination' (*Ars poetica* 242: *series iuncturaque*)—the kind of rhetorical *dispositio* that usually applies to the verbal rather than the subject content of a poem.[17] This kind of 'linkage' is certainly what Horace has in mind when he refers to the 'stringing together' (*verbis serendis*) and 'clever arrangement' (*callida iunctura*) of words earlier in the poem (*Ars poetica* 46–8). But set within the context of his wider consideration of the poet's fundamental task as consisting in the selective rearrangement of old stories and plots, the reference here to creating a poem from stuff that is familiar or well known (*noto*) most obviously applies to story *content* and not (only) to style and language.

---

[15] See Lausberg, Orton, and Anderson 1998: 209–10. Grabes 2014: 769 also acknowledges these early discussions of rhetorical structure and sequence as the ancient forerunners to modern narratological treatments of the same and identifies Horace as one of the key ancient theorists whose work can be read as 'anticipating the later differentiation between chronological and non-chronological narrating'.

[16] Beware the false syllogism that connects Horace's advice here with Aristotle's (*Poetics* 14.1453b 21–5): a poet 'cannot undo time-honoured plots … but he can be inventive as well as making use of traditional stories'.

[17] Rudd 1989: 190.

Thus, it appears that Horace does indeed demonstrate a basic recognition that a new story is composed through the rearrangement and reconnection—the 'linkage and combination' or *series iuncturaque*—of pre-existing story stuff (*fama*) and the rearrangement of story material into an emplotted narrative. But he does not need Aristotle or the *Poetics* in order to achieve this.

The longstanding but misrepresentative reception of Horace's *Ars poetica* as a reworking of Aristotle's *Poetics* risks distracting attention from the distinctively Roman and rhetorical character of Horace's ideas on narrative. It also risks overshadowing the marked affinities between Plato's Socrates and Horace's own narratological *persona* on the subjects of poetry and storytelling.[18] For, not only do both writers mediate their poetological and narratological precepts through distancing frames (Socratic 'irony' and Horatian satire respectively), both share a common concern with the rhetorical and affective impact of poetry upon its audiences.

Like Plato's Socrates, Horace emphasizes the ethical and moral responsibilities incumbent upon the poet, whose work should influence his audience positively through the representation of good characters behaving well (*Ars poetica* 196–201, 312–15; cf. Plato, *Republic* 3.396c–e). Like Socrates, he repeatedly emphasizes the importance of reader response (*Ars poetica* 102–3, 240–3; cf. Plato, *Republic* 3.395c– 96a).[19] In particular, Horace echoes Plato's (Socratic) concerns regarding the psychological and ethical impact of poetry (*Ars poetica* 333–4):

> Poets either want to educate or to entertain,
> or to tell what is both pleasurable and proper in life.

Poets and poetry, Horace claims, aim either to benefit their readers pedagogically or didactically, or to bring them pleasure, or to do both—offering a mixture of entertainment and education. In each case it is the impact upon the reader that is important. And, as in Socrates' discussion of poetry in the *Republic*, there is an important ethical dimension to this position. While Socrates was concerned that mimetic poetry might teach its hearers, readers, and performers bad habits by exposing them to bad role models and characters behaving badly (*Republic* 3.395d–396a), Horace suggests that poetry can teach its readers how to live well, how to live a good life, by showing and telling them what is fit and proper (*idoneus*). Both Plato's Socrates and Horace, then, share a

---

[18] See Herrick 1946 and Golden 2010.   [19] See Cronk 1999.

common interest in what modern narratologists would recognize as narrative ethics. As Jim Phelan notes:[20]

> beginning with Horace's *Ars poetica*, and its dictum that the purpose of literature is to instruct and to delight, [treatises on literature] found a place for ethics. By linking the two purposes, Horace emphasized the interaction of the ethics of the told (and its role in instruction) and the ethics of the telling (and its role in delight).

Rather than 'beginning' with Horace, we can see this ethical dimension as one of the key features of Plato's *Republic*.[21] Indeed, one of the most intriguing aspects of Horace's interaction with Plato's writings appears in the form of a tip (*Ars poetica* 310–11):

> The writings of Socrates/the Socratics will show you material,
> and words will easily follow when material is already provided.

As Sedley has suggested, here the 'attractive possibility is that the reference [to Socratic writings— *Socraticae...chartae*] is in fact to Plato'.[22] Plato's *Ion* and *Phaedrus* have several themes in common with Horace's *Ars poetica* and the material content (*rem*) provided by Plato's Socrates in these works might very well represent the sort of pre-existing 'stuff' that Horace has in mind for easy poetic reworking of his own here. This would include, for example, Socrates' playful discussions of poetic inspiration as a kind of madness (*Ion* 533e–535a and *Phaedrus* 228b–263d3)— an idea which Horace also famously explores in this poem (*Ars poetica* 295–300). More significantly, this would also include Socrates advising us in the *Phaedrus* on the proper form and arrangement of all discourse (*Phaedrus* 264c):

> Every discourse should be organized, like a living organism, with a body of its own, as it were, neither headless or footless, but with a middle and with limbs, all composed in apt relation to each other and to the whole.

Horace similarly insists upon the organic unity of the ideal poem, opening the *Ars poetica* with this explicit consideration and returning repeatedly to the topic of form and composition. Indeed, it is out of this emphasis upon organic unity which Horace's most important proto-narratological precepts and intuitions arguably emerge. The poem opens with Horace anticipating the response of a viewer to encountering the image of a monstrous hybrid that is part woman, horse, bird, and fish—a

---

[20] Phelan 2014: 535.

[21] On narrative and ethics in Plato's *Republic* see Phelan 2014: 534–5, Korthals-Altes 2005: 142, Booth 1961: 385, and chapter 2 in this volume.

[22] Sedley 2014: 119.

picture which also anticipates the reader's response to encountering the strange hybrid that the *Ars poetica* itself represents (1–9):[23]

> If a painter had chosen to put a human head
> on a horse's neck, and covered over with multicoloured plumage
> a random collection of limbs, so that what was a lovely woman at
>   the top
> ended hideously in the tail of a black fish,
> invited to look, could you hold back your laughter, my friends?
> Believe me, dear Pisos, a book would be just like that picture
> if its own vain fancies were so conceived, like a bad dream,
> so that neither its foot nor its head could be related
> to a unified form.

Significantly, Horace's initial representation of this picture describes— indeed, *narrates*—the (hi)story of its production before moving on to imagine its reception as a finished product. We follow the ecphrastic narrative as an artist first paints a human head (a female head, we subsequently discover), then adds the body of a horse, then covers it with feathers, and then gives it a fish's tail.[24] The Latin syntax markedly enhances this impression of narrativity. The flag of the conditional 'if' clause (*si*) is delayed, inducing the reader to approach the first line of the poem as a narrative report: '[Once upon a time…] A painter joined a human head to a horse's neck' (*Humano capiti ceruicem pictor equinam/ iungere*). And the verbs initially relate to the artist's rather than the viewer's activity: he joins (*iungere*) and covers/introduces (*inducere*) his material in a coordinated series of different steps at different temporal junctures.[25]

The head of Horace's own poem thus begins with an image of the very creature that Socrates describes to Phaedrus: a 'living being' that has the head of a woman, the body of a horse, covered with the plumage of a bird, and the tail of a fish (*Ars poetica* 1–5). In what is potentially an inventive and playful misreading of Socrates, Horace's chimera technically conforms to the rules of organically unified composition commended by Socrates in the *Phaedrus*. Horace's chimera too has its own

---

[23] The apt response, Horace suggests, is laughter or derision (*risum*)—a hint perhaps as to how we are to read and respond to the satirical character of the poem itself.

[24] In a much abbreviated form, Horace's ecphrasis here reflects the narrative mode of Homer's account of Achilles' shield—described through an account of its making (*Iliad* 18.476–608).

[25] *OLD s.vv.* There may be a rhetorical allusion here too: according to classical rhetorical handbooks, the first principles of composition involved *invenio* and *dispositio*—the selection and arrangement of material. See Schwindt 2014: 65 for an alternative reading of Horace's 'narrative' here.

body, and is neither headless nor footless. It has a trunk and limbs, with each of these incongruous yet congruous body parts joined in appropriate relation to one another and to the whole. The woman's head aptly joins the neck of the horse (where else should it go?), the horse has the tail of a black fish (it is not sprouting from the woman's nose, or the horse's feathered fetlock). And Horace makes it clear that the painter responsible for this creature has paid attention to its careful composition, so as to join (*iungere*) and connect (*collatis*) its parts into a fantastic whole. In these terms, Horace's chimera—and his own chimerical poem—corresponds perfectly (albeit satirically) with Socrates' precepts on organic unity and synthesis.[26]

Horace's allusion to 'the writings of Socrates/the Socratics' or *Socraticae chartae* (*Ars poetica* 310) also points us towards a potentially satirical engagement with Socrates' precepts on the relative merits of *diegesis* and *mimesis*. There is a distinct stress throughout the *Ars poetica* upon the value of showing over telling, emphasizing the difference in affect upon an audience that can be achieved according to whether we observe it for ourselves (through *mimesis*) or merely hear it reported (through *diegesis*). So, imitating and remixing Socrates' point that 'narration may be either simple narration, or narration through imitation, or a mix of the two' (*Republic* 3.392d), Horace tells his own readers (*Ars poetica* 179–88):

> Things are either acted on stage, or reported.
> The mind is affected less intensely through the ear
> and more through the faithful focus of the eye, and that which
> the spectator witnesses for himself. But you must not put on stage
> things better acted behind the scenes, and you must keep out of
>   sight many actions which a messenger's eloquent report may
>   presently deliver.
> Don't let Medea murder her sons in front of the audience;
> and don't let the evil Atreus openly cook human entrails.
> Don't let Procne be turned into a bird, or Cadmus into a snake on
>   stage.
> Whatever you show me in this way, disbelieving it, I hate it.

There are mixed messages here. We are told that the eyes are a more powerful conduit of emotion and affect than the ears, drawing a clear

---

[26] Lines 1–152 of the poem deal explicitly with matters of unity, transition, arrangement, and organization of material. Laird 2007: 138 notes that Horace's suggestive parallels between the chimaera and his own poem go back to Plato's *Republic* 6.487e–488a where Socrates offers a '*meta*-iconic' *eikon* or image of a painter who makes images of fantastic hybrid creatures to illustrate one of his own arguments.

distinction between the relative merits of showing versus telling—not just on the stage, but in narrative poetry too. Yet the reference to the vivid narrative of the messenger speech, the usual vehicle for conveying grisly scenes to the audience in ancient tragedy, shows Horace's recognition that narrative *diegesis* may be a more effective and affective mode of discourse than *mimesis* in some circumstances. Horace's initial reduction of Socrates' tripartite typology of discourse into two—things shown (*agitur*) and things told (*refertur*)—is quickly reformulated to stress the merits of a third, mixed, kind blending both *mimesis* and *diegesis*, both showing and telling.

Of the many things shown (*agitur*) and things told (*refertur*) in the *Ars poetica*, then, it is Horace's imitation of Plato rather than his reception of Aristotle that calls out for our attention. Horace may even be the first literary critic formally to condense Plato's (Socrates') proto-narratological precepts into a narrower distinction between showing and telling. The first in a long line, as we shall see.

4.3 *Teleute*

Akin to the likeness of the monstrous chimera which takes form in its opening lines (*Ars poetica* 1–5), Horace's *Ars poetica* represents a strange mixture of theories pertaining to both rhetoric and poetics. But the combined precepts it offers on the 'art of poetry' are so commonplace and banal as to hint at parody, with at least one modern critic convinced that the *Ars poetica* is designed as 'an intentionally misleading "instruction booklet"'.[27] It combines elements of different genres, splicing together the epistolary genre with didactic and satire—but insists on the proper preservation of the traditional rules and distinctions of genre. It asserts that 'everything must keep appropriately to the place allotted to it' (*Ars poetica* 92), although it then grants that sometimes, in practice, generic flexibility may be desirable (*Ars poetica* 93–8).[28] It commends poetic order and formal unity in composition (*Ars poetica* 1–37), but arranges its own subject material in an ostensibly haphazard and illogical

---

[27] Frischer 1991: 61. Frischer sees the poem as performing a 'parody of a pedantic member of the grammarian tribe' (61) and the 'inept ramblings of an unreliable narrator' (85).

[28] On the generic hybridity of the *Ars poetica* see Frischer 1991: 87–100. Cf. Rudd 1989: 34. Notable for their absence from Horace's 'poetics' are the important genres of elegy, lyric, didactic, and satire—all of which flourished during the Augustan period, and which (excepting elegy) Horace himself produced. On Horace's supposedly pioneering role in genre theory from a narratological perspective see Kearns 2005 and Pyrhönen 2007.

sequence. As Armstrong observes, Horace's theory of poetry is composed of seemingly 'randomly chosen details, giving no systematic advice at all, and questions of style and metre are always "bleeding" into questions of poet, subject, character and plot'.[29] It is difficult, then, to take the chimerical *Ars poetica* seriously as offering any reliable advice on ancient literary theory and criticism—and even tougher to extract from it any sensible observations on ancient proto-narratological theory.

Just how seriously, then, can we (or are we supposed) to treat the didactic-satiric character of the poem and its 'precepts' on narrative (in) poetry?[30] What are we to make of this chimerical compound, a poem whose opening lines lead its readers to expect a study of the art of painting to follow—an *Ars pictura* rather than an *Ars poetica*? It is not necessary to accept Frischer's view of the poem's voice as belonging unequivocally to the narrative *persona* of 'a ridiculous Aristotelian critic who is a captive of the formalist theories of the Peripatetic Neoptolemus of Parium'.[31] But it is worth remembering that, before writing the *Ars poetica*, Horace had made his name as the author of excoriating iambic and satiric poetry and that the poet-*praeceptor*-narrator of his chimerical *Ars poetica* may not be entirely reliable—particularly as an authority on the Roman reception of Aristotle's narratological insights.[32]

---

[29] Armstrong 1993: 187. Cf. Ferenczi and Hardie 2014: 12 on the 'seemingly capricious order' of the poem and Brink 1971: 86 on the contorted Latin syntax of the opening lines (six words placed before *si* in the clause), which he describes as representing its own 'violation of the law of unity'. Laird 2007: 137–9, however, makes a convincing case for reading the opening and closing parts of the poem—its head (*caput*) and foot (*pes*)—as parts of an organized and organic unity.

[30] On this debate see the essays collected in Ferenczi and Hardie 2014. Hardie (43) asks: 'Should we take at all seriously Horace's purported aim to provide practical instruction in how to achieve the status of a *perfectus poeta*, any more than we take seriously Virgil's profession in the *Georgics* to teach how to be a successful farmer?'

[31] See Frischer 1991: 65 and Brink 1963.

[32] On the 'mischievous wordplay' and 'sophisticated conceit' of Horace's *Ars* see Laird 2007: 138 and especially Barchiesi 2001: 144–7 and 1994: 135–8.

5 Ancient narrative theory in practice

> *There are three forms of literary art, says Plato: the dramatic* (dramatiken), *where the poet consistently distinguishes* (eudokimei) *himself [by speaking] through the characters behind/beneath whom he hides; the* amimetic (amimeton), *such as Phocylides' [art]; and the mixed* (mikten), *such as Hesiod's.*
>
> b scholion to *Iliad* 2.494–877

5.1 *Arche*

The ancient scholia (literally, 'little scholarly discussions') appear as literary critical observations and notes preserved in and around the lines of ancient Greek and Roman texts.

Their comments reflect and refract a broad range of ancient literary, textual, and philological views, incorporating diffuse ideas and material predominantly from Alexandrian, Hellenistic, and Roman sources—but also integrating comments and criticism from much earlier and much later periods. A complex cross-fertilization of concepts and comments operated between the ancient critics and the ancient theorists: Plato's *Republic*, along with Aristotle's *Rhetoric*, *On Poets*, and *Homeric Problems* (if not the *Poetics*) would have been known to several of the scholiasts and their sources, and Horace would have known the works of the Alexandrian and Augustan scholia critics, while his own *Ars poetica* would have been known to later commentators. But the chain of reception is inextricably tangled here, and even when the scholiasts name their theoretical interlocutors, it is not always an unequivocal sign of direct engagement.

The corpus of ancient Greek scholia treats a wide spectrum of canonical ancient texts, from the narrative poetry of Homer, Hesiod, and Theocritus, the tragedies of Aeschylus, Sophocles, and Euripides, the philosophical treatises of Plato, Aristotle, and numerous others. The scholia comments consider technical questions of textual criticism and philology, as well as more literary-critical questions concerning textual exegesis, and so have plenty to say about narratological issues.[1] There is even a degree of incidental narrativity in some of the scholia comments. In their editing and athetizing of ancient narratives such as Homer's *Iliad*, marking up lines in the text which are 'not to be read', the scholia critics paradoxically draw their reader's attention to the potential existence of multiple alternatives to the critically sanctioned storyline and approved storyworld. Thus, in Aristarchus' infamous athetization of an allusion to Achilles' homoerotic relationship with Patroclus (*Iliad* 16.97–100; discussed in more detail below, section 5.2), the direction that four lines are not original and are therefore 'not to be read' as part of Homer's epic serves to highlight those very lines and that very relationship as part of an alternative storyline, projecting a parallel counterfactual (or counterfictional) storyworld in which Achilles' character is indeed recast as the lover of Patroclus.[2]

Together with fragments of commentaries like those of Aristarchus, the bT scholia on the *Iliad* make up by far and away the most extensive and detailed of the extant exegetical material, offering a particularly rich source for narratological study. It is from these scholia that most of what we think we know about the application of narratological theories in antiquity derives and, as such, they will provide the main focus for discussion and analysis in the first part of this chapter; while in the second part we turn to a later Latin commentary on Virgil's *Aeneid* to examine ancient narratological theory put to practice in the exegesis of a Roman epic.

---

[1] The Homeric scholia are conventionally organized into three groups based on their content: A, bT, and D. The A group (collating the comments of the Augustan scholars Aristonicus and Didymus, and the second-century CE scholars Herodian and Nicanor, whose comments are based largely on the earlier work of the Alexandrian scholar Aristarchus) focus predominantly on textual questions. The bT scholia, incorporating material from a variety of sources and periods (including the first-century CE commentator Heraclitus and the third-century CE Neoplatonist Porphyry) focus on exegetical issues. The D group (the oldest) represents a diverse mix of lexical interpretation and plot summary. The bT scholia also correspond closely with a fourth group sometimes known as the G (or Ge) scholia. The *locus classicus* for this corpus is Erbse's 1969–88 seven-volume collection (for the A, bT—excluding Porphyry's work, and Ge scholia); van Thiel's 2000 collection includes the D scholia. In the following discussion I specify the group or groups to which any individual Homeric scholion cited belongs, but not its location in Erbse or van Thiel. On the Homeric scholia see Nagy 2011.

[2] Cf. Hexter 2010: 34: 'Even as you follow a particular critic who rejects this line or that, the line(s) remain(s) there as excluded, as silenced, as banished, as ghosts. In other words, readers of Homer already in the time of Virgil dealt ... with a text in which lines and words could bear divergent meanings ... This is reading under the sign of athetesis.'

5.2 Ancient narratological terms and concepts in the Homeric scholia

Received readings of the scholia repeatedly stress their value as illustrations of ancient literary theory in practice.[3] But the scholia reception of Plato, Aristotle, and Horace is far from straightforward. A paratext on the back cover of René Nünlist's study of the critical terms and concepts used by the ancient Greek scholia suggests, for example, that:[4]

The evidence of the scholia significantly adds to and enhances the picture that can be gained from studying the relevant treatises (such as Aristotle's *Poetics*): scholia also contain concepts that are not found in the treatises, and they are indicative of how the concepts are actually put to use in the progressive interpretation of texts.

The case for Aristotle's influence on the Homeric scholia is also set out by Francesca Schironi, who sees a clear connection to Aristotle's *Rhetoric* 'and above all' to his *Poetics* in the scholia work attributed to the Alexandrian critic Aristarchus—although some of the parallels she identifies, such as 'the theory that the *Iliad* and the *Odyssey* are creations of one poet' and 'the importance of the principle of consistency (Homer does not contradict himself)', are hardly exclusive or central to Aristotle.[5] Indeed, Schironi herself acknowledges that there are several important aspects of the *Poetics* with which Aristarchus does not seem either familiar or interested, including Aristotle's ideas about *muthos*.[6]

Roos Meijering's influential dissertation similarly sees the Greek scholia as essentially responding to a set of Aristotelian norms as described in the *Poetics* and considers it probable that the terms and concepts used by the ancient scholia 'reflect a basically Peripatetic theory of poetry' which 'found [its] way into the scholia via Alexandrian scholarship'.[7] Although Nünlist, Schironi, and Meijering are all careful to stress the complexities of any potential relationship between ancient theories and their application in the ancient Greek scholia, each goes on to highlight the primary influence of Aristotle's *Poetics*, and assume that the scholia somehow put into practice essentially Aristotelian theories of narrative.

---

[3] On narrative theory in the ancient (especially Homeric) scholia, see Nünlist 2009a and 2009b (to which this chapter is indebted), Schironi 2009, de Jong 1987: 10–14, Meijerling 1987, Richardson 1980, and Duckworth 1931.

[4] Nünlist 2009b: i. See also Nünlist 2009a: 70: 'Aristotle so to speak provides the theory, the scholia give actual examples.'

[5] Schironi 2009: 279 (this work also includes a useful bibliography).

[6] Schironi 2009: 290 n. 31.

[7] Meijering 1987: 133. References to Aristotle's influence *passim*.

Such assumptions are widespread. For Irene de Jong, the premise made by the ancient scholia on *Iliad* 1.8–9 that the *diegesis* (or narrative discourse proper) of Homer's epic begins only at line 8, after the proem and invocation of the Muse, 'reminds one of Aristotle' (although she does not specify which bit).[8] N. J. Richardson similarly detects Aristotle's 'considerable influence' upon the Homeric scholia and assumes 'the ultimate derivation of much of the literary criticism in the Scholia from Aristotelian principles'.[9] In particular, he regards the scholia comments upon Homer's careful plot structuring and arrangement of incidents as being directly influenced by Aristotle's *Poetics* and as representing 'an elaboration of the Aristotelian view which the Scholia follow, [although] they do not put it so explicitly'.[10] He further maintains that 'the Scholia follow closely the lead of Plato and of Aristotle' in viewing Homer as a proto-tragedian, suggesting:[11]

The power to portray emotion and evoke feeling is the most important link between Homer and tragedy, according with the Aristotelian view of tragedy as arousing 'pity and fear', and the Scholia are full of comments on Homer's ability to create sympathy in this way... [w]here they echo the Aristotelian theory of κάθαρσις [*katharsis*].

Plenty of comments in the Homeric scholia consider questions of sympathy (*sumpatheia*) as it pertains to the emotions of the poet-narrator, his characters, and his audience. But this 'fellow-feeling' is very far indeed from Aristotle's complex theory of *katharsis* as it is set out in the *Poetics* (6.1449b 28). In fact, the extant Homeric scholia typically comment on pity (*eleos*) and fear (*phobos*) in order to emphasize and praise Homer's judicious amelioration of these emotions rather than their arousal, suggesting very different priorities to those encountered in the *Poetics*.[12] In the marked absence of any discussions of Aristotelian *katharsis* (explicit or implicit) in the scholia we instead find frequent references to the empathetic anxiety (*agonia*) experienced by characters and readers that Homer expertly relieves.[13]

Like Richardson's, George Duckworth's pioneering study of focalization in ancient literary criticism also views the scholia as broadly 'following

---

[8] De Jong 1987: 10–11, presumably referring to *Poetics* 24.1460a 5–11.

[9] Richardson 1980: 265–6. *Contra* see Lucas 1968: xxii: 'Neither before nor after the alleged loss of Aristotle's esoteric writings does the *Poetics* seem to have been widely read'; and xxiii: 'there is no passage earlier than the fourth century A.D. of which it can be asserted with confidence that it is derived directly from the *Poetics*.'

[10] Richardson 1980: 268.   [11] Richardson 1980: 270 and 274.

[12] Cf. Nünlist 2009b: 139–49 on emotional effects discussed in the scholia.

[13] Cf. bT scholion to *Iliad* 8.217a.

the Aristotelian tradition' in their frequent observations upon Homer's dramatic qualities.[14] But Duckworth acknowledges that it is most probably Aristotle's *Rhetoric* which serves as the key influence and intertext here: Book 2 of Aristotle's *Rhetoric* explains how to perform and elicit fear in an audience through judicious manipulation of anticipation, stressing the value of incidents and occurrences that are 'contrary to expectation' in arousing emotions of pity and fear, and offering several examples drawn from Homeric epic. Yet, as Duckworth allows, even Aristotle's *Rhetoric* is by no means an uncomplicated source of authority in these scholia readings: 'In their defence of Homer's technique of foreshadowing the future...the scholiasts depart from Aristotle's theory of fear; they show their approval of Homeric foreshadowing by pointing out that the Homeric audience could not endure too great an uncertainty concerning the ultimate outcome of the epic, but demanded an anticipation of the future free from fear.'[15]

We should be circumspect, then, in assigning any direct relationship between Aristotelian narrative theory and *praxis* in the scholia. Although some ostensibly Aristotelian or quasi-Aristotelian theories do pop up in the exegetical scholia, the overwhelming majority of Aristotle's theoretical propositions do not appear—an absence which should serve as a caution against mapping any direct relationship between the ancient narratological theory of the *Poetics* and the practice of the scholia. The fact that Aristotle's technical term for plot (*muthos*) is not picked up and used by any of the extant scholia seems especially important in this context;[16] this is, after all, the most important principle articulated in the *Poetics*, the fulcrum upon and around which Aristotle's other narratological precepts are developed. Where it is mentioned in the scholia, the term *muthos* always retains its more generalized meaning of fiction or myth.[17] Aristotle's definition of *muthos* as the narrative arrangement or synthesis of incidents, events, and actions (*Poetics* 6.1450a 3–4) finds no purchase in the scholia. Where *sunthesis* and its lexical cognates are found, it is typically in descriptions of the rhetorical arrangement or composition of individual words and phrases rather than the stuff of story.[18] As for Aristotle's insistence that all poetry is a form of *mimesis*,

---

[14] Duckworth 1931: 338 n. 63.

[15] Duckworth 1931: 338 n. 63. On focalization in the scholia see also Nünlist 2009b: 116–34.

[16] Cf. Nünlist 2009b: 24 n. 7.

[17] See for example the T scholion to *Odyssey* 10.20.

[18] See Meijering 1987 on ancient Greek theories of rhetorical form. The late first-century BCE rhetorician Dionysius of Halicarnassus records that his ancient predecessors distinguished between subject matter (*pragmatikon*) and style (*lektikon*), assigning the business

there is no evidence at all to suggest that the scholia critics recognize or accept this theory; their references to *mimesis* typically take the form of notes commenting upon mimetic character speech as distinguished from diegetic narrator speech, according to Socrates' rather than Aristotle's definition of the term.[19] Likewise, and despite their considerable concern for the emotional impact of the narratives under their consideration, the Homeric scholia have no apparent awareness of or interest in Aristotle's theory of *katharsis* (*Poetics* 6.1449b 28).[20] Nor do they share Aristotle's ideas on the importance of recognition or *anagnorisis* (*Poetics* 10.1452a 18–21). And when they employ the term *peripeteia* it is in a 'non-technical (i.e. non-Aristotelian)' sense, to mean a 'sudden change' or narrative turning point rather than, as in Aristotle, a tragic transformation or 'reversal of fortune' (*Poetics* 6.1450a 31–4).[21] The extant scholia have nothing to say about Aristotle's theory of plot climax or *desis* and denouement or *lusis*: when the scholia refer to *lusis* it is typically to designate the 'solution' or answer to a textual or exegetical problem.[22] Their frequent designation of narrative details and incidents as probable and/or necessary similarly has nothing to do with causality or plot structure (*Poetics* 9.1451a 35–7), but with questions of plausible characterization or *ethos* (*Poetics* 15.1454a 25–36) and athetization—of whether it is probable (or necessary) that a character should do or say something, and whether such lines should accordingly be marked as 'not to be read'.[23]

In this vein, the second-century BCE Alexandrian scholar Aristarchus athetizes the poignant last words spoken by Achilles to Patroclus as he prepares to go into battle, on the grounds that they are not compatible or consistent with Achilles' character as it is represented elsewhere in the *Iliad*. As he bids farewell to Patroclus, Achilles wishes that every other man on the battle line, both Trojan and Greek, could die so that they two could be alone (*Iliad* 16.97–100). Aristarchus considers this wish to be out of character for Achilles and, since Homer is too perfect a poet to

---

of arrangement (*oikonomia*) to the level of subject matter and the business of composition (*sunthesin*) to the level of style (Dionysius, *On the Admirable Style of Demosthenes* 51).

[19] See Nünlist 2009b: 94–115. [20] *Contra* see Richardson 1980: 274.

[21] See Nünlist 2009b: 268, discussing *peripeteia* (considered a Homeric invention) in the bT scholia to *Iliad* 2.1516. Cf. Meijering 1987: 277 n. 106.

[22] Cf. Nünlist 2009b: 11–12.

[23] So, Aristarchus athetizes Odysseus' address to the ordinary rank and file at *Iliad* 2.200–6 on the grounds of social class: 'such words are appropriate for kings but not for the rank and file' (schol. *Iliad* 2.192a). The advice that Thetis gives to her son Achilles at *Iliad* 24.130–1 is athetized on the grounds of age (and possibly gender) appropriateness: 'because it is inappropriate for a mother to say to her son "it is a pleasant/good thing to have sex with women"' (schol. *Iliad* 24.130–2a).

make such a mistake, considers these lines must have been inserted into Homer's text by another hand (schol. *Iliad* 16.97–100). Aristarchus does not object to the possibility of a homoerotic or pederastic relationship between Achilles and Patroclus because of any objection to inconsistency or indecorum in Homer's representation of Achilles' sexuality: it is rather the (mis)representation of Achilles' (lack of) sympathy for his fellow Greeks and his express wish that he and his lover might be the only two left in their storyworld that is deemed improbable and therefore 'not to be read'.

Aristotle certainly stresses in the *Poetics* that a character must be represented with consistency and his or her behaviour and speech patterned according to the same principles of probability and necessity that govern a plausible plot (*Poetics* 15.1454a 25–36). However, this Aristotelian link is never made explicit in the extant scholia and it is more likely that their discussions of consistency in characterization are shaped by ancient theories of rhetoric than by those of poetics— especially the exercises of *ethopoeia* or 'speaking appropriately in character' described in ancient rhetorical handbooks.[24]

Remarkably, the scholia have very little to say about the pleasures of poetry, focusing predominantly upon the painful state of suspense (*agonia*) from which a good storyteller relieves his audience, rather than upon the narrative pleasures (*hedone*) that Aristotle repeatedly stresses in the *Poetics*.[25] And, like many modern critics, the scholia critics are either ignorant of or ignoring of Aristotle's observations on the narration of simultaneous events. Aristotle in the *Poetics* claimed that 'epic . . . since it is narrative, is able to show many things happening at the same time' (*Poetics* 24.1459b 22–7). But the scholia critics largely disagree—one commenting upon Homer's attempt to establish a simultaneous series (rather than sequence) of multiple events in the transitional opening scene(s) of *Iliad* 22, that 'to say everything at the same time is impossible' (bT scholion to *Iliad* 22.131). So much for the scholia demonstrating Aristotelian theories of narrative in practice, then.

The scholia reception of Plato's narratological precepts is no less complex. The Homeric scholia—not unexpectedly, given Socrates' own use of Homer in the *Republic* to illustrate his narrative theory—do occasionally allude to Plato, and generally follow Socrates' broad use of the term *diegesis* (and its related forms) in *Republic* 3 to describe different types of narration and narrating within a text. But they show little regard

---

[24] See Nünlist 2009b: 246–54.
[25] Cf. *Poetics* 13.1453a 36, 14.1453b 11, 23.1459a 21, and 26.1462b 13. See also Nünlist 2009b: 144, discussing the rarity of the Aristotelian concept and term in the scholia.

for Socrates' subcategorizations of this genus. So, *diegesis* in the scholia refers generally to any kind of narrative discourse, including the main narrative spoken by the poet-narrator (*haple diegesis* in Socrates' terms), as well as embedded narratives and speeches spoken by characters (in Socrates' typology, *diegesis dia mimeseos*).[26] Occasionally, however, Socrates' tripartite typology of *diegesis* (simple, mimetic, and mixed) is reformed into a simple binary differentiating simply between *mimesis* and *diegesis* or *mimetikon* and *diegematikon*. So, the Homeric bT scholion on *Iliad* 19.282–302 (a passage alternating between narrator and character speech) comments upon the restrained yet detailed objectivity of the poet-narrator's *diegesis* and contrasts this with the emotional subjectivity of the *mimesis* through which Homer presents Briseis' moving lament for Patroclus:

The passage, being of a mixed/middle character (*mesou characteros*), is phrased seriously in the narrative (*diegematikoi*) part where it is graphic (*graphikos*), and in the mimetic (*mimetikoi*) part it is sympathetic (*sumpathes*) and sad.

Notice here that, even in the mode of simple narration or *diegesis*, Homer is still considered to be a highly affective narrator, depicting a 'graphic' scene which not only tells but 'shows' his own point of view. And in his sympathetic *mimesis* of Briseis' speech, Homer seems to this scholia critic to combine his own point of view with that of his character, sympathetically sharing this focalization of the tragedy of Patroclus' death.[27]

Elsewhere, as in the b scholion to *Iliad* 2.494–877, we find more explicit acknowledgement of Plato's Socratic theory of narrative being put into practice—but once again we find the terms of that theory adapted for use:

There are three forms of literary art, says Plato: the dramatic (*dramatiken*), where the poet consistently distinguishes (*eudokimei*) himself [by speaking] through the characters behind/beneath whom he hides; the amimetic (*amimeton*), such as Phocylides' [art]; and the mixed (*mikten*), such as Hesiod's.

Here the critic points to Plato as the authority in distinguishing between those genres, types, and parts of a narrative in which a poet-narrator

---

[26] *Diegesis* (and its related lexical forms) is used in the Homeric scholia on the *Iliad* to describe (a) the story or narrative (1.8–9, 10.558–63, 14.153, 17.301–3, 20.410, 21.34); (b) direct speeches (1.366); (c) embedded narratives (1.366, 9.232, 11.677–761, 19.101); and (d) storytelling (2.494–877, 12.175–81, 14.347–51, 17.648). *Apangelia* is also used in comments on the poet-narrator's story-telling, particularly the detailed description of an activity (e.g. hand-to-hand fighting at *Iliad* 16.116 and 17.605; or domestic chores at *Iliad* 9.212 and 18.346). Cf. Nünlist 2009b: 368–89.

[27] Cf. Nünlist 2009a: 101–2; *contra* see Richardson 1980: 276.

speaks as himself (*amimeton*) 'without impersonation/*mimesis*', those in which he speaks in impersonation of his characters (*dramatiken*) 'dramatically', and those in which he does both. Yet the narratological terminology adduced here departs significantly from its alleged Platonic source. The mode of simple narration that Plato's Socrates identified as *haple* is represented here as a variant mode not of *diegesis* but of *mimesis*: as *amimeton*. Similarly, the scholion describes the Homeric poet-narrator as speaking *amimeton* (as himself, in the first person) as he asks the Muses to aid him in remembering and recounting the catalogue of all the ships and all their captains who set sail for Troy (*Iliad* 2.484–93).[28] In comments such as these, Plato's theories seem decidedly Aristotelian. So much for the scholia straightforwardly demonstrating 'Platonic' or 'Socratic' theories of narrative in practice, then.

5.3 Modern narratological terms and concepts in the Homeric scholia

Although they do not appear to have been familiar with Aristotle's technical term for plot (*muthos*), the ancient scholia critics do work with a clear distinction between what modern narratologists would recognize as *syuzhet* or *discours* and *fabula* or *histoire*—between the plot of a particular narrative and its (re)arrangement of pre-existing story material.[29] But the terminology that the scholia employ in discussing these core concepts varies widely and maps only imperfectly onto equivalent modern models.

The scholia critics generally share the intuition that there are two fundamental narrative levels: (1) the invariable stuff of story, held in common by all poets (*logos*); and (2) its variable treatment in individual stories told by particular poets (*lexis*).[30] Plato famously drew a distinction in his *Phaedrus* (236a) between *heuresis* and *diathesis*, between finding the material for an argument or a story and its composition, in one of the first and most important definitions of the relationship between rhetorical (and literary) content and form. Aristotle in his

---

[28] Cf. Nünlist 2009b: 133 for the view that 'the distinction between author and narrator . . . seems to be unknown to ancient critics'. *Contra* see Whitmarsh 2009.

[29] On *hupothesis* as plot see Meijering 1987: 99–133, and Nünlist 2009b: 24 n. 5.

[30] Cf. Plato's *Ion* 531c–d, 532a, and *Republic* 3. Nünlist 2009b: 23–68 offers an excellent analysis of the scholia on plot—although he does not take account of Plato. Cf. Meijering 1987: 135.

Rhetoric, likening the compositional principles of rhetoric to those of poetry (*Rhetoric* 3.1.1403b 3), drew a similar distinction between knowing what to say and how to say it (*Rhetoric* 3.1.1403b 1–3).[31] The first-century BCE rhetorician Hermagoras of Temnos elaborated on both of these models and described content and form respectively as *heuresis* and *oikonomia*.[32] These terms were then further adapted by the Augustan historian and rhetorician Dionysius of Halicarnassus, who designated *heuresis* (in the sense of preparation of raw material) and *oikonomia* (in the sense of arrangement or management of content) as relating exclusively to the treatment of subject matter rather than to style. Thus, in the ancient scholia we find *oikonomia* used in a way which overlaps broadly with modern conceptions of plot and emplotment—that is, the management or arrangement of raw subject material (*pragmatikon*).[33] The etymology of *heuresis*—the preliminary preparation by way of finding and selecting story content—is also suggestive in pointing to the potential source for that raw material: that is, a pre-existing common reserve of narrative stuff, or 'myth-kitty'.[34]

Hermagoras' rhetorical model of *oikonomia* as the organization of pre-existing story stuff maps relatively well onto modern narratological definitions of plot—and onto its broad equivalents, *syuzhet* and *discours* (or *récit*). Dionysius' more complex account of *oikonomia* also makes sense in these terms, given that his focus on linguistic/stylistic (*lektikon*) content and form parallels his description of subject (*pragmatikon*) content and form. Both accounts of *heuresis*, however, subtly yet significantly diverge from modern notions of *fabula*—defined by Shklovsky as 'material for *syuzhet* formulation' and by Prince as 'the set of narrated situations and events in their chronological sequence; the basic story material (as opposed to plot or *syuzhet*)'.[35] For both Hermagoras and Dionysius, and for the scholia critics who adopt their terminology, the raw story stuff of *heuresis* is always already partially pre-formed and prepared, pre-existing as part of a traditional meta-*fabula*, the multifaceted universe of ancient Greek myth out of which individual

---

[31] It seems to be in this context in which Aristotle criticizes Euripides for 'managing' (*oikonomei*) his tragic plots badly: *Poetics* 13.1453a 29–30.

[32] See Meijering 1987: 135–6 on Hermagoras' rhetorical model of content and form. On *oikonomia* see also Grisolia 2001.

[33] Cf. Aristotle's definition of plot (*muthos*): *Poetics* 6.1450a 3–4.

[34] As Aristotle advises us, a poet can be inventive as well as making good use of traditional tales (*Poetics* 14.1453b 21–5), and a *muthos* can comprise the organization of either invented or pre-existing story stuff into plot (*Poetics* 1.1447a 8–9).

[35] Shklovsky 1965b: 57. Prince 2003 *s.vv.*

storyworlds are formed.[36] In this context, *heuresis* is not so much opposed to *oikonomia* as it is its (chrono)logical and formal precondition and in the extant scholia does not represent the re-configured plot but rather its pre-figuration.

The scholia also use the term *hupothesis*, which potentially corresponds to a conception of *fabula* as subject matter or story. Nünlist suggests that a common formulation indicating that a feature threatens 'to destroy the story' (*lusein ten hupothesin*) points to the ancient critics' distinction between a generalized *fabula* and a particularized plot.[37] However, the extant evidence shows that the term *hupothesis* is never paired in contrast with any equivalent term for plot and is, indeed, used in several cases simply as a synonym for *oikonomia*.[38]

Although we struggle to identify a closely corresponding terminology, we do find plenty of evidence in the scholia of intuitions about the structure of narrative which are analogous to modern conceptions of *fabula* as a distinct diegetic level. This is particularly well illustrated by scholia comments about the arrangement or *oikonomia* of a narrative's story or *hupothesis*.[39] The Homeric scholia repeatedly show their appreciation for Homer's careful arrangement and emplotment of his traditional story material, and especially his decision to begin his *Iliad* in the middle (*in medias res*)—or, as the scholia see it, towards the end (*in ultimas res*)—of the story. Praising Homer for his admirable manipulation of temporal order in his narrative of the Trojan War, and contrasting this with the dull linearity of other versions, one ancient critic notes (schol. B *Il.* 2.494–877):[40]

The poet is marvellous. He leaves out no part of the story (*hupothesis*), but narrates all events at a timely moment in reverse order (*anastrophe*): the conflict between the goddesses, the abduction of Helen, and the death of Achilles. Chronological/linear narrative (*taxin diegesis*) belongs to the newer poets and the historians, and is lacking in poetic quality.

The scholia critic here clearly recognizes that Homer's narrative (*diegesis*) represents the skilful management of a traditional *fabula* or

---

[36] In this respect *heuresis* corresponds to Petrovsky's notion of *syuzhet*. The meta-*fabula* configured by the interlocking stories found in the corpus of ancient Greek myth suggests obvious parallels with the twenty-first-century narrative universes (and franchises) of *Marvel* and *DC* comics.

[37] See Nünlist 2009b: 67.

[38] See Nünlist 2009b: 24 n. 5. The term also seems to be used in Philodemus (*On Poets* 2.62; cf. 5.5) to denote plot. See *LSJ s.vv.* II.3.

[39] The equivalent term *taxis*—in later rhetorical handbooks contrasted with *oikonomia* to differentiate between the 'natural' and 'unnatural' order of words or narrative—is only occasionally used by the scholia. Cf. scholion B *Il.* 2.494–877 and Nünlist 2009b: 24.

[40] Cf. Nünlist 2009b: 88.

hupothesis concerning the fall of Troy. The *Iliad* tells of the events of just a few days towards the end of the Trojan War, beginning *in medias res* in the tenth year of the war and ending with the death and funeral of Hector—that is, beginning after the infamous Judgement of Paris and concluding before the fall of Troy. This critic favourably contrasts Homer's narrative anachrony with the chronolinear storytelling found in Greek history and post-Homeric epic. This critic implicitly opposes *taxis* with *oikonomia* to contrast Homer's skilful representation of the *fabula* in an 'unnatural' order (*oikonomia*) with the dull representation of the same subject matter in its 'natural order' (*taxis*) by other poets. Similarly, in the Pseudo-Plutarchan *De Homero* (2.162), we find Homer again praised for the unnatural arrangement and order of his plot:[41]

> The principal feature of [Homer's] technique is the arrangement/unnatural order (*oikonomia*) which he demonstrates throughout his poetry and particularly in the beginnings of his works. In beginning the *Iliad* he does not go back to the remote past, but to a time when things were gaining impetus and about to reach a climax. The less interesting incidents that had happened earlier are briefly referred to elsewhere in incidental narrations (*paradiegesato*).

This critic not only recognizes Homer's plot as comprising the anachronical rearrangement of a traditional *fabula*, but notices the narrative effect and affect of that arrangement: the plot of the *Iliad* focuses upon exciting events as they lead up to a climactic moment in the traditional story, relegating less exciting moments 'that had happened earlier' to the margins of the central narrative, into a 'para-narrative' (*paradiegesis*)—comprising the digressions which do not form part of the central narrative plot (or *syuzhet*) but which do form part of the story (or *fabula*).[42] Examples of such *paradiegesis* in Homer's *Iliad* would include the poem's numerous analepses or flashbacks: Nestor's nostalgic stories;[43] the history of high-status or 'significant' objects such as Agamemnon's sceptre (2.101–8); background episodes or myths such as the Judgement of Paris (24.27–30); and the incidental 'obituaries' that add pathos to the deaths of so many warriors on Troy's battlefield.[44] In modern narratological

---

[41] Also discussed in Meijering 1987: 146–8. Pseudo-Plutarch, we know, is certainly familiar with Aristotle's dialogue *On Poets*. There are also parallels here with Horace *Ars poetica* 146–50.

[42] Horace takes the view that Homer leaves these incidental details out altogether (*Ars poetica* 146–50). Cf. Aristotle's *Rhetoric* 1417a2. On *paradiegesis* and analogous terms in the scholia (especially *epidiegesis* and *parekbasis*) see Nünlist 2009b: 64–6.

[43] See, for example, the scholia to 1.260–73, 7.132–57, 11.670–762, 23.629–43.

[44] The scholia comment explicitly on these 'obituaries'. See, for example, the scholia to *Iliad* 11.226 and 11.242–3 (the death of Iphidamus) and 20.383 (on the death of Otrynteides).

terms, such backstories are characterized as external analepses, flashbacks to incidents outside the temporal reach of the *Iliad*'s main plot.[45] But this scholion seems less interested in the temporal location of these incidents at the level of the *fabula* than in their location at the level of the *syuzhet*, describing these analepses as *paradiegesis*—that is, conceptually *beside* (rather than *outside* or *behind*) the central storyline.[46] The term *paradiegesis* thereby recognizes that what makes such analeptic (and potentially proleptic) story material meaningful and affective is not its temporal location in terms of story time but its location in terms of discourse time, and the narrative juxtaposition of parallel past and present moments.

As these examples discussing *taxis* and *oikonomia*, *hupothesis* and *paradiegesis* suggest, and as the recent work of Nünlist has confirmed, the Greek scholia employ a highly eclectic technical vocabulary (borrowing heavily from the rich lexicon of ancient rhetorical theory) and are aware not only of key narratological phenomena such as the differences between plot and story, but of the various stages involved in the building and arrangement of a storyworld. What is more, they not only recognize and describe devices such as focalization, but identify secondary (internal or embedded) and anonymous focalization.[47] They are also interested in prolepsis (flashforward or foreshadowing) and in analepsis (flashback or backshadowing) of various different kinds—akin to the variants described by Genette as 'repeating' and 'completing' analepsis (described by the scholia as *anakephalaiosis* or recapitulation, and *anaplerosis* or completion).[48]

The scholia are consistently inconsistent in their use of different terms to describe similar narratological features. To take just one telling example concerning prolepsis, the ancient scholia employ more than ten different terms to describe this narrative feature, in addition to

---

[45] Genette 1980: 40–54.

[46] The term *paradiegesis* might usefully be contrasted with a related scholia term: *hupodiegesis* or sub-narrative, which typically indicates a subordinate but concurrent (rather than prior) storyline embedded as a strand inside the main narrative—such as the story of Meleager narrated by Phoenix in Book 9 of the *Iliad* (cf. schol. to *Iliad* 9.529a). Cf. Nünlist 2009b: 263.

[47] See in particular Nünlist 2003: 61: 'ancient literary critics regularly treated questions of focalization, although they neither had a specific term for the concept nor discussed it in its own right'.

[48] Nünlist 2009a: 66. See the AbT scholia to *Iliad* 1.366 for a recapitulating or repeating analepsis; and the bT scholion to 4.251 for a completing analepsis. See also Genette 1980: 51–61. Prince 2003: 79 defines completing prolepses as those which 'fill in later gaps resulting from ellipses in the narrative', repeating prolepses, or advance notices, as those which 'recount ahead of time events that will be recounted again'.

describing and discussing the phenomenon periphrastically.[49] However, careful scrutiny suggests that these various expressions do not simply (re)describe the same narrative phenomenon that modern narratologists call 'prolepsis': that is, 'anachrony going forward to the future with respect to the "present" moment; an evocation of one or more events that will occur after the "present" moment... an anticipation, a flashforward, a prospection'.[50] Rather, the scholia seem to be concerned with Homeric prolepses less in terms of their anachrony than in their *affectivity*.

The scholia critics certainly recognize the temporal interruption to the narrative order that different kinds of prolepses introduce, and fully appreciate that different kinds of prolepses cover a different 'reach', extending to a future point in time which may be near or far relative to the present moment of the narrative (the 'now' of either discourse or story time), and which may fall inside or outside the central plot and timeline of the narrative. So, the scholia notice that Andromache's pathos-filled anticipation of the future awaiting her son Astyanax (*Iliad* 22.473–515) proleptically (through *proanaphonesis*) looks forward to future events which will fall outside of the *Iliad*'s immediate plot but which nevertheless form part of the traditional story of the Trojan War and the *fabula* of Homer's narrative. Similarly, the foreshadowing of the death of Achilles (not included within the plot of the *Iliad* but frequently anticipated) prompts the scholia critics to note the affective quality of this feature and to suggest that such prolepses are employed by the Homeric poet-narrator (and by his internal character-narrators) in order to stimulate an emotional response—such as sadness, sympathy, or pity.[51] This is certainly how the scholia respond to scenes such as Achilles complaining to his mother about the poor hand fate has dealt him (1.352), or Thetis seeking recompense from Zeus on behalf of her ill-fated son (1.505). In each case, the anticipation of Achilles' not-quite-imminent death is employed by an internal speaker with clear intentions and motivations: to move an internal audience towards pity and sympathetic action. The scholia, not unreasonably, extend this affective response to Homer's external audience too and treat the

---

[49] See Nünlist 2009b: 368–86 for a comprehensive glossary of the literary critical terms used by the Greek scholia. Prolepsis as a feature in ancient criticism and commentary has been widely discussed in the secondary literature: in addition to Nünlist 2009a and 2009b, see Meijering 1987: 204–9, Richardson 1980: 269 n. 9, and Duckworth 1931.

[50] Prince 2003: 79 *s.vv.* See also Genette 1980: 40–78 and de Jong 2005a: 20: '[T]he scholia speak of proanaphonesis or prolepsis (anticipation or foreshadowing), seed (hint or advance mention), and paraleipsis (leaving out of details to be told at a later, more effective moment), terms which will become part and parcel of modern narratology.'

[51] See the bT scholia to *Iliad* 1.505, 1.352, 18.88–9, and 18.458.

prolepsis as a purposeful communicative act, designed to produce a similar emotional response in both internal and external audience sets. Indeed, the Homeric scholia frequently blur the affects experienced by internal and external narratees, assuming that the same narrative devices employed to sway Homer's characters apply to Homer's readers too.[52] Thus, the great majority of the ancient scholia critics assume that both the Homeric poet-narrator and his internal character-narrators aim to relieve suspense by strategically managing their audience's expectations, easing audience fears by placing the prospect of future calamities just beyond the horizon of the present narrative timeline.[53]

With prolepses as with other narratological phenomena, the ancient scholia seem to focus primarily upon describing the affectivity of such features. The emphasis upon rhetoric rather than poetics in their theoretical foundations drives the ancient critics to go beyond simply noting the narratological dynamics of features such as prolepsis to consider and comment on what they are for, what such devices do to audiences, how and why they are employed by the poet-narrator in his communication exchange with readers and auditors. And it is in this regard, above all, that the scholia reveal their most 'modern' narratological intuitions. For, in focusing upon the impact and affectivity of ancient narrative, in the way that readers and audiences receive and respond to narrative phenomena, they nicely anticipate the rhetorical poetics and priorities of modern narratology.

5.4 Ancient commentaries

Some sets of scholia upon ancient texts offer extensive enough notes to be considered commentaries in their own right and offer a more expansive overview of what one ancient critic describes as *narrantis officium*—the business of narrating.[54] One of the most complete of such commentaries, that attributed to the late fourth- or early fifth-century CE grammarian Servius, treats a set of literary texts: Virgil's first-century BCE Latin poems, the *Eclogues*, *Georgics*, and *Aeneid*. Two versions of Servius' Virgil commentary survive, the longer version of which (probably dating from the eighth century CE) is known variously as *Servius Auctus*, *Servius Danielis*, *DServius*, and *DS*; the shorter version known simply as *Servius*

---

[52] See the examples discussed in Nünlist 2009b: 135–56.
[53] See Duckworth 1931.   [54] Servius Auctus 2.11.

or *S* (and in some contexts, the 'Harvard' Servius).[55] Both forms of the Servius commentary clearly draw upon much earlier commentaries and scholia dealing with Virgil's poems (notably that of an earlier fourth-century CE commentator, Aelius Donatus) and share similar priorities and processes with those evinced in the Greek scholia—although their differences are also significant. Like the Greek scholia, these Latin commentaries demonstrate a clear familiarity with Plato's Socratic 'poetics' and some of the embryonic theories of narrative discussed in the *Republic*. Thus:[56]

We are aware of three types of poetic expression. In the first, only the poet speaks—this is the case in three books of the *Georgics*. The second type is dramatic in which the poet never speaks—this is the case in comedies and tragedies. The third type is mixed, as is the case in the *Aeneid*. For there, the characters who are introduced speak, as well as the poet.

An introductory comment to the first line of Virgil's *Eclogues* 3 also refers explicitly to Socrates' tripartite distinction in *Republic* 3 between simple, mimetic, and mixed narrative modes, translating these descriptions into corresponding Latin modes in which 'only the poet speaks' (*tantum poeta loquitur*), the 'dramatic' (*dramaticum*), and the 'mixed' (*mixtum*).[57] However, it is Horace's *Ars poetica* which leaves the most discernible mark of influence upon the ancient commentaries to Virgil's *Aeneid*.

The preface to the Servius Auctus commentary discusses the structure of Virgil's narrative in terms of some of the key principles outlined in the

---

[55] The modern editing of the Servius and extended Servius Auctus commentaries continues to challenge successive generations of classical philologists and there is as yet no wholly satisfactory edition on which to draw. The most accessible (and least frustrating for those approaching the text with narratological interests) remains the Thilo and Hagen edition (2011), which seeks to distinguish the shorter Servius (or S) text from the expanded Servius Auctus or Servius Danielis (or DS) text by printing the additional comments of the extended work in italics. Deletions, errors, and 'corrections' by the various hands contributing to the Servius Auctus text over several centuries are occluded by such an approach but this loss is compensated for by the clarity of the text's general presentation. See Mountford and Schultz 1930, Williams 1966–7, Lazzarini 1984 and 1989, and Murgia 2004. Given that both versions of 'Servius' represent composite texts, collating the comments of various ancient critics responding to Virgil's *Aeneid* across several centuries, I have tried to avoid attributing views to 'Servius' and have instead emphasized the plural form of any observations.

[56] Servius Auctus on Virgil, *Eclogues* 3.1. The formulation clearly shows the reception of Socrates' proto-narratological theory of narrative discourse consisting of three key forms, as it is described in *Republic* 3.

[57] The commentaries on the *Aeneid* refer occasionally to other Platonic dialogues (such as the *Symposium* at line 6.444) and demonstrate awareness of (neo)Platonist philosophy (as at line 3.68). In the *Aeneid* commentary there is one reference (at line 5.81) to Aristotle's *Physics*, but the Servius commentaries show no overt engagement with Aristotle's *Poetics*, further confirming the obscurity of this text in late antiquity.

Ars poetica and offers a number of revealing insights into the turning of narratological theory into practice by the contributors to ancient Latin commentaries:

It is clear what kind of poem this is: it is in the heroic/hexameter metre and in the mixed mode (*actus mixtus*) where the poet speaks and introduces other characters speaking too. It is heroic because it consists of divine and human characters, combining truth with fiction; for it is obvious that Aeneas came to Italy, but it is accepted that Venus speaking to Jupiter or the visit from Mercury are fictional constructs. It is in the high style, which consists of elevated diction and serious ideas. We know there are three kinds of narrative (*genera dicendi*)—the low, the middle, and the high. Virgil's intention is to follow Homer and to praise Augustus through his ancestors...The order (*ordo*) is also obvious, although some say superfluously that the second is first, the third second, and the first third, because Troy falls first, then comes the wandering of Aeneas, and then he arrives at Dido's lands; they are unaware that this is the art of poetry (*artem poeticam*), so that by beginning in the middle of things (*a mediis incipientes*) through narration (*per narrationem*) we return to the beginning (*prima*) and sometimes we anticipate things that are about to happen, as if through prophecy. Horace gives this very advice in the *Ars poetica*: 'so the poet says now what ought to be said just now, and postpones or omits many things for the time being'. It is accepted that Virgil has done this expertly.

Although there is no explicit theorization of any of the narrative features treated in the Servius or Servius Auctus commentaries, these prefatory remarks to the treatment of the *Aeneid* can be seen to outline the synthesis of a coherent theoretical framework which the ensuing analysis then puts into practice.

Horace's influence is immediately evident in the commentators' classification of the *Aeneid* as typical of the 'high style', but an echo of the fourth-century CE grammarian Aelius Donatus suggests that earlier Greek authorities on narrative theory may be shaping the views of the commentators here too.[58] Certainly, Socrates' typology of narrative discourse as outlined in Plato's *Republic* has helped to inform the assessment here of the *Aeneid* as a straightforward example of mixed discourse (Socrates' *diegesis di' amphoteron*) 'where the poet speaks and introduces other characters speaking too'. The direct citation and quotation of Horace's *Ars poetica* (43–4) also demonstrates the importance of theory to the ancient commentators and the criticism directed towards those critics who unnecessarily argue for a reordering of the first three

[58] The Servius commentaries refer to the three styles of narrative discourse—the plain (*humilis*), middle (*medius*), and high (*grandiloquus*). The influence of Donatus may be evident in this mode of analysis. Cf. Brummer 1912: 14. See also Dietz 1995.

books so as better to preserve the chronological structure of the narrative is particularly revealing. These dolts, the preface suggests, do not recognize that such narrative anachrony represents the 'art of poetry' (*artem poeticam*), and should better acquaint themselves with Horace's narratological precepts on the advantages of beginning a story *in medias res*; of exploiting strategies of delay, anticipation, and omission; and of using flashback and flashforward, playing with order, time, and narrative levels in order to tell a more compelling story.[59] The preface, with its clear commitment to such Horatian precepts, prepares us then for the commentaries' subsequent attention to Virgil's storytelling technique in general and in particular to the question of how to order and arrange Aeneas' story.[60]

5.5 Ancient narratological terms and concepts in the Servius commentaries

Given the narrative complexity of Virgil's epic, its Homeric-style flash-backs and flashforwards, its intricate timelines, and multiple plot lines, it is perhaps unsurprising that the commentaries devote significant attention to the order in which the story of the *Aeneid* is narrated.[61] They appear to be especially interested in Virgil's narrative economy, and the ways in which the story of Aeneas is not merely emplotted but effectively 'edited'. So, when Aeneas (as internal narrator) relates through analepsis the fall of Troy and the 'Odyssean' adventures that bring him and his fellow exiles to Carthage in the first three books of the epic, the commentators analyse this character's narrative technique closely—as if

---

[59] Several points in the main commentaries also refer explicitly to Horace's *Ars poetica* and cross-references suggest that the Horatian precepts and other narratological 'rules' applied in the preface and Book 1 are to be carried forward in the reading of the rest of the epic. Cf. 1.8, 1.223, 1.267, 1.382, 1.683, 1.748, 6.34, 6.660, 9.761, 10.653, 12.83.

[60] An awareness of the proto-narratological framework for the collected comments in these works goes some way towards acquitting 'Servius' of the pedantry charges that the commentaries have often invited. See for example Casali 2008, Falco 2000: 131, Knight 1958: 3, and Hinds 1998: 109 n. 14.

[61] The Greek scholia pay attention to what Meijering classifies as 'logical preparation' (1987: 182–208) whereas the Latin commentators seem less interested in this narratological device. A rare example in the Servius commentaries appears in the commentary to line 11.777 in relation to the rich suit of armour worn by an enemy that will attract the downfall of the female warrior Camilla: 'Sensibly the long description of the armour looks forward, so that Camilla may justly seem to be inflamed with desire for it.' The critic also seems to infer an embedded focalization here: the narrator's detailed description of the armour focalizes Camilla's (womanly) desire to possess it herself. Cf. Nünlist 2009b: 34–45.

finding there a meta-narratological model for Virgil's own epic technique. They observe how, despite Dido's request that he tell everything from the very beginning (*Aeneid* 1.753–6), Aeneas gives two reasons as to why he cannot tell her (or us) his whole story: it is too long for the time available and it is too sad to tell (2.9: *et duas causas praetendit, quibus dicit non posse universa narrari, dolorem et tempus*). Thus, when he agrees to tell the story 'briefly' (*breviter*), the commentaries observe that it should be read in the light of Dido's entreaty at the end of Book 1 that he should tell all (*Aeneid* 1.753–6). In this light, the commentators see the point of Aeneas' narrative 'brevity' as demonstrating (2.11):[62]

AND BRIEFLY (*et breviter*):... not the wishes of Dido, but the business of narrating (*sed narrantis officium*). And to some there appears to be a case of hysteron-proteron (*hysterologia*) here. By 'highest/best' (*supremum*) he means the last (*postremum*), the final. For he narrates (*narrat*) the destruction of Troy having left out what came before.

There is no straightforward Latin (or Greek) equivalent for the word 'narrator' and, as we have already seen, ancient theorists, critics, and commentators typically refer to the author or poet when discussing the work of the narrator. But in this commentary we see 'the business of narrating' *(narrantis officium)* highlighted as a specific area of concern and critical consideration. Here we see, too, not only an interest in narrative economy (the selection and organization of episodes to form a coherent—and in this case summary—plot) but in the dramatic arrangement of incidents leading up to a climactic ending: literally leaving the best (which here, the critics helpfully explain, means the worst) until last.[63] And although Horace is not directly cited here, the description of this form of *hysterologia* (or hysteron-proteron) certainly points back to the precepts on narrative order and arrangement in the *Ars poetica*.

Horace's influence can again be detected in a later comment upon a different kind of internal narrative: that describing the 'indescribable pattern' or 'unnarratable text' (*Aeneid* 8.625: *non enarrabile textum*) depicted on Aeneas' famous shield—where, once again, the narrator leaves the worst until last, casting Augustus' victory over Cleopatra at

---

[62] Note that the line numbering used in these commentaries does not always correspond precisely with that found in modern editions of the *Aeneid* and may be a line or more out.

[63] The commentary to line 1.363 and Venus' story of how Dido came to found Carthage shows a similar interest in narrative economy and order. Venus introduces her story as 'a long tale of wrong, with long digressions' and she promises to outline briefly only 'the main chapters of the story' (*Aeneid* 1.341–2). The commentaries note (to line 1.363 but embracing Venus' story in full) that 'it is permitted to tell that story in another order'.

Actium at the centre of its decorative and narrative schema. According to the ancient commentators, the shield is aptly described as 'indescribable' since it ambitiously purports to narrate the entirety of Rome's history, 'the history of Italy, Rome's triumphs, every future generation of Ascanius' line, and the battles they were to fight in sequence' (*Aeneid* 8.626–9).

As the commentators note, the poet-narrator does not (and could not) describe all of this (*nec tamen universa descripsit*) because of the great length of time it would take to do so and the detrimental impact this would have on the 'speed of the narration' (*narrationis celeritas*). What is more, it is to maintain the tempo of his narrative, they suggest, that Virgil deviates from the pattern of his Homeric predecessor here and narrates the 'unnarratable' ecphrasis as he does: in Homer, each of the individual scenes depicted on the shield is 'depicted/narrated as it happens' (*illic enim singula dum fiunt narrantur*)—that is, in the present tense and at the same time as it is being forged into the metal (*Iliad* 18.468–607); in Virgil, individual episodes (*singuli*) are narrated in the pluperfect and seen only when they have been completed (*perfecto opere*) as Aeneas takes up his finished shield to examine its narrative design.[64] For Virgil's Augustan audience, of course, the future episodes prophesied on Aeneas' shield have all long been completed and belong to the pluperfect past. For Homer's audience (ancient and modern) the scenes depicted on Achilles' shield represent an idealized atemporal fusion of past, present, and future.

However, the Servius commentators seem less interested in the differences that Homer and Virgil effect through their different approaches to the narrative focalization of these ecphrases: Homer describes the scenes on Achilles' shield as Hephaestus crafts them, producing the effect of impersonal or zero-level focalization, whereas Virgil has Aeneas turn his uncomprehending gaze over each part of the shield's story (*Aeneid* 8.626–731), so that we see each familiar story through Aeneas' fresh eyes in a striking instance of complex or embedded focalization. It is, however, strictly upon the economy, order, and tempo of narration at work in this famous ecphrasis that the Servius commentaries maintain their own focus.

---

[64] Smith 1997: 178 suggests that 'the shield is difficult to conceptualize as an objet d'art, for its primary function is not that of a picture but that of a narrative'. On the complex relationship between narrative and set piece description in the *Aeneid* see Fowler 2000, especially 66–9. Lessing 1984: 125–35 offers an influential reading of Homer's shield (cf. also the discussion of Servius at 245).

The commentary to line 8.625 highlights a marked interest in the details that are left unnarrated in the production of a satisfactory narrative—that is, in the effective arrangement of events and the gaps between them, the proper selection and synthesis of a coherent and unified plot out of the raw mass of 'unnarratable' elements that make up the story and which it is the business of narrating (*narrantis officium*) to edit and reorder. The back-story of how Dido came to found Carthage, the story of Aeneas' wanderings after the fall of Troy, and the history of Rome as depicted on Aeneas' shield, each engage the commentators in an analysis of how Virgil elects to arrange and synthesize this material into the plot of the *Aeneid.*

In the commentary to line 1.223 (echoed again in 2.668), Horace's *Ars poetica* is directly cited in the context of Virgil's achronological ordering of material:[65]

THE END (*finis*). Either of the narrative (*fabularum*) or the day, since it follows shortly after 'Aeneas tossed and turned throughout the night'. It is well known that Virgil does not always describe the beginning or ending of the day, but either leaves it to be understood, as in this example, or indicates it by action suited to the time period. For it is not poetically sophisticated to squeeze out every detail; as Horace says in his *Ars poetica*: 'As a true translator you will take care not to translate word for word' (*nec verbum verbo curabis reddere fidus interpres*).

The art of narrative discourse and the business of narrating, this commentary unexpectedly suggests, is akin to that of the translator. It is a mark of poetic sophistication (*poetica callopistia*) not to narrate every little detail and event in its chronological order; the best narrators avoid offering an unabridged reproduction of the original story material just as the best translators do.[66] They remind us that the business of narrating is the selection and transformation of key actions and events from history, and involves translating a source text, where episodes are set in their familiar and natural order (*ordo naturalis*) of causal-temporal sequence, into a new and aesthetically pleasing narrative order (*ordo artificialis*). Or, in modern narratological terms, that the business of narrating involves the translation of *fabula* into *syuzhet* or *histoire* into *discours.*

---

[65] Cf. Horace, *Ars poetica* 133–4.

[66] The commentary to 2.668 aptly reminds Virgil's readers and critics that 'the poet need not state everything that happens, for he will describe the day, but not the night before'. Homer, the paradigm of narrative economy in the Greek scholia (and in Aristotle), is praised in the commentary to *Iliad* 1.223 for not describing every single minute. Cf. the discussion of narrative schemata and scripts in Chapter 11.

5.6 **Modern narratological terms and concepts in the Servius commentaries**

Servius and Servius Auctus are interested in many other issues beside the *artem poeticam* behind Virgil's narrative technique: their glosses offer guidance on grammatical and linguistic features, particularly poetic forms and figures, and obscure or archaic words; explanations of mythological, historical, and geographical references; interpretations of philosophical, political, and religious aspects of the poem; and observations on intertextual allusions and parallels. In keeping with the commentary tradition both ancient and modern, this exegesis focuses principally upon helping readers of Virgil to make better sense of his syntax and grammar, his more obscure references and allusions, his occasional contradictions and numerous complexities. Yet, as the preface to the *Aeneid* commentary already suggests, and as Gianpiero Rosati's and Don Fowler's path-breaking work has persuasively demonstrated, the Servius commentaries also show a keen interest in narrative issues, especially those relating to focalization (including complex and 'embedded' focalizations).[67] Both versions of the commentaries regularly note those occasions on which Virgil (through indirect discourse) expressly manifests his empathetic or sympathetic subjectivity through apostrophes, questions, exclamations, epithets, and adjectives. What is more, they devote careful consideration to questions of focalization in response to the numerous cases in Virgil's poetry where these issues are unclear and the attribution of a speech act or point of view is contentious.

However, the responses of these ancient critics to key narratological questions are sometimes counterintuitive to a modern reader. So, in the commentary to line 2.733 of the *Aeneid*, an important line in Aeneas' account of his dramatic flight from Troy, the commentaries purport to advise on 'who sees' and 'who speaks'—anticipating questions that will become fundamental to narratological interrogations in the twentieth century after Genette's *Narrative Discourse*.[68] Ancient editions of the *Aeneid* (indeed, of any text) would not have included the punctuation marks that guide modern readers, and advice on questions of this kind is typical of the ancient commentary. At this point in the text, Aeneas

---

[67] Rosati 1979 and Fowler 1997. Cf. Fowler 2000 where he explores the issue of focalization in Virgil's *Aeneid* in the context of free indirect discourse (FID)—also discussed in Laird 1999. Genette 1988: 129 considers the Servius and Donatus commentaries on Virgil as a prototype of a genre schema based on style and content.

[68] Genette 1980.

(as internal narrator) is telling Dido and her companions (his internal narratees) how Troy came to fall and how he managed to escape the burning city, together with his father and son. Within this predominantly first-person narrative Aeneas has already spoken several times in voices other than his own, and here he briefly enters into a dramatic, mimetic mode of narration, and speaks two lines (*Aeneid* 2.733–4, highlighted in the text below) as if in his father's voice (*Aeneid* 2.730–6):

> And now I was nearing the gates, and it seemed I'd made it
> all the way through, when suddenly to my ears came the sound of
>   heavy feet
> seeming to be close by and, peering through the darkness,
> my father cries: '**My son, run my son; they're coming.**
> **I see their glittering shields and gleaming armour.**'
> At this, I run in terror as some unfriendly power seized
> my muddled wits…

> *iamque propinquabam portis omnemque videbar*
> *evasisse viam, subito cum creber ad auris*
> *visus adesse pedum sonitus, genitorque per umbram*
> *prospiciens 'nate,' exclamat, 'fuge, nate; propinquant.*
> *ardentis clipeos atque aera micantia cerno.'*
> *hic mihi nescio quod trepido male numen amicum*
> *confusam eripuit mentem…*

Most modern commentators and editors, responding to what appear to be pretty obvious textual cues as to which character sees and speaks these two lines, straightforwardly take the focalizer who sees the shields and armour in line 2.734 to be Aeneas' father, Anchises: the first main verb (*propinquabam*, I was nearing) clearly refers to Aeneas; the second main verb (*exclamat*, he cries) is in the third person and clearly refers to Anchises (as *genitor*, father); the present participle (*prospiciens*, peering) describes a contemporaneous action and its subject is similarly Anchises; so, in the absence of any linguistic direction otherwise, the main verb (*cerno*, I see) logically and syntactically takes Anchises as its subject (this verb is in the present tense, distinguishing it from Aeneas' past tense reportage using predominantly imperfect and perfect verbs). What is more, Aeneas' brief mimetic impersonation of Anchises appears to reach a logical conclusion at the end of line 2.734, with the deictic shift signalled by the start of the following line (*hic*) strongly suggesting that it is here that Aeneas drops his first-person *mimesis* and picks up his own first-person internal narration again to describe his reaction to Anchises' alarm—that is, he momentarily loses his head and runs in terror.

The Servius Auctus commentary to 2.733 sees things rather differently though:

I DISCERN (*cerno*): lots of people ask by which character/*persona* 'I discern' may be spoken. But those looking into the matter more deeply attribute 'I discern' to Aeneas, since he himself seems to have spoken this line.

Unfortunately, the commentary does not provide any further details of what exactly 'those looking into the matter more deeply' might have seen, or what theories of narrative they might have considered to justify this attribution. But that they should do so and reach such a different solution to those modern editors and commentators making a similar investigation is intriguing. The Servius Auctus commentary does not explicitly or unequivocally affirm the attribution of *cerno* (I see) and its point of focalization to Aeneas here (according to its own scholarly conventions, it merely reports what other experts have decided) but it does forward an interpretation of these lines which, though contrary to modern judgements, is syntactically and logically possible. So what is there in the text—and this part of the narrative—to justify giving the focalization and expression of line 2.734 to Aeneas rather than Anchises? What do the ancient commentators see that we don't?

Removing the modern punctuation, we both have the same Virgilian text for these lines, but our insights into its narrative discourse produce very different readings. Speculation (aptly) is our only option here. Perhaps these ancient critics are responding to the vivid first-person narration of this highly dramatic scene: believing himself to be on the brink of escape, Aeneas hears the approaching footsteps of the enemy behind him, he is alerted to the imminence of danger by his father's cry, at which he turns and sees for himself the threat closing upon them, graphically figured by the clash and flash of their weapons, and at the sight of this peril fast closing in upon himself and his family, he loses his head and runs in terror. In this context, the first-person expression and focalization conveyed by *cerno* (I see) fits persuasively with reference to Aeneas: it is, perhaps, more dramatically satisfying for this line to be 'narrated' by him rather than 'spoken' by his father. There are also plausible syntactical reasons for attributing the focalization of this line to Aeneas: as the suspense of the scene builds, the narrative moves from the past tenses typically associated with reportage in Latin poetry and prose, into the more vivid present tense (*exclamat*, he cries; *cerno*, I see; *trepido*, I flee in terror), making the two first-person present tense verbs here (arguably) part of a coherent narrative and syntactical unit describing Aeneas' own reactions to the danger encountered in this scene. Those ancient critics who decided to attribute this line to Aeneas have good grounds for doing so, and, in the absence of any external referent to which we can appeal in order to confirm with absolute assurance whether it is Aeneas or Anchises who sees and speaks this line, its attribution must remain a matter of interpretation.[69]

Yet, the Servius and Servius Auctus commentary on line 2.733 illustrates, with striking clarity, the very practical consideration that had to be given by ancient readers to questions of who sees and who speaks in a narrative discourse, given the lack of modern punctuation to resolve such questions on their behalf. This key difference between ancient and modern modes of textual presentation has important narratological implications. The readers and critics of unpunctuated narratives (like those listening to the recitation of a narrative text) must become acute observers of all the textual and narrative cues that are available to them if they are to attribute points of view and acts of speech appropriately. And, what is more, they must pay particular attention to cases involving complex or embedded focalization, where such attribution is not immediately obvious.

In the Servius commentaries (as in the scholia) metaphors, similes, epithets, apostrophes, and related features are all typically associated with the voice of the narrator rather than with his characters. Occasionally, however, the scholia show awareness of what Fowler characterized as a type of 'deviant focalization'.[70] Amidst a dramatic battle scene (12.486) the Virgilian narrator interjects with an expression of fear and dismay at the sight of the enemy wreaking havoc against the Latin coalition led by the hero Aeneas, exclaiming: 'Alas, what could he do?' (*heu, quid agat?*). But this interjection and its focalization belong also to the character Aeneas, through whose eyes we witness the enemy's success on the battlefield here. The Servius commentaries emphasize the difficulties in making sense of these words in the context of the narrative, pointing out that some readers and critics take them as a sympathetic interjection spoken by the poet, and 'others take them as spoken by Aeneas' character, as if he had said "Alas, what should I do?"'. The commentaries do not suggest which alternative is more acceptable, but the possibility that line 12.486 offers an embedded focalization is clearly allowed here.[71]

---

[69] Analysis of parallel cases in the commentaries fails to illuminate any standard processes by which the ancient critics attributed points of view and acts of speech.

[70] Fowler 1997 and 2000.

[71] Similar cases of questionable attribution appear in the commentary to lines 10.507, where the grief-stricken apostrophe (*o dolor*) might be attributed either to the poet-narrator or to the comrades who carry Pallas' dead body home; and 9.37, where: 'Some read "The enemy is here, come on!"; others think "come on!" is spoken not by one character to another but that the poet himself cried out as if with the impulse of the matter and imagination.'

The Servius commentaries detail several similar cases and evince a sophisticated appreciation of the different narrative levels and perspectives that Virgil's *Aeneid* displays—even suggesting theoretical and quasi-narratological 'rules' that readers can apply to help clarify such questions of complex focalization. So, in the commentary to line 1.23 of the *Aeneid* an explanation is offered as to why Juno is represented as 'remembering the old war' at a point in the narrative when, in terms of both story time and discourse time, the Trojan war could hardly be characterized as 'old' (*veteris*). The commentaries seek to explain this temporal anomaly, not as a case of authorial anachronism, but as a case of complex focalization, as follows:[72]

OLD WAR (*veteris belli*): as pertaining to Virgil, meaning 'ancient'; if you refer it to Juno, meaning 'waged for a long duration' (that is, for ten years). A view should be referred to a character when s/he speaks it (*tunc autem ad personam referendum est, cum ipsa loquitur*); when there is no character speaking, it is referred to the poet (*ad poetam refertur*). In this case, therefore, 'old/ancient' must be understood as relating to the character (*persona*) of the poet. So the poet himself in another part [of the poem] says 'they admire Aeneas' gifts, they admire Iulus and the blazing face of the god', referring in part to himself, and in part to the Tyrians, who were not aware that he [Iulus] was a god.

The commentaries pass over the hint from Virgil that this description of the Trojan War might offer readers an insight into the mind of Juno—described here significantly as 'remembering' or 'mindful' (*memor*)—and they simply ignore the word *memor* in their comments on the line. To a modern reader it seems perfectly reasonable that the description of the war should relate to Juno and represent this character's point of view. The commentaries, however, are unwilling to allow the possibility of embedded focalization in this particular case and direct the reader to take the adjective and its attendant viewpoint as straightforwardly representing that of the narrator, Virgil, for whom (writing more than a thousand years after the event) the Trojan War was certainly 'ancient' history. The possibility that Juno's view of the war might be shown here is dismissed by the commentators because it is not the character Juno who speaks these words. Indeed, the Servius and Servius Auctus commentaries both style their responses to this line as in accordance to some narratological rule or formula, using the Latin gerundive (*referendum est*—'should be referred' and *intellegendum*—'must be understood') to indicate the necessity rather than simply the plausibility of this interpretation: s/he

---

[72] This example is also discussed by Fowler 1997: 76.

who speaks will indicate s/he who sees—voice and point of view must correspond.

The example that the commentators give to support this rule, however, is thorny. It also comes from the first book of the *Aeneid* (1.709–10), describing an incident in which the god Cupid disguises himself as Aeneas' son Iulus and attends a banquet hosted by Dido and her Tyrian nobles. The reader, along with Virgil as omniscient poet-narrator, all know that Iulus is not really present in this scene, but the Tyrians do not. Therefore, when the narrator observes that they 'admire Iulus and the blazing face of the god' the focalization (and point of view) is bifurcated: the admiration directed towards 'Iulus' (= Cupid in disguise) represents the view of the Tyrians ('who were not aware that he was a god') and the admiration directed towards the 'god' represents that of Virgil. Rather than attribute that bifurcation or split point of view to Virgil alone—even though it is clearly 'the poet himself' who speaks this line—the commentaries allow the prospect of a more complex kind of focalization to function here, claiming that Virgil is 'referring in part to himself, and in part to the Tyrians'. Indeed, patient explication is given as to which point of view should be attributed to whom at each narrative juncture:

[709] THEY ADMIRE AENEAS' GIFTS (*mirantur dona Aeneae*): this is attributed to the Tyrians. THEY ADMIRE IULUS: the one they [i.e. the Tyrians] think is Iulus.

[710] THEY [ADMIRE] THE BLAZING FACE OF THE GOD (*flagrantisque dei vultus*): this is attributed to the poet (*hoc ad poetam refertur*). DECEPTIVE WORDS (*simulataque verba*): arranged to give an impression of Iulus Ascanius. This too should be attributed to the *persona* of the poet.

Numerous cases of such exceptions to the theoretical 'rule' established at line 1.23 follow, in which embedded or bifurcated focalization (bifocalization?) is explicitly acknowledged in passages of ostensibly straightforward narration—that is, 'where there is no character speaking'. So, in the commentary to *Aeneid* 4.141, the focalization of Aeneas' beauty described by the poet-narrator is straightforwardly attributed to the infatuated character Dido:

HANDSOMEST (*pulcherrimus*): from the mind/perspective (*ex animo*) of Dido; for so he appeared to her. Virgil gives different kinds of epithets to Aeneas: when he shows piety, he calls him 'pious'; when he shows bravery, he calls him 'mighty'.

The commentaries see the adjective here as unequivocally representing Dido's point of view, on the grounds that it would be incongruous for the poet-narrator to describe the story's hero in this way, but perfectly reasonable for a (female) character in love to do so.[73]

A more complicated example, set within a passage of internal dialogue, concerns Turnus' apparent self-pity in an address to his sister Juturna, where he refers to himself as her 'pitiable brother' (*fratris miseri*). The commentary to this line (12.636) advises that 'this is poor (*humile*), if you take it as coming from the *persona*/character of Turnus: therefore "pitiable" must be referred to the mind of the sister'. The commentaries assign the point of view expressed by the sympathetic adjective to Juturna on the grounds of a narrative ethics of decorum, it appears: it is appropriate for a sister to regard an unfortunate brother in this way, but not for a male protagonist to so regard himself.[74]

In each of these examples, the ancient commentators appeal to a set of normative narrative concerns which are remarkably close to those employed by modern narratologists. They seek to identify the voice and point of view of a narratorial *persona*, and to distinguish these from those of the narrative's characters. What is more, in the absence of a Latin term with which to identify the 'narrator' as such, they describe the narrator as another *persona* or 'character' performing a function (that of author or poet) within the narrative, conducting the 'business of narrating'. This is sophisticated stuff.

In modern narratology, as Fludernik has argued, 'the narrative text is frequently regarded as a tissue of conflicting "voices" that overlap and need to be unravelled by the reader and literary critic'.[75] This is precisely what these ancient commentaries set out to do and, through their critical expertise, to help Virgil's readers to do. The Servius and Servius Auctus commentators, it emerges, are no less ready than modern readers of the *Aeneid* to highlight those parts of the poem in which multiple voices and competing viewpoints are evident, and throughout both commentaries our attention is drawn to moments at which the character of the poet-narrator reduces the distance between his narrating *persona* and that of his characters by indicating his sympathy for their point of view. The commentators find such subjectivity on the part of the epic narrator not only characteristic of Virgil's narrative style (*ut solet*, 12.452) but admirable (*mire*, 9.397). They appreciate that at some (especially heightened) moments in the narrative, the voice and the viewpoint of the narrator may be seen to coincide with those of a character—even if that character

---

[73] This is also one of the examples discussed by Rosati 1979: 556.

[74] Notice that in this instance the commentators are content to attribute a point of view to a character's mind, but were not open to the same in the case of Juno at 1.23.

[75] Fludernik 2001: 622. See also Pascal 1977.

is not then speaking—as embedded focalization (even deviant focalization) collapses the distance between the poet-narrator and his narrative.

Concerns with narrative distance of this kind run throughout the Servius commentaries, coming particularly to the fore at moments when, as the Latin critics have it, the poet-narrator appears to be 'speaking to his own times' (3.701: *ad praesens tempus locutus est*) or 'reflecting his own time' (3.84: *ad tempora poeta respondit*) rather than reflecting the time and temporality inhabited by his characters within the storyworld of the *Aeneid*. The commentators carefully note when Virgil uses names or terms which might suggest a mistaken anachronism on the part of the poet-narrator.

There are numerous examples identifying anachronistic 'continuity' errors, with a prominent cluster appearing in the commentaries to Book 8 which, significantly, tells of Aeneas' visit to the future site of Rome: precisely the place in the story where we would expect the poet-narrator to refer to anonymous ancient spots by their contemporary Augustan names, whether carelessly projecting Rome's topographical present onto its past, or deliberately foreshadowing its future Augustan glory.[76] Although some ancient commentators appear to regard these 'anachronisms' as simple errors on the part of the poet-narrator, the theoretically informed narratological sophistication hinted at in the Servius commentaries suggests that a less nitpicking and more nuanced appreciation of Virgil's narrative technique may be at work here.[77]

The critical term that the ancient commentators use to identify these instances of Virgil's temporary (and temporal) closing of the distance between narrator and narrative is *prolepsis*—a difficult term to translate in the context of Latin narrative discourse and commentary. As we saw, the concept of prolepsis features prominently in the Greek scholia, where it typically describes a flashforward or foreshadowing in the narrative, whether internal to the main narrative (such as Odysseus' homecoming in the *Odyssey*) or external, alluding to an event falling outside of the narrative but within the compass of its wider story arc (such as Odysseus' 'gentle death', prophesied but not included in the main plot line of the *Odyssey*). But this is not quite the same sense in which prolepsis appears

---

[76] Cf. 8.347 ('"Tarpeian seat" is an anachronism: for these two names were given to the hill afterwards'); 8.361 ('the Roman forum is where the speakers' platform now is. But he has committed anachronism here too, for it was called this [only] later on'). Similar anachronisms are noted at 7.797 and 9.9.

[77] In a multi-authored, composite work, such as the Servius or Servius Auctus commentary, we necessarily encounter competing views and interpretations of prolepsis. In the commentary to line 1.2, for example, at Virgil's reference to 'Lavinian shores', we are advised: 'some authorities would, unnecessarily, wish this to be an anachronism'.

to be used by the Latin commentators in their readings of Virgil's *Aeneid*. It seems—as is so often the case with narratological terminology—that the definition and use of the term changes significantly when it enters the hands of a different set of critics.

The later Latin term *prolepsis* (this word is not found in classical Latin) clearly represents a translation and transliteration of the Greek, but in Latin it becomes a technical term applied to rhetorical figures of speech and does not usually transfer to narrative contexts.[78] The rhetorical application of the term properly describes a speaker's prediction and refutation of a counter-argument, as in 'You may say I'm a dreamer, but I'm not the only one.' There are, however, no instances at all in the Servius commentaries on the *Aeneid* where the term prolepsis is used in this sense. In rhetorical theory prolepsis can also describe the premature use of a word at the syntactical level, as in the classic example of hypallage at *Aeneid* 1.69, where Juno asks Aeolus to 'overwhelm the sunken ships' but where we might more logically expect a request 'to sink the overwhelmed ships'. Significantly, the Servius commentaries observe this wordplay as an instance where 'the sense order is reversed' but do not describe this as a rhetorical or syntactical prolepsis. Nor is prolepsis used in this sense anywhere else in the ancient *Aeneid* commentaries.

In Book 6, however, the term prolepsis is used to describe the chronologically premature use of a word at the story level rather than at the syntactical level. Having completed his journey through the Underworld, Aeneas returns to his ships and the fleet sets sail for the harbour of Caieta; except, as we learn at the beginning of the next book (*Aeneid* 7.1–4), the harbour is not yet called Caieta: it will only later take this name in honour of Aeneas' old nurse, Caieta, who dies there shortly after the fleet arrives. The poet-narrator's reference to Caieta as a place name in *Aeneid* Book 6 is therefore premature, prompting the commentaries to note (6.900):

TO THE HARBOUR OF CAIETA (*ad Caietae portum*): prolepsis from the character/*persona* of the poet (*a persona poetae prolepsis*): for it was not yet called Caieta.

---

[78] Quintilian (9.2.16) uses the term *prolepsis* (in Greek) to describe a rhetorical technique of deflecting potential opposition or objection by anticipating—and dismissing—it. Significantly, he translates the Greek *prolepsis* with the Latin word *praesumptio*. In rhetoric, the term *anticipatio* can be used synonymously with *prolepsis*, but on the single occasion on which *anticipatio* is used in the Servius commentaries (6.359), it describes a straightforward case of what we would recognize as anachronism: the ghost of Aeneas' former helmsman, Palinurus, speaks of 'Velia's harbour' (*Aeneid* 3.366) although this Greek harbour would not then have been known by a Roman name but by its Greek name, Ἐλέα (Elea or Elia). The Servius commentaries explain that 'this is anachronism which, as I said above, is forgivable if it is [voiced] from the *persona* of the poet, but totally unacceptable if voiced by another'.

The qualification of the prolepsis here as coming from the hindsight (that is, the viewpoint and temporality) of the poet-narrator is significant. For it invites (and itself performs) a reading which redeems the anticipatory naming of 'Caieta' not as an anachronistic error on the part of the poet-narrator but as a deliberate foreshadowing of an event occurring later on in the story. This is not exactly a kind of rhetorical prolepsis, and it is not precisely the same kind of proleptic flashforward described in the Greek scholia: the narrative of the event foreshadowed in *Aeneid* 6.900 immediately follows (7.1–4). And yet, it shares qualities with both figures. This concept of prolepsis seems to combine elements of the term found both in the Greek scholia and in the later Latin and Greek rhetorical schools to form a new narratological application which we might well translate as 'proleptic anachronism', reflecting a concern with story and discourse time.

Indeed, the crucial position of the prolepsis—or proleptic anachronism—found in the penultimate line of Book 6, at exactly the midpoint of the twelve-book epic, confirms the narratological rather than the rhetorical emphasis of this figure for the Servius critics. The proleptic naming of Caieta helps to bridge the book division between the first and second halves of Virgil's narrative: as Aeneas' ships drop metapoetic anchors and the story comes to a temporary pause, Caieta anchors the present to the past, the Odyssean first half of the story to the beginning of its Iliadic second part. The fact that Ovid (himself a virtuoso in negotiating narrative continuity across book divisions) gleefully flags up this potential bit of historical anachronism in an infamous 'misreading' of Virgil also suggests that there is an important narratological aspect to Virgil's aetiological anachronism here, to which the later commentators are similarly responding. In his own mini-*Aeneid* in Book 14 of the *Metamorphoses*, Ovid 'corrects' Virgil by describing the arrival at Caieta as the moment when 'Trojan Aeneas arrives at the shore which **did not yet** bear the name of his nurse' (*Metamorphoses* 14.156–7: *Troius Aeneas sacrisque ex more litatis/litora adit **nondum** nutricis habentia nomen*).[79]

In this light it is significant that the Servius commentaries explicitly contextualize the *Aeneid* and its author within a wider historical 'grand narrative'—the foundation story of the Roman Empire and its first *princeps*. The preface to the *Aeneid* commentary regards the intention to 'praise Augustus through his ancestors' as one of Virgil's key ambitions for the poem, as its final cause. The ancient commentators clearly

---

[79] Cf. Hinds's elegant reading (1998: 109).

recognize that Virgil's epic narrative has an ultimate *telos* which reaches into 'the poet's own time' and they seem satisfied that the vatic poet-narrator should sometimes have privileged, proleptic, knowledge of the future.[80] However, they are less happy when that knowledge appears to extend to characters within the narrative. So, when Aeneas tells of the final stages of his journey to Carthage and of sailing past famous landmarks at the end of Book 3, the ancient commentators criticize the fact that he lists places yet to be founded (3.699–704). The commentary to line 3.703 notes that here Virgil 'looks to his own time, not to that of the work', adding that 'he frequently does this but now the same thing is a fault because these details are narrated from the *persona* of Aeneas'. In this context, the proleptic foreshadowing that might positively be attributed to the omniscient poet-narrator is treated negatively (as historical anachronism) because it is attributed to an internal character-narrator. What is more, the ancient critics have here identified two distinct temporalities at work within the narrative of the *Aeneid* (one pertaining to the poet-narrator and a second pertaining to the 'work') and set limitations as to what might appropriately be narrated within each temporal frame. Thus, what superficially appeared to be a pedantic concern with Virgil's anachronisms turns out to represent a sophisticated set of narratological interests in narrative time, focalization, and distance—and a proleptic anticipation of future concerns with internal narrators and focalizers.

5.7 *Teleute*

Viewed as practising proto-narratologists, the critics of the ancient Greek scholia and later Latin commentaries offer us ample evidence to rethink and redeem their reputation as dusty pedants. Their work is clearly informed by the prevailing narratological theories of the day—the scholia by Plato and Peripatetic 'Aristotelianism' if not directly by the *Poetics*, and the Servius commentators by Horace too. They and their readers have recourse to a complex lexicon of specialized narratological terms and concepts (as knotty as anything dreamed up by the Russian formalists

---

[80] Cf. Thomas 2001: 93–121. For a nicely nuanced discussion of the 'anomalous focalization' that the epic's various prolepses open up, see Reed 2009: 129–30. Barchiesi 1994 and Fowler 1997 also see Virgil's prolepses as integral components of his highly teleological narrative. Zetzel 1981: 118 notes 'the curious logic, not peculiar to Servius, which permitted knowledge of the future to the poet or to a god, but never to a human speaker'.

or French structuralists) often freely adapted from ancient theories of rhetoric. In this rhetorical-narratological context, they show a keen interest in matters of affect and cognition, in the ways that stories are formed so as to produce particular affects upon an audience, presenting a fascinating glimpse into 'the business of narrating' as understood by ancient theorists and critics.

6 Russian formalism

It is simply Aristotle's old theory of literature.
Boris Tomashevsky, 'Letter
to Shklovsky' (1925)

6.1 *Arche*

Modern genealogies of narratology tend to locate its origins with the structuralist project of the 1960s and document the evolution of narrative theory only back thus far.[1] But long before there were structuralists, there were formalists. Emerging from the aesthetic movements of Saint Petersburg and Moscow in the revolutionary period *c.*1914–29, and most associated with the work of Viktor Shklovsky, Mikhail Petrovsky, Boris Tomashevsky, and Vladimir Propp, the pioneering narratological theories of Russian formalism have come to play a significant role in the history of narratology, as well as in the reception and transmission of classical theories of narrative poetics. While the German and Anglo-American theorists of the period were busy focusing their narratological attentions upon the novel, the Russian formalists—early adopters of critical approaches to the new narrative art form of cinema—widened their analytical horizons to examine narrative form much more broadly, considering the evolution and morphology of the anecdote, the short story, the novella, and novel, as well as poetry, drama, and film. In so doing, they not only introduced some of narratology's foundational principles but re-interrogated and re-introduced some key Aristotelian theories into narrative theory. Working independently, yet in close parallel to European and American narratologists in the first half of the twentieth century, the Russian formalists share with those narrative theorists a common foundation: Aristotle's *Poetics*.[2]

A long letter from Tomashevsky to Shklovsky, written in 1925, published in 1978, but hitherto untranslated, acknowledges the awkwardly self-conscious Aristotelian affiliations of the Russian formalists – as seen in the epigraph to this chapter. In this letter Tomashevsky playfully

---

[1] Cf. Fehn, Hoesterey, and Tatat 1992, Herman 1999, and Fludernik 2005a.
[2] See Todorov 1977: 247–67 on the 'methodological heritage of formalism' and its impact upon structuralism.

chides Shklovsky (his friend, colleague, and fellow 'formalist') for labelling his book on the theory of literature as a pioneering formalist study. He would, he writes, expect such a review from a journalist, but not from a friend:[3]

> There should be no misunderstandings between you and me. My *Theory of Literature* lies entirely outside the bounds of the formal method, outside scientific analysis, outside the usual questions. It is simply Aristotle's old theory of literature...I would not dwell so much on this misunderstanding if it were not pregnant with certain consequences. "The Formal school" is not a theory of literature. We should keep that firmly in mind. By the way, I recently attended a scholarly and clever paper...which construed the formal method precisely as a theory of literature, precisely as a justification of the right of Aristotle's poetics to exist, and as such coming many centuries late. The entire paper was addressed to Alexander of Macedonia's schooldays.

The ludic and contradictory character of Tomashevsky's professed attempts to 'set the record straight' with Shklovsky here makes it difficult to identify the precise nature of his views on either 'formalism' or Aristotle's *Poetics*. Tomashevsky's own work, he alleges, is not part of the formalist project (which does not, he says, represent or offer a 'theory of literature'—tellingly, the title of his own book), and does not mechanistically seek to map its conclusions onto to a pre-prepared formalist grid (literally, 'little squares'). It is not original, nor particularly scholarly, he claims in the letter: he wrote it for a popular audience, based on old lecture notes, and as such *it is simply Aristotle's old theory of literature*—another 'formalist' narrative poetics famously configured of old lecture notes.

Amidst these protestations Tomashevsky clearly identifies himself and his project with that of Shklovsky, referring to 'our disciples', despite the fact that it is the 'formalist' Shklovsky who has supposedly offended Tomashevsky in praising the originality of his *Theory of Literature* as a groundbreaking formalist study. Tomashevsky also claims to have been impressed by a recent 'clever' attempt to align the formalist method with Aristotle's *Poetics* (represented as a 'theory of literature' analogous to his own).[4] Precisely where we are to align either Tomashevsky's or Shklovsky's literary critical affinities in the light of this letter is far from

---

[3] Tomashevsky 1978: 385–6. Steiner 2014: 32 argues that 'the formalists themselves resented any parallelism drawn between their poetics and Aristotle's, and they certainly would have rejected the label "neo-Aristotelian"'. In this view Steiner perhaps overlooks what he later acknowledges as 'the complex trope of irony' informing Russian formalist discourse (2014: 8).

[4] Tomashevsky's description of the paper he attended as 'clever' (*khitrom*) carries negative connotations—of 'craftiness' and an attempt at deceit—but the playfulness of the letter means that the paper's author could well have been Shklovsky himself.

clear, but the simultaneous avowal and disavowal of formalist and Aristotelian correspondences foregrounds and acknowledges a complicated sympathy between these two pioneering approaches to narrative and narrative theory.

As Tomashevsky's letter reminds us, the 'formalist' label was initially attached to the Russian narratologists by their detractors and was not a term ever wholly embraced by these theorists themselves.[5] In fact, some—like Propp and Petrovsky—preferred to characterize their brand of narratology as 'morphological' rather than formalist.[6] This self-identification highlights important links between the theories of narrative developed by the Russian formalists and some of the theories of the novel promoted by their near-contemporaries working in Germany in the early part of the twentieth century—notably the morphologists Bernard Seuffert, Wilhelm Dibelius, and the classical philologist Otmar Schissel von Fleschenberg.[7] In particular, the German theorists worked with clear-cut (quasi-classical) distinctions between narrative disposition and composition—terms which correspond closely with the distinctions between narrative *fabula* and *syuzhet* that would subsequently be drawn by the formalists.[8]

The Russian formalists certainly shared with their German counterparts a common concern with literary form over literary content.[9] They were concerned with the how rather than the what, the device rather than the material, the manner rather than the matter, *Gestalt* rather than *Gehalt*, discourse rather than story, narration rather than narrated, and—in the terms they themselves introduced to narratology—in *syuzhet*

---

[5] See Steiner 2014.   [6] See Erlich 1955: 627.

[7] See Doležel 1990: 124–46, who views Dibelius as influencing Propp in his designation of character as 'a certain function of the whole' (134). However, it is worth noting that amongst the many publications of the formalists, only Eichenbaum mentions Dibelius in his 1927 account of the origins of formalism and only then to dismiss any influence or correspondence. Schmid 2010: 176 also suggests that the German philologists may have asserted some (qualified) influence upon the Russian formalists. Propp reveals his own indebtedness to the German schools when he writes (1984: 73): 'I should have spoken not of morphology but of a much more narrow and accurate concept, that of composition, and should have entitled the book *Composition of the Folk Wondertale*.'

[8] In the discussion that follows, *fabula* and *syuzhet* (transliterated elsewhere as *sjuzhet*, *sujet*, *sjužet*, *syuzhet*, or *suzet*) have been translated according to the familiar convention that maps the Russian *fabula* onto the English story, and *syuzhet* onto plot. These are far from uncontentious translations, however. See Lowe 2000: 5–6 and 18–19. On the indebtedness of *fabula* and *syuzhet* to German morphological models of disposition and composition see Sternberg 1973: 23–69. According to Schissel's definitions of these terms (1910: vi), 'disposition' described the natural, logical, and chronological pattern of raw narrative material or story stuff (*Stoff*), with 'composition' describing the artificial, artistic, rhetorical arrangement of that stuff.

[9] Key studies of Russian formalism include Schmid 2010, Volek 1985, Hansen-Löve 1978: 238–63, and Garcia Landa 1998: 32–80. Eichenbaum's 1965 survey remains an excellent introduction and overview.

(plot) rather than *fabula* (story).[10] But, unlike their German predecessors, the Russian formalists were also interested in the reception and reading of literature, the readerly response to and processing of narrative. So, according to one of the early innovators in Russian formalism, '*Art is a way of experiencing the artfulness of an object; the object is not important.*'[11] Like Aristotle's *Poetics*, the objective of Russian formalist poetics was to understand poetry 'not in terms of what it is, but in terms of what it is for'.[12] The Russian formalists were interested in literary and narrative affect and in theorizing the devices and patterns—specifically 'the commonly accepted rhetorical figures, and all those methods which emphasize the emotional effect of an expression'—that impact upon the reader, viewer, or listener.[13] Shadowing ancient concerns with the cognitive and emotional effects of narrative as well as anticipating the rhetorical and cognitive turns in postclassical narratology, the point of narrative art for the Russian formalists was 'to recover the sensation of life; it exists to make one feel things, to make the stone stony'.[14] The point of their narratology was to reveal how and why narrative achieves this effect.

6.2 **Victor Shklovsky**

It is to Victor Shklovsky's theory of plot, first fully outlined in his 1921 essay 'Sterne's *Tristram Shandy* and the Theory of the Novel' (subsequently included in his 1929 collected essays, *O teorii prozy*, *On the Theory of Prose*), that modern narratology traces the origins of one its core

[10] The dominant translation of these terms (promoted by Lemon and Reis 1965) renders *syuzhet* as plot and *fabula* as story. The equivalents are problematic. As Sternberg 1978 points out, *syuzhet* refers to the narrative discourse (or text) as a whole, while plot describes a textual abstraction. But Brooks is happy with this translation of the pair (1984: 326): '*sjuzet* as used by such Russian formalists ... [is] an abstraction and reconstruction of the logic of the narrative text, and in this sense quite close to Aristotle'.
[11] Shklovsky 1965a: 12, emphasis in original.
[12] Erlich 1955: 179. Erlich's remains one of the best studies of Russian formalism and its narratologies. Erlich does not, however, share my view of the 'Aristotelianism' of this school.
[13] Shklovsky 1965a: 8–9.
[14] Shklovsky 1965a: 12. Tynyanov also deserves a brief mention here. Rejecting the delineations of *syuzhet* and *fabula* described by his fellow formalists, Tynyanov sees *fabula* as 'the entire semantic (conceptual) basting of the action', a cognitive construct effected by the imagination of the reader, hearer, or spectator who cooks it up in the process of 'searching for the story'; *syuzhet*, on the other hand, represents the structure through which the *fabula* is made accessible: 'the story's dynamics, composed of the interactions of all the linkages of material (including the story as a linkage of actions)—stylistic linkage, story linkage, etc.' (Tynyanov 1981: 95–6). For Tynyanov, both *fabula* and *syuzhet* co-exist in the reader's mind.

concepts—the distinction between story (*fabula*) and plot (*syuzhet*). Shklovsky is initially interested in the workings of narrative in so far as this helps him to illustrate and develop his ideas about 'defamiliarization' (*ostranenie*)—a project at the heart of the Russian formalist project.[15] Shklovsky observes that the basic pattern of any story (*fabula*) essentially reproduces a *familiar* pattern, imitating the sorts of temporal and causal sequence of events found in real life. But there is nothing artistic, poetic, or literary in such patterns. Shklovsky's translators, Lemon and Reis, put it well in their commentary:[16]

Story is essentially the temporal-causal sequence of narrated events. Its formula, capable of infinite extension, is always "because of A, then B." ... Such is the pattern of the story, each event coming in the order in which it would occur in real life and the events bound each to each in a cause-and-effect relationship. This, to return to the notion of defamiliarization, is the familiar way of telling something; but precisely because it is the familiar way, it is not the artistic way.

Unexpectedly, Shklovsky marshals Aristotle—and 'Aristotle's old theory of literature'—in support of this theory of 'defamiliarization' as that which renders a story artistic, claiming: 'According to Aristotle, poetic language must appear strange and wonderful.'[17]

For Aristotle it is non-standard, unfamiliar diction which turns ordinary language into poetry (*Poetics* 22.1458a 20–3): 'Strange and wonderful is the diction that uses exotic language (by "exotic" I mean loan words, metaphors, contractions, and all deviations from the norm).' But, for Shklovsky, it is plot which transforms story into poetic or literary narrative through the artistic process of re-arranging, re-presenting, and explicitly distorting familiar patterns so as to render them strange and wonderful. Narrative devices such as parallel storylines, digressions, prolepses and analepses, unexpected beginnings *in medias res* or *in ultimas res* all contribute to the effects of defamiliarization. And for Shklovsky, plot rather than story is interesting because it is only through plot (*syuzhet*) that these devices come into play. Rajnath aptly summarizes the implications of this theory of defamiliarization for the Russian formalists thus:[18]

Ordinary language is to poetic language as story is to plot. Poetic language disrupts ordinary language just as plot disrupts story. Ordinary language is the logical and sequential order of words just as story is a logical arrangement of motifs.

---

[15] See Sher in Shlovsky 1990: xviii–xix on the range of meaning and suitable translations for Shklovsky's neologism *ostranenie*.

[16] Lemon and Reis 1965: 25, ellipsis in original.

[17] This passing reference to Aristotle appears in 'Art as Technique', Shklovsky 1965a: 22.

[18] Rajnath 1996: 34.

Accordingly, Shklovsky describes the *syuzhet* as 'a phenomenon of style', likening the *syuzhet* and its operations to musical orchestration and 'rhyme':[19]

> The methods and devices of plot (*syuzhet*) construction are similar to and in principle identical with the devices of, for instance, sound orchestration. Works of literature represent a web of sounds, movements, and ideas.

It is the principles guiding the formation and configuration of this web which most concern Shklovsky and not its actual form or content. Indeed, this disinterest in material form and content is what seems to have motivated his drawing of that crucial distinction between *syuzhet* and *fabula* in the first place. It is important to remember that until Shklovsky redefined their relationship, the Russian terms *syuzhet* and *fabula* were broadly interchangeable, both equally referring to stories, narratives, and/or plots.[20] In his earlier works this is how Shklovsky himself uses the terms, with *syuzhet* a straightforward synonym for *fabula*. But as he sought to articulate and emphasize the privileged status of *syuzhet* as transforming process rather than as product, as construction rather than content, Shklovsky sets up the term *fabula* (story) as antonym to *syuzhet* (plot), suggesting:[21]

> The idea of *syuzhet* is too often confused with the description of events—with what I propose provisionally to call the *fabula*. The *fabula* is, in fact, only material for *syuzhet* formulation.

This cautious 'provisional' proposal establishing a tentative distinction between two levels of narrative, between story (*fabula*) and plot (*syuzhet*), marks a decisive moment in the history of narratology.

In line with his appeal to Aristotle as anticipating and authorizing his own theory of 'defamiliarization', a few critics have noted a degree of correspondence between Shklovsky's definitions of *syuzhet* and Aristotle's notions of *muthos*.[22] The parallels are certainly suggestive: both Shklovsky and Aristotle identify plot as the organizing principle that configures the stuff of story into narrative discourse through its 'arrangement of incidents' (cf. *Poetics* 6.1450a 2–4); both assume a hierarchical relationship between plot and story; both consider that a writer or poet principally demonstrates his artistry through his construction of plots (cf. *Poetics* 9.1451b 27–30); and both see the plot as the primary vehicle

---

[19] Shklovsky 1990: 45–6.   [20] Volek 1985: 142.   [21] Shklovsky 1965b: 57.
[22] See Schmid 2009a: 36, Sternberg 1978: 307 n. 15, and Garcia Landa 1998: 27. Cf. Prince 2003: *s.vv.* 'The distinction between *mythos* and *logos* is suggestive of that between ... SJUZET and *FABULA*.'

through which a writer or poet reaches the goal of narrative and achieves an emotional impact upon an audience.

Shklovsky himself admits no Aristotelian parallel for his dyad of story (*fabula*) and plot (*syuzhet*) but his writings reveal an extensive and nuanced engagement both with Aristotle specifically and the classical canon more generally. In the collected essays of his 1929 *Theory of Prose*, Shklovsky quotes extensively from Aristotle's *Poetics*—including substantial excerpts from chapter 14 (1453b 11–1454a 15) and chapter 17 (1455a 34–1455b 15).[23] In a highly self-reflexive literary-critical essay on the ostensibly plotless discourse of literary-critical essays and anecdotes, he suggests that such writings do effectively 'plot' in their necessary selection and arrangement of subject material, and he references Aristotle as already anticipating the 'formal causes' of this important point:[24]

The plot distorts the material by the very fact that it selects it . . . This is especially noticeable in the history of Greek literature, whose themes focus on the conflicts obtaining in a specific number of families. The formal causes for this focus were already pointed out by Aristotle. The anecdotes which we shall now relate concerning our contemporaries have their origins in the depths of the ages.

Like Aristotle, Shklovsky cites Homer, Aeschylus, Sophocles, and Euripides. But he also offers examples drawn from Menander, Plautus, and Terence, as well as Virgil, Ovid, Apuleius, and Petronius.[25] He repeatedly stresses the fundamental affinity between ancient poetry and the modern novel, emphasizing continuity through change in maintaining the principle that[26] 'Greece has not left us a theory of the novel, but it has left us both novels and novelistic schemata.'

Shklovsky also shows a detailed familiarity with the literary criticism of Alexander Veselovsky and Thaddeus Zielinsky, responding in particular to Veselovsky's theories of ancient to modern literary evolution and to Zielinsky's ideas about narrative continuity in Homer.[27] Indeed, Shklovsky is often persuaded by the secondary scholarship to misread or overlook key evidence from the very ancient sources that he likes to cite as authorities for his theories and observations. In a famous essay discussing the chaotic simultaneous action narrated in *Tristram Shandy*,

---

[23] Shklovsky 1990: 43–5. His quotations are taken from Appelrot's 1893 Russian translation and commentary of the *Poetics* (as discussed below, section 6.6).

[24] Shklovsky 1990: 206. Cf. *Poetics* 13.1453a 15–22, 14.1453b 14–39, and 15.1454a 1–15.

[25] Shklovsky 1990: *passim*.   [26] Shklovsky 1990: 206.

[27] See Veselovsky 1876 and Zielinksy 1899–1901: 317–28.

Shklovsky refers to the controversial Homeric 'continuity of time principle' or 'Zielinsky's Law' (*'Sukzessionsgesetz'*), observing:[28]

Homer never shows two simultaneous actions. If by force of circumstances they ever had to be simultaneous, they were reported as happening in sequence. Only the activity of one character and the "standing pat" (that is, the inactivity) of another can occur simultaneously.

Shklovsky makes essentially the same point in his reading of the narrative interlacing technique of *Don Quixote*, contrasting Cervantes's sophistication with Homer's supposed primitivism, and arguing:[29] 'Zielinsky has demonstrated that simultaneity of action is not admissible in the *Odyssey*. Although parallel narrative lines do exist in the storyline (Odysseus and Telemachus), yet the events unfold alternately in each line.'

In both of these parallel instances, Shklovsky ignores Aristotle's observation that 'in tragedy it is impossible to represent different parts of the story simultaneously, as it is only possible to show that part of the story which the actors are performing onstage; whereas, in epic, because it is narrative, several parts can be represented as being performed at the same time' (*Poetics* 24.1459b 23–7). Shklovsky also overlooks (with Zielinsky) the several occasions in Homer where the so-called 'continuity of time principle' is not observed and synchronous events are, in effect, narrated.[30] Yet, the nod to Zielinsky (and to Homer) turns out to be an important factor in shaping Shklovsky's understanding of the ways in which plot (or *syuzhet*) temporally distorts and rearranges the stuff of story (*fabula*). His reading of Zielinsky and misreading of Homer help to mould Shklovsky's own theory that '"Literary time" is clearly arbitrary; its laws do not coincide with the laws of ordinary time.'[31] From this position he goes on to observe that a story (*fabula*) possesses a basic linear chronological structure (mirroring that found in day-to-day life or 'ordinary time') that is radically different to the artificial patterning of time produced by the treatment of that same story material in a narrative plot (*syuzhet*). Indeed, the 'displacement of time' brought about by the emplotment of a narrative turns out to be central to Shklovsky's theory of

---

[28] Shklovsky 1990: 150. Sher's awkward translation ('standing pat') reflects Shklovsky's awkward reading of Zielinsky here. For a nuanced critical discussion of Zielinsky's Law see Scodel 2008. Auerbach 1974: 3–23 shares Zielinsky's views and the belief that Homer 'knows no background. What he narrates is for the time being the only present' (4).

[29] Shklovsky 1990: 101. Cf. de Jong 2001b: 589–91.

[30] *Odyssey* 4.847, 8.438–48, 13.185–9, 15.295–495, 16.1–3, 17.492–3, and 21.188–244. See also de Jong 2001b: 589–91.

[31] Shklovsky 1965b: 36–7.

the relationship between story and plot, *fabula* and *syuzhet*, as well as to subsequent narratological treatments of time and narrative.[32]

Shklovsky is in no way a lazy reader of classical texts or classical scholarship, however. Criticizing Zielinsky's interpretation of the typical abduction and recognition plot found in the Greek novel and in Menandrian New Comedy as rooted in 'an actual phenomenon' (as, Zielinsky supposes, part of the social reality of child exposure and kidnap in the ancient world), Shklovsky points out that by the fourth century BCE such plot devices were already familiar *topoi* of the literary and dramatic tradition and as such please audiences because they draw attention to their own internal metatheatricality and narrativity rather than alluding to or imitating an external actuality.[33] It is this self-awareness of poetic plotting and narrative reflexivity which Shklovsky represents as characteristic of the ideal, most artistic, pleasurable story form:[34]

Why does the recognition scene in the plays of Menander, Plautus and Terence take place in the last act, when the spectators have already had a presentiment by then of the blood relationship binding the antagonists, and when the author himself often notifies us of it in advance in the prologue? ... Why is it that, in fashioning an *Art of Love* out of love, Ovid counsels us not to rush into the arms of pleasure? A crooked road, a road in which the foot feels acutely the stones beneath it, *a road that turns back on itself—this is the road of art*.

Shklovsky is profoundly interested in affect, in the cognitive pleasure that a narratee feels in recognizing the processes of *poiesis* through which a story is mediated, through which (in Shklovsky's terms) *fabula* is distorted and transformed into *syuzhet*. These principles underpinning the pleasures of plot lead Shklovsky to the appreciation and analysis of distinctly anti-Aristotelian plots and narrative devices, such as those displayed in Sterne's *Tristram Shandy* (the focus of Shklovsky's 1921 study of story and plot in the novel). Here, the simultaneous detailed familiarity and considered disregard which Sterne and his characters demonstrate towards Aristotelian poetics provides an excellent illustration of the 'crooked road' upon which Shklovsky's encounters with the classics are routed—as well as providing a suggestive model for Shklovsky's own reception of the precepts outlined in the *Poetics*. In particular, Sterne's tale within a tale, 'translated' from the Latin by the novel's eponymous protagonist-narrator and narrated by a pedantic Aristotelian character named Hafen Slawkenbergius, offers some insights into the way in which Shklovsky's theory of plot distinguishes itself from

---

[32] Shklovsky 1965b: 29.   [33] Shklovsky 1990: 37.
[34] Shklovsky 1990: 15, emphases added.

Aristotle's by re-arranging, re-presenting, and distorting that familiar model. Indeed, Shklovsky takes care to distance himself from the Slawkenbergian approach to narrative by elsewhere reminding his own readers (parenthetically) that when he himself refers to what 'Aristotle says' he is decidedly 'not quoting him as Holy Writ'.[35]

In Sterne's novel, the writer and critic Slawkenbergius tells—in a miniature parody of *Don Quixote* (another of Shklovsky's favourites)—the tale of two lovers and one very large nose. While telling his tale, Slawkenbergius begins to analyse the dramatic plot of his own story using quasi-Aristotelian terminology:[36]

> Haste we now towards the catastrophe of my tale—I say Catastrophe (cries Slawkenbergius) inasmuch as a tale, with parts rightly disposed, not only rejoiceth (gaudet) in the Catastrophe and Peripeitia of a DRAMA, but rejoiceth moreover in all the essential and integrant parts of it—it has its Protasis, Epitasis, Catastasis, its Catastrophe or Peripeitia growing one out of the other in it, in the order Aristotle first planted them—without which a tale had better never be told at all, says Slawkenbergius, but be kept to a man's self.

In a strictly chronolinear plodding plot (the dull antithesis to Sterne's own exaggeratedly, ingeniously chaotic narrative) Slawkenbergius moves from Protasis 'or first entrance—where the characters of the Personae Dramatis are just touched in, and the subject slightly begun'—on to the Epitasis, 'wherein the action is more fully entered upon and heightened, till it arrives at its state or height called the Catastasis, and...the ripening of the incidents and passions for their bursting forth in the fifth act...[which] constitutes the Catastrophe or Peripeitia'. This movement, he advises his readers, involves 'bringing the hero out of a state of agitation (as Aristotle calls it) to a state of rest and quietness'.[37]

Sterne's Slawkenbergius is clearly a strict adherent to the principles set out in the *Poetics*. At one level his own tale slavishly respects Aristotelian values: each of its story elements is appropriately related ('with parts rightly disposed'); it covers all the 'essential and integrant' parts of a successful drama, with each component logically and persuasively connected as part of an ordered unity ('growing one out of the other'). And in this careful plotting it could hardly be more different to Sterne's own tale, infamous for its digressions, temporal displacements, and narrative disorder. But, of course, what renders Slawkenbergius' love story strange and

---

[35] Shklovsky 1965b: 33 and 1990: 197.

[36] Sterne 1761: Vol. 4, 1–59. Extract from 58. The peculiar spelling of '*peripeitia*' here is Sterne's. Note too that *protasis, epitasis, catastasis*, and *catastrophe* have their provenance in late antiquity, and none of these terms is actually found in the *Poetics*.

[37] Sterne 1761: Vol. 4, 58–9.

Sternian (and so, of interest to Shklovsky) is the self-reflexive, fragmented, and digressive character of its telling at another level. By integrating an Aristotelian commentary on his storytelling within that very storytelling, Slawkenbergius draws more attention to his narrative technique than to his tale, to the process rather than to the product. As Shklovsky puts it, in their very different appeals to Aristotle, both Sterne and Sterne's Slaw-kenbergius 'lay bare' their storytelling technique to the reader.[38] They make us feel the storiness in the story. And there is, perhaps, no better analogue to Shklovsky's own playful reception of Aristotle. Like Sterne, Shklovsky constantly draws attention to the dialectics and plotting of his own narrative theory, to the digressive—even parodic—relationship between himself and his classical predecessors. In Shklovsky's *Theory of Prose*, as in Sterne's *Tristram Shandy*, then, we encounter Aristotle's theory of poetry 'defamiliarized' and *muthos* made strange.

6.3 **Mikhail Petrovsky**

Within just a few years, Shklovsky's own theory of narrative would itself undergo a similar process of defamiliarization, with Mikhail Petrovsky's radical reworking of Shklovsky's theory of prose. Petrovsky elects to invert the definitions of *syuzhet* and *fabula* so recently established by Shklovsky, declaring:[39]

I want to use the word *syuzhet* in the sense of the *material* of the work of art. The *syuzhet* is, in a sense, the system of events, of actions (or a single simple or complex event), which was available to the writer in a particular form, which is, however, not yet the result of his own individual creative work. I would like to describe the *poetically* handled *syuzhet* with the term *fabula*.

Petrovsky appears to have simply relabelled story as *syuzhet* ('the material of the work') and plot as *fabula* ('the poetically handled *syuzhet*'). But there is much more to this defamiliarization of Shklovsky's dyad. In the redefinition of plot not as the poetic process of 'handling' raw story material (Shklovsky) but as the material end result of that process, the final 'poetically handled' work itself (Petrovsky), we see a new accent upon material rather than formal cause. Plot has not only

---

[38] Shklovsky 1965b: 27. In his autobiography Shklovsky explicitly identifies himself as a writer like Sterne: Shklovsky 2002: 57–8.
[39] Petrovsky 1925: 197, emphases in original. Translation Schmid 2010: 180.

taken on here entelechial attributes (as that which realizes the potential
of the stuff of story) but story has itself taken on some of the attributes of
plot (as that which already has 'a particular form').[40] Petrovsky even
defines his idea of *syuzhet* (story) as a 'system' of events and actions,
echoing Aristotle's definition of *muthos* as the *mimesis* of action
(*praxis*) and the arrangement (*sunthesis*) of incidents (*pragmata*) (*Poetics*
6.1450a 2–4).

The Aristotelian character of this important redefinition of *syuzhet*—
Schmid describes it as 'Petrovosky's Aristotelian formulation'—is unmis-
takeable (and not least of all in the way in which it recalls Aristotle's own
deliberate redefinition of Plato's distinction between *diegesis* and *mimesis*
in the *Poetics*).[41] The overtly Aristotelian character of Petrovsky's formulations brings his notion of *syuzhet* (story) much closer in tenor to
Shklovsky's *syuzhet* (plot) than his basic description of the term initially
suggests. He has not then simply reversed Shklovsky's binary terms but
refined them—with an Aristotelian twist.

This twist is further ratcheted in Petrovsky's 1927 essay examining the
morphology of the novella, published in an edited collection under the
suggestive Latin title, *Ars poetica*. Here plot (Petrovsky's *fabula*) is
identified as 'the artistic structure' of a narrative, which 'is organically
linked to its composition, with the device of exposition, i.e., the development of its story'.[42] In contrast, story (Petrovsky's *syuzhet*) is described
as 'a transformation of life, as of raw material ... above all, story (*syuzhet*)
is selection'.[43] It is important to notice, however, that Petrovsky's story
(*syuzhet*) is not directly equated with that raw story material but
is instead identified as its transformation. For Petrovsky, *syuzhet*
(story) is already one step removed from the raw reality of life, and
represents both a 'selection' and a 'system'—qualities it shares with the
kind of plot suggested by Shklovsky's *syuzhet* and Aristotle's *muthos*.
Both *syuzhet* and *fabula* in Petrovsky's model are mimetic constructs;
syuzhet (story) re-presents life, and *fabula* (plot) re-presents that representation. In making these refinements to Shklovsky's model of *fabula*
and *syuzhet*, Petrovsky reveals his sophisticated understanding
of Aristotle's theory of plot—and adds an important third level to

[40] Petrovsky is likely to have been influenced by Zirminsky (1923: 6) in this. Zirminsky's
1923 model of *fabula-syuzhet* had already hinted at a correlation between Aristotle's
definition of plot (*muthos*) as the 'soul (*psuche*) of tragedy' (*Poetics* 6.1450a 38) and the
idea that the *syuzhet* represents the actualization of the *fabula*. Schmid 2010: 180 identifies
Petrovsky's narratological innovation here as the 'shift of emphasis from *energeia* to *ergon*
that became key to the entire later reception of the *fabula-syuzhet* dichotomy'.
[41] Schmid 2010: 180.   [42] Petrovsky 1987: 25.
[43] Petrovsky 1987: 24–5.

his narrative model: life—story—plot. He has used Aristotle's theory of narrative as a mode of *mimesis* to refine Shklovsky's theory of narrative.[44]

Just as it was for Aristotle, the affect stimulated in the reader through all of this is a priority for Petrovsky. Throughout his work, connections between different structural parts of the story and the various plot devices through which the story is developed are all viewed in the context of their reception and cognition by a reader or listener. He stresses:[45] 'Everything must be directed toward the attention of the listener (resp. the reader) being completely absorbed by the unravelling of the narrative, so that the impression drawn from the [narrative] will be unified and continuous.' And once more he appeals to Aristotelian ideals of the perfect plot: he represents narrative, at the levels of both *syuzhet* and *fabula*, as incorporating the equivalent of Aristotle's *desis*, the tying of the narrative knot which builds up through complication (*zavjazka*) to a moment of heightened tension or *peripeteia* (what Petrovsky calls *naprjaženie*), followed by the untying or denouement (Aristotle's *lusis*) and final 'resolution' (Petrovsky's *razvjazka*).

But Petrovsky moves beyond Aristotle in seeking to understand the ways in which narratives both manipulate and depend upon their audience's sense of time and temporality. He reminds us that story (*syuzhet*) is the selection and transformation of key actions and events from real life, set in their familiar and natural order (*ordo naturalis*) of causal-temporal sequence, identified by Petrovsky as 'disposition'. Plot (*fabula*) is the artistic or poetic structure given to this selection, the aesthetically motivated organization of this story material into an artificial and unfamiliar order (*ordo artificialis*), identified by Petrovsky as 'composition'. Petrovsky thus emphasizes that underpinning Shklovsky's *fabula/syuzhet* model and his own is a fundamental assumption about the different ways in which time and temporality are patterned in different narrative levels. Like Shklovsky, Petrovsky sees the *fabula* (in his terms) as the temporal rearrangement of the chronological storyline of the *syuzhet*, the manipulation of its timeline and (crucially) the reader or audience's perception of time so as to affect interest and suspense.[46] And in this respect a fundamental affinity rather than dissimilarity between the theories of Petrovsky and Shklovsky is revealed: both of these narratologies are essentially concerned with the ways in which

---

[44] Shklovsky 1965b: 12.   [45] Petrovsky 1987: 26.
[46] See Aumüller 2009 for a more detailed discussion of Petrovsky's narratology.

narrative form functions in its impact upon the receiver, the way in which narratives operate to 'make one feel things'.[47]

6.4 **Boris Tomashevsky**

In a groundbreaking work on the structure and sequence of narrative, Boris Tomashevsky offers his own distinctively Aristotelian take on the structural relations between story and plot.[48] Illustrating this narratological theory with a diverse selection of literary examples (including Pushkin, Swift, Tolstoy, and H. G. Wells, as well as contemporary detective fiction and Tarzan movies) Tomashevsky, in the words of his translators, brings Aristotle's *Poetics* 'up to date'.[49]

In the most accessible and influential chapter of his 1925 *Teoriya literatury* (*Theory of Literature*) on 'Tematika' or 'Thematics', Tomashevsky offers a detailed analysis of the core components which combine to effect (in his terms) a unified, motivated, thematic plot—and in so doing, offers a broadly comprehensive framework and technical vocabulary for narratological analysis that reveals a profound indebtedness to and close reading of Aristotle's *Poetics*. Like Aristotle, Tomashevsky distinguishes between basic modes of narration—the 'omniscient' (in which 'the author knows everything, including the hidden thoughts of the characters'); the 'limited' (in which 'the whole tale is filtered through the mind of the narrator'); and the 'mixed' (in which the protagonist is 'covertly . . . the narrator').[50]

Aristotle, as we saw in Chapter 3.2 and 3.7, developed his model of narrative mode without the explicit term or concept of 'narrator', whereas Tomashevsky seeks to differentiate between the omniscient 'objective' narrator and the character-based 'limited' narrator. Tomashevsky's examples make it clear that he does not necessarily seek to distinguish here between what modern narratologists (after Genette) might characterize as heterodiegetic, homodiegetic, or autodiegetic narrators, and his passing reference to the covert narrator does not obviously anticipate the kind of distinction between covert and overt

---

[47] Shklovsky 1965b: 10–12.

[48] Lemon and Reis (1965: 62) directly compare the comprehensive scope of Tomashevsky's narratology to that of Aristotle: 'Perhaps the only comparable piece of criticism easily available to Western readers is Aristotle's *Poetics*.' Garcia Landa (1998: 43) also notes that Tomashevsky's affiliations are openly Aristotelian.

[49] Lemon and Reis 1965: 71 n. 8.

[50] Tomashevsky 1965: 75. Cf. *Poetics* 3.1448a 18–23.

narrators and narration that Chatman later develops.[51] Instead, the pattern of Tomashevsky's narrator model is distinctively classical, and the allusions to *Poetics* 3 (and, indeed, back to Plato's *Republic*) are marked. As we've seen, both Aristotle (*Poetics* 3.1448a 18–23) and Plato's Socrates (*Republic* 3.392d) sought to distinguish between simple, mimetic, and mixed modes of narrative, identifying the different levels of narratorial mediation effected in each mode. Tomashevsky eschews any technical discussions of *mimesis* in this context, but his distinctions between simple authorial or narratorial reporting, character speech or narration, and the combination of both in 'mixed systems' closely parallel those of his ancient models.

In fact, the voice of Aristotle can be heard covertly authorizing and informing several aspects of Tomashevsky's poetics, from the cognitive and emotional effects of narrative, to the role of *peripeteia*, and the tying and untying of 'knots' in the story.[52] But what, above all, Tomashevsky seems to take from Aristotle is his emphasis upon the importance of meaningful causal compositional connections between actions and events—a unity which Tomashevsky sees, significantly, functioning at the level of both *fabula* and *syuzhet*. Although his definitions do change slightly over time to become somewhat fuzzier, Tomashevsky initially defines story or *fabula* as the 'aggregate of mutually related events', noting that 'no matter how the events were originally arranged in the work and despite their original order of introduction, in practice the story [*fabula*] may be told in the actual chronological and causal order of events', whereas in the plot or *syuzhet*, 'events *are arranged* and connected'.[53]

In an oft-cited footnote to this section of the 1925 text (cut from later editions), Tomashevsky distils his distinction between *fabula* and *syuzhet* further still: 'In brief, the story [*fabula*] is the "action itself", the plot [*syuzhet*], "how the reader learns of the action".'[54] But in the revised fourth edition from 1928, Tomashevsky presents a modified picture of this dyad, stressing the relationship rather than the difference between *fabula* and *syuzhet*:[55]

a *fabula* presents a more or less unified system of events that emerge from, and are linked to, one another. The totality of the events in their reciprocal internal

---

[51] See Chatman 1978.

[52] On *peripeteia* compare Tomashevsky 1965: 72 and Aristotle, *Poetics* 11.1452a 21–1452b 13; on the tying and untying of 'knots' see Tomashevsky 1965: 72 and Aristotle, *Poetics* 18.1455b 24–35.

[53] Tomashevsky 1965: 66–7, emphases in original. On the evolution of Tomashevsky's definitions see Schmid 2010: 184–5.

[54] Tomashevsky 1965: 67 n. 5.

[55] Tomashevsky 1967: 134. Translation in Schmid 2010: 185, emphases in original.

concatenation is what we call *fabula*...It is not enough to invent an entertaining chain of events and limit them with a beginning and an end. These events need to be *arranged*, put into a certain order, be portrayed, by making of this *fabula* material a literary combination. The artistically organized arrangement of events in a work is what we call *syuzhet*.

These core principles and precepts of the *Teoriya literatury* have obvious roots in Aristotle's *Poetics*. Indeed, Tomashevsky's definition of *syuzhet* as the 'artistically organized arrangement of events' reads as if it were a direct translation of Aristotle's definition of *muthos* as the 'arrangement of incidents' (*sustaseos ton pragmaton*: *Poetics* 7.1450b 22). His caution that 'It is not enough to invent an entertaining chain of events and limit them with a beginning and an end' similarly evokes Aristotle, *Poetics* 7.1450b 25–34.

Tomashevsky claims that a narrative text displays an overall unity that is based upon the careful arrangement of smaller units and sub-units, the tiniest 'atomic' element of which he describes as a 'motif' (*motiv*). He further distinguishes between two different pairs of motifs: the 'dynamic' (those actions which keep the plot moving by changing situations) and the 'static' (the temporal and spatial contexts through which the plot moves); the 'bound' (the essential, core elements of plot which perform 'objective functions' in a narrative) and the 'free' (those elements which are non-essential, incidental to the plot). In these terms, any variation in the bound motifs will result in a different story; any variation in the free motifs will merely result in a different telling of essentially the same story.[56]

Aristotle makes the same point (*Poetics* 8.1451a 30–6):

the arrangement of the component incidents of the plot must be such that if anything is moved or removed the unity of the whole is disrupted and broken. For, if the presence or absence of a thing makes no obvious difference, it is not a component part of the whole.

Tomashevsky maintains that motifs must be introduced and patterned within a narrative text according to the particular order demanded by the Aristotelian logics of causal and temporal sequence.[57] He even suggests a practical way to distinguish between free and bound motifs and their relative importance to a narrative 'by retelling the story in abridged form, then comparing the abridgement with the more fully

---

[56] Tomashevsky 1965: 68. In his distinctions between static and dynamic motifs, Tomashevsky is also influenced by Alexander Reformatsky 1973. Cf. Todorov 1969 and his focus upon narrative periods of equilibrium and imbalance.

[57] Tomashevsky 1965: 67. Cf. *Poetics* 15.1454a 33–1454b 7.

developed narrative'.[58] This is, in fact, precisely what Aristotle does in his abridged *katholou* of the *Iphigenia* story (*Poetics* 17.1455b 3–12) and his *idion* of the *Odyssey* (*Poetics* 17.1455b 17–23).

Building upon this Aristotelian framework (and, of course, Shklovsky's narratological foundations), Tomashevsky goes on to characterize story (*fabula*) as the aggregate of these motifs, and plot (*syuzhet*) as their thematic ordering and arrangement. Thus, we find Tomashevsky eliding event with motif in his description of *fabula* as comprising both 'the aggregate of mutually related *events*' and 'the aggregate of *motifs* in their logical, causal-chronological order', and in his definition of *syuzhet* as comprising both those same '*events* … arranged and connected [sc. thematically]' and 'the aggregate of those same *motifs* but having [sc. thematic] relevance and order'.[59]

In this schema, motifs are synonymous with the raw incidents and events that form the basis of story (akin to Aristotle's *pragmata*). For Tomashevsky (as for Petrovsky), *fabula* is always already subject to some kind of mediation even before its arrangement and emplotment in and by *syuzhet*, and the motifs/events which make up the stuff of story are already pre-patterned in some kind of connective order which is not merely chronological but also causal. In a move away from the Shklovskian model, in which *fabula* was typically seen to denote the raw, undigested, pre-literary stuff of story with *syuzhet* describing its arrangement, Tomashevsky forwards a more sophisticated (and Aristotelian) theory in which *fabula* is already partially cooked, already part of a preliminary narrative system.

Appreciating Aristotle's influence upon Tomashevsky helps us to better understand the nuances of his model of narrative structure and his understanding of what it is that sets apart the chronologically and causally related events and motifs of story (*fabula*) from the chronologically and causally related events and motifs of plot (*syuzhet*). For Tomashevsky, what distinguishes *fabula* from *syuzhet* is the *thematic* arrangement and *synthesis* of motifs and elements in the latter. That is, the representation of actions and events through a mediating perspective which recognizes not only their temporal-causal links but their thematic interconnectedness. Aristotelian notions of plot as *sunthesis* underpin Tomashevsky's understanding that events must be put into a certain

---

[58] Tomashevsky 1965: 71. Meister 2003: 20 offers a useful summary of Tomashevsky's definition of the motif as 'a descriptive concept whose function lies in the hermeneutic reconstruction of the *syuzhet*; it identifies … something that introduces motion into the overarching complex of the *fabula* or *syuzhet*'.

[59] Tomashevsky 1965: 66–8, emphases added.

order to qualify as plotted narrative (*syuzhet*); Aristotelian notions of *mimesis* support the understanding that for the stuff of *fabula* to become the stuff of *syuzhet* it must be mimetically, artificially, *synthetically*, represented, its separate elements and motifs combined 'to produce a definite structure unified by a general thought or theme'.[60] This is, in a sense, the 'theme' of Tomashevsky's work.

The idea of 'theme' itself is, of course, a subject famously ignored by Aristotle in the *Poetics*.[61] As Heath has observed:[62]

Aristotle does not ever discuss the thematic structure of tragedy and epic; he apparently does not think (as many modern critics seem to do) that a tragedy is 'about' some philosophical or moral topic. If a tragedy is 'about' anything, in Aristotle's view, it is about the events which make up the plot.

This, I would argue, is precisely how Tomashevsky reads Aristotle: the thematic structure of a narrative is the same thing as the unified pattern of events which form the *muthos*—or *syuzhet*.[63] We can see in Tomashevsky's repeated emphasis upon thematic unity a reflection of Aristotle's repeated emphasis upon plot unity in the *Poetics* (particularly at 8.1451a 15–35), where Aristotle argues that unity of plot does not consist in the superficial unity of a story chronologically following the life or episodic adventures of one hero (such as Odysseus), or even of one major event (such as the Trojan War), but in the appropriate selection and arrangement of related incidents. Aristotle criticizes those poets who have attempted to compose a Heracleid or a Theseid, following the life stories of Heracles or Theseus, and praises Homer for recognizing that 'the incidents in a man's life are infinitely diverse and cannot be reduced to a unity' (8.1451a 15–18). However, Aristotle's praise for Homer stops short of acknowledging the actual source of plot unity in Homer's narratives: their unifying themes. Homer selectively centres his *Odyssey* upon the single action and theme of Odysseus' homecoming and his *Iliad* upon the single action and theme of Achilles' wrath. The identification and importance of these overarching themes to their respective epics is clearly signalled in the opening lines of each poem (so should not be dismissed as anachronistic retro-projections), but Aristotle has nothing directly to say here or elsewhere on unity of

---

[60] Tomashevsky 1965: 62.
[61] See Belfiore 2000 on Aristotle's marked lack of interest in what modern critics would identify as 'themes'. She argues (60): 'Aristotle's events, unlike Propp's functions, or Bremond's ordering of roles, or Beardsley's themes, are actions, without ethical or psychological coloring, and without thematic interpretation.'
[62] Heath 1989: 45.   [63] Tomashevsky 1965: 63.

theme per se. It is Tomashevsky who nuances the Aristotelian model of plot as 'an arrangement of incidents' by positing theme as the principal unifying agency of *muthos*.

Rather than characterizing Tomashevsky's reception of Aristotle as bringing the *Poetics* 'up to date', then, we might rather see the 'Thematics' as adding more to the story. Tomashevsky takes Aristotle's dynamic model of *muthos* and develops it into his own model of *syuzhet*. More so than any of his fellow Russian formalists, he translates Aristotle's core narratological concepts into a critical and technical idiom which will go on to shape the themes of modern narratology.

6.5 **Vladimir Propp**

Propp remains perhaps the best known of the Russian formalists, recognized for his innovative work on Russian folktale narratives and the relationship between their invariant story elements or 'functions' and variable features or 'motifs'. Propp's indebtedness to classical models may not be immediately obvious, but his borrowings from Petrovsky and Tomashevsky are clearly evinced in his focus upon the fundamental building blocks of the Russian folktale. We can therefore see Propp's work as representing a fulcrum both in the reception of Russian formalism and in the reception of Aristotle's *Poetics*—whose influence upon Propp (albeit heavily mediated) remains under-acknowledged.

Propp's 'story grammar' as set out in his *Morphology of the Folktale* (*Morfologiya skazki*), first published in 1928, is based on the premise that in the traditional Russian folktale (at least, in the hundred or so he analyses):[64]

The names of the *dramatis personae* change (as well as the attributes of each), but neither their actions nor functions change. From this we can draw the inference that a tale often attributes identical actions to various personages. This makes possible the study of the tale *according to the functions of its dramatis personae*. We shall have to determine to what extent these functions actually represent recurrent constants of the tale. The formulation of all other questions will depend upon the solution of this primary question: how many functions are known to the tale?

---

[64] Propp 1968: 7–8, emphases in original. Propp goes on to define function as follows (1968: 21): 'Function is understood as an act of a character, defined from the point of view of its significance for the course of the action.' The point of view issue is particularly problematic and never adequately addressed by Propp. For a neat summary of Propp's story grammar see Schmitz 2007: 44–7.

Evoking Aristotle's theory that *dramatis personae* are the products of plots, and that their narrative status is therefore essentially functional (*Poetics* 2.1448a 1), Propp famously goes on to define thirty-one such core functions, patterned around the actions of a core list of *dramatis personae*, including: the hero; false hero; opponent; donor; dispatcher; princess; and her father. Despite criticisms that his highly schematic narratological model works only for a very specific type of narrative (some but not all Russian folktales), Propp's 'functions' make an important contribution to the history of narrative theory. In his highly influential structuralist study, Lévi-Strauss would later translate Propp's functions into his 'mythemes' to develop an innovative analysis of the Oedipus myth, and Greimas would reformulate Propp's functions into his structuralist narrative grammar comprising six paired 'actants': the hero and his search for an object; the sender and the receiver; the hero's helper and the opponent.[65] Indeed, Propp would later identify his own project as structuralist rather than formalist in conception. In a later essay defending his work, he claimed:[66]

> The structuralist...detects a system where the formalist inevitably fails to see one. The method elaborated in *Morphology* makes it possible to rise above the plots and study the genre of the wondertale as a whole.

Propp certainly adopts and adapts some of the core concepts proposed by his formalist predecessors (although his notion of 'motif' is significantly less nuanced than Tomashevsky's) and shares a common interest with Petrovsky in story composition, but he is much more interested in content and story stuff, and much less concerned with form and plot (or its impact upon audiences) than his fellow formalists. He uses their foundational terms somewhat differently too—another hint that his priorities are differently oriented. For Propp, the *fabula* is conceived as a genre-specific story skeleton which can be dressed up in myriad differently themed costumes or plots. For Propp, the term *syuzhet* (as its Russian etymology prompts) is taken to refer to thematic 'subjects' as they appear in the Russian folktale. In fact, Propp represents his project straightforwardly as 'a comparison of the themes [*mezsjuzetnoe*

---

[65] Lévi-Strauss 1955 and Greimas 1983. Greimas's actants are Proppian rather than Aristotelian in conception. Propp 1968: 64 already notices that several of his functions work in paired oppositions: 'prohibition—violation, reconnaissance—delivery, struggle—victory, pursuit—deliverance'. Bremond's work (1966) similarly exhibits a primarily Proppian rather than Aristotelian character in its analysis of various narrative 'functions' and their sequencing to form plot.
[66] Propp 1984: 72. For Propp's debt to Goethe see Doležel 1990: 143–6. On Propp's affinities with Petrovsky see Steiner 2014: 70–83.

sravnenie] of these tales'.[67] He does not therefore draw the same kinds of distinction between *syuzhet* and *fabula* that we find in the work of the other Russian formalists.

Yet this is not because he is uninterested in such distinctions or in matters of form and plot. It is simply that for Propp, the syntactical structure of the *fabula* takes priority over that of the *syuzhet*. Propp sees both a temporal and logical priority to the story stuff which plot transforms into narrative. His morphological schema for the Russian folktale even hints that lying behind his cast list of *dramatis personae* and functions there exists an abstract 'protoplot' or theoretical 'prototale' for this genre—a common ancestral source which different plots transform into different stories.[68] We see something like this in Aristotle's description of the *idion* of the *Odyssey* and the *kalothou* of the *Iphigenia* in the *Poetics*. There Aristotle reconstructed the core of each myth (drawing upon familiar plots) in order to identify the abstract 'prototale' for each story, as made up of their essential dynamic incidents or functional motifs.[69]

There are numerous examples of such echoes from the *Poetics* in *Morphology of the Folktale*. To begin with, Propp shares with Aristotle the same basic intuitions regarding the priority of plot over character: that is, the notion that narrative essentially involves the representation of 'people in action' (*Poetics* 2.1448a 1).[70] What is more, as Kafalenos points out, each function in Propp's invariant sequence is 'perceived as a logical necessity: at each stage in a sequence that begins at the onset of a problem and leads to its resolution, only events with certain outcomes (e.g., events that fill a specific one or two functions) can move the situation closer to resolution'.[71] It is important to remember that Propp defines a function both as 'an act of a character, defined from the point of view of its *significance for the course of the action*' and as an action defined 'according to its *consequences*'.[72] Just as Aristotle stressed that there should be not just temporal connections between events but causal connections (*Poetics* 10.1452a 18–21)—that is, events and actions

---

[67] Propp 1968: 19. As Kafalenos 2006: 473 notices, Propp does not meaningfully distinguish between *fabula* and *syuzhet*.

[68] Toporov 1985: 261.

[69] On Propp's 'Ur-type morphology' see Doležel 1990: 141–6.

[70] Cf. Rimmon-Kenan 1983: 34 and Brooks 1984: 15. Belfiore 2000: 46 offers a potentially misleading reading of both Propp and Aristotle in her claim: 'Propp reverses Aristotle's theory that "tragedy is imitation not of human beings but of actions," by writing that stories are about characters who act.'

[71] Kafalenos 2006: 205. See also Doležel 1990: 144 on Propp's 'functional polyvalence'.

[72] Propp 1968: 21 and 67, emphases added.

with consequences—so Propp too stresses the causal and consequential patterning of incidents in his model of narrative functions.

Underpinning this emphasis upon con-sequence in Propp's morphology is a similarly Aristotelian emphasis upon a plot's basic tripartite structure (*Poetics* 7.1450b 25–34). The chronolinear arrangement that Propp assigns his thirty-one functions follows a clear trajectory from beginning, to middle, to end: an 'initial situation' gives rise to an initiating action (in Propp's model, 'one of the members of a family absents himself from home'); an interconnecting sequence of actions ensues (Propp's 'functions' and 'connections') effecting some form of 'complication'—the equivalent of Aristotle's *desis*; until a narrative 'peak' is reached (Propp's nineteenth function)—the equivalent of Aristotle's *peripeteia*; a further sequence of functions leads to a 'solution' (Propp's twenty-fifth function in which the 'task is resolved')—Aristotle's *lusis*; and the hero's 'recognition'—or *anagnorisis*; swiftly followed by a resolution (a happy ending for the hero).[73] Thus, Propp's 'functions' can be, and arguably ought to be, understood in Aristotelian terms as marshalling the events and actions which make up the character-driven plots of Russian folktales into coherent logical and causal sequences. Indeed, Propp's *Morphology* can be understood as itself performing an important mediating (or donor) function in helping to transfer Aristotelian principles of plot into modern structuralist narratology.

6.6 *Epeisodion* (On translation)

The Russian edition of Aristotle's *Poetics* enjoying the widest circulation in the early decades of the twentieth century was Vladimir Appelrot's 1893 popular text and translation, *Aristotel: Ob iskusstve poezii* (*Aristotle: On the Art of Poetry*).[74] Glossing his translation of the facing Greek text, Appelrot offers the occasional parenthetical clarification of Aristotle's ideas and concludes the work with a brief set of commentary notes for each chapter. It is highly likely that both Petrovsky and Tomashevsky accessed Aristotle via Appelrot, whether reading the original Greek or

---

[73] Propp 1968: 25–65. It is often observed that the final sequence of Homer's *Odyssey* maps neatly onto Propp's functional sequence 23–31, including the double resolution that Aristotle described at *Poetics* 13.1453a 31–2. We should also note here the similarities between Propp's consequential functions and Reformatsky's work on the structural division of narrative into distinct episodes and their core motifs.

[74] The text was significantly revised and reprinted in 1957 and again in 2000. The discussion above is based on the 1893 version.

the Russian translation, and it is certainly from this edition of Appelrot's translation and commentary of the *Poetics* that Shklovsky quotes at length in his essays and in his *Theory of Prose*.[75] Shklovsky is not always careful to distinguish Aristotle's theories from his own, and in his discussion of 'framing as a device of deceleration' the quotation of a hefty section of *Poetics* 14.1453b 13–1454a 13 (running to fifty-seven lines and four sizeable paragraphs set across two pages in the Russian text) is particularly difficult for the reader to recognize as such. The blurring between Shklovsky's ideas and those of Aristotle is further muddied by the (playful?) littering of internal quotation marks throughout the piece. Given the importance of Appelrot to Shklovsky's work then, this translation and commentary are worth examining in a brief excursus here for the potential insights they help to yield into the Aristotelean affinities of Russian formalist narratology. For, as is the case with any translation, Appelrot's rendering of Aristotle's *Poetics* is also a reading and Appelrot's interpretation of the *Poetics*' precepts helps to lay bare the ancient foundations of one of the key features of formalist Russian narratology—the distinction between *fabula* and *syuzhet*.

As we've seen, *fabula* and *syuzhet* are broadly interchangeable in the Russian lexicon and before Shklovsky imposes his own stamp upon them as separate narratological terms they are used synonymously to describe story, plot, and narrative.[76] Yet, in his work Appelrot opts for consistent lexical equivalence and elects to fix *fabula* as his own preferred translation for Aristotle's *muthos*.[77] To highlight the significance of this move let us observe that, by contrast, English translators until the late 1960s typically used a variety of terms, rendering *muthos* as plot, story, myth, theme, or even as action—sometimes pointedly, sometimes assuming that these terms function synonymously in the context of Aristotle's *Poetics*.[78] Like their English counterparts, Russian translators also used *syuzhet* (сюжет), myth (миф), and *fabula* (фабула) interchangeably: Zakharov's translation of the *Poetics* from 1885, and Novosadskiy's from 1927, both use *syuzhet* (сюжет) as well as myth (миф), and *fabula*

---

[75] Shklovsky is notoriously poor at identifying his sources, but the Russian original of his *Theory of Prose* clearly uses the Russian translation of Appelrot (1929: 47–9 = Appelrot 1893: 29, 37).

[76] *Oxford Russian Dictionary s.vv.*

[77] Appelrot uses *fabula* a total of forty-seven times in his translation, each time as a direct synonym for or gloss upon Aristotle's *muthos*.

[78] Downing 1984 offers a detailed if flawed survey of Aristotle's varied use of *muthos* and the attempts of English translators to render its equivalents.

(фабула) to translate Aristotle's *muthos* ($\mu\hat{\upsilon}\theta o_S$), treating the three terms as more or less synonymous.[79]

Significantly, Appelrot uses the term *syuzhet* (сюжет) only four times in his main text: twice in parenthetical glosses (to distinguish 'perform-ance' from 'story'; and to clarify Aristotle's reference to killing family members 'in a story'); and twice to supplement Aristotle's Greek by offering a translation that offers greater clarity, by referring, for example, to 'the story of Iphigenia' rather than simply to 'the *Iphigenia*', and to 'tragic stories' rather than simply 'tragedy'.[80] In none of these instances is Appelrot's use of *syuzhet* offered as a translation for Aristotle's *muthos* or any other specific term in the Greek, and this term is used exclusively as referring to 'story'.

Appelrot does occasionally use the term myth (миф) to translate Aristotle's *muthos* but only in those contexts where it is clear that Aristotle is referring specifically to a traditional myth and never as a simple or more general synonym for story, narrative, or plot.[81]

As a consequence of these lexical choices, *fabula* becomes fixed as the restricted term for *muthos* as 'plot' in Appelrot's translation of Aristotle. For Appelrot (and Aristotle) the *muthos/fabula* is 'the proper arrange-ment of incidents...the first and most important thing in tragedy' (*Poetics* 7.1450b 22–3); *muthos/fabula* is the organizing and selecting principle which transforms incidents and events into a coherent, pleas-ing, and probable unity (*Poetics* 8.1451a 15–35). In thus separating and circumscribing the semantic range of *syuzhet* and *fabula* in his transla-tion of Aristotle, Appelrot not only helps to position the *Poetics* as a text concerned primarily with plot, but anticipates the important separation and distinction between these key terms that would subsequently be drawn by the Russian formalists.

For Shklovsky's sustained close engagement with Appelrot's trans-lation of the *Poetics*, considered alongside his commitment to the principles of 'defamiliarization', invites us to see his own pioneering distinction between *fabula* and *syuzhet* as an 'estrangement' of Appelrot's differentiation—and thus as a kind of defamiliarization of Aristotle's principles. In Shklovsky's theory of plot, *fabula* is re-designated as story

---

[79] See, for example, Novosadskiy's translations of *Poetics* 13.1453a 37, 14.1454a 12, and 1454a 15.

[80] See Appelrot 1893: 19, 29, 37, and 41 (there are no equivalent references in the Greek). Given the relative scarcity of *syuzhet* in Appelrot's translation, it seems more than coinci-dental that both of the extended quotations that Shklovsky uses contain this term (compare Shklovsky 1990: 47–8 and 49 with Appelrot 1893: 28–9 and 37).

[81] See, for example, Appelrot's translations of *Poetics* 4.1449a 19, 5.1449b 4, 5.1449b 7, 9.1451b 24, 13.1453a 18, and 14.1453b 22.

stuff and *syuzhet* re-presented as plot in order to make these terms strange, to highlight their new status as important terms of literary criticism. There thus emerges a plausible rationale for Shklovsky's decision to take *fabula* as story 'material' and *syuzhet* as story 'formulation' in his model—despite the fact that the Russian term *syuzhet* can denote story material, that is 'subject' or *syuzhet* matter, whereas *fabula* cannot.[82]

Positing a (possible and plausible?) connection between Appelrot's translation and Shklovsky's interest not only in separating the narrative functions of *fabula* and *syuzhet* but in radically redefining their relationship also helps to make sense of Petrovsky's subsequent inversion of Shklovsky's model. In reversing the polarity of Shklovsky's *fabula* and *syuzhet* in his own theory of narrative poetics, Petrovsky returns to the original distinctions between plot and story drawn by Appelrot, with *fabula* once more designating plot and *syuzhet* story. Petrovsky, as we saw, was a more faithfully 'Aristotelian' formalist than Shklovsky and his writings, despite the absence of direct quotation, are infused with Aristotelian formulations and allusions—at least one of which makes the connection between Aristotle, Appelrot, and the foundational principles of Russian formalism plainly manifest.

Appelrot offered the following observation in his commentary to *Poetics* 9.1451b 1–32, which is (improbably enough) Aristotle's chapter treating the merits of narrative probability and necessity in structuring events in different kinds of stories:[83]

Even if the poet sticks to relating real-life events, his artistry is manifested in their creative selection, the distinctions he makes between what is essential and what is incidental, and his handling of the story (*obrabotke syuzhet*).

There is nothing in Aristotle's *Poetics* setting out this thesis in quite these terms. But in the writings of Shklovsky, Petrovsky, Tomashevsky, and their fellow formalists, this theory and this formulation (re)appear as a central tenet. Real-life events, whether historical or fictional, are seen to comprise the basic stuff of story (*syuzhet*), which is transformed into literary or historical narrative (*fabula*) through the artistic process of handling, selecting, rearranging, and emplotting that material. Or, as Petrovsky, writing in 1925, puts it:[84]

---

[82] Lowe 2000: 5 n. 4 also observes the etymological perversity of Shklovsky's new terminology.

[83] Appelrot 1893: 75.

[84] Petrovsky 1925: 197. Translation in Schmid 2010: 180.

The *syuzhet* is, in a sense, the system of events, of actions ... not yet the result of [the writer's] own individual creative work. I would like to describe the poetically handled *syuzhet* with the term *fabula*.

Is there any probable connection between these two theories—between Appelrot's reworking of Aristotle and Petrovsky's reworking of Shklovsky? Or is this link simply the sort of *post hoc ergo propter hoc* fallacy that Aristotle himself identifies as a common syllogism? Certainly, as Aristotle warns, 'It makes all the difference whether a thing happens because of, or only after, its antecedent' (*Poetics* 10.1452a 20–1). But 'we enjoy even coincidental events which only appear to have happened by design' (*Poetics* 10.1452a 4–7). So, perhaps we can take pleasure in recognizing Aristotle's unexpected role in shaping Russian formalist approaches to narrative and narratology whatever the 'real' story.[85]

6.7 *Teleute*

Shklovsky's notion of defamiliarization (*ostranenie*) appears as both critical concept and operation in the narratologies of Russian formalism. We encounter Aristotle's *Poetics* made strange in each new iteration of its reading and reception by the Russian 'neo-Aristotelians', with each (r)evolution itself configuring a self-conscious reaction of some kind to a contemporary theorist, no less than to Aristotle himself. Through these various iterations, however, familiar Aristotelian priorities and principles remain essentially unchanged: the primacy of plot, of form synthesizing raw story content, of unity, and the ultimate importance of final cause—the experience and affect of the narrative as it is cognitively processed by an audience. Thus, the Russian 'neo-Aristotelians' continue to follow Aristotle's lead in seeking to explore and explain the ways in which narratives work to 'make one feel things'.[86]

[85] Erlich 1955 offers a brief overview of the immediate influence and reception (or lack thereof) of Russian formalism in Europe and the USA. Beyond a couple of obscure papers published in French and English in the late 1920s, the earliest transmission of Russian formalist ideas to the West appears to have come through Wellek and Warren in the 1940s.
[86] Shklovsky 1965a: 10–12.

7 Neo-Aristotelianism

> *The rhetorical approach to stories and storytelling has its roots in Aristotle's* Poetics *with its definition of tragedy as the imitation of an action that arouses pity and fear and leads to the purgation of those emotions. Although Aristotle's treatise is appropriately called* Poetics *because he is primarily concerned with identifying and analyzing the principles of construction underlying effective tragic drama, his definition makes rhetoric part of poetics by linking tragedy to its effect on its audience.*
>
> James Phelan, 'Rhetoric/Ethics' (2007b: 292)

7.1 *Arche*

The Chicago school formalists, also known as the neo-Aristotelians, coalesce as a distinctive group of critics with broad literary and narratological interests in the 1930s, headed by Ronald Crane and his colleagues, most notably Norman Maclean, Richard McKeon, and Elder Olson.[1] Vaunting their polemic opposition to the (then) more popular brand of formalism practised by the Yale 'New Critics', the neo-Aristotelians adopted a highly distinctive approach to the analysis of narrative literature—the legacy of which would eventually outshine and outstrip that of their New Critical opponents. The label 'neo-Aristotelian' seems to have been first coined by Burke, who describes the work of Crane, Maclean, and Olson thus in his 1945 *Grammar of Motives*.[2] But the group had already been tagged as such in a 1944 essay pitting the new 'Aristotelian' criticism coming out of Chicago against the new 'Platonist' criticism coming out of Yale.[3]

Whatever its origins, the 'neo-Aristotelian' label was not one which the Chicago school group itself initially embraced. In his introduction to the 1952 collection of essays showcasing the work of the school, *Critics and Criticism Ancient and Modern*, Crane takes some pains to

---

[1] Crane 1952: 1 describes them as 'a group of friends who came to know one another at the University of Chicago in the middle thirties'.
[2] Burke 1945: 470.   [3] Trowbridge 1944: 538.

defend this new critical theory and methodology from charges that it represents 'a species of pseudo-Aristotelian formalism' or dogmatic 'neo-Aristotelianism'.[4] In fact, the label that Crane himself uses most often to describe the collective Chicago school project is simply that of 'Aristotelianism'. As was the case for the so-called Russian 'formalists', the enduring tag of 'neo-Aristotelianism' to describe the approach of Crane and his circle is not one coined or encouraged by the earliest members of the group itself.

However, both the name and the broadly Aristotelian principles of the group stuck. Successive generations of theorists and critics would subsequently align themselves with the Chicago school approach, refining and expanding its distinctive 'neo-Aristotelian' priorities and poetics with each iteration. The first generation and the pioneering work led by Crane and his colleagues would be succeeded by a second generation, principally associated with Sheldon Sacks, Ralph Rader, and Wayne Booth. A third generation—still very much engaged in shaping the landscape of narrative theory—is represented by David Richter, Peter Rabinowitz, and Jim Phelan, who follow Booth in developing a predominantly rhetorical theory of narrative. Phelan himself also proposes some candidates for an emerging fourth generation, signalled by the recent narratological studies of Gary Johnson, Katherine Nash, Dan Shen, Katra Byram, and Kelly Marsh.[5] Indeed, the exceptional interdisciplinary work of Phelan and his colleagues at the Project Narrative Institute in Ohio suggests that a case might even be made for identifying this as the new home of the neo-Aristotelians and for recognizing a dynamic 'Ohio school' as continuing the Chicago school project and as representing the current power base in rhetorical narrative poetics.[6]

The ongoing work of this distinctive neo-Aristotelian narratological tradition spanning more than eighty years of criticism presents a particularly rich reception case study, then, illustrating the ways in which what begins as a powerful direct engagement with a body of ancient narrative theory becomes diffused and diminished over time. The early narratological pioneers of the Chicago school promote their reception of Aristotle's poetics in a polemicized mode of resistance to the New Critical caricature of 'Aristotelianism' as a narrowly mechanistic kind of formalism. Rejecting what they portray as the modern instantiation of an outmoded 'Hellenistic-Roman-Romantic tradition' and

---

[4] Crane 1952: 2.   [5] Phelan 2015.
[6] https://projectnarrative.osu.edu/.

instead adopting Aristotle as a patron and the *Poetics* as a key intertext, Crane and his colleagues appropriate a figurehead who paradoxically supplies their project at once with an ancient authority and a certain counter-cultural, anti-establishment credibility.[7] But for ensuing generations of the Chicago school, different conflicts and different authorities come to demand different responses. Indeed, for the second (and apparently now also for the fourth) generation of neo-Aristotelians it is the first generation that represents the site of established authority and thus invites resistance and challenge in a classically 'Bloomian' (quasi-Oedipal) plot of literary-critical inheritance.[8]

Yet what has made this neo-Aristotelian narratological school cohesive and recognizable as part of a continuing tradition is the ongoing commitment of successive generations to the methodological principles originally adopted by Crane et al. from Aristotle's *Poetics*. Direct engagement with Aristotle and his theories (as distinct from his methodologies) diminishes markedly from the first to fourth generations. In the writings of Crane, Olson, and McKeon, Aristotle appears in some guise on virtually every page. In fact, the first generation *mimesis* of Aristotle's poetics is so convincing that it can be difficult to distinguish the reception from the original: definitions and formulations with a definite Aristotelian source are so well re-presented and assimilated by the first generation neo-Aristotelians that it is not always clear to whom the ideas being forwarded actually belong. But even indirect references and allusions to Aristotle appear much less frequently in the writings of later generations. Booth cites Aristotle largely to refute him; Phelan usually to remind us only that he and his fellow neo-Aristotelians are 'less interested in getting Aristotle right or in being "true" to the *Poetics* than they are in using his treatise as a springboard' to launch their own theories and interpretations.[9] Amongst the fourth generation, despite explicit claims of allegiance to a neo-Aristotelian practice, Aristotle barely merits a mention: generally restricted to a single glancing reference in an introduction, when Aristotle is directly acknowledged it is typically through the mediating lens of an earlier neo-Aristotelian text. Nash's solitary reference to Aristotle is characteristic of this approach, appearing in an introductory overview where he quotes Phelan on the *Poetics*.[10] Similarly, Shen is interested in Aristotle only in terms of the

---

[7] I should note that this championing of Aristotle isn't down to pure bloody-mindedness; Crane (1952: 12) tells us that he and his Chicago colleagues 'feel a strong temperamental affinity' for Aristotle and his poetics.

[8] See Bloom 1973.   [9] Phelan 2015: 137.

[10] Nash 2014: 3, citing Phelan 2007a: 10.

limitations his priorities placed upon the Chicago school inheritance. So, according to Shen's version of this reception history:[11]

The first generation of Chicago critics followed Aristotle in subordinating literary language to the larger structure of the work in a given genre. The basic assumption is that disregarding style or language enables them to focus on the "architecture" of literary works...This tendency was inherited by contemporary rhetorical critics...To [Booth], the earlier Chicago critics' development of Aristotle's method provides "the most helpful, least limiting view of character and event—those tough realities that have never submitted happily to merely verbal analysis".

Shen somewhat overstates the case here in suggesting that earlier generations working in the neo-Aristotelian tradition 'disregarded' style or language—although, as Booth's dismissive reference here to 'merely verbal analysis' indicates, they certainly saw language as subordinate to the larger form and structure of a work—just as Aristotle had seen diction (lexis) as subordinate to plot (muthos) and the structural arrangement (sunthesis) of incidents. Yet the finer point of Shen's charge stands and signals Aristotle's direct influence on the neo-Aristotelian privileging of structure and form over the other parts of a literary work.

However, as Phelan and Richter tell it, it was not a concern with structure but an interest in reader response and related rhetorical narratological poetics which first inspired the neo-Aristotelians, and drew them to the Poetics:[12]

The Chicagoans were drawn to the Poetics in particular because they were interested in the affective experiences offered by reading literature, and they understood Aristotle's treatise as explaining the principles underlying the audience's experience of Greek tragedy. This way of conceiving their project made Aristotle's a posteriori method of reasoning back from their effects constituting that experience to the causes of those effects in the plays of the Greek tragedians more important than his particular conclusions. But this way of conceiving their project also led them to adopt the concept of form underlying Aristotle's famous definition of tragedy...the organizing principle that synthesizes the various aspects of imitation—the objects (the constituent parts of the action: plot, character, and thought), manner (the dramatic spectacle), and means (the speeches of the characters, the songs)—into a larger purposive whole designed to affect its audience in a particular way.

In this version of the story, the first generation of neo-Aristotelians were principally concerned with the affective dynamics of literature and found

---

[11] Shen 2014: 13, citing Booth 1961: 460.
[12] Phelan and Richter 2011: 4, emphases added.

Aristotle's concomitant concerns with tragic *katharsis*—and the formal elements that bring about its affects—in sympathy with their own. This led them to a theoretical template on which to form their own project, adapting ancient schemata from Aristotle's *Poetics* and *Metaphysics* and applying them to modern texts.[13]

We find this same basic *fabula* in the various accounts that Crane himself gives of the genesis of the Chicago school's Aristotelianism, but here the *muthos* is given a slightly different shape, from which slightly different emphases and causal relations inevitably emerge. Phelan and Richter focus on the reverse chain of effect to cause that prompts Crane in his 1950 reading of *Tom Jones* to work backwards from the reader's emotions of relief and pleasure at the happy ending of this novel, through the plot structure that led there, and thus to an 'Aristotelian' moment of climactic recognition and conclusion that plot and its components (action, character, and thought) constitute a unified and teleological whole designed to elicit a specific emotional response from an audience. But Crane himself tells it otherwise. He narrates the story of the Chicago school as a type of conflict narrative, in which the priorities of the neo-Aristotelians are determined in diametric—and dialectic—opposition to those of the New Critics. In this telling, the so-called 'New' Critics (Crane likes to hint that their approach is not really so new[14]) follow a Roman rhetorical tradition focusing upon individual, localized 'configurations of thought or diction' which tend to preclude the analysis of texts 'as concrete artistic wholes with distinctive forms which are analytically more than the sum of their parts';[15] their critical approach tends towards the 'monist' rather than plural;[16] to privilege the abstract rather than the concrete and the a priori over the a posteriori.[17] The 'New' Aristotelians, on the other hand, see language as just one of the multidimensional aspects of literary fiction, and deny its primacy—placing it, like Aristotle, below plot in terms of significance. They are consequently concerned less with parts than with wholes, with the literary work as 'the specific constitution and power of the whole'.[18] And they are prepared to take a holistic, pluralist approach in examining the dynamic forces that structure those parts into such wholes. According to Crane:[19] 'If we are

---

[13] See also Phelan 2007a: 79–85 on the first three 'chapters' of the neo-Aristotelian story.

[14] See for instance the conclusion to his essay 'The Critical Monism of Cleanth Brooks' (1952: 107).

[15] Crane 1952: 14.   [16] Crane 1952: 84.

[17] Crane 1952: 107.   [18] Crane 1952: 15.

[19] Crane 1953: 41. For Phelan (2015: 135) this defining neo-Aristotelian pluralism anticipates the critical and theoretical multi-disciplinarity typical of poststructuralist narratologies.

interested in learning the truth, as [Aristotle] saw it, about poetry and the other related arts, we must read not only the *Poetics* but also the *Rhetoric*, the *Nichomachean Ethics*, the *Politics*, even the *Physics* and the *Metaphysics*.' And, above all, he insists that, if we are interested in learning about narrative poetics, we must appropriate from the *Poetics*, not its universal principles, but its a posteriori methodology. Only by moving backwards from our experience and observations of effects and affects, can we track their probable and necessary conditions, and understand their causes.

7.2 **Ronald Crane**

The particular emphases that would come to define the Chicago school's neo-Aristotelianism are already taking shape in a relatively early piece written by one of its founding figures, Ronald Crane. In an entry on 'English Neo-Classical Criticism' for the 1944 *Dictionary of World Literature* (reprinted in the 1952 collection *Critics and Criticism*) Crane assesses the strengths and weaknesses of the enduring 'neo-classical' critical tradition, and in so doing signals his own sympathies for a neglected 'Aristotelian' strand within that tradition. He characterizes neo-classicism as 'a poetics rhetorically conceived' whose 'basic historical affinities were Roman rather than Greek', pointing out that 'its favorite masters were Horace rather than Aristotle (for all its many debts to the *Poetics*) and Quintilian rather than Longinus (for all the enthusiasm many of its adherents felt for the treatise *On the Sublime*), and that its typical devices of analysis and evaluation owed more to the example of rhetoric…than they did either to philosophy or to poetics'.[20] Although that characterization of neo-classicism as a *rhetorically* conceived poetics would become a fitting description of the second and third generation of the Chicago school (particularly championed by Booth and his followers), Crane signals here his own intuition that the over-dependence upon a limited range of rhetorical (and particularly Roman) paradigms and tools compromised neo-classicism's scope and effectiveness as an approach to literature. He is also critical of the neo-classical 'Platonic' focus upon 'what poets or artists ought to do rather than with what they have done and hence may do'.[21] For Crane, such an a priori, deontic, and 'top-down' approach to poetics is fundamentally flawed, and his own

---

[20] Crane 1944: 195–6.   [21] Crane 1944: 195.

'Aristotelian' preferences for an a posteriori inductive methodology becomes one of the most important principles of the Chicago school approach to narratology. He appears to have some sympathy with the neo-classical interest in articulating the particular *pleasures* of literary texts, but he again finds fault with the neo-classical critics for their methodology in this regard—their general failure to concentrate on the forms and processes that produce such pleasure, or to take into proper consideration the role of audiences in the co-poiesis of meaning and affect. This fundamental failure Crane sums up as the neo-classical neglect of those formal elements that 'had constituted, for Aristotle, the distinctive principle of poetics as the science of imitations'.[22]

Not only does this early essay nicely illustrate Crane's nuanced understanding of classical literary criticism and its neo-classical reception, it also neatly highlights the key correspondences between Crane's own formalist poetics and those set out in Aristotle's. Both conceive of poetics as a 'science', indeed as a science helping to distinguish between different types and modes of discourse. Both treat rhetorical theory as one instrument amongst many rather than as the best or only tool fit for purpose in the practice of that scientific enterprise. Both regard an a posteriori inductive approach as the most effective methodology for that science to follow. Both recognize the importance of audience affectivity. And both consider the dynamics of form to represent a (if not *the*) key focus to the theory and *praxis* of poetics.

However, despite these significant affinities, Crane's own theory of poetics does not represent a straightforward imitation of Aristotle's *Poetics*. Crane's poetics are 'neo-Aristotelian' rather than classically 'Aristotelian'. In one of his best-known papers, 'The Concept of Plot and the Plot of *Tom Jones*' (1950), Crane explains how his concept of plot is at once aligned with and yet different to that of Aristotle's:[23]

[S]tructure is only the matter or content of the plot and not its form; the form of the plot—in the sense of that which makes its matter into a definite artistic

---

[22] Crane 1944: 195. In his major work, *The Languages of Criticism* (1953), of which he devotes almost a quarter to an analysis of Aristotle's poetics (broadly conceived and received), Crane reiterates these key points: Aristotle is credited with developing 'a productive science of poetry' (54); Crane aligns his own method of 'inductive and causal analysis' with Aristotle's (164); he compares their analogous approaches to analysing 'the pleasures of poetry' (58–60); he favourably contrasts Aristotle's approach to plots and poetics with Plato's (39); and he insists upon the valuable pluralism of Aristotle's poetics, enhanced by its borrowings of terminology from physics, metaphysics, ethics, rhetoric, biology, and psychology (41–2).

[23] Crane 1950: 68. In his introduction to *Critics and Criticism*, this formulation is recast as 'working *or* power' and 'form or "power"' (1952: 21, emphasis added).

thing—is rather its distinctive "working power," as the form of the plot in tragedy, for example, is the capacity of its unified sequence of actions to effect through pity and fear a catharsis of such emotions... It follows, consequently, that the plot considered formally, of any imitative work is, in relation to the work as a whole, not simply a means—a "framework" or "mere mechanism"—but rather the final end which everything in the work, if that is to be felt as a whole, must be made, directly or indirectly, to serve.

For Aristotle, as we saw, the plot (*muthos*), defined as the *mimesis* of action (*praxis*) and the arrangement (*sunthesis*) of incidents (*pragmata*) (*Poetics* 6.1450a 2–4), was the first principle which had to be grasped before any meaningful analysis could be made of the other parts of poetry—namely action (*praxis*), character (*ethos*), and thought (*dianoia*). For Aristotle, plot was 'the first principle (*arche*) and the soul (*psuche*) of tragedy' (*Poetics* 6.1450a 38), with each of the other parts deemed hierarchically subordinate to that first principle and to each other.[24] As 'the structure of the incidents' and the framework subsuming the other parts, plot was necessarily 'the first and most important part of tragedy' (*Poetics* 7.1450b 21–2).

But for Crane, something is missing from this account of plot as structure. It is too mechanistic, too focused on the discrete workings of discrete parts, too centred upon content and matter. Something else is required if we want to explain how a tragic plot and its contents work together not as separate parts but together as the synthesized, unified, whole that Aristotle insists is necessary for such a plot to achieve its intended affects upon its audience—for it to realize its intended *telos* or 'final end'. For Crane, therefore, it is not the architectonics, content, or structure but the dynamic, synthetic, form of the plot that must be taken as the first—and final—principle of poetics. Indeed, Crane appears to find a way to reconcile logically here Aristotle's claim that plot is simultaneously the *alpha* and *omega* of poetry, its first and final principles, both of which are somehow 'the most important': as the arrangement of incidents, the plot (*muthos*) 'is the first and most important part of tragedy' (*Poetics* 7.1450b 21–2); but at the same time, so Aristotle tells us, 'the incidents and the *muthos* are the end goal (*telos*) of tragedy, and the end is the most important thing of all' (*Poetics* 6.1450a 22–3).

Crane pulls off this reconciliation with a bold bit of dynamic synthesizing of his own. For Aristotle's *Poetics* to achieve its own intended *telos* and final cause by providing an effective model of poetics, Crane perceives that

---

[24] Cf. Crane 1950: 63 n. 7 for a neat summary of how plot, character, thought, and diction fit together in the *Poetics* 'in a causal sequence of form-matter or end-means relationships'.

it must be taken as working not in isolation but together with the other elements of Aristotle's philosophy. His allusions to form in relation to its force as a 'working power' and a 'final cause' in the study of *Tom Jones* already anticipates this synthesis, but in his subsequent writings he shows his own 'Aristotelian' workings more clearly. In his 1953 monograph, *The Languages of Criticism*, he explicitly characterizes the 'working power' of form as *dunamis*, appropriating a key term from Aristotle's *Rhetoric* and *Metaphysics*.[25] He suggests that Aristotle 'gives us a formula which specifies not merely the three material components necessary to the existence of wholes of this kind but also the distinctive *dynamis* which is the actuality or form of their combination'.[26] In the case of a tragic plot, for instance, the particular form or *dunamis* is what drives the whole towards its kathartic affect upon the audience in their experience of pity and fear. Thus, for Crane, form is not structural or material but rather a dynamic force; it is 'that principle, or complex of principles, which gives to the subject-matter the power it has to affect our opinions and emotions in a certain definite way such as would not have been possible had the synthesizing principle been of a different kind ... [and] which we can warrantably assert was the actual final cause of its composition'.[27]

The 'final end' we saw described in the 1950 discussion of form is now characterized in Crane's 1953 work as 'the actual final cause'. Crane's redefinition here is now more closely informed by Aristotle's discussions of the four different 'causes' that he deems the foundation of any analytical investigation in his *Metaphysics* and *Physics*. If we are to come to terms with Crane's reception of the *Poetics*, then, we need to appreciate how Aristotle's theory of the four causes intersects with his theory of poetry.[28]

In the *Physics*, Aristotle maintains that proper knowledge is tied to understanding of *aition*: we can only claim proper understanding of a thing when we know the answers to how and why (*because* of what?) it exists (*Physics* 2.194b 17–20).[29] So, in order to gain proper knowledge of a narrative we must understand:[30]

1. The material cause (*tropos*)—that is, the bronze of a statue, the language of a narrative;

[25] See especially *Rhetoric* 1 and *Metaphysics* 9.   [26] Crane 1953: 53.
[27] Crane 1953: 66.   [28] Cf. Phelan 2015: 138.
[29] The same argument is mounted in Aristotle's *Posterior Analytics* 71b 9–11 and 94a 20.
[30] See *Metaphysics* 5.1013a. Aristotle offers a varied selection of examples (a bronze statue, a silver cup, a piece of music, a child, and walking) to illustrate these four causes. The bibliography on Aristotle's *aitia* is vast, but see in particular Hankinson 1998 and Schofield 1991.

2. The formal cause (*eidos*)—that is, the shape of a statue, the form of a narrative (its synthetic pattern of plot, character, thought, and diction);
3. The efficient cause (*metabole*)—that is, the technique of bronze-casting, the narrative style (the dramatic, tragic, or comic manner);
4. The final cause (*telos*)—that is, the particular purpose or end goal of the statue (to serve as commemoration or decoration, as may be), the ultimate aim of the narrative to move its audience (to pity, fear, laughter, or some other affect).

We can map these four causes against the taxonomy that Aristotle used to distinguish between different kinds of *mimesis* in the *Poetics*, where we find him putting into practice the very principles of inquiry that he advocates in the *Physics* and *Metaphysics*. This taxonomy would thereby relate to: (1) *the material cause*—the media of imitation, such as rhythm, language or melody (*Poetics* 1.1447a 21-2); (2) *the formal cause*—the type of plot and the objects of imitation, such as serious or unserious characters in action (*Poetics* 2.1447b 29–1448a 1); (3) *the efficient cause*—the manner or mode of imitation, such as the mixed narrative-dramatic mode of Homeric epic, pure narrative, or drama (*Poetics* 3.1448a 18–23); and (4) *the final cause*—the aim or purpose of the imitation, which is an appropriate audience affect, such as *katharsis* achieved through the experience of pity and fear for the audiences of tragedy (*Poetics* 6.1449b 28).

For Crane and his fellow neo-Aristotelians, then, Aristotle's taxonomy in the *Metaphysics* is synthesized with that of the *Poetics* in order to produce a general model of narrative (and poetry) as *synolon* or 'formed matter'. As one of the third generation of the Chicago school critics, David Richter subsequently explains, literary works in this model are conceived as 'syntheses in which plot, character, and thought (the formal cause) give shape to language (the material cause), using various techniques or devices of disclosure (the efficient cause), in order to create an object with the power to affect readers in determinate ways (the final cause)'.[31] Richter's summary is particularly useful because it avoids the pitfall into which some critics fall of conflating the efficient cause—the manner or mode of representation—with the author. David Herman's summary, for example, distinguishes between 'the efficient cause (= the author), the final cause (= effect on readers), the material cause (= the language), and the formal cause (= the mimetic content)'.[32] Although in the *Metaphysics*, Aristotle does include agents, as 'the producer' is generally the

---

[31] Richter 2005: 57. See also Phelan 2015.
[32] Herman 2005: 28.

efficient cause 'of that produced' (5.1013a 30–3), and so invites us to take the poet as (one of) the efficient cause(s) of the poem, further discussions of this subject in both the *Physics* (2.195b 21–5) and *Metaphysics* (5.1013b 6–9) reveal that Aristotle places greater emphasis upon the technique rather than the technician, the artistry rather than the artist, in his taxonomy. It is somewhat wide of the mark, then, to equate the efficient cause with the author alone—particularly given how little attention Aristotle correspondingly pays to the agentive or authorial aspect of poetic composition in the *Poetics*.

The first generation of the Chicago school neo-Aristotelians attempts to resolve this issue by adapting Aristotle's taxonomy and distinguishing between subsets of 'internal' and 'external' elements within two of his causes. The efficient and final causes, they reason, both involve an external agency—author and audience, respectively—as well as internal features that are inherent in the mode and in the *telos* of the work, conceived as 'a kind of entelechy of the artifact'.[33] The result is something of a fudge, but it does succeed in creating carefully circumscribed roles both for the author and the audience in their subsequent textual analyses. In deliberate contrast to the prevailing New Critical theories of the period in which the only 'cause' of literary fiction deemed significant was the linguistic element of the material cause, the neo-Aristotelians thereby realized the *telos* of their own project, with a four-cornered causal methodology that enabled them to consider the linguistic, formal, modal/intentional, and teleological/affective dynamics of literary fiction and its narratives.

Thus, and as Crane himself acknowledges in his introduction to the 1952 collection that sets out the Chicago school 'neo-Aristotelian' agenda, the Aristotle that we encounter in the work of Crane, Olson, et al. is not necessarily recognizable as the Aristotle who is familiar to classicists. According to Crane, 'It may not, indeed, except in a general way, be Aristotle at all.'[34] What Crane and his fellow Chicago school neo-Aristotelians do consider to be distinctively and unassailably Aristotelian about their project, though, is their appropriation of his methodology, his a posteriori inductive approach to poetics. This, far more so than the conclusions and the theories Aristotle derives from the application of

---

[33] Herman 2005: 33 n. 7. See also Trowbridge 1944: 546: 'Since they do not inhere in the object itself, the efficient and final causes are external. These external causes, while not entirely disregarded, are subordinated in the *Poetics* to the internal causes. Horace and Longinus, by contrast, focus upon the external causes—Horace emphasizing the final cause or purpose, defined as an effect upon the audience; Longinus dealing primarily with the efficient cause, the mind or soul of the poet.'

[34] Crane 1952: 17.

this methodology in the *Poetics* (or the *Metaphysics*), is ultimately what defines the neo-Aristotelian reception of Aristotle.

7.3 Wayne Booth

Amongst the second generation of neo-Aristotelians, Sheldon Sacks and Ralph Rader remain broadly faithful to the Aristotelian narratological principles set out by Crane, and their work continues to focus largely upon the affective dynamics of narrative form—although they significantly expand the range of texts considered under this general rubric. Sacks offers a new taxonomy of the novel, seeking to distinguish between the particular features of satires, apologues, and 'action' texts, predicated upon their central objects of representation and upon the ethical beliefs and sympathies evinced towards those objects by the author. Rader meanwhile picks up on three literary forms signally excluded both from Aristotle's own and the first generation neo-Aristotelian purview: history, biography, and lyric.

This is not to say that Sacks and Rader simply replicate the theories and approaches of the first generation and apply them to new situations. Rader points out that unity and coherence do not in or of themselves produce literature or 'literary pleasure', and in order to understand how narrative fiction elicits its particular affects 'we must remember what Aristotle teaches' and consider the ethical and moral contexts determining its patterns of cause and effect, necessity and probability.[35] Rader tries this out in an essay (written in 1981 but not published until 1999) offering a nuanced critique of Crane's reading of *Tom Jones*, arguing that Crane's classic description neglects 'the historico-ideational dimensions of that form'.[36] For Sacks too, Crane's resistance to any mode of analysis that might be open to charges of succumbing to intentional or affective fallacies led him to under-appreciate the shaping influence of context upon the dynamics of form and affect. In his major work of literary theory, *Fiction and the Shape of Belief*, Sacks therefore argues (explicitly *contra* Crane) that 'the ethical beliefs, opinions, and prejudices of novelists do not shape their novels, but rather have a discernible and vital shape within those novels'.[37]

---

[35] Rader 2011: 117–18.
[36] Rader 1999: 47. On Rader's contribution to narratology and literary theory see Phelan and Richter 2010.
[37] Sacks 1964: 69.

For Sacks and Rader, then, ethics emerge as an important addition to the methodological framework developed in the first iteration of the Chicago school poetics, with its keen interest in final causes and audience affect. For their contemporary, Wayne Booth, however, it is not primarily ethical but rather rhetorical concerns that demand fresh attention in this context, and his major work *The Rhetoric of Fiction* (1961) marks a significant change in direction for the neo-Aristotelians. Booth's own 'Aristotelianism' is not always visible in this study, but its fundamental Aristotelian affinities are retrospectively highlighted in his later works, including a playful piece written for Amélie Rorty's 1992 edited collection *Essays on Aristotle's Poetics* in which Booth claims that 'I could never have written *The Rhetoric of Fiction*, or any of the evaluative portions of subsequent works, without pursuing a version of the method I extract from the *Poetics*.'[38] Here, Booth not only impersonates Aristotle, critically reviewing the *Poetics* and its legacy *in propria persona*, but closely aligns his own rhetorical priorities with those evinced in the *Poetics*—albeit a text unabashedly appropriated as Booth's own, and 'reconstructed as if Aristotle were our contemporary'.[39] Thus, the Boothian Aristotle (or Aristotelian Booth) reminds us that his theory of narrative and dramatic poetry is essentially a rhetorical theory, its methods oriented towards a better understanding of works of literary fiction through a better understanding of their final cause: that is, their communicative (or rhetorical) impact at the point of reception as 'unified experience'.[40] Indeed, this version of the *Poetics* goes further than Crane et al. in positing that 'the means (medium), the object (the stuff imitated), and the manner' work together 'to further the effect, or "end"'—the material, formal, and efficient causes each subserve the final cause, which in this model involves a final product (a mimetic 're-made piece of life') 'that is *experienceable*'.[41] This *telos* proves crucial to Booth's reception of the *Poetics*, underpinning his major claim that Aristotle is first and last concerned with 'formed matter as unified experience'; which entails the treatment of literary fiction 'neither as an abstract form, neither as a statement of ideas or themes or meanings—not as

---

[38] Booth 1992: 404. Booth acknowledges in a later work that Aristotle's *Rhetoric* was something of a late addition to his bibliography on this topic (2004: 498): 'The Russian formalists had back in the 1920s discovered—as I learned only much later—the indispensability of rhetorical studies in all criticism of literature. But did the Russians...or even Aristotle enter my study as I labored on a dissertation demonstrating the "unity" of the disunified *Tristram Shandy*? Not at all.'

[39] Booth 1992: 387.

[40] Booth reiterates that literary fiction is first and foremost an act of communication between author and audience (1961: 55, 73, 89, 105, 387–8).

[41] Booth 1992: 383.

form on the one hand and content on the other, but rather as *a composition to be experienced*.[42] The final cause is the *ultimate* cause for which poems and narratives are produced. Therefore, 'It is only in relation to their functions, or ends, that we can ever hope to distinguish good from poor makings' and 'all appraisals of any composed form must be referable to the distinctive end that dictated, however mysteriously, its making'.[43]

This significant refinement to the Aristotelianism of the first generation of the Chicago school (who had treated the final cause as playing no more or less fundamental a role in its poetics than the other causes) consequently prioritizes the rhetorical dynamics of form—the power that moves a work of literary fiction to move its audience. Accordingly, in his *Rhetoric of Fiction*, Booth set out to reconceive the neo-Aristotelian poetics of narrative as a *rhetoric of narrative*. He argued that every formal aspect of a given narrative will have been chosen and organized by its author so as to realize a desired end, to make a particular impact and to affect an audience in a particular way: the choice of material or subject (the *Odyssey* or *The Penelopiad*), the choice of where to begin and end (*ab ovo*, *in medias res*, or *in ultimas res*), the selection and suppression of elements from the raw story stuff, the temporal patterning and sequencing of cause and effect (prolepses, analepses, and anachronies), the decision to narrate the story by showing and/or telling (the choice between dramatic and narrative modes), the point of view adopted, the epithets and adjectives employed to describe characters and situations, are all *rhetorical* choices in Booth's model: for an 'author cannot choose to avoid rhetoric; he can choose only the kind of rhetoric he will employ'.[44]

Booth supplies a framework and lexicon that allows him to foreground the operations relating to these rhetorical choices—those devices that configure the 'work as the product of a choosing, evaluating person rather than as a self-existing thing'.[45] Deciding that none of the existing terms (such as persona, mask, or narrator) adequately characterize this authorial proxy and allow us to distinguish properly between the author and his 'implied image', Booth describes as the 'implied author' the narrative agent who 'chooses, consciously or unconsciously, what we read'.[46] Booth's controversial concept thus posits the implied author as

[42] Booth 1992: 393–4, emphasis in original.
[43] Booth 1992: 389 and 391.
[44] Booth 1961: 149; similarly, an 'author can to some extent choose his disguises, he can never choose to disappear' (20).
[45] Booth 1961: 74–5.
[46] Booth 1961: 75. See Nünning 2005 for a summary of the critical opposition to Booth's concept of the implied author. Cf. Kindt and Müller 2006 on the ongoing controversy.

personifying the textual 'core of norms and choices', orienting a corresponding 'implied reader' towards the appropriate 'moral and emotional' import of each of the text's constitutive elements of action and character: 'it includes, in short, the intuitive apprehension of a completed artistic whole'.[47] What is more, this concept of the implied author as a kind of anthropomorphized moral compass pointing the implied reader towards the (implied) purposive ends of the text as a whole allows Booth to extend the reach of his rhetorical-narratological model and to introduce corresponding terms and concepts such as 'reliable' and 'unreliable' narration. Thus, a narrator will be '*reliable* when he speaks for or acts in accordance with the norms of the work (which is to say, the implied author's norms), *unreliable* when he does not'.[48]

It is instructive here to ask how far the 'norms' of Booth's own work reliably or otherwise accord with those at the core of the neo-Aristotelian project. He certainly shares their inductive, a posteriori, methodology; his stated purpose in *The Rhetoric of Fiction* is to 'free both readers and novelists from the constraints of what novelists *must do*, by reminding them in a systematic way of what good novelists *have in fact done*', and he develops his model by examining in depth and detail the rhetorical devices evidenced in a wide range of literary texts.[49] Deeply critical of the New Criticism, he dismisses the notion that there ever existed a work of literary fiction fully corresponding to any 'Platonic notion' of a perfect—that is, rhetoric-free—narrative or dramatic form; indeed, Booth aims to persuade his readers that 'all great literature has in fact made use of rhetoric'.[50] To illustrate this claim, he examines the extensive rhetorical elements found in ancient narrative and dramatic poetry, pointing out that even in the 'mimetic' texts of Greek tragedy, where we might expect the action to be entirely 'shown' without recourse to rhetorical commentary and manipulation of the audience's emotions, we find rhetorical devices to the fore. He notes that 'nearly one-fourth of *Agamemnon* is given over to commentary by the chorus when no other characters are present and when no internal decisions or actions are at stake', arguing that the rhetorical purpose served by this choral commentary is to remind the audience that it is watching a play and to offer it prompts as to how to respond appropriately to what is unfolding on the stage in

---

Tynyanov's concept of 'literary personality' (1981: 75) anticipates Booth's 'implied author'; Iser's 'implied reader' (1972) offers the counterpart.

[47] Booth 1961: 73. On the relationship between implied author and reader see also Chatman 1990: 75.

[48] Booth 1961: 158–9, emphases in original.

[49] Booth 1961: xv, emphases added.

[50] Booth 1961: 98.

the main scenes.[51] However, he finds Aristotle an unsupportive ally in mounting this argument. Aristotle may acknowledge in the *Poetics* that 'poetry always works upon an audience, and thus always has a close relationship to rhetoric', but he is critical of any and all obviously 'separable rhetoric ... because it is "extraneous"'.[52]

Taking issue with Aristotle for this alleged blindness to the rhetorical import of all narratorial decisions, and the impossibility of separating 'extraneous' from 'essential' rhetorical devices, Booth analyses the different ways in which all implied authors can be seen—implicitly or explicitly—to manipulate the emotions of their audiences:[53]

Though Aristotle praises Homer for speaking in his own voice less than other poets, even Homer writes scarcely a page without some kind of direct clarification of motives, of expectations, and of the relative importance of events ... [and] we move through the *Iliad* with Homer constantly at our elbow, controlling rigorously our beliefs, our interests, and our sympathies ... to insure that our judgment of the "heroic", "resourceful", "admirable", "wise" Odysseus will be sufficiently favorable.

With these classic illustrations, Booth is able to turn Aristotle's implicit preference for showing over telling, dramatic over narrative representation (or *mimesis* over *diegesis*), on its head, demonstrating that showing has *always* been an effect of telling (*mimesis* an epiphenomenon of *diegesis*), in which the narratorial role is rhetorically configured so as to more or less efface itself. Once again, Aristotle is a useful stalking horse:[54]

The poet [Aristotle says] "should speak as little as possible in his own person". But why, then, speak at all? If Homer is better than the others for appearing rarely—though as we have seen already he appears far more often than Aristotle's comment would suggest—can we not out-Homer Homer by not appearing at all, by *showing* everything and *telling* nothing?

For Booth, Aristotle's inductive methodology in the *Poetics* may be sound, but the conclusions he draws on this account are not. Although Booth will later credit Aristotle with providing the methodological template for his own findings in *The Rhetoric of Fiction*, at this point in the story Aristotle is ancient history. Staking out a new claim in the nascent field of narratology, Booth has no need of Aristotelian concepts such as

---

[51] Booth 1961: 99.   [52] Booth 1961: 93.
[53] Booth 1961: 4–5. Cf. 183 on Virgil's style.
[54] Booth 1961: 93, emphases in original. Cf. Booth 1961: 154 on the limitations of the showing/telling binary: 'Like Aristotle's distinction between dramatic [mimetic] and narrative [diegetic] manners, the somewhat different modern distinction between showing and telling does cover the ground. But the trouble is that it pays for broad coverage with gross imprecision.'

synolon and *eidos*, or the four causes and their *dunamis*; he has his own terms to coin. And it is these concepts—the *implied author* and the *unreliable narrator*—rather than Aristotle's that will go on to become indispensable terms in the critical and narratological lexicon taken up by the third generation of the Chicago school.[55]

7.4 **David Richter, Peter Rabinowitz, and James Phelan**

Three names stand out as leading lights of the third generation of the Chicago school neo-Aristotelians: David Richter, Peter Rabinowitz, and Jim Phelan. All three directly position their work as a continuation of the 'Aristotelian' poetics developed by Crane et al., and all three engage in close dialogue with each other's work, often co-writing pieces together. But it is Booth with his rhetorical poetics who proves to be their most important interlocutor from the Chicago school tradition. His insistence that all analyses of poetic (that is, composed) form be configured in terms of their experienced, affective, ends inaugurates a rhetorical turn that continues to shape the contemporary narratological landscape.[56]

David Richter develops Sacks's ideas about the form of the novel to explore in much greater depth and detail the rhetorical means by which novelists manipulate form in order to achieve their purposive affects upon audiences, thus developing a model much closer to Booth's than to Sacks's in his study *Fable's End: Completeness and Closure in Rhetorical Fiction* (1974). Booth's influence is also evident in Richter's more recent work on film, where he examines the rhetoric and ethics of cinematic narratives—thereby continuing the commitment of the second generation to widen the sphere of texts and authors illuminated by their poetics out beyond that of the novel.[57] Yet, alongside this correspondence with Sacks and Booth, Richter is also unmistakably a 'grand-pupil of Crane' (as he describes Phelan[58]), inheriting Crane's nose for literary history as well as his taste for Aristotelian 'causes'—and putting both to good use in his study *The Progress of Romance: Literary Historiography and the Gothic Novel, 1790–1830* (1996).

[55] Booth revisits these rhetorical narratological themes in his 1988 study *The Company We Keep*.

[56] See Phelan and Richter 2010 and 2011, and Phelan and Rabinowitz 2012.

[57] Cf. Richter 2005.   [58] Richter 2005: 58.

As a neo-Aristotelian literary historian, Richter is particularly well attuned to the critical and theoretical historiography in which his own work is located. He notices, for example, the 'convergence' of ideas between ostensibly disparate schools—between 'formalists like Tynyanov and Shklovsky, neo-Aristotelians like Crane and Rader, reception theorists like Iser and Jauss'.[59] Exhibiting the same pragmatic approach to theoretical pluralism as that championed by Crane and the first generation of neo-Aristotelians, Richter finds something worth taking from each. Richter also remains loyal to the neo-Aristotelian commitment to an a posteriori rather than a priori critical methodology. In one of the rare direct references to Aristotle's *Poetics* that appear in his writings, Richter aligns his own 'empirical' approach to the Gothic novel with Aristotle's inductive approach to tragedy, noting:[60] 'Tragedy, in Aristotle's *Poetics*, is... a set of texts with a family resemblance generated by different authors within a time frame, and what Aristotle thinks he knows about them is not deduced from foreknown general principles of aesthetics but is rather inferred from common features in the texts and their reception.' Thus, Richter's work affirms its own 'family resemblance' to the neo-Aristotelian set.

Another member of this familial group, Peter Rabinowitz, is equally recognizable as such—as the immediate pupil of Booth and another 'grand-pupil of Crane'. Booth had recalibrated the formalist poetics of the first generation neo-Aristotelians with its focus on authors 'making form', and transformed this into a rhetorically inspired poetics—albeit still formalist in inflection—which focused on authors instead 'making readers'.[61] In his pioneering work 'Truth in Fiction: A Reexamination of Audiences' (1977), and *Before Reading* (1987), Rabinowitz picks up on this concept of authors and texts 'making readers', and interrogates the role that rhetoric plays in the dynamics of this complex author–reader relationship. Rabinowitz goes much further than Booth in his investigations into the poetics of reader-response, but never strays too far from his neo-Aristotelian roots. He is highly critical of the the apolitical principles of the New Critics and their heirs, condemning their adherence to an overly simplistic (monist) view of 'theme' as the predominant aspect of their poetics.[62] His methodological principles are unequivocally inductive and a posteriori, explicitly focusing 'less on the abstract possibilities of reading and writing than on what readers and writers have in fact done with narratives'.[63] Although he is sceptical of some of Aristotle's conclusions (such as Aristotle's perceived emphasis upon the final cause

---

[59] Richter 1996: viii.   [60] Richter 1996: 168–9.   [61] Booth 1961.
[62] Rabinowitz 1987: 4–7.   [63] Rabinowitz 1987: 3.

as the pre-eminent force determining narrative form), Rabinowitz welcomes the Aristotelian principle that literary interpretation should involve 'study not of *what* a work means but of *how* it comes to mean'— that is, in Aristotelian terms, its 'causes'.[64] There is even a passing resemblance to Aristotle's four causes in Rabinowitz's own proposition of the four kinds of 'rules' that shape our reading and response(s) to a narrative text: (1) the rules of *notice*, recognizing some parts of the text as more salient and noteworthy than others; (2) the rules of *signification*, signalling the wider thematic, semiotic, and hermeneutic relevance of key details; (3) the rules of *configuration*, organizing discrete textual elements and incidents into logically related plots and subplots; and (4) the rules of *coherence*, synthesizing textual parts into a unified and coherent whole. Like Crane and like Aristotle before him, Rabinowitz's primary concern with audiences and readers ultimately causes him to be concerned with the underlying rules that govern narrative patterns of form and structure—with *muthos* and *sunthesis*.

The third and most prolific member of this neo-Aristotelian triumvirate is Jim Phelan, whose work similarly, though more explicitly than that of Rabinowitz and Richter, finds a synergy in the rhetoric and poetics of narrative. In fact, he characterizes his 2007 study *Experiencing Fiction: Judgments, Progressions, and the Rhetorical Theory of Narrative* as 'an effort to write a third chapter to [the] narrative of the neo-Aristotelian movement by putting the poetic and the rhetorical strands of the tradition back together in the construction of a rhetorical poetics'.[65] Phelan is characteristically overt in declaring his neo-Aristotelian (and ultimately Aristotelian) heritage, and his extensive body of work is tattooed with signs of this inheritance. Thus:[66]

Defining narrative as somebody telling somebody else on some occasion and for some purposes that something happened, I emphasize the purposes of the somebody telling (the implied author) in relation to the somebody who is told (actual audiences who take on the roles of authorial and narrative audience). However, since we can discover purposes only through their realization in the matter of narrative as shaped into form, I seek to understand the various components of that matter (style, character, perspective, narration, plot, temporality, place, and so on) and their multiple ways of interacting... In this respect,

---

[64] Rabinowitz 1987: 8, emphases added.
[65] Phelan 2007a: 81.
[66] Phelan 2015: 146. Cf. Phelan 2007a: 86 and 2007b: 287: 'the rhetorical theorist defines narrative as somebody telling somebody else on some occasion and for some purpose(s) that something happened'. Cf. Barthes's claim (1975: 260) that 'a narrative cannot take place without a narrator and a listener (or reader)'.

rhetorical poetics draws on the earlier generations' interest in formal construction and the affective power of literature.

Variations on this key definition of narrative as 'somebody telling somebody else on some occasion and for some purposes that something happened' are found across Phelan's writings. Its emphasis upon the purposeful and communicative—that is, rhetorical—quality of narrative, the rhetorical function pertaining to both the telling and the told (in terms of author and audience but also story and plot), is of the utmost significance here. For, as Phelan makes clear, in this narratological model these rhetorical dynamics can only be accessed and analysed through their realization in the poetics of a particular form; hence, the characterization of this model as a 'rhetorical poetics'.

We can, as does Phelan himself, align these rhetorical poetics and their priorities with the rhetorical turn initiated by the second generation of neo-Aristotelians, and we can even see this concern with audiences and affect as originating in Aristotle's *Poetics*.[67] But we might also acknowledge the wider context—the so-called 'contextualist' turn—which in the late 1970s and early 1980s similarly recognized the importance of these issues in and for narrative theory. The contextualist narratologist Barbara Herrnstein Smith sees no connection between her own narrative theory and that of Aristotle's *Poetics*—although she does take issue with the 'lingering strain of naive Platonism' that she perceives in the structuralist narratological tradition, against which she stakes her own position.[68] Nor does she identify any specifically 'rhetorical' quality to her approach. Yet there are important parallels between Smith's view of narrative as a communicative discursive act, requiring analysis as such, and that of Phelan's. Thus, in a 1980 essay Smith argues for the necessity of developing alternatives to the structuralist narratological models then prevailing:[69]

one in which narratives [are] regarded not only as *structures* but also as *acts*, the features of which—like the features of all other acts—are functions of the variable sets of conditions in response to which they are performed. Accordingly, we might conceive of narrative discourse most minimally and most generally as verbal acts consisting of *someone telling someone else that something happened*.

---

[67] Cf. Phelan 2007b: 207: 'The rhetorical approach to stories and storytelling has its roots in Aristotle's *Poetics*... [which] makes rhetoric part of poetics by linking tragedy to its effect on its audience.'

[68] Smith 1980: 213. Cf. 216, 220, and 228.

[69] Smith 1980: 231–2, emphases in original.

We might also see Smith's legacy no less than Aristotle's in the description that Phelan and Rabinowitz offer of their approach as rhetorical narrative theorists who:[70]

look at narrative primarily as a rhetorical act rather than as an object. That is, we see it as a purposive communication of a certain kind from one person (or group of persons) to one or more others ... *Narrative is somebody telling somebody else, on some occasion, and for some purposes, that something happened to someone or something.*

We should perhaps be hesitant, then, about plotting too strictly a linear chain of reception linking the rhetorical narrative poetics of the third generation back to the first iteration of the neo-Aristotelian project, where literary texts were unequivocally conceived not as 'discourse' or as verbal 'acts' but as made 'objects' and in which 'rhetoric' was part of the 'Hellenistic-Roman-Romantic tradition' of literary criticism against which Crane's 'neo-Aristotelianism' was explicitly targeted.[71]

Having authored several histories of the Chicago school, Phelan himself knows well the discontinuities between—no less than the contradictions within—each generation. In fact, he attributes one of the substantive weaknesses of the first generation to their self-contradictory relationship with the *Poetics*, the gap between theory and *praxis*.[72] They claim that it is Aristotle's a posteriori methodology that matters most in their reception of this foundational text, that it is his inductive logic leading him to identify causes from effects (and, of course, their affects) that inspires their own work. It is, after all, precisely this claim to have borrowed Aristotle's general *methods* rather than his particular *conclusions* that helps legitimize their application (and those of ensuing generations) of Aristotle's theory of the poetics of Greek tragedy to the novel and other modern narrative media. Yet, along with that core a posteriori methodology they inevitably import a set of basic a priori assumptions:

1. that diction is subordinate to plot;
2. that texts cannot properly be understood through the atomization of their several parts but must be viewed as a unified whole;

---

[70] Phelan and Rabinowitz in Herman et al. 2012: 3, emphases in original. Phelan's latest book (2017) is also aptly titled *Somebody Telling Somebody Else*.

[71] See especially Crane 1952: 15.

[72] Phelan 2007a: 83.

3. that the *telos* is the shaping force of that whole;
4. that we can only claim proper understanding of a thing when we know the answers to how and why it exists—that is, when we comprehend each of its four *causes*.

One of the great virtues of Phelan's own work, as of the third generation of the Chicago school as a whole, however, is its willingness to acknowledge these contradictions and tensions in the neo-Aristotelian reception of the *Poetics*—and to find pragmatic solutions that work around them.

Phelan's work on the 'tensions' (caused by gaps between tellers and audiences in terms of knowledge, beliefs, opinions, and values) that drive narrativity in his 2005 study *Living to Tell about It* offers an apt illustration of this. Here we find no direct engagement at all with Aristotle but we do encounter a (neo-)Aristotelian inductive a posteriori methodology and a model of narrative which is not only rhetorically but *teleologically* configured, with a clear orientation towards the formal and structural dynamics of the whole narrative working towards a purposive affect upon its narratees—both real and implied. Aristotle is at once endorsed and ignored.[73]

Refining the concept of the 'unreliable' narrator first proposed by Booth—again signalling partial endorsement and partial rejection of Booth and his (unreliable?) accounts of that 'unreliable narrator'—Phelan observes two distinct kinds of unreliability in narration: one kind concerning ethical (mis)judgement and one factual (mis)representation, each kind impacting upon the relationship between the reader and the narrator differently. Phelan therefore develops and tests the hypothesis that unreliable narration is not, as Booth's model proposes, a binary but a spectrum, involving a range of resources and, most importantly, affects, raising important rhetorical and ethical questions about the ways in which readers respond to narrators (mis)reporting and (mis)perceiving events.[74]

Beyond its value as a sophisticated theory of the narrator function in literature, Phelan's reception of Booth's reception of Crane's reception of Aristotle exposes the way in which critics and theorists are also narrators in their own way. In this reception story, each narrator-theorist-critic signals different degrees of endorsement and/or departure from a previous theoretical position in his own evaluative, interpretative (narrative?) reportage. In fact Phelan, a highly self-reflexive author, explicitly

---

[73] Phelan, however, does return to Aristotle in his 2017 study of 'probable impossibilities' (2017: 34–6).

[74] Phelan 2007b: 289–90. In this model, unreliable narration proceeds by the 'tensions' prompted by gaps between tellers and audiences in terms of knowledge, beliefs, opinions, values, etc.

describes his work in *Living to Tell* as 'an indirect telling, through that odd form of observer narration we call rhetorical criticism, of [his own] activity as a reader'.[75] Thus, Phelan signals to us, his own readers, that his neo-Aristotelian interlocutors have to various degrees provided a spectrum of reliable to unreliable reports and readings in a rhetorical-narratological model of reception that demonstrates, perhaps, why the neo-Aristotelian approach to narrative poetics has proven itself to be so 'reliable' a model over successive iterations—and why its values and judgements continue to inform the latest narratologies.

7.5 *Teleute*

The 'rhetorically conceived poetics' of narrative that successive gener-ations of the neo-Aristotelians have worked to place at the forefront of twenty-first-century narratology reminds us that Aristotle's *Poetics* was, in several respects, always already a rhetorically oriented theory. Its concern with purposively shaping plots in order to realize a particular audience experience and affect shows an interest not only in 'making form' but in 'making readers', an awareness of narratives not only as structures but as communicative acts, which stretches back over three millennia. Ultimately, however, it is not Aristotle's theory—either of poetics or rhetoric—that marks this neo-Aristotelian reception as such. It is, instead, Aristotle's inductive, a posteriori methodology that stands out as the most valuable thing bequeathed and inherited across the generations. That, and the equally remarkable gift of regarding tradition as opportunity rather than as restraint, and reception as a dynamic rather than a passive process, as an evolving co-poiesis.

---

[75] Phelan 2005: 204.

8 Prestructuralism

> *The successful application of any art is a delightful spectacle, but the theory too is interesting.*
>
> Henry James, 'The Art of Fiction' (1894: 376-7)

8.1 *Arche*

Although the 'prestructuralists' Henry James, E. M. Forster, Percy Lubbock, and Franz Stanzel were not part of the same critical circle, and although their theories of the novel did not directly shape the narratological 'structuralism' of the 1960s and 1970s, their individual, cumulative, and collective contribution to modern narratology is significant. No less significant is their indebtedness to the proto-narratologies of Plato and Aristotle. We should be cautious, as with our ancient theorists and critics, not to assume *post hoc ergo propter hoc* correlations between these early twentieth-century narratologists and their classical predecessors—especially when apparent correspondences and influences are unacknowledged, as in the writings of James and Lubbock. Yet, the 'prestructuralists' help us to realize nuanced and new appreciation of ancient theories of narrative. Their allusions to and appropriations of the classics help to shed new light on to some of the more controversial and complex aspects of both the *Republic* and *Poetics*, and upon their twentieth-century reception in narrative theory.

8.2 Henry James

In his introduction to Henry James's *Art of the Novel*, Richard Blackmur explicitly likens the work to Aristotle's *Poetics* in both its ambition and its flaws.[1] The analogy is apt. *The Art of the Novel*, a collection comprising James's own prefaces to his novels, shares something of the 'lecture notes' character of the *Poetics* as well as its concern with theorizing the 'art' or *techne* of fiction. What is more, Aristotelian precepts pervade

---

[1] Blackmur in James and Blackmur 1937: vii.

James's critical writings on this narrative art, including his essay 'The Art of Fiction'.[2] James shares Aristotle's fundamental position that a work of narrative fiction is mimetic, drawing analogies between the art of the painter and the art of the novelist on the basis of their (purportedly) shared interest in re-presenting reality:[3]

The only reason for the existence of a novel is that it does attempt to represent life. When it relinquishes this attempt, the same attempt that we see on the canvas of the painter, it will have arrived at a very strange pass. It is not expected of the picture that it will make itself humble in order to be forgiven; and the analogy between the art of the painter and the art of the novelist is, so far as I am able to see, complete. Their inspiration is the same, their process (allowing for the different quality of the vehicle), is the same, their success is the same.

Like Aristotle, James also distinguishes between the art of the novelist (or epic poet) and that of the historian on the basis of their (purportedly) very different modes of mediating and imitating reality: both Aristotle and James privilege fiction's mimetic ability to re-present the typical and universal rather than the actual and historical.[4]

Alongside their mutual view of narrative as *mimesis*, James similarly shares Aristotle's (and, for that matter, Plato's Socrates') understanding of a narrative text as a quasi-organic, unified entity, claiming:[5]

A novel is a living thing, all one and continuous, like any other organism, and in proportion as it lives will it be found, I think, that in each of the parts there is something of each of the other parts.

Compare this with what Aristotle has to say about narrative poetry (*Poetics* 23.1459a 16–24):[6]

[T]he plot must be constructed as in tragedy, dramatically, focused upon a single piece of action that is whole and complete in itself, with a beginning, middle, and end, so that like a single living organism it may produce its own particular form of pleasure.

---

[2] James demonstrates much less affinity with Plato's (Socratic) approach to narrative, carefully skirting discussions of narrative ethics. In 'The Art of Fiction' (1894: 404) he concludes: 'I have left the question of the morality of the novel till the last, and at the last I find I have used up my space.' There is, however, a distinctly Horatian tenor to his analogies between painting and poetry (1894: 378) and his declaration (1894: 381): 'Literature should be either instructive or amusing.' Cf. Horace, *Ars poetica* 333–4.

[3] James 1894: 378. Aristotle also draws analogies between *mimesis* in poetry and in painting: *Poetics* 1.1447a 18–27, as does Horace, *Ars poetica* 1–6.

[4] Cf. *Poetics* 9.1451a 38–b 11.

[5] James 1894: 392. Cf. Herman 2005: 26.

[6] Cf. James 1937: 106 on the distinctions between narrative and dramatic forms.

Or with Plato's *Phaedrus* (264c):[7]

Socrates: Every discourse should be organized, like a living organism, with a body of its own, as it were, neither headless or footless, but with a middle and with limbs, all composed in apt relation both to each other and to the whole.

James returns repeatedly to the importance of this kind of unity in the novel, albeit diverging from Aristotle in his view that drama 'reaches its effects of unity ... by paths absolutely opposite to the paths of the novel'.[8] James's own ambition as a novelist, he tells us, is to be able to say, 'My several actions beautifully become one' through the careful 'working out of the detail of that unity ... the order, the reason, the relation of presented aspects'.[9]

Amongst his other Aristotelian affinities, James clearly shares the understanding that rational and relational selection, synthesis, and arrangement is central to successful artistic (especially narrative) composition.[10] However, these comparisons help to highlight that James does not share a concept of plot that is quite like Aristotle's notion of *muthos*. Indeed, it appears that James's concept of action provides the closest analogy to Aristotle's plot. For James 'the soul of a novel is its action'.[11] For Aristotle 'the *muthos* is the first principle and the soul of tragedy' (*Poetics* 6.1450a 38).

Recalling Aristotle's insistence upon the practical and theoretical primacy of plot, James writes in *The Art of the Novel*:[12] 'I might envy, though I couldn't emulate, the imaginative writer so constituted as to see his fable first and to make out its agents afterwards.' Aristotle had, of course, proposed that it would theoretically be possible to have a tragedy without character, though not without plot (*Poetics* 6.1450a 23–4). And amongst his more practical recommendations on poetic *praxis*, he had advised that a poet should construct his *muthos* first, laying out its general structure (*katholou*), next arranging its sequence of episodes (*epeisodia*), and only then supplying named characters (*onomata*) as

---

[7] Cf. Horace, *Ars poetica* 8–9 for a similar instance upon (quasi-organic) unity of form.
[8] James 1937: 320.   [9] James 1937: 88.
[10] See in particular James 1894: 398 on 'rearranging' and some qualifications to the view that 'art is essentially selection'. Other notable 'Aristotelianisms' in James include his insistence upon consistency of characterization (1937: 37; cf. Aristotle, *Poetics* 15.1454a 32–6) and his recommendations regarding the careful treatment of 'wonder, ghosts, and the supernatural'. Cf. James 1937: xxi and 256. Cf. Aristotle, *Poetics* 24.1460a 11–14.
[11] James 1921: 25. See also James 1937: 88, where he discusses the pleasure 'of handling an action (or, otherwise expressed, of a story)'.
[12] James 1937: 44.

the narrative's agents (*Poetics* 17.1455a 21–1455b 13). For James, evidently, it is character that must come first, before either story or plot.

Yet, this is not to say that James's own view of the centrality of character is wholly at odds with Aristotle's. Notice that he refers to characters in this context as 'agents'—that is, as actors engaged in the action of the 'fable'. Aristotle too sees story, plot, and character as intricately and dynamically linked. Elsewhere in the *Poetics*, Aristotle insists that mimetic art represents 'people in action' (*Poetics* 2.1448a 29) and this key principle informs Aristotle's treatment of both plot and character (*Poetics* 6.1449b 35–1450a 5):

> Tragedy represents action and is acted by actors, who must necessarily have certain qualities of character and thought—for it is these which determine the quality of their actions; thought and character are the natural causes of any action and it is in virtue of these that all men either succeed or fail.

Albeit without the same interest in or recognition of the interrelation of character and plot, James also sees an inextricable link between character and action:[13]

> What is character but the determination of incident? What is incident but the illustration of character? What is either a picture or a novel that is *not* of character?

> ... It is an incident for a woman to stand up with her hand resting on a table and look out at you in a certain way; or if it be not an incident, I think it will be hard to say what it is. At the same time it is an expression of character.

Unexpectedly, perhaps, James also shares Aristotle's views on the best 'kinds' of characters to employ in the novel. Aristotle, throughout both his *Poetics* and *Rhetoric*, had privileged representations of familiar and universal character types over the representation of unique psychological personalities. He had even recommended that characters be drawn from a small pool of great mythological families (*Poetics* 13.1453a 18–22). James too claims to prefer character 'types', declaring in *The Art of the Novel*: ' "Kinds" are the very life of literature', repeatedly emphasizing the value of examining the universal through minute study of an individual 'great'.[14] As Blackmur explains:[15]

> Being concerned with the tragedies of the high intelligence and the drama of the socially and intellectually great (much as the old tragedies dealt death to kings

---

[13] James 1894: 392. Cf. Scholes and Kellogg 2006: 160.
[14] James 1937: 111.
[15] Blackmur in James and Blackmur 1937: xx, emphasis in original.

and heroes) he argues for using the *type* of the historical and contemporary great and against using the actual historical or contemporary figure.

It is impossible to determine the precise extent to which James draws his own rules on the art of the novel from Aristotle's *Poetics*—if at all. James's precepts on realism, action, and character may be Aristotelian, quasi-Aristotelian, or pseudo-Aristotelian. Yet the parallels—whether coincidental or otherwise—can help to cast light upon some of the nuances and *aporiae* of Aristotle's proto-narratology. For example, Aristotle argued that 'the poet should speak as little as possible in his own voice, since this is not mimetic' (*Poetics* 24.1460a 7–8), praising Homer in particular for allowing his characters rather than his narrator to take centre stage in his 'dramatic' epics. James argues that the focal 'centre' of a novel should be a character rather than a narrator figure. Reflecting his own narrative practice, James prefers a character (through whose eyes the reader sees and learns) rather than a narrator (who tells) to provide the central point of focalization in a novel.[16] This preference may help us to better appreciate one of the more contentious observations that Aristotle makes in the *Poetics*, when he complains that non-Homeric epic poets 'play a part/act as themselves throughout their poems and only occasionally and briefly try *mimesis*' (*Poetics* 24.1460a 8–9): all the extant evidence indicates that this is nonsense. But perhaps, like James, we might see Aristotle's privileging of character over narrator speech as marking a preference for character over narrator focalization and a character-based centre for the (mimetic) presentation of the narrative. In which case, it may be particularly apt that James designates such character-focalizers as narrative 'mirrors' and 'reflectors'—that is, as the agents through which the reader accesses the novel's storyworld *mimesis*.

James's notes on his own successes and failures regarding the mimetic re-presentation of his characters as universal 'types' can also help to illuminate Aristotle's notes in the *Poetics* concerning 'universalism' and its merits.[17] Aristotle claims that poetry, in contrast with history, deals with 'the universal' (*katholou*). The universal equips an audience with the knowledge that a leads to b, that x causes y, and that in the plot of Homer's *Iliad* Achilles' anger is likely—'in accordance with probability

---

[16] In this context, James's writings provide us with one of the earliest considerations (in English) of point of view in narrative. Admittedly, when James uses the formulation 'point of view' he is typically pointing to writerly opinion or attitude, but he does discuss—albeit, not under these rubrics—what modern narratologists would recognize as 'focalization' or POV.

[17] See Leonard 2015 on the 'universal' humanism(s) of tragic narratives and their reception.

or necessity'—to result in death and tragedy. The universal is also, therefore, what prepares an audience to experience suspense and relief, pity and fear, through their anticipation of what Achilles' words and actions (and those of the *Iliad*'s wider cast of agents) are likely to bring about. As Heath points out:[18]

to recognise a tragic plot as an imitation of what would happen in accordance with necessity or probability, we must know what would happen necessarily or probably. It seems, therefore, that the cognitive processes involved in the grasp of poetic action presuppose an understanding of the world, rather than producing it.

James's theories on the role of the universal in narrative fiction follow this same line of reasoning but make a further Aristotelian connection. Critiquing his own character, Roderick Hudson, and his own failure to fully secure the reader's 'understanding' and 'sympathy' in this characterization, James suggests:[19]

The very claim of the fable is naturally that he [Roderick] is special, that his great gift makes and keeps him highly exceptional; but that is not for a moment supposed to preclude his appearing typical (of the general type) as well; for the fictive hero successfully appeals to us only as an eminent instance, as eminent as we like, of our own conscious kind.

James has, it seems, either interpreted or intuited Aristotle's recommendation that characters should not only be of eminent and universal types, but that they should be 'like us' (*Poetics* 2.1448a 5–6). Elsewhere, James talks of the 'truth and strength' that comes from 'the complete recognition' of such 'kinds' on the part of the reader.[20] These observations—regardless of their actual Aristotelian provenance—help our further recognition that Aristotle's emphasis upon the universality of poetry has wide-reaching implications for his *Poetics*. The universal or *katholou* impacts upon our narratological understanding of Aristotle's precepts on character and characterization (*ethos*), on the probability (*eikos*) and necessity (*anangke*) of their actions, and thus on the plausibility of plot. It also aids our understanding of Aristotle's intuitions regarding the cognitive processing of plots by an audience and the ways in which effects such as tension and relief, and affects such as pity, fear, and sympathy, might be achieved by the narrative. That is, by playing

---

[18] Heath 1991: 13.

[19] James 1937: 12. James also considers 'type' of place (8), reminding us that this is something Aristotle overlooks in his own consideration of 'types'.

[20] James 1937: 111.

upon the audience's pre-existing experiences and understanding of the universe and its universals.

8.3 **Percy Lubbock**

We encounter several of James's theories of narrative reworked and refined by his friend Percy Lubbock, whose still influential study *The Craft of Fiction* (first published in 1921) sets out to organize the Jamesian 'art' of fiction into a more methodological and technical 'craft'. Although this shift in emphasis upon the form and technique of narrative is broadly in line with Aristotelian ideas of poetic *techne*, and although Lubbock shares with both James and Aristotle a preference for the dramatic mode of narrative presentation, the tenets of Lubbock's central theory turn out to be more closely aligned with those of Plato's (Socratic) poetics than Aristotle's *Poetics*.

Lubbock derives several of his key terms from James ('scene', 'panorama', 'reflector') and also adopts several of James's quasi-Aristotelian values, notably: consistency in characterization; unity and singularity of form; the ordered arrangement of story stuff into narrative; and the relative importance of action over that of characters and their inner lives.[21] So, echoing Aristotle on the relative tiered values of *praxis*, *ethos*, and *dianoia*, Lubbock suggests: 'That is what the [novel] is to show— action essentially, not the picture of a character or a state of mind.'[22]

This last 'Aristotelianism' is particularly significant because its hierarchical ordering of action over character and state of mind is ostensibly at odds with the position that Lubbock leads us towards in the rest of his work. For Lubbock, as for Aristotle and James, action is certainly important and the dramatic mode of story presentation is unequivocally the best: 'other things being equal, the more dramatic way is better than the less', Lubbock maintains.[23] But he ultimately rejects the primacy of action and the purely action-based 'dramatic method' of narrative presentation on the grounds that this involves unacceptable sacrifices in terms of restricted access to the interiority of characters and

---

[21] See Lubbock 2014: 29 on consistency; 23 on unity and singularity of form; 62–3 on the ordered arrangement of story; 134 on the primacy of action.

[22] See Lubbock 2014: 98. Cf. 80–4 on 'images of thought... expressing the story in their [the characters'] behaviour'.

[23] Lubbock 2014: 76.

their thoughts. In his final chapter, he concludes that the dramatic story is:[24]

> limited to so much as the ear can hear and the eye see. In rigid drama of this kind there is naturally no admission of the reader into the private mind of any of the characters; their thoughts and motives are transmuted into action ... [I]t is not a form to which fiction can aspire in general.

The formula privileging 'action over character over state of mind' which attracts Lubbock in theory (as supporting his preferences for dramatic presentation of the story; for 'showing' over 'telling') proves too restrictive in practice. Indeed, given Lubbock's Jamesian preferences for a mixed mode of narration which is presented sometimes from an authorial narrator's perspective and sometimes from a character's point of view (*pace* James's 'reflector' characters), his ultimate rejection of the purely dramatic mode is unsurprising. Such a mixed mode offers the reader access to the subjective thoughts and feelings of characters, but without forgoing the more objective commentary of a narrator.

In Lubbock's theory of narrative poetics, then, we can see a closer affinity to Plato's (Socratic) narratology than to Aristotle's. Lubbock's formal distinction between telling and showing, between 'pictorial' and 'dramatic' modes of narration, between 'summary' and 'scene', recalls Plato's parallel distinctions in his *Republic* between 'diegetic' and 'mimetic' forms of narrative. For Plato, as we saw, 'narration (*diegesis*) may be either simple narration, or imitation, or a mixture of the two' (*Republic* 3.392d). Lubbock, who is familiar with a much wider range of diegetic fiction than Plato, introduces a fourth type of narration to this tripartite model: (1) third-person authorial (akin to Plato's *haple diegesis*, or what modern narratologists would recognize as heterodiegetic) narration; (2) first-person (what modern narratologists would recognize as homodiegetic) narration; (3) third-person narration blended with the point of view of a central 'reflector' character (akin to Plato's *diegesis di' amphoteron*); and (4) purely dramatic narration (akin to Plato's *diegesis dia mimeseos*).

Lubbock's model is ostensibly crafted according to the foundational principle of point of view—ranked according to the relative degree of (im)mediacy determined by 'who sees' (an 'impersonal' narrator, a 'personal' character-narrator, both narrator and character, or characters only). But his four categories are equally determined by 'who speaks'. So, he defines his character-narrator point of view as 'telling the story in the first person ... [where] the characterized "I" is substituted for the loose

---

[24] Lubbock 2014: 127.

and general "I" of the author'.[25] Similarly, he defines the mixed mode as that in which: 'Sometimes the author is talking with his own voice, sometimes he is talking through one of the people in the book.'[26]

Again, echoes of Plato talking through Socrates can be plainly heard here. Socrates' distinction in *Republic* 3.392e–393b between simple and mimetic narrative is based upon voice: the narrator speaks in his own voice and produces simple narration; or he imitates the voice of a character speaking as if he were someone else and produces mimetic narration; or he shifts back and forth between the two. This is not to say that Lubbock is necessarily familiar with this passage in the *Republic*, or that his binaries 'telling and showing' or 'summary and scene' map perfectly onto Plato's *diegesis* and *mimesis*. They don't. But the fact that we can see both Aristotelian and Platonic/Socratic principles and intuitions paralleled and refined in Lubbock's writing is significant in aiding our understanding of how these ancient narratological intuitions find their way into twentieth- and twenty-first-century theories of narrative. The quasi-Platonic and quasi-Aristotelian tenor of Lubbock's critical theory helps to render the ideas of these ancient narratologists always already familiar. Whether or not Lubbock (or James) derived any actual influence from the *Republic* or *Poetics*, the like-mindedness or *homophrosyne* that we witness in the treatment of core narratological motifs asserts its own dynamic of reception here.

8.4 **E. M. Forster**

While the 'Aristotelianism' found in James and Lubbock was unacknowledged as such, in the series of lectures that comprise his *Aspects of the Novel*, E. M. Forster places the *Poetics* very squarely in his sights.[27] And he does not hesitate to pull the trigger.[28] Aristotle gets both barrels in Forster's famous discussion of character and, in Forster's view, Aristotle's wrongheaded views thereon:[29]

"Character," says Aristotle, "gives us qualities, but it is in actions—what we do— that we are happy or the reverse." We have already decided that Aristotle is

---

[25] Lubbock 2014: 65.   [26] Lubbock 2014: 36.

[27] For Forster's reception of Lubbock see especially Forster 1927: 78–9. Forster responds to James as a novelist rather than as a critic or theorist.

[28] Day 2007: 223 similarly suggests (although without developing the point) that 'Forster formulates his views about the novel in reaction to Aristotle's *Poetics*.'

[29] Forster 1927: 83.

wrong and now we must face the consequences of disagreeing with him. "All human happiness and misery," says Aristotle, "take the form of action." We know better ... There is, however, no occasion to be hard on Aristotle. He had read few novels and no modern ones—the *Odyssey* but not *Ulysses*... and when he wrote the words quoted above he had in view the drama, where no doubt they hold true.

Forster's criticisms are based not on allusions to a received Aristotelian tradition, but on a key passage from the *Poetics* (6.1450a 16–21) and its specific rendering in Bywater's contemporary translation, from which Forster quotes here:[30]

Tragedy is essentially an imitation not of persons but of action and life, of happiness and misery. All human happiness or misery takes the form of action; the end for which we live is a certain kind of activity, not a quality. Temperament gives us our personal qualities, but it is in our actions—what we do—that we are happy or the reverse. In a play accordingly they do not act in order to portray temperament; they include temperament for the sake of the action. So that it is the action in it, that is, its plot, that is the end and purpose of the tragedy; and the purpose is everywhere the chief thing. Besides this, a tragedy is impossible without action, but tragedy does not have to represent the inner qualities of characters—their respective temperaments.

Bywater translates Aristotle's *ethos* (character or characterization) as both 'character' and 'temperament' here. What is more, he uses both terms to interpret Aristotle's controversial claim (literally) that 'there could be tragedy without character' (*Poetics* 6.1450a 24) as a more subtle point about tragedy's option to represent or not to represent the inner lives of its characters. In this reading and translation, Aristotle's much-debated claim that 'character' is inessential to drama is made to accord with rather than to contradict his core principle that drama represents 'people in action' (*Poetics* 2.1448a 29).[31] The logical consistency offered by this interpretation is attractive. It also helps us to appreciate why Aristotle insists in his parallel discussion of character in epic that (*Poetics* 24.1460a 5–11): 'Homer after a brief prelude/proem/preamble at once brings onstage a man or a woman or some other figure/character (*ethos*)—none of whom are lacking in character (*aethe*) but who all possess character (*ethos*).' If *ethos* means for Aristotle both 'character'

[30] Bywater (1909) translates Aristotle's technical term *muthos* with a twinned alternative as 'Fable or Plot'. A second edition is issued in 1920 with a preface by Gilbert Murray who steers readers towards the second term, noting that Aristotle uses the word *muthos* 'practically [sc. *but not quite*] in the sense of "plot"'.

[31] Other translations of the *Poetics* foster an internal contradiction between the precepts of *Poetics* 6.1450a 24 and 2.1448a 29: cf. *ad loc* Butcher 1955, Bywater 1909, Fyfe 1927, Else 1957, Hardison and Golden 1968, Janko 1987, and Halliwell 1999.

and 'personality' or 'temperament', then his points regarding Homer's characterful characters take on greater narratological significance.[32] Restricted (as he appears to be here) by the technical lexicon at his disposal, Aristotle is not making contradictory or redundant claims about characterful characters in Homeric epic. He is making an important point about what an audience sees or does not (need to) see in and through the characters represented in drama and epic. He is making an important point about point of view.

True, Aristotle is more interested in action than in character: in his model, 'temperament' or psychology drives agents to action and reaction which, in turn, drives the plot. A drama (or epic narrative) must have agents in order to have action in order to have plot, but an audience need not have access to the psychological forces motivating those agents into action. However, we should remember that Aristotle identifies *dianoia* (the representation of character 'thought' in order to 'demonstrate or declare a view': *Poetics* 6.1450a 5–6) as the third key component of tragedy, following plot and character in order of importance. Therefore Forster is quite justified in seeing Aristotle's treatment of character, *pace* Bywater, as concerning not only the mechanics of plot but also the dynamics of its presentation: that is, the viewpoint through which an audience witnesses a set of agents act out a plot and work through what Forster describes (with unusual praise for the *Poetics*) as 'the triple process of complication, crisis, and solution so persuasively expounded by Aristotle'.[33]

Indeed, this interpretation emerges even more clearly as Forster continues his critique of Aristotle, contrasting the restrictions facing the dramatist and the options facing the novelist when it comes to focalization:[34]

The speciality of the novel is that the writer can talk about his characters as well as through them ... [where] all that matters to the reader is whether the shifting of attitude and the secret life are convincing, whether it is πιθανόν [persuasive, plausible] in fact, and with his favourite word ringing in his ears Aristotle may retire.

---

[32] See Gill 1986 and 1998 on the distinctions between 'character' and 'personality'.

[33] Forster 1927: 85.

[34] Forster 1927: 84. The influence of Lubbock is also at work here. Forster has already summarized the thesis of Lubbock's *Craft of Fiction* (1927: 78) thus: the 'novelist, he says, can either describe the characters from outside, as an impartial or partial onlooker; or he can assume omniscience and describe them from within; or he can place himself in the position of one of them and affect to be in the dark as to the motives of the rest; or there are certain intermediate attitudes'. Forster himself questions the significance of point of view (1927: 79–80).

Forster's emphasis upon consistency and plausibility in this consideration of point of view in the novel demonstrates an obvious affinity with the core principles of the *Poetics*—despite focusing upon a narratological phenomenon that is barely touched upon by Aristotle. In fact, Forster's retirement of Aristotle at this juncture proves to be somewhat premature. For, as he turns his lecture from the subject of character towards the topic of plot, Aristotelian principles once more come to the fore.

In his consideration of the processes by which a writer selects and shapes his raw material into a meaningful novel, Forster identifies three stages: the development of 'story', of 'plot', and of 'pattern' (which further embraces 'rhythm').[35] At the level of 'story' the presentation of material is structured chronologically: story represents sequential or episodic narrative, 'the chopped-off length of the tapeworm of time'.[36] Indeed, Forster's definitions of story correspond closely with narratological definitions of *fabula*—described by Prince, we recall, as 'the set of narrated situations and events in their chronological sequence; the basic story material (as opposed to plot or *syuzhet*)'.[37] Plot, on the other hand, introduces causality to that basic chronolinear arrangement:[38]

> Let us define a plot. We have defined a story as a narrative of events arranged in their time-sequence. A plot is also a narrative of events, the emphasis falling on causality. "The king died and then the queen died" is a story. "The king died, and then the queen died of grief" is a plot. The time-sequence is preserved, but the sense of causality overshadows it. Or again: "The queen died, no one knew why, until it was discovered that it was through grief at the death of the king." This is a plot with a mystery in it, a form capable of high development.

Aristotle's distinction between simple and complex plots reappears here as a distinction between the simple, chronolinear, story and the more complex, temporal-causal plot. In the *Poetics*, Aristotle had advised that the incidents and actions making up a plot should not be linked by mere temporal succession but be motivated by probable or necessary cause (*Poetics* 9.1451a 35–7). He insisted that the actions that make up a coherent, unified, plot 'should be the necessary or probable result of the preceding action' since 'it makes all the difference whether any given event is a case of *propter hoc* or *post hoc*' (*Poetics* 10.1452a 18–21). It is not enough for Aristotle or Forster that events merely follow each other in temporal (*post hoc*) sequence; there must be a causal (*propter hoc*) connection between them because, from the audience's perspective, this

---

[35] Forster 1927: 36 also refers to the 'pre-story' to denote the flashback sequence in which characters fill in some of the plot's backstory.

[36] Forster 1927: 85. [37] Prince 2003: *s.vv.* [38] Forster 1927: 86.

arrangement is more artistic and more affective. In Aristotle's terms, this form of plot structure appeals to the audience's sense of wonder. In Forster's terms, it appeals to the reader's intellect. And if this temporal-causal arrangement is also well formed, it will produce a narrative 'pattern' which further appeals to the reader's sense of beauty. Thus: 'Whereas the story appeals to our curiosity and the plot to our intelligence, the pattern appeals to our aesthetic sense, it causes us to see the book as a whole.'[39]

There is nothing dealing with Forster's model of 'pattern' in precisely these terms in the *Poetics*, but in his discussions of the requisite qualities and patterns that make a plot well constructed (*sunestotas*) it may be significant that Aristotle saw the most important of these as 'wholeness' (*Poetics* 7.1450b 25–34). What is more, an appreciation of such 'wholeness' was, for Aristotle, precisely what enables us to see the 'beauty' (*kalon*) of a good plot and a well-ordered narrative.

Forster's lectures on the novel, then, do not simply follow Aristotle's lectures on poetry in a temporal sequence of reception (*post hoc*). There is a clear causal (*propter hoc*) connection between them. A connection, moreover, which firmly establishes the *Poetics* as part of the 'pattern' of modern narratology.

8.5 **Norman Friedman**

The sum of Norman Friedman's contribution to the history of narratology is far greater than his two slender articles on point of view and forms of plot, respectively, might suggest. His influence on Stanzel and more recently on Schmid on the subject of perspective is particularly significant.[40] What is more, Friedman acknowledges his own influences as deriving from two important and interrelated sources: from Plato and Aristotle, and from the neo-Aristotelians Olson and Crane.[41] Friedman's

---

[39] Forster 1927: 150.

[40] See Stanzel 1955 and 1984, and Schmid 2010.

[41] See in particular Friedman 1967, where he notes his indebtedness to the Chicago school, especially to Olson and Crane's definitions of 'scene', 'speech', 'story', and 'plot' (149 n. 4). Friedman owes his categorization of plot types (plots of 'fortune', 'character', and 'thought') directly to Crane. Cf. Crane 1950: 66: 'we may say that the plot of any novel or drama is the particular temporal synthesis effected by the writer of the elements of action, character, and thought that constitute the matter of his invention . . . and it follows also that plots will differ in structure according as one or another of the three causal ingredients is employed as the synthesizing principle. There are, thus, plots of action, plots of character, and plots of thought.'

work thus represents a key nodal point in the reception and transmission of ancient theories of narrative, helping to establish the authority of the *Republic* and *Poetics*, in particular, in questions of plot and point of view.

As might be anticipated from Friedman's admiration for the emerging Chicago school, Aristotle's *Poetics* plays a major role in his essay on forms of plot. For Friedman, as for Aristotle, 'the important thing about a literary work is not the story it tells' but its arrangement into 'an organic whole'; 'the principle of unity which governs the selection and arrangement of parts'; 'the crucial chain of cause and effect leading [the protagonist] from one condition to another'.[42] Such a plot in Friedman's model, again evoking Aristotle's key tenets, must also be formed in accordance with 'the necessary and the probable' if it is to be 'intelligible, vivid, and moving' and so achieve its proper purpose, which is to achieve a particular emotional effect upon and affect within its audience.[43]

Indeed, it is this emotional audience reaction which Friedman identifies as the key to classifying different forms of plot. In his *Poetics*, Aristotle had considered in detail only the simple and complex forms of tragic and epic plots, focusing upon the type of character, the type of transformation, and the audience affect presented in different genres.[44] Friedman, synthesizing both Crane and Aristotle, determines that these principles ought to apply to more nuanced categorizations of form than that of genre alone, on the basis that:[45]

a good man achieving good fortune, a good man suffering bad fortune, a bad man achieving good fortune, and a bad man suffering bad fortune … produce different effects and therefore comprise different kinds of plots.

He goes on to define and describe fourteen different forms of plot under three category headings: plots of 'fortune', comprising action plots, pathetic plots, tragic plots, punitive plots, sentimental plots, and admiration plots; plots of 'character', comprising the maturing plot, reform plot, testing plot, and degeneration plot; and plots of 'thought', comprising education plots, revelation plots, affective plots, and disillusionment plots. These categories and their sub-groups are obviously contentious.[46] Friedman's tripartite distinction between plots of 'fortune', 'character', and 'thought' attempts to squeeze the entire Western canon of narrative literature (from Sophocles' *Oedipus*, through Shakespeare's *Richard III* and Dickens's *Great Expectations*, to Roald Dahl's *Beware of the Dog*)

---

[42] Friedman 1967: 146.   [43] Friedman 1967: 152.

[44] Aristotle, *Poetics* 10.1452a 13–17.

[45] Friedman 1967: 157. Cf. Aristotle, *Poetics* 13.1452b 27–1453a 10.

[46] Chatman 1978: 88 is among those sceptical of Friedman's classifications.

into pigeonholes that are necessarily constrictive. Nevertheless, this focus upon three distinctively Aristotelian features of narrative—fortune (akin to *peripeteia*), character (*ethos*), and thought (*dianoia*)—illustrate the rich potential in the appropriation of Aristotle's theory of poetry and its application to a narrative form undreamt of in his philosophy: the novel.

And this matters, because Friedman's appropriation is not merely a borrowing, but a nuanced development of Aristotle's framework. Aristotle had treated the core component parts of a tragedy as comprising plot (*muthos*—the emplotted action or *praxis*), character (*ethos*), and thought (*dianoia*). But Aristotle made only a limited investigation into how these component parts might work *together* to achieve tragedy's particular *telos*, inspiring its audiences to experience feelings of pity and terror. In his analysis, Friedman fixes this. He shows that Aristotle's emphasis upon the meaningful arrangement or *sunthesis* of plot parts can be applied to other parts of narrative—(change of) fortune, character, and thought—too. He can then go on to demonstrate that it is through the mutual interaction of these phenomena that the final form of a narrative plot is determined. Efficient cause and final cause complement each other, with any one of these three elements ultimately dominating the dynamics of the plot and so characterizing its effect and its form.

The effect of a plot upon its audience (one of the principal interests of the Chicago school) is also a prominent concern in Friedman's work on narrative point of view. And once again, Friedman begins his own analysis by historicizing the phenomenon. He suggests that the study of perspective or point of view has an ancient history, rooted in classical rhetoric.[47] In fact he traces the origins of this concept back to Plato's *Republic* and the distinction drawn there by Socrates:[48]

between "simple narration" on the one hand and "imitation" on the other. When the poet speaks in the person of another we may say that he assimilates his style to that person's manner of talking; this assimilation of himself to another, either by the use of voice or gesture, is an imitation of the person whose character he assumes. But, if the poet everywhere appears and never conceals himself, then the imitation is dropped and his poetry becomes simple narration.

As this synthesis of Socrates' discussion of *diegesis* and *mimesis* in the *Republic* suggests, Friedman is a close reader of Plato's ancient theory of narrative. He even notices that Plato conveniently ignores the narrative components of tragedy in his discussion of the mimetic mode—the

---

[47] Friedman 1955: 1161.
[48] Friedman 1955: 1162. He also adduces the example of Aristotle, *Poetics* 24.1460a 5–11, in Bywater's translation.

'choral comment and messenger-narration'.[49] Here Friedman recognizes
that the key distinction Plato draws is between two core modes of
narrative presentation or *diegesis*: he does not simply conflate Plato's
terms with the popular distinction between 'telling' and 'showing',
although he does subsequently introduce these topoi into his framework.
What's more, Friedman's perceptive reading of Plato's (Socratic) preference for simple over mimetic narration appropriately identifies the
grounds of that partiality as rooted in the intuition that simple narrative
offers a more effective—if not affective—mode of story presentation than
the mimetic because it can claim access to the widest frame of perspective, the widest 'angle of view' in Friedman's terms. In the haplodiegetic
or heterodiegetic mode, the narrator does not pretend to be anyone else,
but he or she does pretend to be capable of knowing and seeing
everything—a position which Friedman terms narratorial 'omniscience'
(which may be 'editorial' or 'neutral').

Following Plato's example in the *Republic* (where Socrates 'rewrites' a
scene from Homer's *Iliad*: *Republic* 3.392e–393b—discussed in Chapter 2)
Friedman rewrites a couple of passages from Hardy's *Tess of the D'Urber-
villes* to show the key differences in these two modes, stressing the
narratorial option to offer a distanced external perspective in which events
and descriptions are '*narrated* indirectly as if they have already occurred—
discussed, analyzed, and explained'; or to offer an internal character's
more immediate point of view in which events and descriptions are
'presented *scenically* as if they were occurring now'.[50] These illustrations
help Friedman to show that it is perspective (rather than dialogue, as
Plato's Socrates sees it) which is the marker between (simple) 'narrative'
and what Friedman terms (immediate) 'scene'.[51]

Friedman's crucial distinction between 'narrative' and 'scene', then, is
configured as a direct response and correction to the distinction between
simple and mimetic narration articulated in Plato's *Republic*. Following
Plato's own theory and methodology, Friedman persuasively refocuses
our attention away from the question of 'who speaks?' and towards the
question of 'who sees—and how?' in the presentation of a story, to
conclude that it is not voice but viewpoint which determines the affectivity of a narrative—its mediacy or immediacy, its narrative or scenic
quality. Friedman's neo-Aristotelian sympathies ultimately—and
appropriately—lead him back to Plato.

---

[49] Friedman 1955: 1162. Aristotle makes the same oversight in his *Poetics*.
[50] Friedman 1955: 1173, emphases in original.
[51] Friedman 1955: 1169–70.

8.6 **Franz Stanzel**

Franz Stanzel's work pulls together the several narratological strands of his predecessors into a much more systematic theory; a theory, moreover, not merely of the novel but now distinctively of narrative.[52] He draws his influences from a varied pool: he cites James, Lubbock, Forster, and Friedman as shaping his views on mediacy, and Hamburger's work on narrative function and Lämmert's theories of narrative temporality as informing his related thinking on narrative situations.[53]

However, it is Plato whom Stanzel repeatedly identifies as the key authority providing the 'conceptual nucleus' of his own theory and typology of narrative.[54] In his refinements to various prestructuralist theories of narratorial mediacy (the variables attending first-/third-person narration; internal/external point of view; and telling/showing, etc.), Stanzel explicitly configures his own approach as something of a return to 'the beginnings of literary theory' and to the basic distinctions between *diegesis* and *mimesis* ostensibly found in Plato's *Republic*.

Plato's Socrates, as we saw, identified three key types of narrative discourse based upon whether a poet-narrator speaks directly in his own voice (*haple diegesis*); whether he imitates and dramatizes the voice of a character and speaks as if he were that character (*diegesis dia mimeseos*); or whether his voice alternates between these two modes (*diegesis di' amphoteron*).[55] For Stanzel, too, it is not 'how' a story is narrated that matters so much as 'who' narrates it. Downgrading the primacy of labels such as scene and summary, showing and telling, Stanzel therefore proposes:[56]

to shift the emphasis of [narrative] definition from the textual categories (scene, summary) to the agents of transmission (teller, reflector)... whether a personalized narrator (teller-character) or a figural medium (reflector-character) serves as the agent through which the narrated events reach the reader.

Like Plato's Socrates, Stanzel concludes that there are three key modes of narration, one 'reportlike', one 'scenic', and one 'hybrid'. What's more, he maintains that the distinctions between these three modes 'can be

---

[52] See Cohn 1978, Genette 1988, and Chatman 1990 for critiques of Stanzel.

[53] See Hamburger 1973 in which she draws an important category distinction between third-person narration ('epic' or 'mimetic fiction') and first-person narration (a 'feigned reality statement'); and Lämmert 1967 in which he attempts a comprehensive taxonomy of narrative types predicated on their treatment of temporality.

[54] Stanzel's bibliography for *A Theory of Narrative* (1984) includes Plato's *Republic*, but not Aristotle's *Poetics*.

[55] Plato, *Republic* 3.392d.   [56] Stanzel 1955: 6.

reduced to one basic difference: the author's presence in or absence from the narrative'.[57] In a voice strongly reminiscent of Plato's Socrates, Stanzel reminds us that when 'the author withdraws behind his characters' we find that 'the reader no longer faces a narrator *in persona*; as in a play the reader seems to find himself before a scene'.[58] It is, therefore, primarily the absence or presence of the author-narrator (over and above any textual phenomena such as description or direct speech) which determines the 'type' of narrative discourse—or, as Stanzel describes it, the type of 'narrative situation'.

This typology allows Stanzel to develop his elegant 'typological circle', which places three possible 'narrative situations'—the first-person, authorial, and figural—around a continuum. In the first-person narrative situation, the events are related by a 'narrating and experiencing I', a 'teller-character' who offers a predominantly internal perspective with a necessarily limited point of view. The authorial narrative situation is typified, in contrast, by the presence of a third-person teller-character and the dominance of an external and omniscient perspective. And the third, figural narrative situation is characterized by the dominance of the (Jamesian) 'reflector-character' mode, offering a restricted point of view but able to offer both external and internal perspectives.

Underpinning the nodes of separation and intersection at each point around Stanzel's narratological compass is the understanding that *diegesis* and *mimesis* 'evoke different attitudes of spatio-temporal orientation in the reader'.[59] In Homeric epic, for example, the narrator or teller-character is (for the most part) temporally and spatially distanced from the narrative and its events, and the audience experience the same levels of spatio-temporal distance. In Greek tragedy, on the other hand, the 'experiencing characters' are much closer to the action in both time and space, and, again, the audience share similar levels of spatio-temporal immediacy and nearness to the drama.

However, Stanzel intentionally avoids contrasting the novel with drama in terms of narrative (im)mediacy, just as he carefully avoids privileging one narrative situation, person, perspective, or mode, over any other.[60] The compass of his 'typological circle' (despite diagrammatically orienting the 'teller-character' as the equivalent of north and the 'reflector-character'

---

[57] Stanzel 1955: 23. Stanzel is careful to insist here that 'Presence and absence are not taken here in the epistemological sense... They refer to the author's visibility in the narrative or to his withdrawal behind the fictional world.'

[58] Stanzel 1955: 163. Elsewhere (Stanzel 1984: 143), he distinguishes between the 'personalization and impersonalization of the narrative process'. Cf. Plato, *Republic* 3.392e–393b.

[59] Stanzel 1984: 66.   [60] See Stanzel 1984: 244 n. 2.

as south) imposes no obvious hierarchy and presupposes no preference for any particular narrative form. In fact, the circular spectrum of narrative possibilities that Stanzel's circle inscribes stresses the porosity of its key boundary 'distinctions' and the potential for overlap between them. Stanzel's 'circle' thus helps to illustrate that *mimesis* and *diegesis* are not—and never were—part of a binary system. Plato's Socrates may have used his narrative typology ostensibly to argue for the ethical superiority of *diegesis* over *mimesis*. Or, rather, for 'plain', 'unmixed', or 'simple' (*haple*) *diegesis* over 'mimetic' (*dia mimeseos*) *diegesis*. But Stanzel's reception of that typology reminds us that the *Republic* ultimately presents us with a sliding scale of more or less ethically acceptable forms of both *mimesis* and *diegesis*, determined by the degree to which the author-narrator is more or less present and visible in the narrative—and the concomitant distance or nearness of that mediating narratorial presence.[61] Like Stanzel's tripartite 'typological circle' of narrative situations, Plato's typology of narrative discourse is similarly plotted upon a spectrum of diegetic possibilities.

8.7 *Teleute*

The 'prestructuralists' are very far from representing the close-knit community of critics and theorists we find working under the banners of Russian formalism and neo-Aristotelianism. Yet their ideas about the form and function of key narratological phenomena such as plot, action, and character—and their preferences for *mimesis* over *diegesis*, showing over telling—make a significant contribution to the early twentieth-century (re)naissance of narrative theory in Europe and the US. Among this disparate group, James and Lubbock evince only indefinite Aristotelian affinities, but their precepts—whether or not influenced by ancient poetics—help to establish an environment in which Aristotelian and Platonic (Socratic) theories find a ready and receptive audience. On the other hand, Forster adopts a decidedly anti-Aristotelian stance, but his work similarly helps prepare the ground on which subsequent theorists and critics are able to build. The prestructuralists, then, play a major role in opening up a channel of communication between the ancient and modern worlds of narratology, through which ideas can freely flow.

---

[61] Plato, *Republic* 3.396c–e.

9 Structuralism

> *Recognition* (anagnorisis) *and change* (peripeteia)...*follow on as
> the necessary or probable result of the preceding action.*
>
> Aristotle, *Poetics* 10.1452a 16–20

9.1 *Arche*

The structuralist turn in narratology is famously inaugurated by the
publication of a special edition of the French journal *Communications*
in 1966, featuring contributions from Roland Barthes, Algirdas Greimas,
Claude Bremond, Umberto Eco, Tzvetan Todorov, Gérard Genette, and
the film theorist Christian Metz. In contrast to their 'formalist' predecessors (from whom they import the key concepts of *fabula* and *syuzhet*—
now broadly reformulated as *histoire* and *discours*), the 'structuralists' saw
themselves as part of a close circle, explicitly engaged in the collective
endeavour of the 'structural analysis of narrative' (*l'analyse structurale du
récit*).[1] They repeatedly emphasize not only the mutuality of their individual 'structural' approaches, but their common indebtedness to 'structural' anthropology and to 'structural' linguistics.[2] The influence of the
structuralist linguistic paradigm, in particular, would come to define the
structuralist project and its attempt to describe a narrative 'grammar' to
account for the structure and logic of story and its stories.

Following Saussure's crucial distinction between *langue* (the abstract
system of language, its general grammar and syntax) and *parole* (language in action, its individual speech acts), the structuralist project
initially focused its attention less upon the construction of actual stories
than upon the abstract structuration of 'story'.[3] Thus Bremond tries 'to

---

[1] See Benveniste 1966.

[2] On the defining structuralist contribution to classical narratology see Fludernik 1996,
Herman 1999, Mathieu-Colas 1986, Chatman 1978, and Prince 1995. See also Culler 1975.
See Adams 1989 and Sturgess 1989 for two particularly scathing responses to Culler's own
contributions to narratology. Like the Russian formalists, the structuralists are also influenced by the German morphological tradition, especially Hamburger 1973, Müller 1968,
and Lämmert 1967.

[3] An analogous use of these distinctions between *langue* and *parole* appears in Lévi-
Strauss's work on myth (1955), in which an individual instantiation of a myth (e.g.

reconstruct the syntax of human behavior as exemplified in narrative, to trace the succession of "choices" which this or that character inevitably has to face at various points in the story'.[4] And Greimas proposes 'to describe and sort out characters in narrative not on the basis of what they are but on the basis of what they do (hence the name of actants), inasmuch as they partake in three main semantic axes, which incidentally have their replica in the sentence (subject/object, attributive clause, circumstantial clause)'.[5] Todorov and Barthes, as we will see, similarly base their theories of narrative upon the principle that stories are structured according to the same syntactical patterns and using the same semantic units as the sentences which form them. And it is not until Genette takes Proust's novel, *À la recherche du temps perdu*, as the central case study for his pioneering *Narrative Discourse*, that narrative *langue* and *parole* are effectively considered together.

Indeed, what distinguishes the work of Genette—and, to a lesser degree, Todorov and Barthes—from that of his structuralist peers is a greater willingness to recognize that narrative discourse is not reducible to the sum of its grammatical parts. Narrative as *langue* may function like a language, but the corollary to this metaphor is that individual narratives must function as *parole*, as speech acts performing a purposeful attempt at communication. Todorov, Barthes, and Genette take on board more fully than some of their colleagues the position of linguist Benveniste in acknowledging this important application of the narrative 'grammars' they seek to identify. In the annotated bibliography included in the special 1966 edition of *Communications*, the entry for Benveniste defines his contribution to the structuralists' narratological project thus:[6]

[Benveniste] presents several concepts of paramount importance for the theory of narrative: namely, the existence of two levels of enunciation, that of *discours* and of *histoire*. The *histoire* is "the presentation of the facts that occurred at some point in time without any intervention of the speaker in the story". The *discours*,

---

Sophocles' *Oedipus*) is distinguished from (and understood within the context of) the wider cultural schema of ancient Greek 'myth'. Fludernik 1996: 16 offers the reminder that narrative is not, however, 'a speech act in the ordinary sense'.

[4] See Barthes 1975: 252 and Bremond on 'the logic of narrative possibilities' (1966: 407). Cf. Booth 1961 on the importance of rhetoric to such poetic 'choices'.

[5] See Barthes 1975: 257 and Greimas 1983 and 1987. Brooks 1984: 14–17 offers a short synthesis of Greimas's work, emphasizing its limitations.

[6] Communications 1966: 168. On the structuralist reception and reworking of Benveniste's principles see Culler 1975: 197–200. See Kawashima 2011 on the limitations of Benveniste's linguistic model and its non-translatability to Greek or Latin texts (which do not display the same patterns of person or tense in direct and indirect discourse found in French). Benveniste's emphasis upon speakers influencing listeners here invites us to draw parallels with the rhetorically inflected narratology of the neo-Aristotelians. Cf. Chapter 7.1.

in contrast, is defined as "every utterance that assumes a speaker and a listener, and a speaker's intention to influence the listener in some way".

Benveniste's distinction between two *levels* of enunciation, *histoire* and *discours* (which Todorov pairs—rather too neatly—with the Russian formalist terms *fabula*, 'what actually happened', and *sujet*, 'what the reader reads'[7]), are signalled here as key terms of art for the structuralists. But we should not overlook the concomitant emphasis here upon a further concept 'of paramount importance for the theory of narrative': that of narrative discourse *qua* discourse—an act of communication between narrator and narratee. This emphasis reaffirms Benveniste's own somewhat muddy consideration of *discours* and *histoire* not as levels but as modes of 'enunciation': for Benveniste, the mode of *histoire* (that of 'story', for which Benveniste offers the examples of history and prose fiction) is distinguished from *discours* (best exemplified by dialogue) precisely by the occlusion of its role as interpersonal communication. Where *discours* is marked by its subjectivity and immediacy, its clear indicators of space and time, and the dynamics of a speaker and an addressee (an 'I' and a 'you'), *histoire* is marked (along with its predominant use of the third person, and the preterite and pluperfect tenses) by the absence of these features.[8] According to Benveniste, in the apersonal mode of *histoire*, 'There is in fact no longer even a narrator. The events are set forth as they occurred in the story. No one speaks here; the events seem to recount themselves.'[9]

There is a suggestive link here back to Plato's *Republic* where Socrates distinguished between those passages in Homeric epic where the poet-narrator speaks in his own voice as himself (*legei te autos*) in the mode of simple *diegesis* (*haple diegesis*), and those sections when he speaks in dialogue, in the voice of someone else (*allos tis*), in the mode of *diegesis* through *mimesis* (*Republic* 3.392e–393b). Despite the slight variation in emphasis, the same key point is being made by both Plato's Socrates and Benveniste, namely that narrative shifts between two fundamental registers, sometimes imitating natural speech and sometimes adopting a special storytelling manner. Although Benveniste himself does not exploit the correlation between his own model of *histoire* and *discours*

---

[7] Todorov 1966: 126. Cf. Volek 1985: 154–5 for criticisms of the structuralist appropriation of these terms.

[8] Cf. Genette's summary of Benveniste's theory (1976: 8–9).

[9] Benveniste 1966: 241. There are significant parallels between Benveniste's model of apersonal *histoire* and Lubbock 2014: 58 (emphases added): 'Certainly [Maupassant] is "telling" us things, but they are things so immediate, so perceptible, that the machinery of his telling, by which they reach us, is unnoticed; *the story appears to tell itself.*'

and that of Socrates' *diegesis* and *mimesis*, the structuralists do pick up on the connection and use it as another link in the chain that they set out to forge between the new science of narratology and its ancient origins.

9.2 **Roland Barthes**

According to Barthes, Aristotle was the first structuralist narratologist:[10]

Poetics has three patrons: Aristotle (whose *Poetics* provides the first structural analysis of the levels and the parts of the tragic oeuvre), Valéry (who insisted that literature be established as an object of language), Jakobson (who calls phatic any message which emphasizes its own verbal signifier). Poetics is therefore at once very old (linked to the whole rhetorical culture of our civilization) and very new, insofar as it can today benefit from the important renewal of the sciences of language.

Barthes's own pioneering contribution to the structural analysis of narrative was first published in 1966, opening the special issue of the journal *Communications* with an induction into the principles and theory of structuralism's new grammar of narrative. Barthes makes clear in this programmatic work his indebtedness to the Russian formalists (especially to Tomashevsky and his theory of thematic 'motifs', and to Propp and his theory of narrative 'functions'), as well as to Lévi-Strauss, who had developed Propp's theories on the morphology of the Russian folktale in his structural analysis of the Oedipus myth.[11] For Barthes, these 'proto-structuralist' narratologies had firmly established the framework for his own project: confirming that all narratives share a common semiotic structure which the tools of linguistics help to identify and analyse. Proceeding on the basis that, like the sentences from which it is built, narrative discourse also 'has its units, its rules, its "grammar"', Barthes sets out a working hypothesis that narrative can be regarded as 'a large "sentence"'.[12] He therefore proposes to break down the semiotic structure of narrative into three interrelated syntactical levels: 'function' (borrowing the term from Propp and Bremond); 'action' (adapting this term from Greimas and applying it to the level of characters as agents or actants); and 'narration' (the speech act or discourse, modifying the term this time from Todorov).[13] Underpinning each of these levels we find a direct appeal to Aristotle.

---

[10] Barthes 1989: 172.   [11] Lévi-Strauss 1955.   [12] Barthes 1975: 240–1.
[13] Barthes 1975: 243.

Admittedly, Barthes does not himself draw a connection between Aristotle and his own narrative 'functions'—which he subdivides into two classes, comprising narrative units which function as 'nuclei' (the 'cardinal' functions) and units which function as 'catalyses' (the 'complementary' functions). These nuclear and catalytic functions are closely equivalent to Tomashevsky's bound and free 'motifs' respectively, as well as to Aristotle's *idion* and *epeisodia* in the *Poetics* (17.1455b 17–23).[14] Indeed, Barthes's subsequent explanation of the grammar which links these functional units together to form a coherent narrative (or, as he puts it, 'the narrative syntagm') clearly signals the Aristotelian principles governing this model.[15] Propp and Tomashevsky (already influenced by Aristotelian poetics, as we've seen) inform Barthes's primary classification of the basic units of narrative structure. But it is Aristotle who guides Barthes in his thinking through the ways in which these functional units are arranged and combined in narrative discourse, their ordered connection and relation, their emplotment and (in Aristotle's terms) their *sunthesis*.

Barthes identifies the fundamental and functional mainspring of narrativity as a 'confusion between consecutiveness and consequence, what-comes-after being read in a narrative as what-is-caused-by…a systematic application of the logical fallacy denounced by scholasticism under the formula *post hoc, ergo propter hoc*'.[16] Aristotle had already discussed this fallacy and stressed that in an effective *muthos* events should be the necessary or probable result of the preceding action (*Poetics* 10.1452a 18–21). Barthes's innovation is to realize that narrativity actively flourishes in ambiguity, in the space opened up by the question of whether or not these events are connected causally or merely temporally. He dismisses Propp's insistence upon chronological order as the governing principle of story syntax and observes that Aristotle, writing two thousand years earlier, had already noticed the importance of logical over chronological connection.[17] The crucial question posed by Aristotle as to 'whether any given event is a case of *propter hoc* or *post hoc*' thus becomes the key to Barthes's understanding of narrative emplotment.

At the level of story or *histoire*, chronology and temporal sequence dominate. At the level of plot or *discours*, causal logic and consequence dominate. In fact, it is worth noticing that, although Aristotle and

---

[14] Barthes 1975: 247–9.   [15] Barthes 1975: 251.
[16] Barthes 1975: 248. See also Prince 2003: 11 on causality: 'According to Barthes (following Aristotle), the confusion between consecutiveness and consequence, chronology and causality, constitutes perhaps the most powerful motor of NARRATIVITY.'
[17] Barthes 1975: 251.

Barthes themselves make very little of this distinction between story and plot, the fundamental separation of narrative into two interconnected discursive planes proves to be of central importance in their general understanding of how narratives work, of how the syntax and *sunthesis* of plot functions. Aristotle had ranked the key elements of poetic discourse (in order of significance) as concerning plot (*muthos*), action (*praxis*), character (*ethos*), and thought (*dianoia*), and this same order of priority is followed by Barthes. Having dealt briefly with plot under the rubric of 'function', Barthes effectively telescopes Aristotle's action, character, and thought under the single rubric of 'action'—the plane upon which characters think, plan, and act.[18] He acknowledges the partial influence here of Greimas and his Aristotelian theory of 'actants', but also recognizes the nuancing of Bremond, whose attempt to produce a narrative syntax of character behaviour focuses upon the decisive 'choices' that characters are driven to make and, crucially, to act upon in the unfolding of any narrative. Barthes further suggests that both his and Bremond's interpretation of character resembles Aristotle's *proairesis*, and the rational choice between different options and potential actions.[19] What we encounter in Barthes's discussion of 'action' then is a refinement of several different theories of character—all of which are rooted in Aristotelian poetics. Although Barthes does not accept Aristotle's view of character as something potentially divorced from action, he does accept the view that character is subordinate to action. Character becomes the vehicle through which thoughts, choices, and deliberate actions are transformed into *praxis*—that is, into action and narrative.[20]

The third of Barthes's grammatical levels is that of 'narration', and concerns the telling of the tale, the communication or speech act which motivates and codes the discourse as such. For, as Barthes insists:[21] 'a narrative cannot take place without a narrator and a listener (or reader)'.

This is one of the most important recognitions to emerge from the semiotic foundation of Barthes's structuralist narratology. The linguistic metaphor that treats narrative as a sentence writ large opens up narrative discourse to structural—and structuralist—analysis *qua* discourse in a variety of more or less interesting ways. But the wider implications of this metaphor are more interesting and significant still. For the treatment of narrative as discourse reminds us forcefully that narrative is a mode of

---

[18] Barthes 1975: 258.   [19] Barthes 1975: 252 n. 36.
[20] Barthes 1975: 256. He reminds us: 'In Aristotelian poetics, the notion of character is secondary, entirely subordinated to the notion of plot [*d'action*]. There can be fables [*fables*] without characters, according to Aristotle, but there cannot be characters without fables.'
[21] Barthes 1975: 260, emphases in original.

communication between narrator and narratee, a speech act that aims to produce a certain affect upon its recipient(s).[22]

Once again, Barthes's interest in this 'narrational' level (the communication level) looks back to ancient paradigms. In the *Republic* Plato's Socrates outlined a model of narrative which was concerned principally with the negative effects of narratives upon their audiences. In the *Poetics*, similarly, Aristotle assessed the impact of different kinds of narratives upon their audiences and was concerned with the affects produced by different types of plot. Rather than focusing upon the reception of narrative, however, Barthes centres his attention upon its senders (that is, its narrators), the signs of narratorial presence encoded in the various illocutionary acts they employ in communicating their messages—in particular, their use of 'personal' and 'apersonal' or 'impersonal' modes.[23]

In so doing, Barthes credits Plato rather than Aristotle with the original recognition of different forms of speech (or what he terms 'narrational levels') and their attendant points of view. However, in a self-conscious display of classical erudition, the terms of his subsequent analysis are actually drawn from the late antique Roman grammarian Diomedes' *Ars grammatica* rather than from Plato's *Republic*.[24] What is more, in a footnote glossing these levels, Barthes borrows directly (albeit without reference) from Diomedes, re-describing the Roman theorist's model to characterize three different levels of narration as follows:[25]

Genus activum vel imitativum (no interference with discourse on the part of the narrator: the theater, for instance); *genus ennarrativum* (the poet alone is entitled to speak: aphorisms, didactic poems); *genus commune* (a mixture of the two: the epic poem).

As it appropriates and opens up an ancient typology of narrative discourse and its late antique reception in this way, Barthes's own theory of narrative offers a particularly nice illustration of the dynamics of appropriation and reception at work in structuralist narratology. Ancient theories and theorists are adopted and adapted in order to lend authority to a nascent narratological model, to provide a genealogy, an ancient aetiology for this new 'science' of narratology.

---

[22] In this crucial respect, structuralist narratology thus shares a fundamental affinity with the rhetorically oriented narratology of the neo-Aristotelians. See Chapter 7.1.

[23] Barthes 1975: 262. Barthes seeks to divorce these modes from their conventional designation as 'first-person' (I) and 'third-person' (s/he) linguistic modes. He also discusses and dismisses James's model of character-narrators.

[24] Barthes 1975: 264.   [25] Barthes 1975: 264 n. 58.

9.3 Tzvetan Todorov

It is Tzvetan Todorov who famously coins the term 'narratology' (*narratologie*) for this new 'science' in his 1969 study *Grammaire du Décaméron*, but his contribution to the field of narrative 'poetics' (to use the term he prefers) is significantly richer and deeper than the mere naming of a nascent theory. It is Todorov, for example, who makes the narratological work of the Russian formalists readily accessible to a Western audience for the first time with his 1965 anthology *Théorie de la littérature*, translating selected works by Shklovsky, Tomashevsky, and Propp—and with his patient explication of Russian formalist theories in each of his subsequent works. One of the contributors to the landmark special edition of *Communications* in 1966, it is Todorov who, as editor of the journal *Poétique*, helps to establish structuralist poetics as a formal intellectual discipline. And it is his 1968 essay '*Qu'est-ce que le structuralisme?*' (later expanded and published as '*Poétique*') which serves to define the structuralist project and its scope.[26] It is also Todorov who fosters Dupont-Roc and Lallot in the production of their 1980 French translation of Aristotle's *Poetics*—described by one of its contemporary reviewers as 'Aristotle for the structuralist'.[27] Todorov therefore plays a pivotal part in the reception and transmission of ancient theories of narrative, both directly through his engagements with Aristotle and Plato, and indirectly through his work on the Russian formalists. Indeed, Todorov sees the Russian formalists and his own form of structuralism as explicitly 'linking up with the Aristotelian tradition which, it will be remembered, was concerned to distinguish the pertinent levels and segments of works'; he even claims that these twentieth-century narratological projects are 'closer to the spirit of the *Poetics* than were its sixteenth-century admirers, since in a sense they resume the undertaking at the same point where Aristotle left off'.[28]

This, of course, serves as a convenient valorization of the new 'science' of narratology that Todorov is consciously pioneering. In particular, he views the formalists and thence the structuralists as picking up Aristotle's narratological baton in terms of paying renewed attention to the *muthos* (that is, to the plot or *discours*). It is not the incidents themselves that are interesting to Todorov but their arrangement into a narrative, just as it is not the incidents (or *pragmata*) of tragedy or epic that are interesting to

---

[26] Translated in English under the title *Introduction to Poetics* (1981). See also his 1969 essay in English, 'Structural Analysis of Narrative'.
[27] Rees 1981.   [28] Todorov 1981: xxvi.

Aristotle but their arrangement into a plot (*Poetics* 6.1450a 3–4).[29] Todorov also stresses that narrative (*récit*) involves a mimetic representation of 'reality' and 'real life'—just as it is described in Aristotle's *Poetics* (2.1447b 29–1448a 4). Narrative, for Todorov as for Aristotle, is conceived as inherently mimetic. And, in keeping with this Aristotelian model which treats all narrative discourse as mimetic but allows that some modes and genres are more mimetic than others (in the sense that drama is overtly more mimetic than epic), Todorov goes on to argue that there are two principal modes of narrative (*récit*): 'representation and narration'.[30] He resists the straightforward association of '*représentation*' with the direct speech of characters ('*la parole des personnages (le style direct)*') and '*narration*' with the indirect speech of a narrator ('*la parole du narrateur*'), and he does not use either the term *mimesis* or *diegesis* in this context. However, the Aristotelian (and Platonic/Socratic) influences shaping Todorov's distinction between mimetic representation and diegetic narration are clear:[31]

> The chronicle, or story [*histoire*], it is believed, is a pure narrative [*pure narration*], the author is a simple eyewitness who reports the facts; the characters do not speak; the rules are those of the genre of historiography. However, in drama, the story [*histoire*] is not reported, it is before our eyes (even if we only read the play); there is no narration, the narrative (*récit*) is contained in the dialogue/ imitative speech [*répliques*] of the characters.

Thus, we find in Todorov's categorization of narrative a return to ancient categories of *mimesis* (the equivalent of Todorov's 'representation') and *diegesis* (Todorov's 'narration'), alongside a new focus upon an ancient concern with the speech acts of narrators and their characters.[32]

Accordingly, Todorov identifies distinct grammatical categories for the various speech acts that configure narrative or *récit*:[33] *tense*, concerning the relation between story time and discourse time; *aspect*, the point of view or perspective of the narrator; and *mood/mode*, concerning the type of discourse through which the narrator tells the story. In this schema, the basic distinction between story and plot, *histoire* and *discours*, is fundamental: tense is significant because of the linear chronological order of one and the potential anachrony of the other;[34] meanwhile the closely interconnected categories of aspect and mood

---

[29] Todorov 1966: 126. He attributes the popularization of this Aristotelian distinction to Benveniste and the Russian formalists.
[30] Todorov 1966: 144.   [31] Todorov 1966: 144.   [32] Genette 1980: 30.
[33] Todorov 1966: 138. Todorov subsequently redefines aspect as 'vision' and mood/ mode as 'register' (1981) to clarify these designations. Cf. Genette 1980: 29–30.
[34] Todorov 1966: 138.

are significant because they both point to the narratorial mediation of the story—that is, the narrator's particular point of view and preferences towards showing (representation) or telling (narration) the story.[35]

Within Todorov's schema, narrative is treated as a sentence: verbs represent actions, proper nouns name characters (the agents predicated by those verbs), while adjectives and adverbs describe thought and status (including point of view). Extending the literal implications of this analogy (and with it Aristotle's emphasis upon action as the primary element of plot), Todorov treats the verb element of narrative—the action that drives it—as its fundamental unit.[36] So, just as there can be no proper sentence without a verb, there can be no proper narrative without action. In this model, the narrative verb and its corresponding action can be parsed to reveal narratological insights into tense and temporality, voice and perspective, mood and mode.

Todorov turns repeatedly to ancient narratological paradigms to authorize this linguistic speech-act model, particularly highlighting the a priori methodology that Plato and Diomedes both demonstrate in identifying their theoretical genres in abstract (proto-Genettian) terms of 'who speaks', eschewing the traditional classification of genre according to more concrete phenomena such as metre (epic, tragic, iambic, lyric, elegiac, etc.) or subject (heroic, tragic, comic, erotic, etc.).[37] Todorov's own poetics of prose positions itself as offering a systematic theory of literary discourse very much in the mode of these ancient predecessors, starting from an abstract hypothesis that narrative functions like a language and then testing that hypothesis on actual works.[38] For some structuralists, such as Bremond and Greimas, an abstract linguistic frame is not merely necessary but sufficient to account for the grammar and syntax of narrative. In contrast, and anticipating some of the criticisms that would later be levelled against the structuralist project and its theoretical abstractions, Todorov insists that his own style of structuralist poetics and analysis will refer to actual texts.[39] This important qualification and its practical application in Todorov's writings declare his commitment to analysing both the *parole* and *langue* of narrative alongside one another. Concrete narrative texts are to be the 'stepping stones' in the development of his narrative theory—and of the next critical phase in structuralist narratology.

---

[35] Todorov 1966: 143.

[36] There are obvious parallels between Todorov's structuralist grammar, with its emphasis upon verbs, and Propp's (1968: 7–8) emphasis upon functions.

[37] Todorov 1975: 14.   [38] Todorov 1969: 70–1.

[39] Cf. Todorov 1977: 54–5 for an illustration of this approach based on Homer's *Odyssey* and its exegesis.

9.4 **Gérard Genette**

If the importance of Aristotle and Plato to the structuralist narratological project is initially marked out by Barthes's programmatic introduction to the 1966 special edition of *Communications* and further mapped in Todorov's grammatical schema, it is conclusively established in Gérard Genette's closing contribution to that landmark issue in his essay 'Frontières du récit'. Here Genette grounds his discussion of 'the boundaries of narrative' in the formal distinctions first drawn by Plato's Socrates (and subsequently reformulated by Aristotle) between *diegesis* and *mimesis*.[40]

This crucial distinction between *diegesis* and *mimesis*, and its particular treatment in Book 3 of Plato's *Republic*, crops up again and again in Genette's narratological writing, reworked in a section headed '*Diégésis et mimésis*' in his 1969 *Figures II*, reappearing again in his 1972 *Discours du récit* (a selection of work from *Figures*, translated in 1980 as the canonical—for anglophones—*Narrative Discourse: An Essay in Method*), and re-evaluated once again in his 1983 *Nouveau discours du récit* (translated in 1988 as *Narrative Discourse Revisited*).[41] A diegetic/mimetic binary runs throughout *Narrative Discourse* and provides the conceptual and lexical foundation for Genette's taxonomy of homodiegetic, heterodiegetic, metadiegetic, extradiegetic, and even pseudodiegetic levels of narration—terms which have become common currency in literary criticism. Given the repeated attention Genette pays to this ancient binary between *diegesis* and *mimesis*, a better understanding of the complex, contradictory, and evolving reception of his ancient narratological 'ancestors' (as he himself describes Aristotle) will help to shed light upon some of the fundamental strengths and weaknesses of Genette's major work of narrative theory.[42]

There are three key iterations of this reception process, which show Genette grappling with the proto-narratological tenets of Plato's *Republic* and Aristotle's *Poetics*, and using them to test and refine the structuralist narratologies of his contemporaries. Holding this more immediate horizon of reception in view as we evaluate Genette's reception—and

---

[40] For a summary overview of Genette's reception of Plato and Aristotle see Kirby 1991: 114, who warns: 'Relying on [Genette's] *précis* of the classical models and without scrutinizing the original texts...one might come away with a somewhat distorted conception of their import (and of their symbiotic relationship).' Gibson 1996: 76 argues that Genette's 'narratological undertaking has always been neo-Aristotelian'.

[41] Cf. Genette 1966: 152–6, 1976: 1–5, 1972: 184–6, 1980: 163–4, and 1988: 42–5.

[42] Genette 1988: 153. The reach of Genette's influence—and thus of this reception of Plato and Aristotle—is secured by Genette's own reception and translation at the hands of Prince 2003, Bal 1997, and Rimmon-Kenan 1983.

transmission—of Plato and Aristotle through these various iterations helps bring the details of his engagement with both ancient and more recent interlocutors into sharper focus. It is instructive, therefore, to consider Genette's iterative engagements with Aristotle and Plato in dialogue with the various structuralist perspectives upon *diegesis* and *mimesis* through which these engagements are filtered. Approached in this way, we can see a gradual but clearly marked shift in Genette's eagerness to align his own narratological theories with those of his 'ancestors'.

It begins with a direct response to Aristotle on the thorny subjects of *diegesis* and *mimesis*; it proceeds through a simplification and partial contradiction of that early response; and culminates in what appears to be at minimum a dilution, at most a disavowal, of any meaningful connection between Genette and his classical interlocutors (as his own narrative theory itself takes on that 'classical' status, perhaps). At stake throughout this movement away from his ancient predecessors is an overriding concern with narrative as *diegesis*, or rather as *diegetic*—the key term at the heart of Genette's narratology and that which shapes the contours of his narratological lexicon, providing the stem from which he parses his various diegetic levels of narration. In keeping with Genette's own structuralist grammatical tenets, then, we will follow the morphology of *diegesis* through its several forms in Genette's narratology.

9.4.1 *DIEGESIS* AS *MIMESIS* (PLATO AND ARISTOTLE)

In his 1966 essay circumscribing the domain that belongs to the new science of narratology, we first meet Genette claiming close affinity with Plato and Aristotle and mapping a series of direct correlations between classical poetics and structuralist narratology. He moves deftly between diegetic description of Plato's proto-narratology and extensive mimetic quotation of Plato's words, adopting a 'mixed' mode in his approach to the foundational topic of '*Diégésis et mimésis*'.[43] Indeed, so important is this topic to establishing the boundaries of narrative in this early work that Genette devotes almost a third of his essay to it—and, above all, to its treatment by Plato and Aristotle.

Genette opens with a broad definition of narrative or *récit*, described here as the linguistic 'representation of a real or fictitious event or series of events'.[44] This definition provides us with important clues

---

[43] Genette (1976: 2) quotes extensively from Plato, incorporating significant portions of *Republic* 3.393a 4–393e (itself incorporating sections of Homer's *Iliad*, 1.12–16).

[44] Genette 1976: 1.

regarding the status of representation, events, and language in Genette's narratology; these aspects of narrative (that is, the representation of action in language, rather than, say, story or character) will form the foundational focus of his theory. We proceed, therefore, from the familiar structuralist assumption that narrative works like a language and that its structures can be illuminated by linguistic modes of analysis. But we also proceed from an assumption that narrative is representational—that it is, in Aristotle's formulation, a kind of *mimesis* in words (*Poetics* 1.1447a 13–18). These initial suppositions will provide the Aristotelian grounds (already a variation of Plato's Socratic theory) upon which Genette will develop his own narratology. He will be concerned with narrative as discourse rather than as story, with *discours* rather than *histoire*, *sujet* (the French structuralist transliteration of *syuzhet*) rather than *fabula*. He will also be concerned with establishing the legitimacy of this new project by rooting it firmly within the classical tradition.

In '*Frontières du récit*', then, Genette begins his discussion of *diegesis* and *mimesis* with Aristotle and Plato, unabashedly fusing Plato's *mimesis/diegesis* distinction with Aristotle's, and veiling the major differences in emphasis between the two models.[45] Genette acknowledges that Plato's Socrates had made *diegesis* the genus and mimetic *diegesis* one of the species of narrative, while Aristotle had maintained the reverse. Yet he goes on to claim that, nevertheless, both Aristotle's and Plato's narratological models of *diegesis/mimesis* are 'identical except for a reversal of value'.[46]

On the basis of these supposedly compatible systems, then, Genette insists that both Plato's and Aristotle's distinctions between *mimesis* and *diegesis* (as two opposing styles of narration) map neatly onto a more fundamental distinction between dramatic and narrative modes of representation. So, Genette sees both the Platonic/Socratic and Aristotelian models of *mimesis* and *diegesis* as distinguishing essentially between direct representation (dialogues) and mediated representation (narration); between 'imitation' in which the narrator speaks 'pretending' to have become one of his characters on the one hand, and on the other 'simple narrative' involving 'all that the poet relates "in speaking in his own name"'.[47]

Certainly, both Plato's Socrates and Aristotle saw the dramatic mode as more mimetic than the narrative mode and therefore as more engaging and affective. For Socrates this was precisely what makes

---

[45] Genette 1976: 1.   [46] Genette 1976: 3.
[47] Genette 1976: 2, quoting from Plato, *Republic* 3.393e (and, in the original French version, from Chambry's translation).

drama and mixed modes such as epic ethically dangerous; for Aristotle, this was what makes tragedy superior to epic and Homer (with his dramatic style and penchant for character speech) superior to other epic poets. However, in a move that simultaneously establishes his indebtedness to and independence from his classical predecessors, Genette reverses this polarity. He wants to argue instead for the greater mimeticism—and therefore the superiority—of the narrative mode.[48] So, just as Aristotle had once turned Plato's (Socratic) model of narrative as *diegesis* upside down, inverting Plato's emphases in order to realize his own innovative theory of narrative as *mimesis*, Genette turns both Plato's and Aristotle's theories inside out in order to achieve similar ends.

Taking Homer's mixed diegetic/mimetic representation of Chryses' embassy to Agamemnon as his central illustration, Genette re-examines the fundamental differences between what he later describes as 'Homer's "imitated" discourse—that is, discourse fictively *reported* as it supposedly was uttered by the character' and 'Plato's *"narrativized"* discourse [in which] . . . nothing external distinguishes between what was words in the original and what was gesture, posture, state of mind'.[49]

Genette thus distinguishes between Homer's representation of Chryses' actions and his representation of Chryses' words in order to make the claim that the linguistic representation of a speech act, the discursive representation of character discourse, 'is not, properly speaking, representational'.[50] It is not, as Socrates and Aristotle both suppose, properly *mimetic*. Genette argues that Homer's words do not represent (that is re-present) Chryses' words but literally re-enact them; there is no *mimesis* here, he maintains, because Homer's discourse is 'completely identical with Chryses' discourse'.[51] Pursuing the logic of this a stage further, Genette proposes that the mimetic representation of direct, dramatic, speech acts (fictitious or real) in literary discourse is an anomaly—it is only the discursive representation of non-speech acts (of other kinds of actions and events) which potentially qualifies as *mimesis* in Genette's taxonomy:[52]

Literary representation, the *mimesis* of the classical notions, is thus not the narrative plus the discourses. It is the narrative, and only the narrative. Plato opposed *mimesis* to *diegesis* as a perfect imitation to an imperfect imitation. However, a perfect imitation is no longer an imitation; it is the thing itself. Ultimately, the only imitation is the imperfect one. *Mimesis* is *diegesis*.

[48] Genette 1976: 3.   [49] Genette 1980: 170, emphases in original.
[50] Genette 1976: 3–4.   [51] Genette 1976: 3.
[52] Genette 1976: 4–5.

Genette's radical revision here of the core narratological terms introduced by Plato and Aristotle is deftly done. The concept of *mimesis* appears to be predicated upon a fusion not only of Aristotle's view of narrative as *mimesis* in the medium of language, but also of both the technical and general ideas of *mimesis* found in Books 3 and 10 of Plato's *Republic*. For Plato's Socrates, *mimesis* concerns 'imitation' or 'identification', whether referring to a particular style of *diegesis* (in which the narrator imitates his characters in direct speech) or to literary representation in general (which for Socrates involves a kind of imperfect third-degree *mimesis*, its linguistic imitations three stages removed from the perfect Forms).[53] The logical inference that Genette draws from this broad notion of *mimesis* is that, in the context of representational (that is, linguistically mimetic) literary discourse, *diegesis* is not just the dominant mode, it is 'the only mode'; *diegesis* is both the genus and its only species. For Genette, merely 'transcribing a discourse', the direct re-presentation of a speech act within a speech act, does not involve any kind of mimetic or poetic activity: 'it is the thing itself'.[54] Only the *indirect* re-presentation of actions (including both speech and non-speech acts) in literature can be deemed imitative and thus properly qualify as *mimesis*. Paradoxically, only diegetic narrative is properly mimetic. *Diegesis* is *mimesis*. Or, as Genette subsequently argues in *Narrative Discourse*:[55] '*mimesis* in words can only be *mimesis* of words. Other than that, all we have and can have is degrees of *diegesis*.'

9.4.2 *DIEGESIS* AS *HISTOIRE* (BENVENISTE)

The conclusion drawn in his 1966 essay that *diegesis* is *mimesis* is explicitly predicated upon—indeed, logically necessitated by—Genette's understanding that both Plato and Aristotle treat all literary discourse as inherently mimetic. Accordingly, both Plato and Aristotle, Genette contends, draw an implicit boundary between representational and non-representational literature. Genette argues that in both Plato's and Aristotle's schemata '*poiesis* = *mimesis*'.[56] And it is on these grounds,

---

[53] Cf. Plato, *Republic* 3.392d and 10.595c.

[54] Genette 1976: 4. Cf. Genette 1988: 42: 'there is no imitation in narrative because narrative ... is an act of language'.

[55] Genette 1980: 164. We must distinguish then 'between narrative of events and "narrative of words".'

[56] Genette 1976: 8. Genette 1993: 7 returns to this same idea. The connection is certainly authorized by Aristotle's text, but Genette is likely to be appropriating this equation from Hamburger (1973: 7–8).

according to Genette, that Aristotle excludes lyric and elegiac, didactic and panegyric from his survey of (mimetic) poetry.[57]

At this juncture, Genette draws his narratological ancestors into dialogue with one of his more immediate interlocutors, the linguist Benveniste, and the morphology of his key term *diegesis* undergoes an unhappy mutation. Genette notices in Plato and Aristotle's distinction between representational (mimetic) and non-representational (non-mimetic) poetry a direct correspondence with Benveniste's analogous distinction between narrative (or story) and discourse.[58] In tragedy and epic we predominantly encounter indirect representation and therefore we have, in Benveniste's terms, reported narration; in lyric and elegy we find instead direct 'utterance' and therefore, in Benveniste's terms, we have discourse.[59] The proem to Homer's *Iliad* ('Sing, goddess...') is therefore non-narrative discourse; that is, in the terms Genette borrows from Benveniste, an utterance assuming the presence of a speaker and a listener, and therefore exhibiting the characteristics of *discours* rather than *histoire*.[60]

Benveniste defines *histoire* as 'the presentation of the facts... without any intervention of the speaker in the story' and *discours* as 'every utterance that assumes a speaker and a listener'.[61] So, the enunciation 'Chryses begged Agamemnon to release his daughter' involves a bald reportage of facts by an apersonal narrator: it is *histoire* in Benveniste's terms. Contrariwise, the enunciation 'Sons of Atreus, give me back my daughter' directly evokes a speaker and listener(s): it is *discours* in Benveniste's terms. By seeking to map Benveniste's linguistic modes *histoire* and *discours* onto a classical schema of representational and non-representational modes, Genette draws an implicit correlation between Benveniste's *histoire* and Plato's *diegesis* (technically, Socrates' *haple diegesis*), and between Benveniste's *discours* and Plato's *mimesis* (technically, Socrates' *diegesis dia mimeseos*). Like their suggestive counterparts in Plato's schema, Benveniste's *histoire* and *discours* are styles or modes of telling (whether conceived as enunciating or narrating). As such, they are not easily compatible with the usual structuralist concepts of *histoire* and *discours*, which (conceived as equivalents to the formalist *fabula* (story) and *syuzhet* (plot) or the Platonic *logos* and *lexis*) concern not modes but levels of narrative—what is told and how it is told,

---

[57] Genette 1976: 8.   [58] Genette 1976: 8.
[59] Benveniste 1966. Cf. Communications 1966: 168.
[60] Genette 1980: 37 n. 9. Cf. 1980: 220 n. 19 on the relative closeness or distance, vividness and immediacy of various (French) verb tenses in Benveniste's linguistic schema.
[61] Benveniste 1966. Cf. Communications 1966: 168.

respectively. Ostensibly, then, this correspondence introduces a new tier of unnecessary complexity to Genette's concept of *diegesis*—and to his notion of the structuralist concept of *histoire*.[62]

Genette wants to maintain the structuralist distinction (with terms borrowed from Benveniste) between two levels of *récit* (narrative): 'narrative as discourse' (*discours*) and 'narrative as story' (*histoire*).[63] And he additionally wants to use the term *diégèse* (borrowed from Plato and Aristotle) as a direct equivalent to *histoire* to describe the story level of narrative. He subsequently explains that 'with the same meaning ("story"), I will also use the term *diegesis*' and that 'I contrast narrative (and sometimes narrating) to story (or *diegesis*).'[64] Not only does *poiesis* = *mimesis* and *diegesis* = *mimesis* in Genette's narratology, then, but sometimes *diegesis* = *récit* and sometimes *diegesis* = *histoire*. This = frustration for many of his readers.

We might put this terminological imprecision down to Genette's twofold application of Benveniste's concepts, *histoire* and *discours*—on the one hand used in reference to two distinct narrative levels (story and discourse, *fabula* and *sujet*), and on the other to two distinct narrative or narrating modes (apersonal reporting and personal utterance). But we might also notice in this twofold approach to the concept of *histoire*, as both a level and a mode of narration, an echo of Socrates' intuition that *diegesis* denotes a concept of narrative that embraces its status as both genus and species. Thus, *diegesis* = *récit* = *histoire*. And thus an ancient formulation unexpectedly helps to balance a modern equation.

9.4.3 *DIEGESIS* AS NARRATIVE PURE AND SIMPLE (TODOROV)

Benveniste's influence in shaping Genette's early understanding of Plato's (Socratic) concept of *diegesis* as both narrative level and mode, as both genus and species, is clearly important, if also complex. But Benveniste's is not the only voice or viewpoint to shape Genette's narratology or his reading and reception of Aristotle and Plato. As Genette's theory of narrative evolves its distinctive character (in parallel with the growing authority of his structuralist peers) into the early 1970s,

---

[62] Elsewhere, Genette uses the terms *diegesis* (*diègèsis*) and diegetic (*diégèse*) as a direct equivalent both for 'narrative' (*récit*) and for 'story' (*histoire*). See Genette 1966: 152: '*le récit (diègèsis)*'; and 158: '*un récit (une histoire)*'.

[63] Genette 1980: 27 n. 2. Thus, in Genette's vocabulary, narrative becomes a synonym for narrating (*récit* is interchangeable with *narration*), and story becomes a synonym for *diegesis* (*diégèse* is interchangeable with *histoire*); *récit* and *narration* concern the telling (the *discours*), while *diégèse* and *histoire* concern the fiction—'what is told'.

[64] Genette 1980: 27 n. 2 and 1980: 87 n. 1.

he shows a greater inclination to position his ideas as refinements to those of his structuralist contemporaries, and a lesser enthusiasm for reminding us of their classical lineage. As structuralist narratology itself becomes the new 'classic' of narrative theory, Genette need no longer argue so loudly for the critical respectability of either narrative or its grammar.

Barthes and Todorov had already suggested that narrative is structured according to the grammatical categories of tense (dealing with time), aspect (dealing with point of view), and mood/mode (dealing with voice).[65] In *Narrative Discourse*, Genette explicitly adopts and adapts Todorov's key categories, similarly electing to focus upon narrative communication in terms of its order, duration, and frequency (the equivalent of Todorov's and Barthes's tense); its mood (dealing with point of view or aspect); and its voice (the equivalent of Barthes's mode and person, and of Todorov's mood/mode). Genette's narratology thus sets out to provide a taxonomy focusing upon three key grammatical aspects of narrative: its temporal dynamics (order, duration, and frequency), the regulation of its discourse (mood), and the manner of its telling (voice). At the same time, Genette redefines his working definition of 'narrative' (*récit*) into a more Todorovian shape. In his 1966 essay, he had defined *récit* as 'the representation of a real or fictitious event or series of events by language', thereby stressing three key elements of narrative discourse:[66] representation, event, and language. In *Narrative Discourse*, adapting Todorov's distinction between discourse and story, Genette broadly revises the three parts of this earlier definition into three key levels: narrative ('the signifier, statement, discourse or narrative text itself'), story ('the signified or narrative content'), and narrating ('the producing narrative action and, by extension, the whole of the real or fictional situation in which that action takes place').[67]

As we've already seen, Todorov's (formalist) distinction between story and discourse (*histoire* and *discours*) aligns closely with Plato's (Socratic) distinction between *logos* and *lexis*. What is more, Todorov's intersecting levels of aspect and mood/mode work with basic distinctions between representation and narration—equivalent to a mode of showing and telling—which mark an apparent return to ancient categorizations of narrative. Despite the very slight amendments to Todorov's category of mood that Genette proposes for his own schema, his appropriation of Todorov's essentially 'Platonic' categories of diegetic narration and

---

[65] Todorov 1966: 138. Cf. Genette 1980: 29–30. Under the category of tense, Genette (1980: 37) offers a nicely nuanced close reading of the complex 'temporal movement' of the opening lines of the *Iliad* (1.1–11).
[66] Genette 1976: 1.   [67] Genette 1980: 27.

mimetic representation necessarily ties him both to the new science of narratology and to a very much older narratological tradition.[68] Thus, we find Genette's engagement with Todorov necessitating some re-engagement with Plato and Aristotle.

In his 1966 essay (which, incidentally, mentions neither Todorov nor Barthes), Genette had appeared eager simultaneously to appropriate and to destabilize the ancient narratological concepts of *diegesis* and *mimesis*: in Shklovsky's terms, Genette's insistence that *mimesis* is *diegesis* effectively 'defamiliarized' both concepts and made them newly available for the nascent structuralist project. But as that project gains both traction and authority, the inducements to such defamiliarization are reduced and we find the old 'Platonic' concepts of *diegesis* and *mimesis* reanimated in Genette's *Narrative Discourse*. Here, the argument for the mutual substitution of *diegesis* and *mimesis* is put aside, and the terms are straightforwardly used to characterize two distinct modes or moods of narration. Thus:[69]

Plato contrasts two narrative modes, according to whether the poet "himself is the speaker and does not even attempt to suggest to us that anyone but himself is speaking" (this is what Plato calls *pure narrative*), or whether, on the other hand, the poet "delivers a speech as if he were someone else" (as if he were such-and-such a character), if we are dealing with spoken words (this is what Plato properly calls imitation, or *mimesis*)...In these terms, adopted provisionally, "pure narrative" will be taken to be more distant than "imitation": it says less, and in a more mediated way.[70]

The predominantly diegetic summary of *Republic* 3.392d–394d that follows offers little acknowledgement of Genette's earlier reading of this passage and the conclusions drawn there. Instead, Genette offers a fairly unreflective reiteration of Socrates' core narratological principles, slightly reformulated in order to highlight Genette's own: that is, to highlight the unmediated, direct, and dramatic quality of dialogue (which here equals *mimesis*) as opposed to the more mediated, indirect, less dramatic, and more distant quality of narrative (which here equals *haple diegesis*) in this account of narrative distance and mode.[71] However, despite the simplified

[68] Genette 1980: 29–30.
[69] Genette 1980: 162–3. Genette is wrong to claim here that 'Plato goes so far as to rewrite as *diegesis*...a scene which Homer had treated as *mimesis*'; Homer's scene is actually an example of a *mixed* narrative mode. Genette returns again to what he describes as Plato's 'strange rewriting' of Homer at 169–70.
[70] Cf. Genette 1980: 174 on the differences between direct and indirect speech representation.
[71] Cf. Todorov 1966: 144 on the appropriately mimetic designation of character dialogue/imitative speech as '*répliques*'.

Todorovian definitions of *mimesis* and *diegesis* as 'perfect imitation' and 'pure narrative' that Genette offers here and in the ensuing discussion of narrative mode, the role of these key categories in his own narrative theory turn out to be neither 'perfect' nor 'pure'.[72]

9.4.4 *DIEGESIS* AS *DIÉGÈSE* (METZ AND SOURIAU)

In *Narrative Discourse* Genette follows Plato in distinguishing between two modes of narrating: narrative (*diegesis*) and dialogue (*mimesis*). As we've seen, he also follows Benveniste in distinguishing between indirect and direct discourse, and Todorov in distinguishing between two levels of narrative.[73] But these are not the only ingredients in the conceptual cocktail that is Genette's notion of *diegesis*. As an equivalent to *histoire* he also uses the term *diégèse*, advising us: 'With the same meaning ("story"), I will also use the term *diegesis*, which comes to us from the theoreticians of cinematographic narrative.'[74] This reminds us that an additional influence upon Genette's understanding of *diegesis* comes from the structuralist film theorist Christian Metz (fellow contributor to the 1966 special edition of *Communications*), who had devoted a subsection of his essay to the topic of '*Diégèse et film*'.[75] In his relatively short piece for *Communications*, Metz takes for granted our understanding that the term *diégèse* (diegetic) refers to one of the key levels of film narrative, serving as an adjective useful in distinguishing between 'diegetic' elements of the film storyworld and 'extradiegetic' or 'non-diegetic' features (such as a musical score or voice-over). But in an expanded 1968 collection of essays, *Essais sur la signification au cinema*, Metz offers us a more precise definition of *diégèse*, detailing its classical Greek provenance, and describing its conceptual compass within his own narratology (and, by extension, within Genette's):[76]

---

[72] Genette's definition of *diegesis* as 'pure narrative' directly echoes Todorov's '*pure narration*' (Todorov 1966: 144) but the definition of *mimesis* as 'perfect imitation' appears to be Genette's own refinement.

[73] Genette 1980: 27 n. 2.

[74] Genette 1980: 27 n. 2.

[75] Metz 1966: 123. It is worth noting that Genette's concept of *diegesis* is taken from film studies, but his neologism 'focalization' is not. Despite the ostensible equivalence between Genette's notions of 'external focalization' and the camera eye, his theory of focalization is (surprisingly, perhaps) not predicated upon vision or field of view.

[76] Metz 1974: 97–8. The claim here that *diégèse* is derived from the Greek διήγησις, referring to the narrative parts of judiciary discourse, may have directly influenced Genette in drawing his analogy between the use of direct speech in narrative and the use of exhibits in the law courts (1976: 5).

The word is derived from the Greek διήγησις, "narration" and was used particularly to designate one of the obligatory parts of judiciary discourse, the recital of facts. The term was introduced into the framework of the cinema by Étienne Souriau. It designates the film's *represented* instance... that is to say, the sum of a film's denotation: the narration itself, but also the fictional space and time dimensions implied in and by the narrative, and consequently the characters, the landscapes, the events, and other narrative elements, in so far as they are considered in their denoted aspect... [that is] successivity, precession, temporal breaks, causality, adversative relationships, consequence, spatial proximity, [and] distance, etc.

For Metz, the adjectival notion of *diégèse* describes a particular situation of narration, the 'recital' of *récit*, the sum total of a narrative's '*represented* instance'—that is, story combined with plot, *histoire* with *discours*, *fabula* with *sujet*. This is a subtly different concept of *diegesis* to that found in either Plato's or Aristotle's discussions of narrative, although the rhetorical origins of the term to which Metz refers here are evidenced in Plato's *Phaedrus* (266e).[77] This is because Metz's definition of *diégèse* owes less to Socrates than to Souriau, who is credited with inaugurating the use of the adjective *diégétique* to describe the storyworld evoked in film.[78] For example, Souriau characterizes diegetic space as 'the space in which all the events presented take place' or 'the space of the story'; and diegetic time as 'the time in which all the events presented take place' or 'the time of the story'.[79] Souriau's working definition of *diégèse* comprehensively describes the diegetic as '[w]hatever is supposed to happen according to the fiction that the film presents; and all that this fiction implies/entails if it is assumed to be real'.[80] For Souriau, seeking to distinguish between different levels and experiences of 'representation' and 'reality' in film, *diégèse* is used holistically to refer to the mimetic construct presenting an individual storyworld with its particular story logic: its space and time, its characters and events, and its patterns of cause and consequence. This capacious concept embraces both the story that is narrated and its particular emplotment in a given narrative— including, crucially, its temporal dynamics and anachronies (Souriau's 'successivity, precession, [and] temporal breaks'), and the mediation of its narrative information (Souriau's 'proximity' and 'distance').

---

[77] See Halliwell 2014: 132: '[*diegesis*] could apply, for instance, to the section(s) of a courtroom speech in which a litigant provided a version of events relevant to the case: a reference in Plato's *Phaedrus*, 266e, shows that *diegesis* was codified in this sense in some of the first rhetorical handbooks (cf. Aristotle *Rhetoric* 1.1, 1354b 18 and 3.13, 1414a 37–b 15)'.

[78] See Boillat 2009 on the history of *diégèse* in film theory and Genette 1988: 17.

[79] Souriau 1951: 231. Cf. Gaudreault 2009: 166.

[80] Souriau 1951: 240.

This, then, is the cinematic notion of *diégèse* which Souriau hands on to Metz and thence on to Genette as early as 1966. Yet Genette barely mentions either Metz or Souriau in his work: neither are cited in his 1966 essay; Metz (but not Souriau) appears once, introducing Genette's discussion of story time in *Figures III* and its equivalent in *Narrative Discourse*, and again in a footnote dealing with 'diegetic time';[81] and Souriau (but not Metz) appears in *Narrative Discourse Revisited*, as Genette attempts to clarify his use of the term *diegesis*—or rather, *diégèse*. Here, with characteristic understatement, Genette claims:[82]

> My use of the word *diégèse*, partly proposed as an equivalent for *histoire*, was not exempt from a misunderstanding... Souriau proposed the term *diégèse* in 1948, contrasting the diegetic universe (the place of the signified) with the *screen*-universe (place of the film-signifier)... *diégèse* is indeed a *universe* rather than a train of events (a story); the *diégèse* is therefore not the story but the universe in which the story takes place... We must not, therefore (as is so often done today), substitute *diégèse* for *histoire*.

But he protests too much. In signalling the influence of Metz and Souriau, Genette directly equates the diegetic level of narrative with the diegetic level of the Souriauan storyworld. As he explains in a footnote in his 1972 *Figures* (where he again identifies this key term as one 'borrowed from theorists of cinematic language') he describes 'the diegetic' (*diégétique*) as 'the space-time universe of the narrative (*récit*)'.[83] But elsewhere in his work, he maintains this cinematic definition of *diegesis*—or properly, of the diegetic—only when he wants to discuss narrative phenomena (such as description, narratorial intrusion, or metalepsis) which actually or potentially draw the reader's attention to the status of the narrative *qua* narrative. Thus, he distinguishes the 'diegetic universe' from various 'metadiegetic', 'extradiegetic', or 'pseudodiegetic' levels of narration;[84] he identifies descriptions 'as constituents of the spatio-temporal universe of the story' and therefore as 'diegetic';[85] and describes metalepsis as 'the device through which the narrator pretends to enter (with or without his reader) into the diegetic universe'.[86]

Outside of this restricted adjectival application of *diégèse* to comment on quasi-cinematic levels of narrative immersion, however, Genette uses the term to refer not to a storyworld or story universe but simply to the storyline (*histoire*). His distinction between 'narrative order' (*l'ordre narratif*) and 'diegetic order' (*l'ordre diégétique*) suggests that he has in

---

[81] Genette 1980: 33 and 88 n. 3.   [82] Genette 1988: 17–18, emphases in original.
[83] Genette 1972: 48 n. 1.   [84] Genette 1980: 101 n. 33, 228 n. 41, 234–5, 245.
[85] Genette 1980: 94 n. 12.   [86] Genette 1980: 101 n. 33.

mind here a concept of *diégèse* far closer to storyline than to storyworld.[87] This reading is borne out by further references to *diegesis* in his writing: in his analysis of temporal order, contrasting 'the temporal order of succession of the events in the story [*diégèse*] and the pseudo-temporal order of their arrangement in the narrative [*récit*]';[88] in discussions of sequence, in which the 'diegetic sequence and narrative sequence' are explicitly mapped on to the sequence of 'narrative and story';[89] and in his treatment of frequency, in which he similarly draws a contrast 'between the narrative and the diegesis'.[90] In none of these instances does it make sense to conceive of *diégèse* as 'a universe rather than a train of events (a story)'. Despite the detailed corrections and explanations offered in *Narrative Discourse Revisited* for the confusion of terms prompted by his earlier work (particularly in its English translation), Genette's amplifications do not do very much to untangle the issue of what the 'diegetic' actually constitutes in his narratology. Sometimes *diegesis* involves *récit* and *narration*, the telling (the *discours*), while at other moments *diegesis* involves *diégèse* and *histoire*, the fiction or 'what is told', a notion embracing not only the storyline but the representation and regulation (the telling?) of the entire diegetic universe. The conceptual cocktail has reached potentially dangerous levels of toxicity.

9.4.5 *DIEGESIS* AS *DIÉGÉSIS* (PLATO AND ARISTOTLE REVISITED)

In his reconsideration of *Narrative Discourse* (translated in 1988 as *Narrative Discourse Revisited*), Genette endeavours to dilute this mix—or rather to take out some of its more potent ingredients. He insists, in an extraordinary act of revisionism, that his concept of *diegesis* actually has nothing to do with classical Platonic and Aristotelian notions:[91]

Another misunderstanding results from a telescoping of the terms *diégèse*, as we have (re)defined it, and *diégésis*. *Diégésis*...sends us back to the Platonic theory

---

[87] Genette 1980: 43. See also 1980: 50 where he draws a parallel between the 'story line' and 'diegetic content'. In his later work, Genette's concept of the *diégétique* returns to its Souriauan roots and is used predominantly in reference to the 'historical-geographical framework' of a narrative. But see Genette 1988: 154, where he once again seeks to distinguish between 'the narrative' and 'the story—that is, the content or (and for once this word has to be used) the *diegesis*'.

[88] Genette 1980: 35. The translation Lewin gives for *diégèse* here is 'story'.

[89] Genette 1980: 87.   [90] Genette 1980: 113.

[91] Genette 1988: 18. See Bal 1977 for a critique of Genette. She suggests (107) that Genette's question of who sees and who speaks 'concerns that old distinction between showing and telling, or that very much older distinction between *mimesis* and *diegesis*'.

of the modes of representation, where it is contrasted with *mimésis*. *Diégésis* is pure narrative (without dialogue), in contrast to the *mimésis* of dramatic representation and to everything that creeps into narrative along with dialogue, thereby making narrative impure—that is, *mixed*. *Diégésis*, therefore, has nothing to do with *diégèse*... [*diégèse*] is by no means the French translation of the Greek *diegesis*... [and] the French and Greek words unfortunately neutralize each other in the single English word *diegesis*... I (like Souriau, of course) always derive *diégétique* from *diégèse*, never from *diégésis*; others, like Mieke Bal, freely contrast *diégétique* with *mimétique*, but I am not answerable for that offense.

While it may be true that in *Narrative Discourse* Genette principally derives *diégétique* from *diégèse* (where *diégétique* and its various compounds reference a relationship either to the storyworld or the storyline of the 'first narrative' as Genette terms it), it is not true that this derivation always excludes the 'Platonic' term and concept of *diegesis*, or its contrast with the term and concept of *mimesis*.[92] There are, in fact, several references to Plato's *diégésis* and its cognates throughout Genette's work.

In his 1966 essay Genette straightforwardly equates Aristotle's and Plato's *diègèsis*—note *diègèsis* and not *diégèse*—with 'narrative' (*récit*).[93] There, according to Plato's familiar schema, *diègèsis* was both the genus 'narrative' (Genette's *récit*, Socrates' *diegesis*) *and* a species or mode of narration (the equivalent to Socrates' *haple diegesis*, or 'simple narrative'). Accordingly, when Genette refers to 'the diegetic functions [*fonctions diégétiques*] of the description, i.e., the role played by the descriptive passages or aspects in the general system of the narrative [*récit*]', it is clear that he is deriving *diégétique* not from the Souriauan *diégèse* but from the Platonic (Socratic) *diègèsis*.[94]

In *Narrative Discourse* there is also the odd occasion when Genette's references to various forms of the 'diegetic' (in particular the 'heterodiegetic') specifically concern the storyline ('*ligne d'histoire*') rather than the storyworld.[95] He also uses *diegesis* (or '*diégésis*') in the 'Platonic' sense a number of times, although he contextualizes it as such in each case (qualifying it as '*au sens platonicien*').[96] What is more, in each case he draws a contrast between *diegesis* and *mimesis* (also in the 'Platonic' sense). He also translates *diégésis* as Plato's 'pure narrative' as opposed to *mimésis* as 'imitation', and according to what Genette himself describes as a classical or 'millennial opposition between *diegesis* and *mimesis*'.[97]

---

[92] Genette 1980: 48.   [93] Genette 1966: 152–3.   [94] Genette 1976: 6.
[95] Genette 1980: 50.   [96] Genette 1980: 162–6, and 172 n. 16.
[97] Genette 1980: 168.

In *Narrative Discourse Revisited*, we find that ancient opposition refigured once more, and effectively returned to a reduced version of the concept as we first encountered it in Genette's narratology. We find him clarifying his earlier definition(s) of narrative with the claim that 'narrative consists wholly of two discourses...the narrator's discourse and the character's discourse(s)'.[98] This position allows him to reassess the value of the binary *diegesis/mimesis* and to claim that we must remember, 'as Plato did, to read *mimesis* as an equivalent of *dialogue*, with the sense not of *imitation* but of transcription, or...of *quotation*', since in narrative, 'there are only *rhésis* and *diegesis*...the character's discourse and the narrator's discourse'.[99] Apparently, this authorizes Genette to reappropriate the terms of Plato's schema and insist that 'the only acceptable equivalence for *diégésis/mimésis* is *narrative/dialogue* (narrative mode/dramatic mode) which absolutely cannot be translated as *telling/showing*'.[100] We have moved a long way from the notion that *mimesis* is *diegesis*, yet the fundamentally Platonic (or Socratic) tenets of Genette's conceptualization of *diegesis* as narrative—albeit as species rather than genus—persists. The end of the story returns us to its beginning.

9.5 Mieke Bal

Dutch theorist and critic Mieke Bal is not one of the original structuralists. Yet her work falls very much into a parallel groove running alongside the structuralist tradition: it engages closely with the narrative theories of Bremond, Greimas, Barthes, and Genette and is therefore well understood in this structuralist context. Bal is generally renowned for her (frequently controversial) refinements to Genette's narratology, particularly in the area of focalization: she observed that the phenomenon of focalization depends not only upon the question of 'who sees?' but also of 'what is seen?', adding to Genette's distinction between internal and external focalization a supplementary distinction between focalizer(s) and focalized. For classicists, however, Bal is perhaps best known for her supervision in the mid-1980s of Irene de Jong's doctoral research

---

[98] Genette 1988: 11.   [99] Genette 1988: 43, emphases in original.
[100] Genette 1988: 45. Cf. Genette 1988: 42 n. 5: 'The etymology enthusiast will perhaps find solace in the idea that the Latin *dico* has a family resemblance to the Greek *deiknumi* and therefore (?), that *to say is to show.*'

into Homer's 'narrators and focalizers'.[101] Thus, Bal occupies an especially important node in the network of reception connecting ancient and modern narratology to classics.

However, Bal herself is not particularly concerned with classics nor with what Plato or Aristotle might have had to say about narrative and its dynamics.[102] Her best-known work of narrative theory, *Narratology: Introduction to the Theory of Narrative*, makes barely any reference to the *Republic* or *Poetics* across its several revised editions and translations. There is no mention of either Plato or Aristotle in her earliest work dedicated to narrative theory, the 1977 *Narratologie*. This groundwork study, exploring the tripartite structural relationships between text, narration, and story (*texte, récit, histoire*), takes an approach modelled on Greimassian semiotics, arguing that interaction across these levels produces a distinctive kind of narrative semiosis. Bal's 1978 Dutch publication *De theorie van vertellen en verhalen*, which provides the template for various subsequent iterations of *Narratology*, similarly overlooks both Plato and Aristotle as potential precursors in the field. The revised 1980 edition of *De theorie van vertellen en verhalen* and thus its 1985 translation does include a very brief reference to Plato—albeit not the most reliable or close reading of *Republic* 3.392d–394d ever essayed:[103]

In the *Republic*, Plato tried to rewrite fragments of Homer so that they would be 'truly' narrative. The first elements to be discarded were the descriptions. Even Homer himself attempted to avoid, or at least to disguise, descriptions by making them narrative. Achilles' shield is described as it is in the process of being made, Agamemnon's armour as he puts it on.

In fact, this reads as a second-hand summary of Genette summarizing Plato rather than a direct synthesis of Plato ventriloquizing Socrates.[104] Bal's representation of Plato's attempt to translate Homer's mixed narrative in *Iliad* 1.12–16 into a 'truly' narrative mode is particularly misleading, suggesting as it does that 'truly' in this context might equate to Plato's *haple* (simple) *diegesis*. It is also a stretch to claim, as Bal does here, that, in Plato's translation of Homer, 'The first elements to be discarded were the descriptions'; it is the direct character speech that

---

[101] See Bal 1977 for her critique of Genette, and de Jong 1987 on narrators and focalizers. Cf. de Jong 2014 for Bal's influence on narratology in classics.

[102] Cf. Genette 1988: 18.

[103] Bal 1997: 37. Bal also discusses the narrative qualities of Achilles' shield in her 1982 review essay of the Dupont-Roc and Lallot commentary and translation of Aristotle's *Poetics* (Bal 1982: 177).

[104] Cf. Genette 1976: 1–5. Bal also appears to be responding (tacitly) to Genette in her discussion of the dramatic quality of actor dialogue in narrative texts (60); of anachrony at 84–5 (taking the opening lines of Homer's *Iliad* as a case study); and of scene and summary at 109–10 (taking Homer's narrative description of Achilles' shield as an illustration).

Plato's Socrates is first and foremost engaged in removing from Homer's overly mimetic *diegesis*.

Aristotle—or, rather, a glancing reference to 'the Aristotelian tradition'—earns a single bibliographical credit in the 1985 edition of *Narratology*, via Bal's further recommended reading on 'characters' and a direction to consult Walcutt's 1966 study *Man's Changing Mask: Modes and Methods of Characterization in Fiction*.[105] Walcutt's historical survey does not mention Aristotle and it is not clear how or why his study might qualify as particularly 'Aristotelian'—unless Bal is conflating here the 'actantial' model of character embraced by Propp, Greimas, and Bremond with Aristotle's own analogously functional approach to *ethos* and thereby obliquely acknowledging Aristotle's influence upon these later theorists.[106] This does appear to be the context in which Aristotle receives his second mention in the second edition of *Narratology* in 1997, this time in the main body of the text. Discussing the three core interacting elements that give narrative its structure (now formulated as text, story, *fabula*), Bal defines the *fabula* (now broadly equivalent to the formalist's *fabula* and the structuralist's *histoire*, or story—as opposed to *syuzhet*, *discours*, or plot) as follows:[107]

> The *fabula* as a whole constitutes a process, while every event can also be called a process or, at least, part of a process. Theories are sometimes old, if not tenacious. According to Aristotle as well as Bremond, three phases can be distinguished in every *fabula*: the possibility (or virtuality), the event (or realization), and the result (or conclusion) of the process.

The earlier version of this discussion (in the 1985 anglophone edition, and its Dutch precursor) had referred only to Bremond, with no mention of Aristotle.[108] Belatedly, it seems, Bal realizes that Bremond's three phases are translations of Aristotle's observation in the *Poetics* (7.1450b 25–34, already a reworking of Plato's *Phaedrus* (264 b–c)) that a well-constructed plot and the story it tells requires an appropriate beginning, middle, and end. However, it is noticeable that Bal has nothing to say here about Aristotle's more sophisticated proto-structuralist tenets regarding the key processes through which these phases unfold: complication (*desis*, the tying of the plot's central knot); *peripeteia*; and resolution (*lusis*, or the untying of the plot in denouement).

---

[105] I am grateful to one of the Press's anonymous readers for flagging this.

[106] Bal 1997: 226.

[107] Bal 1997: 189. Unhappily, Bal comes up with her own fusion of the conventional formalist and structuralist terms for story and plot; her *fabula* = story = *histoire* = *logos*; her story = plot = *syuzhet* = *discours* = *muthos*. Thus (1997: 7): 'The *fabula* [is] understood as material or content that is worked into a story...a series of events.'

[108] Bal 1985: 19.

Bal's cognizance of ancient theories of narrative, then, is not transparent in the various iterations of her most prominent study, *Narratology*. But this is not to say that these theories, particularly in their Aristotelian form, are not indirectly informing her work. Bal's theory of character and the functional role of character agents in narrative, for example, is clearly influenced by Bremond and Greimas, whose actantial models are quasi-Aristotelian. Once Bal has reformulated Greimas's actantial functions (transforming 'helper and opponent', 'sender and receiver', into 'power and receiver') there may be very little direct trace left of the Aristotelian view that characters are subordinate to and yet drivers of plot, as agents or actors of the action—that is, as *prattontas* (*Poetics* 2.1447b 29), linked etymologically, thematically, and structurally to the action (*praxis*). Bal sees her paradigm of characters as actors as 'a typically structuralist model... conceived in terms of fixed relations between classes of phenomena, which is a standard definition of structure'.[109] Yet Bal's evolution of these structuralist ideas places her theory of character very squarely within an Aristotelian tradition. She even discusses, *pace* Aristotle, the narrative pitfalls and possibilities attending the representation of historical and mythical characters, whose qualities and stories are already well known to us.[110]

Bal's 'structuralist' conception of *fabula* and its differential relationship to her notion of story also has its roots in Aristotelian definitions of plot. She maintains:[111]

A *narrative text* is a text in which an agent relates ("tells") a story in a particular medium, such as language, imagery, sound, buildings, or a combination thereof. A *story* is a *fabula* that is presented in a certain manner. A *fabula* is a series of logically and chronologically related events that are caused or experienced by actors. An *event* is the transition from one state to another state. *Actors* are agents that perform actions.

For Bal, therefore, the *fabula* is the 'material or content that is worked into a story', the various raw elements and events that are 'organized in a

---

[109] Bal 1997: 197. Bal's theory of narrative 'actors' is explicated further at 195–208.
[110] Bal 1997: 120–1. Cf. Aristotle, *Poetics* 13.1453a 16–22.
[111] Bal 1997: 5, emphases in original. Bal's concept of *fabula* is not always satisfactory. In a discussion of *fabula*'s parts or elements, she claims (209): 'Classical tragedy even has rules about time. The time span of its *fabula*, which should not extend beyond one day and one night, thus functions as an aesthetic criterion.' The notion of *fabula* applied here in consideration of an imagined 'classical' rule is incompatible with Bal's definitions elsewhere. See Aristotle, *Poetics* 5.1449b 11–20 for his views on the ideal duration of a tragic *muthos*.

certain way into a story', in which their 'arrangement in relation to one another is such that they can produce the affect desired, be this convincing, moving, disgusting, or aesthetic'.[112]

Aristotle may not have been concerned with the narrative agent or narrator but, like Bal, he too sees characters first and foremost as agents who act (*Poetics* 2.1447b 29). Indeed, in her 1982 review essay of the new Dupont-Roc and Lallot translation of the *Poetics*, Bal herself notes that Aristotle's characters are '*prattontas* which, significantly, means *act-ant*'.[113] Aristotle similarly recognized that narrative *mimesis* might be produced in various expressive 'texts', in media such as language, colour, shape, and sound (*Poetics* 1.1447a 13–27). He too recognized that a *muthos* (the equivalent of Bal's story) involves the particular representation or emplotment of *logos* (*Poetics* 5.1449b 7), wherein *logos* is understood as 'the raw material or argument for a plot'.[114] For Aristotle, therefore, it is the *muthos* that reorganizes that raw material and works it into a narrative, and it is the *muthos* that can be defined as the arrangement (*sunthesis*) of incidents (*pragmata*) (*Poetics* 6.1450a 2–4) or as the poetic rearrangement of the logically and chronologically related elements as they appear in the *katholou* or *idion* (*Poetics* 17.1455a 34–1455b 2) so as to achieve the desired affect (*psuchagogei*) upon an audience (*Poetics* 14.1453b 3–6).

There are some clear affinities between Bal's narratology and the core narratological principles advocated by Aristotle, then, despite the conspicuous lack of direct engagement with the *Poetics* in her *Narratology*. However, in an oft-cited review of the Dupont-Roc and Lallot translation and commentary on the *Poetics*, Bal reveals a less oblique appreciation of Aristotle's proto-narratological precepts. Here she shows herself to be familiar with the nuances of Aristotle's 'cognitive' theories of *mimesis*, his 'actantial' theory of character, and his 'linguistic' theory of mode—the representation of the same material by narrator or character, in narrative or dramatic styles.

In this review essay Bal suggests that Aristotle's *Poetics* has been grossly 'oversimplified' and 'misinterpreted' by generations of its readers, who have especially failed to appreciate the ambiguity, inconsistency, and dynamism of Aristotle's own use of the key narratological term *mimesis*.[115] Given Bal's criticisms of Genette both within this paper (where she fires a number of shots at Genette's 1979 *Introduction à l'architexte*) and elsewhere (she denigrates Genette's concern with the question of who sees and who speaks as a return to 'that old distinction

---

[112] Bal 1997: 7.   [113] Bal 1982: 179.   [114] See Lucas 1968: 91.
[115] Bal 1982: 171.

between showing and telling, or that very much older distinction between *mimesis* and *diegesis*'), these comments about the misreading of the *Poetics* may well be directed particularly towards Genette.[116]

However, there are some problems with Bal's own reading of the *Poetics*. For example, she identifies Aristotle's *muthos* as equivalent to the '*fabula* that forms the content of any literary text'.[117] The connection between *fabula* and/as content here reflects the notion of *fabula* in Bal's own work. But only if we read *fabula* here as that which *forms* (as in shapes) story content can we legitimately equate it with Aristotle's *muthos*. Bal's observation that in Dupont-Roc and Lallot, Aristotle's *muthos* 'is fortunately translated by *histoire* in the narratological sense' is similarly problematic.[118] Bal, *pace* Dupont-Roc and Lallot, here accepts *histoire* as a direct equivalent of Aristotle's *muthos*, although this does not correspond either to *histoire* 'in the narratological sense' (at least, not in the structuralist sense) that she suggests, nor to her equation of *muthos* and *fabula*. The tangle is further complicated by her claim that Aristotle shows a preference 'for story (*fabula*) over character'—where story and *fabula* must logically be taken as equivalent terms both for each other and for *muthos*.[119] In a structuralist narratologist's review of a structuralist narratological translation of the *Poetics* we might expect to find greater sensitivity to the meaning of Aristotle's key technical term for plot.

Instead, and what lends this review essay further significance in aiding our appreciation of Bal's engagement with the classical tradition, is the use she makes here of the opportunity to recycle some of her pre-existing ideas about Aristotle as a structuralist 'semiotician'. Indeed, the piece incorporates several of the arguments and analyses previously aired in a 1981 article (published only in Dutch), '*Aristoteles semioticus*'. Discussing the treatment that Dupont-Roc and Lallot (DL) provide of Aristotle's key narratological concept of *mimesis*, Bal suggests, for example, that one of the praiseworthy features of their translation is its representation of *mimesis* as 'a semiotic concept'.[120] Her semiotic model here is Peirce's, for whom any and every concept is determined by its relational function as a 'sign'—defined by Peirce as that which 'determines an effect upon a person, which effect I call its interpretant, [so] that the latter is thereby mediately determined by the former'.[121] In this context, Bal suggests:[122]

[116] Bal 1977: 107.
[117] Bal 1982: 177. Dupont-Roc and Lallot, as discussed below, translate *muthos* as *histoire*.
[118] Bal 1982: 176.   [119] Bal 1982: 174.   [120] Bal 1982: 172.
[121] Peirce 1998: 478.   [122] Bal 1982: 172.

It is tempting to interpret the concept [of *mimesis*] in terms of Peircian semiotics. *Mimesis* is then regarded as the representation of an *interpretant*, which makes the question of the object irrelevant. It is significant for the procedure of DL's commentary that they do not discuss such a link but encourage the reader to establish it.

Quite how Dupont-Roc and Lallot encourage the reader to such a tempting interpretation is not clear, either from Bal's review or Dupont-Roc and Lallot's commentary. But elsewhere in her review Bal is happy to assert the same principle. Thus, she claims:[123]

Aristotle is not only a very lucid semiotician; parts of his text could pass the highest standards of research in *Rezeptionsästhetik*, as could his well-known psychoanalytical insights. More than that, he connects both currents to the semiotic basis of his theory. Arguing that *mimesis* is a natural need of mankind, he discusses the pleasure of representation in terms that are almost reminiscent of Barthes's *plaisir du texte*.

Similar observations are scattered throughout the piece: Bal describes Aristotle's theory of genres as a 'semiotic' theory, and refers both to 'Aristotle's semiotic thinking' and to 'semiotic point of view' on the subject of character as a theory fundamentally 'brought about by a semantics of binary oppositions' (his emphasis upon high and low characters, for example).[124] She even sees the whole of the second chapter of the *Poetics* (on the *mimesis* of different character types) as 'based on changes within the sign'.[125] Thus, Aristotle the proto-structuralist and proto-narratologist is recast by Bal as Aristotle the proto-semiotician.

Yet arguably the most significant aspect of this direct engagement with Aristotle's *Poetics* remains its exceptional, one-off status within Bal's work. We see nothing quite like it in any of her other, better known narratological studies. And this may well be because the groundwork for those studies is already firmly in place by 1980, before Bal encounters the Dupont-Roc and Lallot translation of the *Poetics* (which is also referenced in her 1981 Dutch essay '*Aristoteles semioticus*'). Thus, it remains a striking anomaly that, of all the structuralist narratologists, Bal emerges as the one least concerned with her classical narratologist predecessors—and yet as the one who would make the greatest impact upon classics through her influence on her pupil Irene de Jong.[126]

---

[123] Bal 1982: 174.   [124] Bal 1982: 177–8.   [125] Bal 1982: 174.
[126] De Jong's 1987 Bal-inspired study of 'narrators and focalizers' in the *Iliad*, along with her narratological commentary on the *Odyssey* (2001b), has helped to establish narratology as a valid and vibrant enterprise in classical scholarship. Her work also helped to make Bal's distinctive brand of structuralist narratology the basic template for the (basic) study of ancient narrative dynamics and form in many cases (cf. reviews of Grethlein and Rengakos

9.6 *Epeisodion* (On translation)

As in the case of Appelrot's 'formalist' Russian translation of Aristotle, there is one translation of Aristotle's *Poetics* which stands out for its particular associations with French structuralist theories of narrative: that of Roselyne Dupont-Roc and Jean Lallot. Published as part of the *Poetique* series edited by Genette and Todorov, and widely (re)viewed at the time as 'Aristotle for the structuralist', it openly acknowledges its indebtedness to Genette, Benveniste, Ricoeur, and other theorists in the broad structuralist tradition, candidly confirming that its translation and commentary necessarily represent a reading (*interprétation*) of Aristotle directly produced in response to and coloured by modern theories of narrative and poetics.[127] Its structuralist credentials are further confirmed by a short preface written by Todorov himself, where he draws an explicit connection between the structuralist narratological project and Aristotle's pioneering theory. Todorov remarks:[128]

It is not much of an exaggeration to say that the history of poetics coincides in its broad outline with the history of Aristotle's *Poetics*... the founding text of literary theory in Europe.

There are, however, some important discrepancies in the coincidences and correspondences that this translation draws between Aristotle's narratology and that of the structuralists. For Dupont-Roc and Lallot, the central argument of the *Poetics* sees poetry as 'the representation of human actions in language', with that representation (*mimesis*) being produced on two discrete levels—*histoire* and *lexis*.[129] Superficially, this would seem to map neatly on to the structuralist distinction between *histoire* and *discours* as the two fundamental levels of narrative (*récit*). Yet, the description of *histoire* that Dupont-Roc and Lallot offer, alongside their insistence that *lexis* is secondary and subordinate to *histoire*, problematizes that easy association. They suggest:[130]

The first and principal level concerns the construction of the story [*histoire*] according to a systematic arrangement... connected according to principles of

2009 by Liveley 2011 and Goldhill 2010). De Jong also helped launch the series 'Studies in Ancient Greek Narrative', and published *Narratology and Classics* (2014).

[127] See Rees 1981.
[128] Todorov 1980: 5. Todorov's encouragement is also acknowledged by the authors in their introduction (1980: 28).
[129] Dupont-Roc and Lallot 1980: 22: '*la représentation d'actions humaines par le langage*'.
[130] Dupont-Roc and Lallot 1980: 22.

necessity and probability; the construction is that of a sketch...the second and subordinate, is the work of the expression (*lexis*).

Genette, as we saw, drew upon the important Aristotelian distinction between narrative content (*logos*) and narrative form (*lexis*), aligning these levels with the structuralist terms *histoire* and *discours* respectively. But this alignment does not fit with the model forwarded by Dupont-Roc and Lallot. For Plato, Aristotle, and Genette *histoire*—the story—may be identified as the 'first' level of narrative and *lexis*—the expression—may be identified as the 'second', in that story content may be conceived (chronologically) as necessarily preceding its arrangement and representation into narrative discourse. But this isn't what Dupont-Roc and Lallot appear to have in mind here. As their Aristotelian definition of *histoire* confirms, they see it as an equivalent to *muthos*—that is, plot: their *histoire* concerns a systematic arrangement (*sunthesin: Poetics* 6.1450a 3–4); according to a probable (*eikos*) or necessary (*anangke*) sequence (*Poetics* 9.1451a 35–7); in a kind of preliminary outline sketch afforded by the plot (*eikona: Poetics* 6.1450b 1–3). This is the very definition of Aristotle's *muthos* in his *Poetics*. And, as a subsequent clarification reveals, this is how Dupont-Roc and Lallot want to use *histoire*, considering 'it best in translating *muthos* to abandon "fable" for "story"'.[131] They have improved on the two key French translations of the *Poetics* published in the first half of the twentieth century which both translate *muthos* consistently as '*fable*'—that is, as 'myth'—without distinguishing Aristotle's technical terminology for 'plot'.[132] But they have signally failed to align their translation with the latest structuralist terminology.

Despite its reputation as 'Aristotle for the structuralist', then, the Dupont-Roc and Lallot translation is not quite all that. What is more, it emerges *from* the structuralist tradition and is not, properly speaking, a translation *for* the key narratologists in this project. It is not always easy to identify those editions and translations of the *Poetics* (or the *Republic*) actually being used by the various structuralists, and thereby to ascertain those readings and interpretations of Aristotle and Plato that play a key role in shaping their theories. However, Genette is more scrupulous than most in referencing his sources, and from these references we can pinpoint at least two of the main classical translations informing his work.

Genette takes care to exhibit his credibility and authority in proposing the readings of Plato and Aristotle that he does. No specific text or

---

[131] Dupont-Roc and Lallot 1980: 27.   [132] Cf. Ruelle 1922 and Hardy 1932.

212 NARRATOLOGY

translation of Aristotle's *Poetics* is credited in '*Frontières du récit*' (although sources are given for the translations of both Homer and Plato) and the Aristotelian translations offered within Genette's analyses may be taken as his own. In *Figures III*, Genette acknowledges Hardy's 1932 edition as his source for the Greek text of Aristotle's *Poetics*, but again the translations he supplies both here and in *Figures II* appear to be his own. Translating *Poetics* 22.1459a 7–8, Hardy offers '*apercevoir les resemblances*', Genette offers '*voir les resemblances*'; for *Poetics* 1.1447b 19, Hardy has '*conveniendrait-il d'appeler l'un poète et l'autre naturaliste plutôt que poète*', Genette has '*il faut appeler l'un poète et l'autre physician plutôt que poète*'; and for *Poetics* 17.1455b 16–17, Hardy gives us '*dans l'épopee ce [les épisodes] sont eux qui donnent á l'oeuvre son étendue*', while Genette gives us '*la longueur de l'épopée tient aux épisodes*'. Genette clearly wants to show us that his is a direct, unmediated engagement with Aristotle's *Poetics* which lets no nuance of the original escape.

The translation of Plato's *Republic* Genette regularly cites is Chambry's respected 1932 edition, an annotated Greek text facing the French translation. And the source of Genette's emphasis upon the essentially mimetic character of narrative—in both Plato and Aristotle's narratologies—may be traced back to Chambry's work. The commentary that Chambry provides to gloss his translation of Socrates' reworking of the passage from Homer's *Iliad* (*Republic* 392d–394d) refers to 'an accepted principle in Greece even before Plato that poetry and art fall within the category of imitation (*mimesis*)'.[133] We find Genette insisting upon the same mimetic character of *poiesis*.[134] However, in his 1972 reading of this passage from Plato, Genette corrects Chambry's translation. He maintains the term *l'imitation* as the best translation of Plato's *mimesis*, but Chambry's '*simple récit*' for *diegesis* becomes '*récit pur*'. As Genette clarifies in a footnote:[135]

The common [sc. Chambry's] translation of *haplé diégésis* as "simple narrative" seems to me a little off the mark. *Haplé diégésis* is the narrative *not mixed* (in 397b, Plato says *akraton*) with mimetic elements, therefore, *pure*.

Genette, it emerges, is not only a nuanced reader of Plato's narratological taxonomy, but wants (to be seen) to engage with its technicalities and terminologies too. What is more, he wants to demonstrate that his engagements with both Plato and Aristotle are as close—as unmediated, as unmixed—as possible; that his dialogues and dialogic engagement with them both represent a *récit pur*.

---

[133] Chambry 1932: 101.   [134] Genette 1976: 2.
[135] Genette 1980: 162 n. 2.

9.7 *Teleute*

The dynamics of appropriation and reception at work in and across the structuralist project tell a fascinating story. In its early phases, ancient theories and theorists are annexed (and altered) so as to provide an authoritative genealogy for the new 'science' of narratology. Barthes looks for 'patronage' from Aristotle, and Genette also assumes the inherited authority of this narratological 'ancestor'. Genette even goes so far as to restage and re-interrogate (repeatedly) the famous Homeric scene that Plato's Socrates took as his foundational *exemplum* in the *Republic*, effectively overturning the Platonic/Socratic and Aristotelian typologies of *mimesis/diegesis* in the process. However, as structuralist narratology grows in stature and gathers its own authority, eventually taking on 'classical' status in its own right, we see a corresponding distance grow up between ancient and modern approaches, culminating in Genette's revisionist disavowal of Plato's *diegesis*, and Bal's attempt to recast Aristotle as a structuralist 'semiotician'. Yet there remains, as Bal acknowledges, a stubborn tenacity in these ancient theories and the voice of Plato's ventriloquized Socrates speaks on in the terminology and taxonomy of Genette's multi-diegetic levels—and in the common literary critical currency his narratology has helped to coin.

10 Poststructuralism

> An end is something that is inevitably or usually the organic result of
> something else but from which nothing else follows.
>
> Aristotle, *Poetics* 7.1450b 29–31

10.1 *Arche*

For the structuralists, Plato and Aristotle served a clear purpose in
helping to authorize and legitimize the new 'science' of narratology,
lending a notion of continuity and credibility to this old style of poetics.[1]
At least, this was the case in the early days.[2] Yet, by the time Bal joined
the conversation in the late 1970s, the critical momentum of the structuralist project was already such that this kind of valorization from the
classics had become unnecessary, and even a tad old-fashioned in its
mode of appropriation—particularly in its easy assumption that the
Poetics, predominantly a theory of ancient Greek tragedy, could provide
the template for a twentieth-century poetics of narrative more broadly.
We might expect the poststructuralists, therefore, to have no need for the
classics, to limit their engagements merely to the odd name check, to
reduce the theoretical nuances of *Republic* 3 and the *Poetics* down to a
much simpler rubric with diluted allusions to 'the Aristotelian tradition'
and the like. It is somewhat unexpected, then, to find the next generation
of narratologists not only (re)turning to Plato and Aristotle, but engaging
in no less depth and detail with ancient theories than their structuralist
and formalist predecessors. Paradoxically, it seems, the willingness of the
poststructuralists to look beyond the confines of twentieth-century linguistics and semiotics for their critical concepts and models re-energizes
narratology's relationship with ancient poetics. At the same time, the
poststructuralist drive to push beyond the established boundaries of
narratology and into a much wider domain of narrative 'texts'—looking
outside the narrow field of literary narrative into media such as film,

---

[1] On the poststructuralist turn in narratology see Nünning and Nünning 2002, Nünning
2003, and Herman 1999.
[2] See Genette 1988: 150–2 on his own reservations about the (blurred) distinctions
between the narratological projects of structuralism and poststructuralism.

music, and visual culture—rediscovers Aristotle's *Poetics* and the anticipation of cross-medial narrative theory found there. Aristotle, we recall, included a wide variety of different genres and media within the theoretical purview of artistic *mimesis*—including epic, tragic, and comic poetry; music sung to accompany the reed pipe, lyre, and panpipes; and even some kinds of dance (*Poetics* 1.1447a 13–27). However, besides tragedy and epic (and comedy in the lost second book), he ended up having very little to say about music or dance, or about the performance elements of tragic drama.

So, as the scope of narratology is more fully rounded out in its poststructuralist phase, different priorities and positions emerge, each with a different style of attachment to the classics. Although her engagement with ancient narrative theory remains limited, Mieke Bal is one of the pioneers here, not only expanding the semiotic principles of her narratology to demonstrate its potential application to stories in different media ('language, imagery, sound, buildings'), and including among her case studies 'non-canonical' works by Duras and Colette, but also questioning the importance of gender in considering those key narratological questions 'who sees?' and 'who speaks?'.[3] Such questions also occupy Susan Lanser in her groundbreaking work on feminist narratology, *The Narrative Act: Point of View in Prose Fiction* (1981), where she brings together some of the core principles of both feminist and narrative theory—and at the same time widens the range of texts and discourses traditionally considered by narratologists in order to include more works authored or narrated by women and non-European voices. With very different emphases but an analogous approach to blending narratology with contemporary theories from other disciplines, Peter Brooks introduces some of the latest ideas in psychoanalytic literary criticism to the narratological toolkit, exploring the ways in which key aspects of narrative and narrativity are psychologically motivated and cognitively processed in his *Reading for the Plot* (1984). But it is Seymour Chatman's *Story and Discourse: Narrative Structure in Fiction and Film* (1978) which prepares the way for this narratological breadth and theoretical diversity by the trailblazing application of narrative theory to film, thereby inaugurating the poststructuralist turn towards cross-textual, contextual, and cognitive approaches to narrative—the three key approaches which still dominate the field today.[4]

---

[3] Bal 1997: 5.

[4] See Meister 2014. Herman 1999: 8 sees a version of contextualism alive and well in postclassical narratologies, where there has been a marked shift 'from text-centred or formal models to . . . models attentive both to the text and to the context of stories'. On

10.2 **Seymour Chatman**

As apparently behoves those pioneering any new kind of poetics, Chatman marks the important move from literature to film as the object of narrative theory with a return to Plato and Aristotle.[5] Indeed, Chatman's *Story and Discourse* is remarkable for its sophisticated engagement with Aristotle's *Poetics* in particular, directed by the highly nuanced 1968 Hardison and Golden translation and commentary—one of the first English translations to identify Aristotle's *muthos* as a specialist term and to translate it consistently as 'plot'.

With Chatman we never get the sense that he is referring to some received notion of 'Aristotle' or the '*Poetics*' in abstract terms. He appeals to the ancient theorists to help bolster his own authority, certainly, but that authority is enhanced by the careful readings he forwards; he takes Aristotle seriously as a narratologist, rather than simply as a name to drop, openly addressing the shortcomings as well as the successes of Aristotle's narratological intuitions, just as he does with the modern theorists drawn in as his principal interlocutors. Chatman treats Aristotle as a serious theorist, worthy of serious critical interrogation. Thus, he challenges the theory of character presented in the *Poetics* and questions the applicability of Aristotelian ethics to modern texts and contexts.[6] Nevertheless, Chatman flags his fundamental sympathies with Aristotle in his Preface, declaring: 'To me the most exciting approach . . . is dualist and structuralist, in the Aristotelian tradition.'[7]

Given that Chatman's primary objective in *Story and Discourse* is to establish the theoretical framework for a cross-medial narratology and a poetics of narrative that is responsive to the particular requirements of film criticism, we might have expected him to find Aristotle's own cross-medial approach exciting too. However, in *Story and Discourse* we are invited to align Chatman's narratology with an 'Aristotelian tradition'— overtly characterized as a fundamentally 'structuralist' approach—that is less concerned with the dynamics of cross-mediality but concerned rather with the dynamics of *histoire* (story) and *discours* (discourse), of *praxis* (action) and *muthos* (plot).

the neo-Aristotelian focus upon context, see Rader 1999: 47, Sacks 1964: 69, and Chapter 7.3 in this volume.

[5] Chatman's engagement with Plato is relatively brief. Cf. 1978: 146 on Plato's distinction between *mimesis* and *diegesis* as the direct equivalent 'in modern terms between showing and telling'. Cf. 1978: 32.

[6] Chatman 1978: 89 and 108.   [7] Chatman 1978: 9.

Chatman's subsequent analysis also encourages us to draw a further connection between these key concepts and Russian formalist notions of *fabula* and *syuzhet*. Initially, he presents the Russian formalist binary as a more primitive and less nuanced model of narrative structure than that proposed either by Aristotle or the structuralists.[8] Aristotle, Chatman insists, works with a tripartite model which distinguishes between the *mimesis* of real-world elements and actions (*praxis*), and their formation into a basic chronolinear story form (*logos*), which provides the raw material for rearrangement and *sunthesis* into a particularized plot (*muthos*).[9] In Chatman's reading, the structuralists, in their turn, work with a model of narrative that sees events transformed into story (*histoire*) through the operations of language, and those storified events are turned into plot through the operations of discourse (*discours*), or 'the modus of presentation'.[10] But as Chatman develops his own distinctive poststructuralist narratology, he begins to run these separate pre-existing traditions together. Discussing narratological conceptions of character, he claims: 'Aristotle and the formalists and some structuralists subordinate character to plot, make it a function of plot, a necessary but derivative consequence of the chronologic of story.'[11] It seems that Aristotle, and the formalists, and the structuralists are to be lumped together as sharing and bequeathing a common narratology. This, of course, makes it easier for Chatman to position his own cross-medial narratology as an innovative (yet respectful) alternative to that classical tradition. But paradoxically, treating the narratological theories of 'Aristotle and the formalists and some structuralists' as a dehistoricized and decontextualized unity in this way also provides the grounds for Chatman's often overlooked secondary contribution to the wider field of poststructuralist narratology: recognition of the significance of *context* in assessing narrative theory and the discourses it describes. Indeed, it is in Chatman's contextualism rather than in his cross-medial approach to

---

[8] Chatman 1978: 20–1. This represents a highly simplified version of the Russian formalist dyad *fabula* and *syuzhet*, whose dynamics are more sophisticated than Chatman allows (see Chapter 6.1–4 in this volume). Chatman appropriates his notion of 'kernels' and 'satellites' (describing essential and non-essential story elements) from Tomashevsky's 'bound' and 'free' motifs (1965), Propp's invariant and variant functions (1968), and Barthes's 'nuclei' and 'catalysers' (1975).

[9] Chatman 1978: 19.   [10] Chatman 1978: 43.

[11] Chatman 1978: 113. The same alignment is also made at 111: 'The views of the formalists and (some) structuralists resemble Aristotle's in a striking way. They too argue that characters are products of plots, that their status is "functional," that they are, in short, participants or actants rather than personages, that it is erroneous to consider them as real beings.' By 120, he has dropped the qualification '(some)'.

narrative theory that the more interesting story of his reception of Aristotle's *Poetics* may be read.

At this juncture it is important to stress that here we run (as so often) into a problem of terminology: Chatman's appreciation for the narratological importance of context does not straightforwardly qualify his own narratology as 'contextualist'. For, although Chatman is responsible for introducing this label to describe this distinctive poststructuralist approach to narrative theory in his 1990 essay 'What Can We Learn from Contextualist Narratology?' he is profoundly critical of the approach in general. Or, rather, he is deeply critical of the contextualist approach as forwarded specifically by Mary Pratt (1977), Barbara Herrnstein Smith (1981), and Thomas Leitch (1986), with some lesser criticism reserved for Susan Lanser. Chatman seems willing to accept the neo-Aristotelian position, as outlined by Smith, that narratology should treat narratives 'as verbal acts consisting of *someone telling someone else that something happened*'.[12] Chatman himself devotes significant energy in treating narrative as a communication act in *Story and Discourse* and draws the very terms of his title from the linguistic paradigm of structuralism, in which narrative was also conceived as a communicative speech act. He is partially sympathetic, too, to the contextualist manifesto, which, in Smith's formulation, declares that the 'someone' to whom the narrative act is directed, the one told, makes sense of the telling through the combined 'contextual' forces of:[13]

(1) his prior knowledge or beliefs concerning the chronology of those implied events as derived from other sources, including other narratives; (2) his familiarity with the relevant conventions of the language in which that narrative is presented (verb tenses, adverbs, and adverbial clauses, and so forth, and comparable time markers in other modes and media); (3) his familiarity with the relevant conventions and traditions of the style and genre of that narrative; (4) his knowledge and beliefs, including cultural assumptions, with respect to how things in general, and the particular kinds of things with which that narrative is concerned, happen and "follow from" each other—that is, his sense of the "logic" of temporal and causal sequence; and (5) certain more or less universal perceptual and cognitive tendencies involved in his processing—apprehending and organizing—information in any form.

However, Chatman balks at the idea that analysis of the 'real world' conditions pertaining to the production of a particularized narrative act and its reception by 'real world' audiences should or could exclude

---

[12] Smith 1981: 227–8, emphases in original. Cf. Phelan 2015: 146.
[13] Smith 1981: 226.

analysis of the product itself and the structures that support its communicative form and function. For Chatman, context matters most in narratology to the extent that it speaks to a certain kind of relativism. That is, 'the relativism inherent in comprehending narratives, not to speak of analyzing and taxonomizing them'.[14] He suggests that 'if we are serious about theory', we must therefore question the context(s) in which we process and investigate narrative—the conventions and traditions, the cultural assumptions, and those more or less universal tendencies that guide the narrative process and its processing.[15] In respecting this principle, Chatman explicitly acknowledges the influence of his structuralist predecessors, Todorov (who was particularly interested in the contextual dynamics of *vraisemblance* in narrative), Culler (who had tackled the contextual contingencies of 'convention and naturalization' in his 1975 *Structuralist Poetics*), and Genette, who had argued that the cultural assumptions and conventions that make narrative processing possible a priori reflect socio-historical, context-specific notions of common sense and commonplaces. Chatman acknowledges too that this process accords with Aristotelian notions of probability: 'What would be called today an ideology, that is, a body of maxims and presuppositions which constitute at once a vision of the world and a system of values.'[16] For Chatman, then, 'context' does not concern the biography of the narrative's author, the materiality of his or her text, or the anthropology of its audience; but 'context' does concern the conventions and traditions, the maxims and presuppositions, that make a narrative narratable in the first place—the a priori conditions that allow us to recognize and process a narrative as such.

So, for Chatman, the conditions of causation according to probability and necessity that Aristotle repeatedly describes as essential to the emplotment of events in a narrative are contextually configured.[17] Chatman points out that Aristotle, like the Russian formalists and French structuralists, understands that a plot twists the chronological order of a 'natural' story sequence, distorting the logic of temporal and causal sequence. Furthermore, it does so according to a set of normative rules governed by notions of what is probable and necessary, or what Chatman labels as Aristotle's 'probabilistic model'.[18] What is more, the contextual forces articulated by Smith in the contextualist manifesto are precisely those forces which determine whether a poet or an audience will deem a

---

[14] Chatman 1978: 89.   [15] Chatman 1978: 89.   [16] Chatman 1978: 50.
[17] Aristotle incorporates this contextual 'probability' theory into his own readings of Homer. Cf. Aristotle, *Homeric Problems* F 144 Rose [Athenaeus 556d].
[18] Chatman 1978: 45–6.

causative sequence of events to be probable and necessary: as Halliwell puts it, the principles of *eikos* and *anangke* constitute Aristotle's 'recurrent criteria of what makes "natural" sense'.[19] It is this culturally contextualized and thus 'naturalized' sense of what is likely or unlikely to happen next in any given plot that underpins Aristotle's insistence that poets represent 'the kinds of things that might happen and are possible in terms of probability or necessity' (*Poetics* 9.1451a 35–7). Similarly 'naturalized' conventions will work to determine whether a character is good or bad, high or low, and whether a plot consequently delivers him to a deserved or undeserved end, and so delivers the audience a satisfying *telos*. According to Chatman, poststructuralist notions of the contextual are 'very close to that of verisimilitude, the ancient appeal to the probable, rather than the actual'. This, in turn, 'explains the technique by which the reader "fills in" gaps in the text, adjusts events and existents to a coherent whole' according to what seems likely or realistic.[20] However, as Chatman warns:[21]

What constitutes "reality" or "likelihood" is a strictly cultural phenomenon, though authors of narrative fiction make it "natural". But of course the "natural" changes from one society to another, and from one era to another in the same society.

The influence of Aristotle's *Poetics* and its 'probabilistic model' of plot upon Chatman's reasoning here is clear—even down to his use of the formulation 'well-formedness' to describe a coherent narrative whole. However, the conclusion that Chatman ultimately draws regarding the temporal and cultural specificity of these contextual plot dynamics is that much of Aristotle and his theory of narrative will therefore have to go.

Aristotle's plot typology, for instance, was grounded upon the *ethos* and fortunes of its lead character. Depending upon the intersection of plot and protagonist, six basic plot types emerge (although Aristotle only discusses four of them), each producing its own particular affect. According to Chatman, then, Aristotle's typology identifies narrative plots in which:[22]

1. a good hero fails—which 'violates probability' and offends our sense of justice;
2. a villain fails—and we feel 'smug satisfaction, since justice has been served';
3. a flawed hero fails—'which arouses our pity and fear';

---

[19] Halliwell 1999: 57 n. 71.   [20] Chatman 1978: 49.   [21] Chatman 1978: 49.
[22] Cf. Chatman 1978: 85. Cf. Hardison and Golden 1968: 179–85.

4. a villain succeeds—which 'violates our sense of probability' and offends our sense of justice;
5. a good hero succeeds—'causing us to feel moral satisfaction';
6. a flawed hero ('like Orestes') fails temporarily—but his 'ultimate vindication is satisfying'.

But these plot types, already contingent on an ancient typology of character (of the kind delineated in Aristotle's *Rhetoric*), only make sense in those (theoretical) texts and contexts where good and bad, hero and villain, noble and base, success and failure, are obvious and clearly defined. For Chatman, temporarily overlooking the complexity of character and ethics in ancient narrative and drama, these plot and character typologies work only 'to the extent that they account for all and only Greek dramas'.[23] Except, of course, they don't. Aristotle's categories no more reflect the sophisticated characterizations in fifth-century BCE tragedy than they mirror those of the late twentieth or early twenty-first centuries CE when audiences may (still) be delighted to see a villainous protagonist succeed or a noble hero fail.[24] As Chatman concedes of modern narratives: 'The worlds of modern fiction and cinema are not two-valued, black and white, ... or to revert to Aristotle's basic dichotomy, how can we know whether a character's situation has improved or worsened in a narrative whose very point is to question the values of the society depicted?'[25]

Although Chatman himself does not pick up on this, Aristotle frames the 'contextualism' of his own character-based plot typology in the insistence that characters should not only behave and speak according to the same principles of necessity and probability which govern a good plot (*Poetics* 15.1454a 32–6) but should also be 'like us'—*homoios*.[26] That is, they should be like the audience, those whom the poet aims to move with his well-formed *muthos* and *ethos*, moving people to pity and fear in sympathy with his mimetic representation of characters *just like them*.

---

[23] Chatman 1978: 92. Cf. 110 for Chatman's analysis of Aristotle on character.

[24] Milton's Satan (*Paradise Lost*), Shelley's Creature (*Frankenstein*), and Nabokov's Humbert Humbert (*Lolita*) anticipate a wealth of similarly 'complex' characters and narratives in contemporary fiction—especially in television storytelling (e.g. Dexter, Tony Soprano, Walter White): cf. Mittell 2015: 118–63.

[25] Chatman 1978: 92.

[26] Aristotle uses this term in various different contexts but its basic frame of reference seems to mean 'people like us' (*Poetics* 2.1448a 5–6, and 13.1453a 5–6). Chatman overlooks the significance of this, perhaps as a consequence of following Hardison's translation of *homoios* in the context of characterization as 'like an individual', displaying 'idiosyncrasies that soften—without obscuring—the general outline', and 'consistency'. See Chatman 1978: 110 and Hardison and Golden 1968: 204.

The ideal story narrative in Aristotle's schema may deal with abstracts and *universals*, but its characters will reflect a *particular* set of cultural interests, values, experiences, and beliefs. As with plot, this contextual character/audience dynamic with its assumptions about shared conventions and traditions, maxims and presuppositions, is what makes such a narrative narratable in the first place.

For Chatman, contextualist approaches to narrative (particularly as conceived by Pratt, Smith, and Leitch) are fundamentally flawed in their assumptions that form and context, process and product, can be understood separately. His own 'Aristotelian' brand of contextualism treats context and structure as inextricably combined and understands that the narrative operations of each depend upon the other. There is something ironic, then, in the fact that what Chatman ultimately takes from Aristotle's narratology and its 'contextual' concerns is the tenet that poststructuralist narratology and its own (post)modern 'contextual' concerns must leave ancient theories of narrative behind.[27]

10.3 **Susan Lanser**

The contextualist turn leads the theory of narrative towards an important juncture in the path of its poststructuralist development. Twenty years after that famous 1966 special edition of *Communications* had established structuralism as the new narratological paradigm, 1986 saw the independent publication of two landmark articles both introducing the prospect of a new feminist narratology: Robyn Warhol's 'Toward a Theory of the Engaging Narrator' and Susan Lanser's 'Toward a Feminist Narratology'.[28] As Lanser convincingly demonstrates, the decontextualized grammar of narratorial modes promoted by the structuralists are inadequate unless qualified by context—such as, whether a given narrative is conceived as performing public and/or private discourse.

Informed by the latest research in sociolinguistics and speech act theory (which stress the importance of function and framing contexts in any act of communication), both Lanser and Warhol are responding to the ahistoricism that characterized structuralist narratology, in which

---

[27] Chatman's work on film narrative goes on to shape the discipline. Cf. Branigan 1984 and 1992, and Bordwell, Staiger, and Thompson 1985.

[28] Lanser's article more so than Warhol's sparked a heated debate on the (in)compatibility of feminism and narratology. Cf. Diengott 1988 (who claims that Lanser's theory 'has nothing to do with narratology': 50), and Lanser's response (1988).

texts were separated from their contexts in the search for a universal
narrative grammar. As Warhol sees it, 'the first practitioners of narratology lifted texts out of their contexts in order to distil from them the
essential structures that characterize all narrative'.[29] One of the primary
aims of feminist narratology is therefore to correct this essentializing and
decontextualizing trend, to look anew at texts in context. Reacting
against the ahistorical priorities of structuralism, the feminist approach
to poststructuralist narratology thus privileges—and politicizes—the
socio-historical conditions in which narrative discourse is produced
and consumed.[30]

Lanser and Warhol are also keen to address and redress the fact that
the canon of literature on which narratology's core principles are
founded is predominantly written and narrated by men. Lanser had
already signalled these issues in her 1981 study of point of view in
prose fiction, *The Narrative Act*, where she had flagged the 'complete
disregard of gender in the formalist study of narrative voice'.[31] Indeed, as
we have seen, the grammatical categories of tense, voice, and mood
adopted by structuralists simply ignored the classification of gender.
Feminist theorists in other fields had already begun to contest the
supposed objectivity of language used in the social, political, and natural
sciences, objecting that 'systems of meaning are never neutral... they
bear the (gendered) marks of their originators and their receivers'.[32]
Feminist literary critics had also already begun to question whether
stories by and about women might challenge the normative assumptions
about narrative dynamics set out in formalist and structuralist narratologies.[33] Laura Mulvey had analysed the ways in which the pleasures,
positionalities, and perspectives available to female audiences of narrative cinema are restricted by predominantly heterosexual male identities
and fantasies 'triggered by the logic of narrative grammar'.[34] While
Annette Kolodny had argued:[35]

---

[29] Warhol 1989: 4.
[30] See Herman 1999 for a useful summary of the contributions made by feminist
narratology to the contextual turn in poststructuralism.
[31] Lanser 1981: 46. [32] Warhol 1999: 342.
[33] Particularly influential in this context are Kolodny 1975 on the gendered biases
implicit in notional 'universals'; Miller 1981 on plausibility; de Lauretis 1984 on the
implicitly gendered patterns assumed to structure desire in narrative; and DuPlessis 1985
on gendered plot structures and dynamics.
[34] Mulvey 1975: 13.
[35] Kolodny 1975: 89. Her observations on the cognitive aspect of this debate are also
prescient, anticipating current debates in cognitive narratology. See also Showalter 1977: 8

A largely male-dominated academic establishment has, for the last 75 years or so, treated men's writing as though it were the model for all writing. In other words, the various theories on the craft of fiction, and the formalist and structuralist models that have been based on this closed tradition but have been offered up as "universals" of fictive form or even (under the influence of the psycholinguists) as emanations of yet deeper structures within human cognitive processes may in fact prove to be less than universal and certainly less than fully human.

For Lanser too, who similarly tends to collapse the formalist and structuralist traditions together in her work, often referring to a unified 'formalist-structuralist' narratology to which feminist narratology offers a corrective, 'the masculine text stands for the universal text'.[36] Her argument highlights that the narratives which have so happened to provide the case studies for narratology have been almost exclusively masculine: from Plato's proto-narratological study of Homer; Aristotle's analysis of Greek tragedy and Homeric epic; through the Russian formalists' work on Sterne, Pushkin, Swift, and Tolstoy; to the structuralists' studies of Balzac, Boccaccio, and Proust. As Lanser points out in *Fictions of Authority*, 'the canon on which narrative theory is grounded has been relentlessly if not intentionally man-made'.[37]

Even those traditional narratives with no identifiably gendered author, such as the Russian folktales studied by Propp and Greimas, encode a certain gender bias—a bias which translates into the supposedly 'universal' categories for which they provide the narratological case studies. Thus, while Propp's quasi-Aristotelian *dramatis personae* and Greimas's corresponding actants are presented as ostensibly gender-neutral categories—the hero, false hero, opponent, donor, dispatcher, et al. (in Propp's model) and the hero, helper, opponent, sender, and receiver (in Greimas's schema)—implicitly gendered dynamics are clearly in evidence. A decidedly male hero is envisaged in both models, and a decidedly heteronormative hero to boot: Propp's *personae* also include a princess (and her father), and his thirty-one functions assume that a wedding between hero and princess marks the functional *telos* of the typical folktale plot.[38]

---

for the view that both formalist and structuralist models blindly ignore questions of gender and narrative.

[36] Lanser 1986: 343.

[37] Lanser 1992: 6. The emphasis here is upon gender rather than ethnicity, but the point could (and would subsequently) be made that narratology's canon is not only male but white, wealthy, able-bodied, and European.

[38] Propp 1968 and Greimas 1983. Notice that Smith (1981: 226, cited above) similarly presupposes a male default reader in her own contextualist manifesto. Cf. Lanser 2014: 207. In their 2015 edited collection, Lanser and Warhol explore the compatibilities of

However, Lanser suggests that it is not in Russian folktales alone (nor only in the theories of Propp and Greimas) that we encounter an implicitly gendered notion of plot. Citing Brewer's psychoanalytically informed analysis of plot as a gendered operation, Lanser invites us to regard plot as a '"discourse of male desire recounting itself through the narrative of adventure, project, enterprise, and conquest . . . [and as a] discourse of desire as separation and mastery"'.[39] We need, she argues, alternative, more capacious definitions of plot, which could help us find ways to talk about the ostensibly 'plotless' narratives so often found in writing by women.[40]

In this context, it is hardly surprising that Plato, Socrates, and Aristotle—ancient avatars of the very 'white, educated men of hegemonic ideology' whose poetics Lanser resists—play no substantive role in this new branch of poststructuralist narratology.[41] There is no clear link in the chain of reception connecting Lanser (or Warhol) back to the ancient world. The 'classical' narratology that Lanser seeks to challenge is that of Genette and Barthes rather than that of Plato and Aristotle. Indeed, the very concept of such a genealogy runs contrary to the fundamental ethos of Lanser's feminist narratology. However, there is a probable chain of causal connection—a *muthos* of sorts—that links Lanser's poetics to Aristotle's. For Lanser's focus upon the gendered dynamics of narratology and its own narratives reminds us that it was Aristotle, the first of the male 'narrative theorists of plot', who is responsible for initially introducing the model of plot that Lanser seeks to resist and refine. The distinctive profile of Aristotle's *muthos* is clearly visible as an inherited characteristic in Lanser's criticism. She writes:[42]

The units of anticipation and fulfillment or problem and solution that structure plot according to narrative theorists of plot assume that textual actions are based on the (intentional) deeds of protagonists; they assume a power, a possibility, that

---

feminist and queer narratologies. On queer narratology see also Farwell 1996, Miller 1992, and Roof 1996.

[39] Lanser 1986: 356. Cf. Brewer 1984: 1151–3.

[40] Lanser's case study here (1986: 346–57) is a fictional coded letter 'On female ingenuity' in which two competing narratives are produced by literally reading between the lines.

[41] Lanser 1992: 6.

[42] Lanser 1986: 360. Rabinowitz makes the same point regarding post-colonial narratives, signalling the affinity between these two poststructuralist narratologies (1987: 224): 'for instance, the aesthetic value of well-roundedness, of consistently returning characters, privileges a certain kind of life and makes other kinds of social reality all but impossible to portray without departing from "good" structure. Well-roundedness might therefore well be incompatible with a realistic slave narrative, since the very point of that narrative might be precisely that you lose your friends and family—indeed, your whole past and any possibility of order, much less progress, in your life—as you are shuffled around.'

may be inconsistent with what women have experienced both historically and textually, and perhaps inconsistent with women's desires.

It was, after all (or, rather, before all), Aristotle who first maintained that a narrative plot is structured around the intentional actions of its protagonist actants (*prattontas*) as they encounter a problem (*desis*), leading them—and the audience—through a structured series of reversals (*peripeteia*), recognitions (*anagnorisis*), and suffering (*pathos*), through to a satisfactory solution (*lusis*). But Lanser points out that plots by and concerning women may display a very different narrative economy, one not based on actions and deeds; one based on different intentions, desires, and motivations; one potentially evincing very different assumptions about what might formally and thematically constitute a problem and its solution. This does not render such narratives 'plotless', or poorly plotted, but differently plotted. To reappropriate Chatman: '[In] Aristotle's basic dichotomy, how can we know whether a [female] character's situation has improved or worsened in a narrative whose very point is to question the [gendered] values of the society depicted?'[43]

It was Aristotle likewise who first established a definition of plot as a temporal-causal sequence of events following the vicissitudes of a male protagonist ('a discourse of male desire' *avant la lettre*) through to a satisfying *telos*.[44] It was Aristotle too who first established the definition of narrative as emplotted discourse, discounting lyric, elegiac, didactic, and panegyric poetry from his purview not only because of their insufficient mimeticism but evidently because of their lack of formal plot (*Poetics* 1.1447a 12–16). It was also Aristotle who thereby first established an exclusively male-authored canon as the foundation for narratology's first precepts, by excluding Sappho and other ancient female lyric poets. In seeking to resist the gender dynamics evidenced in each of these key narratological areas, Lanser's poststructuralist, contextualist, feminist poetics turns out to address not only her structuralist predecessors but Aristotle too.[45]

Indeed, Lanser tacitly reminds us that narratology is itself the product of a particular set of socio-historical conditions and is therefore itself worthy of contextualist consideration. Her approach suggests that

[43] Chatman 1978: 92. Cf. Koldodny 1985: 147: 'what is important about a fiction is not whether it ends in death or a marriage but what the symbolic demands of that particular conventional ending imply about the values and beliefs of the world that engendered it'.

[44] On the ongoing debate as to whether women numbered among the audiences for ancient drama see Goldhill 1997.

[45] There is a suggestive parallel here with Lanser's own reading of 'Female ingenuity', an analogous discourse resisting traditional patriarchal constraints and telling more than one story.

contemporary narrative poetics might look very different if Aristotle had
not taken the decision to exclude Sappho from his survey of canonical
ancient texts. It invites us to speculate on the dynamics of a counterfactual history of narratology, to ask 'what if' Aristotle had allowed lyric and
elegy to qualify as narrative; what if Plato's Socrates had focused his
attention upon the proem of Homer's *Iliad* as well as upon its opening
scene—what might he have made then of the authority attributed there
to the female Muse who provides the basic story that Homer turns into
discourse; what if Socrates' interlocutor in this dialogue had not been
Adeimantus but Diotima? What if we had (not only) Aristotle's *Poetics*
but that of his sister, Arimneste?[46]

10.4 **Peter Brooks**

Peter Brooks in *Reading for the Plot* reveals fewer qualms about returning
to a universal, ahistorical, and traditional model of narrative—and narratology. Brooks's psychoanalytically informed approach to narrative
involves the 'superimposition of the model of the functioning of the
psychic apparatus on the functioning of the text', and so concerns the
fundamental 'narratability' of (the) human experience and identity.[47]
The 'human' in this story is the universal, transhistorical, white, male
subject. Yet, in keeping with the contextualist priorities of the poststructuralist project more broadly (and therefore broadly in tune with Lanser), Brooks actually conceives of his 'anthropological' approach to
narrative as a corrective to the abstract schematics and grammars of
formalism and structuralism.[48] He criticizes such models as too 'static',
too concerned with 'paradigmatic structure', and presents his own, in
contrast, as a turn towards narrative movement, as a concern with
dynamics and 'the play of desire in time that makes us turn pages and
strive towards narrative ends'.[49]

In the light of the work by Lanser, it is impossible not to see this
emphasis upon dynamic movement, the thrusting forward momentum
through narrative twists and turns, the readerly urge that that makes us
desire to turn pages as we strive towards narrative ends, as an overtly
(even naively) gendered quest narrative in itself. Whatever we make of

[46] On the narrative authority of the Muse in ancient poetry and poetics see Spentzou and
Fowler 2002. On gendered approaches to narrativity (and narratology) in the classics see
Lipking 1983, and Liveley and Salzman 2008.
[47] Brooks 1984: 112.   [48] Brooks 1984: 131.   [49] Brooks 1984: xiii.

the gender politics contextualizing Brooks's theory, and whether or not we identify with the collective, unified, dehistoricized, and decontextualized group identified as 'us' here, the *telos* of this desire is significant. Importing Freudian theories about the desires and drives of the 'human' psyche, alongside Lacanian ideas about the metonymic mechanics and dynamics of desire, Brooks stresses the 'human' desire for closure and coherence as the 'motor force' that drives the teleological dynamics of plot from beginning, middle, to end. Or, as Brooks describes it (in another overtly gendered formulation), the 'movement from passivity to mastery'.[50] According to these principles:[51]

Desire is always there at the start of a narrative, often in a state of initial arousal, often having reached a state of intensity such that movement must be created, action undertaken, change begun. The *Iliad* opens with Agamemnon and Achilles locked in passionate quarrel over the girl Briseis, and the *Odyssey* with Odysseus, detained on Calypso's island, expressing the longing of his *nostos*, the drive to return home.

The desire that follows this initial state of arousal builds towards climax and what Brooks characterizes as the 'consummation' of the narrative.[52] But that desirable climax and consummation must be delayed, the gratification of desire 'reached only through the at least minimally complicated detour, the intentional deviance . . . which is the plot of narrative'.[53]

As feminist narratologists protest, Brooks's schema and understanding of desire in narrative is clearly modelled on that of male sexual arousal and orgasm.[54] The classical plot pattern adduced here articulates a paradigmatic story dynamic in which desire may serve as the motor of narrativity, and plot the vehicle, but the driver of both occupies a gendered positionality as male. For all its genuinely innovative insights into the movement of plots and readers, then, Brooks's poststructuralist psychodynamic theory of narrative essentially retells a very traditional story.[55]

This may well be because Brooks's teleological model of narrative and plot is essentially that first articulated in the fourth century BCE by Aristotle. At first Brooks only tentatively suggests that his own 'conception of plot seems to be at least compatible with Aristotle's

---

[50] Brooks 1984: 90 and 98. Cf. Brooks 1977: 78 on metonymy and desire in narrative.
[51] Brooks 1984: 38.   [52] Brooks 1984: 51–2.
[53] Brooks 1984: 104.
[54] See in particular Mezei 1996 for such criticisms.
[55] Brooks's concern with plot 'dynamics' also recalls Crane's concern with '*dynamis*' as the 'working power' that drives plot. Cf. Crane 1950 and 1953.

understanding of *mythos*', but he then goes on to reinforce that compatibility at every opportunity.[56] Indeed, he even characterizes his principal interlocutors and influences from the formalist and structuralist traditions as themselves essentially Aristotelian: he explicitly aligns the Russian formalist concept of *syuzhet* (as deployed by Shklovsky and Tomashevsky) as directly corresponding to Aristotle's concept of *muthos*;[57] he equates Todorov's theory of 'narrative transformation' as analogous to Aristotle's views on the transformative dynamics of metaphor and the tension of cognitively processing resemblance in difference;[58] and he reads Barthes's understanding of the pleasure of the text as something climaxing in a quasi-orgasmic Aristotelian *anagnorisis*.[59]

Fundamental to these readings of his predecessors, and to Brooks's narratology as a whole, is the Aristotelian idea that plot configures the 'dynamic of narrative', and is therefore itself a mode of narrative understanding.[60] For Brooks, as for Aristotle (and, in Brooks's patrilineal model of reception, as for Shklovsky, Tomashevsky, Todorov, and Barthes), plot comprises an artificial rearrangement of story episodes and events into a coherent unity in which there is, crucially, a beginning, a middle, and an end. Brooks quotes at length from Bywater's 1973 translation of the *Poetics* and synthesizes Aristotle's key points on the ideal *muthos* thus:[61]

First, the action imitated by the tragedy must be complete in itself. This in turn means that it must have a beginning, a middle, and an end—a point wholly obvious but one that will prove to have interesting effects in its applications. Finally, just as in the visual arts a whole must be of a size that can be taken in by the eye, so a plot must be "of a length to be taken in by the memory." This is important, since memory—as much in reading a novel as in seeing a play—is the key faculty in the capacity to perceive relations of beginnings, middles, and ends through time, the shaping power of narrative.

Beyond the repeated emphasis here upon 'beginnings, middles, and ends' (the aspect of Aristotle's *muthos* that helps authorize Brooks to forward and defend his own theory of the psychodynamics involved in 'reading for the plot') we notice here a corresponding and no less important emphasis upon memory and perception. The narrative dynamics of memory, in fact, play an integral part in Brooks's psychoanalytical understanding of the narrative dynamics of desire.[62]

---

[56] Brooks 1984: 10.   [57] Brooks 1984: 326–7.   [58] Brooks 1984: 90–1.
[59] Cf. Brooks 1984: 92.   [60] Brooks 1984: 10.   [61] Brooks 1984: 11.
[62] Cf. Brooks 1984: 58 on Lacan and memory; 111 on Lukacs and memory; 285 on Freud on memory; 328–9 on Augustine's and Ricouer's (Aristotelian) take on memory and/as narrative.

In his preliminary definition of terms, Brooks has already suggested that he sees plot as that which leads to narrative understanding.[63] This emphasis upon narrative perception and understanding adds a further key dimension to Brooks's reception of Aristotle's *Poetics*, and one which positions both Aristotle and Brooks as proponents of at once a very old and very new type of narrative theory: that is, cognitive narratology.[64] Underpinning the foundations of Brooks's psychoanalytically informed model of narrative dynamics is the awareness that plots are not passively received but actively processed—together with the comprehension that certain narrative structures prompt and shape those processes. For Brooks, as for Aristotle, the most important of these structures is plot, the temporal and teleological architecture of which allows meaning and coherence to be built out of discrete, metonymic, story units, and the careful synthesis of which allows the end to be delayed. And for Brooks, as for Aristotle, the ultimate goal of this cognitive process is a climactic moment of recognition, of *anagnorisis*—in which we finally recognize the pattern of the story or *fabula* which the *muthos* or *syuzhet* has transformed, in which we thus make (retrospective) sense of the narrative as a whole. It seems strangely appropriate therefore that Brooks's *Reading for the Plot* should mark a final link in the chain of reception that directly connects poststructuralist narrative theory to the proto-narratologies of the *Poetics* and *Republic*. Subsequent narrative theories will refer in passing to Aristotle and occasionally to Plato, but 1984 marks a watershed moment in this reception history. This is the end.

10.5 *Teleute*

The historical and social context(s) responsible for shaping the production and reception of narrative theory turn out to be no less significant than those contexts shaping the structure and operations of individual narratives. Teresa de Lauretis's cross-medial research on 'desire in narrative' notices that:[65]

The "transhistorical," narratological view of narrative structures seems to have given way to an attempt to historicize the notion of narrative by relating it to the subject and to its implication in, or dependence on the social order, the law of meaning; or to the transformative effects produced in processes of reading and

---

[63] Brooks 1984: 10.   [64] See Chapter 11.2.
[65] De Lauretis 1984: 105–6. She also draws on the pioneering work of Mulvey on cinematic narrative (1975).

practices of writing. More often than not, however, those efforts all but reaffirm an integrative and ultimately traditional view of narrativity. Paradoxically, in spite of the methodological shift away from the notion of structure and toward a notion of process, they end up de-historicizing the subject and thus universalizing the narrative process as such.

As did Lanser, de Lauretis takes particular issue with the default assumption that the dehistoricized subject so happens to be male and that the universal experience of narrative and its processes are thereby predicated upon a masculine model of desire. She points to the fact that Barthes's understanding of 'the pleasure of the text' is 'an Oedipal pleasure (to denude, to know, to learn the origin and the end)';[66] that for Robert Scholes, narrative pleasure is analogous to male sexual pleasure, the form and function of both in this model being that 'of tumescence and detumescence, of tension and resolution, of intensification to the point of climax and consummation'.[67] Narratology's own narratives of desire (in this context) exclude female perspectives and positionalities. Indeed, formalist and structuralist theories of narrative and its pleasures come to mirror the gendered structures of traditional narratives and genres: Oedipus' mythical search for truth reflects Propp's folktale quest of hero for princess, replicates Greimas's model of (default male) actant-subject in search of (default female) actant-object, and reproduces Barthes's readerly desire 'to learn the origin and the end'.

Reflecting their own socio-historical moments, formalist, structuralist, and (some) poststructuralist narratologies can be seen to emplot a theory of narrative whose form and function is essentially a type of heroic 'quest narrative'—a story which women and other 'others' may well experience as 'not their own'. In order to show just how implicated narrative theory is in the *mimesis* of the very plots it seeks to explain, de Lauretis herself turns to the world of classical myth to ask:[68]

What became of the Sphinx after the encounter with Oedipus on his way to Thebes? ... Medusa and the Sphinx, like the other ancient monsters, have survived inscribed in hero narratives, in someone else's story, not their own ... She only served to test Oedipus and qualify him as hero. Having fulfilled her narrative function (the function of Donor, in Propp's terms), her question is now subsumed in his; her power, his; her fateful gift of knowledge, soon to be his.

De Lauretis nicely illustrates here the gender dynamics at work in the imbrication between narrative theory and its canon, where theorists,

---

[66] De Lauretis 1984: 107–8, citing Barthes 1975b: 10.
[67] De Lauretis 1984: 108, citing Scholes 1979: 26.
[68] De Lauretis 1984: 109–12.

narrators, and protagonists assume traditional and stereotypically male subject positions. Yet it is striking that in order to make this important point de Lauretis herself turns back to traditional narratives and classical plots, to myths and stories featuring the Sphinx, Medusa, and 'other ancient monsters'. Indeed, in posing her question regarding the Sphinx, she herself (ironically?) occupies a quasi-Oedipal positionality: after all, to ask questions of the Sphinx is to act like Oedipus.

There are several reasons why this return to ancient poetry and to an ancient model of poetics matters. As Brooks argues in *Reading for the Plot* (published in the same year as de Lauretis's *Alice Doesn't*), such returns and repetitions appear fundamental to the operations of plot itself.[69] Adopting Freud's concept of the repetition compulsion, Brooks speculates:[70]

> Repetition in all its literary manifestations may in fact work as a "binding", a binding of textual energies that allows them to be mastered by putting them into serviceable form, usable "bundles", within the energetic economy of narrative.

Such repetition and 'binding' may be seen to work in similar ways in its theoretical manifestations too. Formalist, structuralist, poststructuralist, and feminist narrative theories appear to enjoy and exploit much the same structural and 'energetic economy' as the narratives that they study. A point that is less surprising when we consider that both narrative theory and its objects encode the same drive, an analogous desire, towards understanding—'towards recognition and retrospective illumination' of (the) narrative text. In this light, de Lauretis looks back to Oedipus and Medusa just as she looks back to Barthes and Greimas, in order to 'bind' their energies into the emplotment of her own narrative and theory. The story she tells about gendered desire in narrative is ultimately satisfying *despite* (or is it *because* of?) that return to a trans-historical and decontextualized model of narrative and its dynamics. And it proves to be much the same story for Culler, for Lanser, and for Brooks, in the poststructuralist turn. The end only takes us back to the beginning.

---

[69] Despite their common focus on desire in narrative, neither de Lauretis nor Brooks appear to be aware of (or, at least, to acknowledge) the other's work in these 1984 publications.

[70] Brooks 1984: 101.

11 Postclassicism

11.1 *Arche*

> *It makes all the difference whether a thing happens* propter hoc *or* post hoc.
>
> Aristotle, *Poetics* 10.1452a 21

As Martin McQuillan and several others tell it, the dinosaur of 'classical' narratology died out at some point in the 1980s.[1] In these extinction narratives, narratology's quasi-scientific armour plating ultimately proved no defence against charges of ahistoricism, antifeminism, and decontextualization, while its narrow dietary preferences, primarily comprising paper novels, eventually limited its energy and its wider interdisciplinary and intellectual interactions.

Such reports of narratology's demise turned out to be somewhat premature, however. In a prescient 1997 essay, 'Scripts, Sequences, and Stories: Elements of a Postclassical Narratology', David Herman first mooted both the term and the agenda for a new postclassical phase in the field. And two years later in his 1999 *Narratologies*, he was able to celebrate the fully-fledged renaissance of a twenty-first-century postclassical narratology (carefully distinguished from the notion of a merely poststructuralist phase), marked by a new emphasis upon narrative not as product but as process and closely informed by cognitive, feminist, psycho-linguistic, and rhetorical paradigms.[2] Herman insisted upon the continuities rather than the discontinuities marking this change, upon

---

[1] McQuillan 2000: xi. Cf. Herman 1999 and Prince 2008.

[2] Herman 1999. Cf. Nünning 2003, who extends Herman's basic categories to include cybernarratology (as pioneered by Ryan 2001) and psychonarratology (see especially Bortolussi and Dixon 2003). Among the postclassical narratological sub-species we also find: computational, conversational, cognitive, corporate, diachronic, dramatic, ethical, feminist, film-based, historicist, hyper-textual, legal, linguistic and psycho-linguistic, medical, possible-worlds, post-colonial, performative, psychoanalytic, queer, transgeneric, and unnatural narratologies. However, as Meister sensibly cautions (2014: 624) 'not every approach labeled "narratological" automatically constitutes a new narratology *sensu strictu*.' For a fuller catalogue of the latest neo-narratologies see the range of entries in Hühn et al. 2014. Cf. also Fludernik 2005a, Nünning and Nünning 2002, and Onega and Landa 1996: 12–35.

these postclassical narratologies' refinement rather than rejection of
earlier models, upon evolution rather than revolution in the discipline.
He proposed that[3]

> in its postclassical phase, research on narrative does not just expose the limits but
> also exploits the possibilities of the older, structuralist models. In much the same
> way, postclassical physics does not simply discard classical, Newtonian models
> but rather rethinks their conceptual underpinnings and reassesses their scope of
> applicability.

Thus, in its latest and ongoing postclassical phase, a plethora of interdisciplinary neo-narratologies are not only exposing the limits but also
exploiting the possibilities of older, classical models, rethinking their
conceptual underpinnings and scope of applicability. In much the same
way that McQuillan suggests structuralist narratology's theoretical (and
metaphorical) DNA survived covertly within the tropes of the poststructuralist diaspora, some of the core genetic material bequeathed by Plato's
Socrates and Aristotle appears to have survived intact into the postclassical era too.[4]

   In particular, there is evidence to suggest that in the postclassical 'cognitive turn' and the latest developments in 'natural' and 'unnatural' narratology pioneered by Monika Fludernik, David Herman, Brian Richardson,
Jan Alber, and others, we are witnessing an important reinterrogation of
the basic terms and frames of narratology's earliest discussions. Developing
the poststructuralists' concerns with context, postclassical narratology is
keenly interested in the part that readers and real-world experiences have
to play in the co-poetic functioning of narrative and its narrativity—
reconsidering the psychological and emotional interactions between stories
and audiences, and returning to the ancient debate between Plato's Socrates
and Aristotle regarding the status of narrative as *mimesis*.

11.2 **Monika Fludernik**

Cognitive narratology, broadly conceived as the analysis of mind-
narrative relationships in storytelling, is now a well-established field

---

[3] Herman 1999: 2. He places the same emphasis on the continuities between narratology's classical and postclassical phases in his 1997 study (1048).
[4] McQuillan 2000: xi. Discussing virtual reality (VR) narrativity, for example, Michelle-
Laure Ryan can forward the (Aristotelian) claim that '[i]t is not (the VR system's) business
to tell what happened, but to tell the kinds of things that would happen—what is possible
according to probability and necessity'—Ryan 1999: 117, paraphrasing Aristotle, *Poetics*
9.1451a 35–7, parentheses as in Ryan's original.

within the eclectic domain of postclassical narrative theory and has introduced a radical reconceptualization of traditional narratological paradigms.[5] With some obvious affinities (albeit not always acknowledged as such) with neo-Aristotelian rhetorical-narratological poetics, cognitive narratology examines the mental processes by which the producers and recipients of narratives process them *qua* narrative.[6] It invites us to rethink preconceptions about how narrative is generated and where narrativity is located. Emphasizing the readerly co-poiesis required in all kinds of narrative activity, it demonstrates that narrativization is at once a textual property and a cognitive process. The text (broadly conceived) supplies one set of parameters which cue the mental activation and re-cognition of key story features such as plot and character, and the reader/receiver supplies another set of contextual frames and experiential ('real-world') schemata that translate those cues into a cogent narrative experience. At its most fundamental level, therefore, cognitive theories of narrative maintain that narrativity is configured not through the interactions of *fabula* and *syuzhet*, *histoire* and *discours*, but through the interactions of text and mind.

Manfred Jahn first coined the term 'cognitive narratology' in 1997, but its theory and practice was already writ large in Monica Fludernik's 1996 groundbreaking work on 'natural narratology'.[7] Fludernik rethinks the narratological paradigms of the prestructuralists (especially Stanzel) and structuralists (especially Genette), refining their theories of narrative (as) discourse with research into discourse analysis, cognitive linguistics, and

---

[5] Cf. Herman 2014a and 2014b, 2003, and 2002, Zunshine 2006, Hogan 2003a and 2003b, Emmott 1997, and Fludernik 1996. Recent work on cognitive narratology has been informed in no small part by research into the representation of consciousness and 'other minds', and by philosophical 'possible worlds' theories. On the narrative representation of other minds see especially Cohn 1978, McHale 1978, Banfield 1982, Sternberg 1982, and Fludernik 1993. On possible worlds theories see especially Doležel 1998 and 2010, Ryan 1991 and 2003. Schmid 2010: 23 n. 20 sees Aristotle as the 'founding father' of the possible worlds school of thought.

[6] On the neo-Aristotelian focus upon experientiality, see Phelan and Richter 2011 and Chapter 7.1 and 7.3 in this volume. See also Pirlet 2011: 111 for the view that Brooks's postclassical narratology 'anticipates some of the basic assumptions of cognitive narratology'; and Stewart 2009: 14 for the argument that 'Brooks's work runs parallel to, though mostly independent of, the rise of cognitive narratology.' Cf. the critical debates between rhetorical, feminist, mind-oriented, and antimimetic narratologies set out in Herman et al. 2012.

[7] Other anticipations of narratology's cognitive turn are found in reception and reader-response research (cf. Iser 1972, Jauss 1982, Gerrig 1993) and in the work of Cohn 1978 and Sternberg 1978. It is worth emphasizing that the focus of postclassical cognitive narratology (particularly as theorized by Fludernik, Herman, et al.) is generally not upon the diachronic study of ways in which narrative features can be seen to evolve—along with the mental models and functions of their readers and audiences—over time. For this approach see Boyd 2009.

reception theory. Taking oral and pseudo-oral storytelling modes as her prototypes for the constitutive functions of narrativity (which is conceived here as 'cognitively prior to, and more basic than, other types of narrative'), Fludernik contests the conceptual cornerstones and categories that had become axiomatic for her narratological predecessors.[8] She questions the validity of the foundational premise of both formalist and structuralist models (and subsequent models built thereon), namely that there exists in narrative a defining dichotomy between story and discourse. Indeed, she reminds us that the origins of this supposedly fundamental dichotomy in Aristotle's *Poetics*—where, she suggests, the ancient text 'actually implies the presence of at least three narrative levels: that of the story . . . ; that of the restructuring of that story into a plot . . . ; and the discourse presentation'—actually form part of a discussion of drama rather than of narrative.[9] She acknowledges the usefulness of the traditional story versus plot dichotomy in the analysis of traditional narrative types, and allows for its partial integration into her own theory of narrativity, but points out the limited value of such a frame in the consideration of non-traditional, non-realist, and/or experimental fiction where there may be no anterior *fabula*, no plot, no narrator or reflector figure, no character, no action, no chronological or teleological structure, for the audience to identify. We might, she allows, label such fiction 'anti-narrative' (*pace* Ryan) but suggests instead that we acknowledge the restricted scope of the basic story versus plot dichotomy and rethink its foundational status in the definition and analysis of narrative and narrativity.[10]

By logical extension, Fludernik invites us to do the same in rethinking the status of those narratological figures and frames that stand upon that traditional foundation: the narrators, tellers, reflectors, and mediators; the characters, agents, and actants; the Genettean concepts of narrative level, voice, focalization, and mode (or mood); the whole plot-focused Aristotelian 'events-in-succession theory of narrative'.[11] In direct contradiction to Aristotle's key proposition that it would be possible to have a tragedy without character but not without plot (*Poetics* 6.1450a 23–4), Fludernik even suggests: 'In my model there can . . . be narratives without plot, but there cannot be any narratives without a human (anthropomorphic) experiencer of some sort at some narrative level.'[12] This tacit

---

[8] Fludernik 1996: 16.
[9] Fludernik 1996: 333: 'Thus, paradoxically, narratology has taken its origin from a text of drama criticism, but this foundational frame has been repressed so successfully that drama has now frequently come to occupy the position of narratology's non-narrative Other.'
[10] Cf. Ryan 1992.   [11] Fludernik 1996: 20.
[12] Fludernik 1996: 13.

rebuttal to Aristotle helpfully signals for us the key concept that will perform the same function for Fludernik's narratology as the concept of *muthos* performed for Aristotle's—that is, experientiality.[13] Where Aristotle positioned plot or *muthos* as the essence of (dramatic) narrative, Fludernik positions human experience—the *sine qua non* that configures narrative and narrativity in two interrelating ways.

Fludernik's model of experientiality maintains that a narrative only functions as such through a basic representation of and appeal to an audience's pre-existing familiarity with real-world experience. Audiences assume that narrative time mirrors real-world temporality, that narrators and narrative situations mimic real-world conversations, and that the conditions of a storyworld will reflect those of the actual world unless and until narrative cues force them to make a cognitive readjustment and acknowledge a difference or departure from that actuality.[14] Thus, if a story introduces a strange chimera such as a feather-covered horse with a woman's head and a fish's tail (like that described in Horace's *Ars poetica* 1–9) we supply a real world or natural model for each possible part of the impossible, unnatural whole.

Narrative representation of real-world experience in a storyworld context therefore requires the activation (or recognition/re-cognition) of that experience through what Fludernik terms 'natural' cognitive parameters. The most significant of these parameters is human embodiment, which 'evokes all the parameters of a real-life schema of existence which always has to be situated in a specific time and space frame' while at the same time determining real-world knowledge about 'the motivational and experiential aspects of human actionality'.[15] From this central premise, Fludernik concludes that the fundamental operations of narrative depend upon human experientiality: the goal of narrative is to represent human experience to other humans—who make sense of such representation through the cognitive parameters endowed by their real-world embodiment and concomitant knowledge not only about temporal and spatial situation, but also about motivation, intention, action, and emotional evaluation. After all, as Fludernik observes, 'experience is . . . stored as emotionally charged remembrance, and it is reproduced in narrative form *because* it was [originally] memorable, funny, scary, or exciting'.[16]

Highlighting the fundamental importance of embodied human experience to the dynamics of narrativity (that is, to the processes

[13] Cf. Caracciolo 2014.
[14] Cf. Ryan 1991 on the 'principle of minimal departure'.
[15] Fludernik 1996: 30.   [16] Fludernik 1996: 29, emphasis added.

of narrative representation at the point of production and to their comprehension at the point of reception), Fludernik treats experientiality and narrativity as synonymous concepts. A representation that features high levels of experientiality (motivation, intention, action, and emotion) will demonstrate high levels of narrativity; a representation that features low or no levels of the same (as in a description, a recipe, a factual report) will demonstrate low or zero levels of narrativity—and may therefore fail to qualify as narrative at all. Thus, Fludernik's central thesis suggests:[17]

> The representation of human experience is the central aim of narrative, and it can be achieved both by means of the low-level narrativity of action report and by a variety of telling, viewing and experiencing patterns in sophisticated combination.

For Fludernik, experientiality (defined in her work as 'the quasi-mimetic evocation of "real-life experience"') can therefore be identified as the defining characteristic of narrative and her 'natural' narratology can be forwarded as the definitive theory with which to conceptualize, describe, and analyse its operations.[18]

Unsurprisingly, Fludernik's radical redefinition of narrative and narrativity in these terms has encountered significant resistance and criticism from some quarters, not least of all for its equation of narrative *diegesis* with experiential *mimesis*—blurring a very ancient distinction.[19] Indeed, Fludernik's heuristic definition of experientiality arguably poses more questions than it resolves: How is 'real life' to be understood in this context? Who calls to whom in the communication exchange implied by that 'evocation'? What is at stake in regarding this operation as something (but not quite) like that of *mimesis*?

Fludernik explains that *mimesis* in this context is emphatically not conceived as 'imitation' in a (quasi) Platonic/Socratic sense, but rather:[20]

> Narrative *mimesis* evokes a world, whether that world is identical to the interlocutors' shared environment, to a historical reality or to an invented fictional fantasy. And in so far as all reading is interpreting along the lines of a represented world, it necessarily relies on the parameters and frames of real-world experience and their underlying cognitive understandings. *Mimesis* is therefore here conceived in radically constructivist terms.

This storyworld-building *mimesis* is *mimesis* in the Aristotelian sense: an artistic re-presentation or construction of a possible world or potential reality, recognized (that is, re-cognized) as such through the 'parameters

---

[17] Fludernik 1996: 51.   [18] Fludernik 1996: 12–13.
[19] Cf. Alber 2002, Wolf 2003, and Herman 2014a.   [20] Fludernik 1996: 37.

and frames of real-world experience'. Aristotle, we recall, saw the role of narrative and dramatic poetry (in contrast to that of history or didactic poetry) as the *mimesis* of that which 'might/could happen and which would be possible according to necessity and probability' (*Poetics* 9.1451a 36–8). Telling stories in his model (as opposed to telling *histories*) is not concerned with representing real things that have 'actually happened' (*ta genomena*) but with representing possible things (*ta dunata*) that might. Aristotle's various definitions of narrative *mimesis* therefore highlighted its constructive rather than its imitative operations, its representation not of reality but of possibility.[21] Fludernik places her own emphasis upon experientiality—'the quasi-mimetic evocation of "real-life experience" ... the evocation of consciousness'[22]—in her own account of *mimesis* and its operations, but the core intuition regarding its constructivist character is very close to that of Aristotle's.

Indeed, on the basis of these shared intuitions, Fludernik and Aristotle independently reach similar conclusions about the relative narrative status of different genres. Grading a scale of narrativity ranging from non-narrative texts at one end through minimally narrative and up to fully narrative texts at the other end, Fludernik denies narrative status to (most) lyric poetry on the grounds that it fails her experientiality test: the typical speaker in lyric 'never becomes a character in her own right, never begins to exist within an alternative fictional world'.[23] Aristotle similarly denies mimetic status to lyric poetry (along with elegiac and didactic poetry) on the grounds that poets who narrate their own personal experiences and emotions in their own first-person voice(s) show insufficient mimeticism in their work (*Poetics* 1.1447b). Similar concerns regarding the restricted scope for the operations of *mimesis* also appear to inform Aristotle's views discounting the mimetic status of history (in relation to tragedy or epic) on the premise that history deals with particulars whereas narrative deals with universals (*Poetics* 9.1451b 5–7). Fludernik takes this principle a step further in her own narratology and denies historiographical writing 'proto-typical narrativity' on the grounds that such writing 'consists in a mere calibration of events

---

[21] For the consummate account of Aristotelian *mimesis* see Halliwell 2002.

[22] Fludernik 1996: 12–13.

[23] Fludernik 1996: 355. To support her judgement, Fludernik cites Ryan (1992: 386), who also appears to be echoing Aristotle in the suggestion that lyric poetry is 'concerned with general truths rather than with particular facts'. Cf. Aristotle, *Poetics* 9.1451b on the distinction(s) between history and tragedy. Like Fludernik, both Plato's Socrates and Aristotle similarly seek to grade different types/modes of storytelling: cf. Plato, *Republic* 3.396c–e and Aristotle, *Poetics* 23.1459a 14–17; cf. 24.1459b 33–6.

which are then reported as historical facts'.[24] History, in this model, is considered to lack the crucial element of experientiality, of human consciousness, that is the *sine qua non* of 'natural' narrative.[25]

That both Aristotle and Fludernik should arrive at broadly the same conclusions from following very different paths and theories (albeit on relatively trivial questions of narrative status) should give us pause to consider just how different are their respective approaches. Both build their respective narratologies upon the foundational assumption that narrative and its conventions are fundamentally or inherently (naturally?) mimetic or quasi-mimetic. The cognitive turn in narratology, then, represents in many respects a cognitivist re-turn—a turn back to the analysis of narrative *mimesis* and its relation to real-world experiences no less than to related cognitive understandings earlier articulated by the ancient narrative theorists.

11.3 **David Herman**

Published soon after Fludernik had ushered in the nascent postclassical phase of narratology (and so without any direct engagement with her work), David Herman's 1997 essay 'Scripts, Sequences, and Stories: Elements of a Postclassical Narratology' presented a bold new 'prolegomena for a future narratology'—which still remains an invaluable introduction to the cognitive turn.[26] Here, like Fludernik, Herman is fundamentally concerned with the question of what defines narrative. He thus sets out to examine the particular dynamics of narrative in terms of both its 'narrativehood' (the qualities that allow audiences to identify a story as such) and its 'narrativity' (the formal and contextual elements that give a story its structure and help to qualify a discourse—and parts thereof—as 'more or less' narrative). Again, like Fludernik, Herman looks to the cognitive sciences for fresh insights into the complex processes at play in the interactions between *logos* and *muthos*, *fabula* and *syuzhet*, *discours* and *histoire*—that is: 'how the (form of the) expression side of stories interacts with (the form of) their content side'.[27]

---

[24] Fludernik 1996: 26.   [25] Cf. Fludernik 1996: 24–5.

[26] Herman 1997: 1057. Material from this essay is reproduced as chapter 3 in Herman's 2002 study *Story Logic*. Herman's interdisciplinary work on cognitive narratology continues to push narrative theory into innovative new territory, most recently his 2018 study *Narratology beyond the Human: Storytelling and Animal Life*.

[27] Herman 1997: 1053.

In particular, Herman draws upon some of the latest research into artificial intelligence (AI), notably the theory of 'schemata' or 'scripts'— the idea that the basic operations of machine (and human) learning depend upon correlating new data and experiences with cognate data and experiences already stored in stereotype form in a memory bank. In this model, humans and machines both make sense of the unfamiliar by comparing it with or contrasting it to the familiar—testing its relation to so-called 'knowledge frames' or 'knowledge scripts'.[28] Virgil and Homer, for example, have no need to tell their audiences what happens to their heroes once night falls: we fill in the gap using *situational* 'knowledge frames' or 'knowledge scripts' that tell us that these characters in all likelihood go to sleep until the morning.[29] In the same vein, *personal* knowledge frames or scripts help us understand why and how characters act as they do: why Achilles responds to the death of Patroclus with impious rage, why Dido neglects the building of her own new city when Aeneas arrives in town. *Instrumental* knowledge frames and scripts help us understand how and why Homer's Hephaestus forges new armour for Thetis (and for her son Achilles). And *generic* knowledge frames and scripts help us understand how and why, after Homer, Virgil's Vulcan forges new armour for Venus (and for her son Aeneas)—even though, in this epic, the hero has no obvious need for new kit.[30]

On the evidence of research in the cognitive sciences, Herman suggests that readers and receivers of narrative draw upon an extensive (but not infinite) 'experiential repertoire' in the process of co-creating narrative 'storyworlds' whereby 'previous experiences form structured repertoires of expectations about current and emergent experiences'.[31] His focus upon the reader's 'experiential repertoire' has obvious affinities with Fludernik's focus on 'experientiality' but also looks back to Barthes's consideration of the 'patrimonial hoard of human experiences' as the key to understanding how audiences process the nuclei of particular action and event sequences into stories—that is, how they turn plot parts into

---

[28] See Herman 2002 and Sandford and Emmott 2012 on the interdisciplinary history (and definitions) of script, schema, and frame theory in psychology, linguistics, computing, and cognitive science. 'Script', 'schema', and 'frame' are used interchangeably by most postclassical narratologists. See Ryan 1991 for one of the earliest (and still influential) accounts of the potential synergies between AI and narratology.

[29] Cf. the discussion of narrative economy amongst the ancient scholia and commentaries in Chapter 5.5. The Servius commentary to Virgil's *Aeneid* 2.668 points out that 'the poet need not state everything that happens', and Homer is similarly praised in the scholia to *Iliad* 1.223 for not describing every single minute of every single day and night.

[30] Cf. Herman 1997: 1054 for the idea that cognitive narratology allows us to rethink genre as a mode of script use.

[31] Herman 1997: 1047.

narrative wholes.[32] For Herman, as for Fludernik (as for Barthes), experience—including experience of other stories—is what drives narrativity. Indeed, Herman acknowledges that there is nothing particularly innovative in the view that an audience actively and cognitively participates in the co-poetic production of that narrative in response to cues supplied by the text. He's quite right: Aristotle's *Poetics* was arguing this over two and a half thousand years earlier.[33] But what is original and useful about analysing this co-poetic relation using the tools of AI and cognitive science, Herman suggests, is that these discourses offer new ways to re-describe and explain this process in greater depth and detail. In particular:[34]

The notion of scripts provides a finer-grained vocabulary for describing what earlier narratologists characterized as readers' tendency to organize event sequences into stories... [For] [e]very act of telling arguably requires that a listener or reader use scripts to help set the narrative in motion, to co-create the story.

One of those earlier narratologists and one of the scripts indexed in Herman's own patrimonial hoard of narratological experience here is, of course, Aristotle and his *Poetics*—the blueprint to the foundation of narrative theory in the West. Aristotle stressed that events merely following on from each other in linear temporal (*post hoc*) sequence do not supply sufficient conditions alone to configure a well-ordered plot or *muthos*. The audience must be able to trace a logical and causal (*propter hoc*) consequence between those events. That is, if readers or viewers are to be able to organize actions and event sequences into stories, they must be able to recognize a probable (*eikos*) and/or necessary (*anangkaios*) connection between those actions and events (*Poetics* 9.1451a 37).[35] And in order for that recognition to take place in the storyworld, the audience must already be equipped with knowledge about what constitutes probable or necessary consequence in the real world. Herman's interest is in what happens on both sides of the mind-narrative nexus to make this possible: the scripts and schemata that arm audiences with the knowledge that a causal chain of probable

---

[32] Barthes 1974: 204.

[33] Cf. Heath 1991: 13 on Aristotle's cognitive narratology.

[34] Herman 1997: 1051.

[35] Herman 1997: 1049. For Herman (1997: 1049), similarly, 'the interest and complexity of narrative depends on the merely probabilistic, not deterministic, links between some actions and events'. Cf. Iser 1972 and Sternberg 1978 on readerly co-poiesis in filling 'expositional gaps'.

and/or necessary consequences result when Patroclus dies, when Odysseus gets home, or when Aeneas meets Lavinia.[36]

Herman's ideas about the role of scripts and schemata in the co-production of narratives and narrativity are further developed in his 2002 landmark study, *Story Logic*, where he refines his focus upon readers as co-creators in the making of what he terms 'story-worlds'. Stories and their tellers are seen to design architectural 'blue-prints' (featuring both micro and macro schemes) for the building of such worlds, guiding readers towards their construction through the outlining of key parameters: *when* (time), *where* (space), *who* (charac-ter), *what* (states, events, and actions), *how* (scripts and sequences), and *why* (rationale, relations, and causality). Redefining stories as 'storyworlds'—that is, as the 'mental models of who did what to and with whom, when, where, why, and in what fashion'—Herman can therefore argue:[37]

[The] *storyworld* points to the way interpreters of narrative reconstruct a sequence of states, events, and actions not just additively or incrementally but integratively or 'ecologically'; recipients do not just attempt to piece together bits of action into a linear timeline but furthermore try to measure the significance of the timeline that emerges against other possible courses of development in the world in which narrated occurrences take place.

Herman's concept of storyworld, then, is not too far removed from the technical concept of *muthos* in Aristotle's *Poetics* in its own emphasis upon readerly co-poiesis in the synthesis of incidents (re)constructed into a coherent and unified whole, according to a series of probable or necessary connections—that is, not just 'additively or incrementally'. For both Herman and Aristotle, the fundamental question of 'what makes a narrative a narrative' (or a plot a plot) is resolved at 'the level of coding *combinations*'—or, in Aristotle's terms, at the level 'of the synthesis/arrangement of incidents' (*sunthesin ton pragmaton*: *Poetics* 6.1450a 3–4).[38] And in both accounts, that coding, as we've seen, relies upon a complex interaction between mutually constitutive storyworld 'blueprints' and real-world knowledge 'frames' or 'scripts'.

---

[36] Cf. Booth 1961: 126. These knowledge scripts work on various levels, cuing the audience's recognition of event and action sequences both large and small, as in Aristotle's observation in his *Homeric Problems* (F 144 Rose [Athenaeus 556d–e]) that readers of the *Iliad* recognize the probability that 'Agamemnon did not acquire a great volume of wine just so that he might get drunk' but as a mark of kingly prestige.

[37] Herman 2002: 5 and 14, emphasis in original.

[38] Herman 2002: 49, emphasis in original.

Aristotle and Herman (and Fludernik) are fundamentally concerned with the narrative representation or modelling of storyworlds whose blueprints rely upon cuing parallels to real-world experientiality.[39]

Thus, Herman's postclassical cognitive narratology reveals that the blueprint for its own configuration is drawn, at least in part, upon the palimpsest of a classical 'script'. A script which similarly defines and analyses storyworld representations as co-poetic creations cued into and by real-world experience. A script which defines and analyses narrative *qua* narrative on account of its mimetic qualities. And I emphasize this mimetic focus to both Herman and Fludernik's respective narratologies not to suggest that here we merely find 'old wine in new wineskins', but to reiterate the tenacity of the theory that, first and foremost, narratives 'are all, on the whole, kinds of *mimesis*' (*Poetics* 1.1447a 13–18) and the persistence of Aristotle's idea that this first principle is the key to narrative poetics.[40]

11.4 Jan Alber and Brian Richardson

This emphasis upon narrative (as) *mimesis* in the postclassical cognitive turn has recently been challenged by a group of theorists who query whether such mimetic models of narrativity can 'really' tell us the whole story about narrative and its dynamics. Proponents of the latest unnatural or antimimetic narratology point out that there is a significant body of narrative fiction (ranging from the comedies of Aristophanes in the fifth century BCE to the postmodernist fiction of the twenty-first century CE) for which natural and mimetic theories of narrative fail adequately to account.[41] Their stated goal is not to produce a specialist postmodern or postclassical poetics to describe only unnatural or antimimetic narratives, but to supplement and reframe existing theories in order to develop a more comprehensive narratology capable of embracing a wider spectrum of narrative fiction.

Thus, Jan Alber and Brian Richardson (often writing together, along with Stefan Iversen and Henrik Skov Nielsen) configure their own narratology—explicitly *contra* Fludernik and Herman—as 'unnatural'

---

[39] Herman 2002: 331.

[40] James 1999: 378 saw the role of the novel as an 'attempt to represent life'; Todorov 1966: 144 also claimed that narrative (*récit*) involves a mimetic representation of 'reality' and 'real life'.

[41] Cf. Richardson 2002, 2012, and 2015, Alber and Heinze 2011, and Alber 2014.

and 'antimimetic'. They argue for a fundamental rethinking of what they see as the mimetic bias prevalent in over two and half thousand years of narrative poetics, beginning with Aristotle and returning to prominence in the latest cognitive narratologies.[42] We need, Alber suggests, to resist the 'mimetic reductionism' that assumes a comprehensive theory of narrative can be produced by correlating storyworld experience with real-world experience.[43]

The cognitive turn in postclassical narratology, as we've seen, draws many of its insights from the premise that a storyworld, the characters who act within it, and the act of its narration, all correlate with real-world scripts and schemata. But, as Alber points out in his groundbreaking study of 'impossible storyworlds', this is not true of all narrative:[44] 'Many narratives confront us with bizarre story worlds which are governed by principles that have very little to do with the real world around us.' Indeed, literary history offers a rich tradition of narratives that involve 'non-mimetic' storyworlds, 'impossible' minds, and 'unnatural' narration—such as those which do not observe real-world conventions regarding time and space (Aristophanes' comedies, or the Greek novel); those in which characters metamorphose into somebody or something else (Apuleius' *Metamorphoses*, or Ovid's *Metamorphoses*); and those in which some kind of breach between storyworld and real world occurs (as in metalepsis) or some physically, logically, or otherwise impossible act of narration features (Aesop's talking animals, or Homer's divinely inspired 'omniscient' narration in the *Iliad* and *Odyssey*).[45]

Yet, as these non-mimetic examples from the classical canon serve to illustrate, not all narrative phenomena and features that are humanly, technically, or logically impossible, that are unnatural or unrealistic, are always received as such. Ancient audiences may (or may not) once have been struck by the strangeness of Aesop's talking animals, or the Homeric narrator's omniscience, his astonishing memory and impossible knowledge, including of other minds. But over time these devices have become naturalized or conventionalized so that they are unlikely to strike modern readers as anything out of the ordinary.[46] Indeed, these ancient

---

[42] For an accessible overview addressing the question 'what really is unnatural narratology' see Alber, Iversen, Nielsen, and Richardson 2013.

[43] Alber et al. 2010: 115.

[44] Alber 2009: 79.

[45] On metalepsis in classical literature see Matzner and Trimble (forthcoming).

[46] Thus, Richardson asks—with rather too many negatives (2012: 96): 'If the flight to the moon in Lucian's *Verae historiae* is unnatural, are comparable space voyages penned by Jules Verne or H. G. Wells equally unnatural? There seems to be no question that a realistic story of space flight in a contemporary setting is not an example of an unnatural narrative.'

examples force us to question the cultural, historical, and individual specificity (as well as stability) of the categories placed at the heart of unnatural narratology—and thus the claims made for and by it. Context is crucial here.[47]

Aristotle, we recall, suggested that Homer speaks non-mimetically whenever the poet-narrator speaks 'in his own voice' (*Poetics* 24.1460a 5–11)—that is, in the brief proems that we find introducing the *Iliad* and *Odyssey*, and in various other first-person invocations to the Muses in the poems. The ancient Greek scholia similarly recognized the Homeric poet-narrator as speaking *amimeton* ('non-mimetically') as he asks the Muses to aid him in the superhuman feat of remembering and recounting the catalogue of all the ships and all their captains who once set sail for Troy (*Iliad* 2.484–93).[48] Each of these instances of Homer's non-mimeticism are potentially metaleptic, crossing the line between story-world and real world and drawing the audience's attention to the fact that a physically or mnemonically impossible act of narration is about to follow. At what point, then, does non-mimetic become antimimetic— and vice versa?

Alber seeks to acknowledge such difficulties head-on in his own heuristic definition of 'unnatural' narrative. He restricts the label 'unnatural' to impossible (that is, 'non-actualizable' in the real world), happenings and situations in the storyworld—in a move analogous to Aristotle's treatment of the impossible (*adunatos*) and illogical (*alogos*) incidents of Homeric epic in *Poetics* 24 and *Homeric Problems*. What is more, Alber draws a line distinguishing conventionalized or naturalized forms of the 'unnatural'—whose features (such as magic, or time travel) are familiar to us from our experience of them in epics, fairytales, science fiction, and the like—from those forms that still retain their 'defamiliarizing' potency (such as polychrony, or second-person narration) and which, for the time being at least, succeed in surprising us as strange and unusual in postmodernist and experimental fiction.[49] In fact, Alber sees an important cognitive dimension to this (de)familiarization process, pointing to the ways in which readers 'try to approach the unnatural by reshuffling and recombining existing scripts and frames', thus leading to

---

[47] Cf. Chatman 1978: 49 on the strict cultural specificity that determines what is realistic, natural, probable, or likely in any given narrative context.

[48] b scholion to *Iliad* 2.494–877.

[49] In this respect, Alber's unnatural narratology has much in common with Shklovsky and the Russian formalist theory of 'defamiliarization'.

the transformation of narrative impossibilities into possibilities cuing and cued by new generic schemata.[50]

Richardson takes a slightly different approach, however. For him, unnatural narratives are those 'that violate mimetic conventions by providing wildly improbable or strikingly impossible events; they are narratives that are not simply nonrealistic but antirealistic'.[51] Indeed, Richardson typically prefers to use the term 'antimimetic' to describe his own mode of unnatural narratology, maintaining that only narratives evincing actively defamiliarizing phenomena can be deemed 'unnatural' in a meaningful sense. Accordingly, he maps a tripartite typology of narrative mimeticism, ranging from the simply mimetic at one end of the spectrum (in which the represented storyworld, characters, events, and narration mirror the real world—as in the modern realist novel); the non-mimetic (in which the storyworld, characters, events, and/or narration deviate in some way from the real world but still comply with familiar narrative conventions—as in Homeric and Virgilian epic); and the antimimetic (which self-consciously eschews all of the above, revelling in the unfamiliar and fantastic—as in Menippean satire and Aristophanic comedy):[52]

Thus, in a mimetic text, a horse can easily carry a human rider for twenty miles on a good day with decent roads; in a non-mimetic text a flying horse can carry a prince across the countryside; and in an anti-mimetic text like Aristophanes' *Peace*, the protagonist, who wishes to speak with the gods, is transported by a giant dung beetle up to the heavens in a parody of Euripides' *Bellerophon*—even as he urges that the audience refrain from passing gas so as not to misdirect his mount.

Indeed, one of the most remarkable aspects of unnatural or antimimetic narratology is the forceful reminder it affords that there is nothing new or particularly postmodern about unnatural or antimimetic narratives: classical texts and authors demonstrate plenty of unnatural narration—this is not a phenomenon reserved for postmodern or experimental modern fiction. Alber discusses the talking animals in Aesop's *Fables* as one example of such ancient unnatural narration.[53] Richardson repeatedly looks back to the unnatural antimimeticism of Attic

---

[50] Alber et al. 2010: 129. See also Alber and Heinze 2011 on the diachronic dynamics of unnatural narratives and of genre.

[51] Richardson 2012: 95.

[52] Alber, Iversen, Nielsen, and Richardson 2013: 102.

[53] Alber 2014. Cf. Nielsen 2011, who also offers Apuleius' *The Golden Ass* as an example.

comedy and Menippean satire (especially Aristophanes and Lucian's 'proto-postmodern' *True History*). Richardson even suggests:[54]

Had Aristotle's lost work on comedy survived, and if it did contain an account of the collapsible chronologies of the dramas of Aristophanes (where those trips to Hades and Cloudcuckooland always happened much too rapidly)... we might have had a better appreciation of non- and anti-mimetic temporal construction ... [and] we might now occupy a more capacious critical position.

We might—although Aristotle has little enough to say about the complex chronologies of Homeric epic or Attic tragedy in the version of the *Poetics* that has survived, and reconstructions of the lost section from the *Poetics* dealing with comedy do not (yet) promise any particularly rich insights into Aristophanes' comic (anti)*mimesis*.[55]

There are limitations to the promise of this new 'unnatural' or 'anti-mimetic' narratology too. Herman, for example, points out that it fails fully to acknowledge the complexity of *mimesis* and its effects, and therefore gets trapped within an unsophisticated network of binary oppositions that assumes straightforward dichotomies and equivalences between categories such as the (un)natural, (non)mimetic, (un)realistic, and (un)conventional.[56] Eva von Contzen attributes some of the shortcomings of Alber's and Richardson's work to the structuralist paradigm that, in her view, it reproduces, and suggests that their aim to provide a comprehensive narratology applicable to a wide spectrum of narrative fiction is misleading:[57] 'The proclaimed breadth of unnatural narrative... seems to be reduced to one narrative mode—that of parody or satire—and it is not quite clear to what extent unnatural narratology is but a new name for this well-known phenomenon, which is essentially transgressive.' Variations in the definitions and applications of key terms by different theorists have also invited criticism—an all too familiar problem in the history of narratology, as we've seen. Indeed, it is even possible to object that the texts and phenomena that Richardson, Alber, Iversen, Nielsen, et al. are attempting to account for under the headings of 'unnatural' and 'antimimetic' might be more appropriately and straightforwardly designated as 'anti-narrative' (or as exhibiting 'weak narrativity') in that they actively resist the usual mechanics and dynamics of

---

[54] Richardson 2002: 58. See also Richardson 2015: 93–8 and Bowie 2004 on narrativity in Aristophanes.
[55] See Janko 1984 and Heath 1989.
[56] See Herman et al 2012: 223. Cf. Fludernik 2012, Petterson 2012, and Klauk and Köppe 2013.
[57] Von Contzen 2017: 8.

POSTCLASSICISM **251**

storytelling.[58] How well and to what extent such a theory of (anti)narrative can help us to rethink the fundamental principles of narratology—and thereby release new readings of (real?) narratives—has yet to be proven. However, for classicists, an exciting opportunity is afforded by these theories of 'unnatural' and 'antimimetic' narrative to release new readings of those genres and texts traditionally excluded from the purview of ancient and modern 'natural' and 'mimetic' narratologies (not only Aristophanic comedy and Menippean satire, but lyric and elegy too), as well as to look again at 'unnatural' representations of time and space, and antimimetic phenomena such as metamorphosis and metalepsis in 'natural' narratives (such as epic and tragedy).[59]

11.5 *Teleute*

Plato's Socrates questioned the power of storyworlds to shape (for good and bad) the real world—and recommended the exclusion of most forms of poetry from his ideal republic as a consequence. He may have had a point. The latest research into cognitive narratology, both mimetic and antimimetic in orientation, informed by emerging insights into artificial intelligence and machine learning, acknowledges that the co-poiesis involved in storymaking has effects on and in the real world too. Readers work on narratives to co-create storyworlds, cued by real-world frames and scripts, but narratives also work on their readers to reshape the cognitive parameters of those real-world schemata. Lubomir Doležel suggests that 'in order to reconstruct and interpret a fictional world, the reader has to reorient his cognitive stance to agree with the [story] world's encyclopedia'; but that cognitive reorientation, in turn, changes the knowledge that the reader has stored in her 'actualworld encyclopedia' too.[60]

For readers and receivers of narrative theory, as for readers and receivers of narratives, an analogous feedback system reorients the frames and scripts of our knowledge and understanding of narratology.

[58] Cf. Herman et al. 2012: 224 and 233 and Ryan (1992), where she first introduces the term 'anti-narrative'. On 'weak narrativity', in which 'at the same time that our sense of narrative is being solicited, it is also being frustrated', see McHale 2001: 164.
[59] For the potential of such an approach see Wolf 2013, Whitmarsh 2013, de Jong 2009, and the essays collected in Matzner and Trimble (forthcoming) on metalepsis as an 'unnatural' device in ancient narrative texts. See the essays collected in de Jong and Nünlist 2007 on time and in de Jong 2012 on space.
[60] Doležel 1998: 181.

Plato and Aristotle—and the broader canon of classical narrative and its poetics—form the foundation of modern narratology, so it is unsurprising (indeed, 'natural') that we find the designs of these classical blueprints providing the frames and scripts for so many modern stories about storytelling.[61] But, in turn, those modern narratologies provide new schemata that feed back into our better understanding of their ancient precursors. And our narratological encyclopedia, both ancient and modern, are mutually enriched with each reorientation.

As we've seen in the preceding chapters, one of the dominant scripts to emerge from this diachronic study of narrative theory is the knowledge that ancient narratologies and narratologists consistently evince a cognitively inflected approach to narrative poetics and a marked concern with the ways and means through which authors and audiences co-produce and co-process stories. Yet, as we've also seen, ancient narratologists display very different theories and intuitions about these cognitive dynamics—about readers' access to other minds, about the rhetorical and narrative cues that trigger affective responses, and about how narrators and narratees work together to configure narrativity through various degrees of co-poiesis. The story plotted out in the preceding chapters therefore both affirms and poses something of a challenge to cognitive approaches to narratology: it questions the reliability or otherwise of assuming that there might exist a trans-historical, trans-cultural, gender-neutral unity that we can usefully identify as 'human' cognition or experience. It questions the temporal, cultural, and contextual specificity (and defamiliarization) of concepts such as probability and necessity, possibility and impossibility; and highlights both the historicity and the mutability of what may or may not be deemed natural and unnatural, mimetic and antimimetic, about a narrative. Thus, in narratology's latest postclassical phase, we may not only recognize the blueprints and schemata of ancient 'classical' narratologies but re-cognize both old and new world models. After all, as Aristotle suggested (*Poetics* 6.1450a 31–4), all good stories depend on some form of *anagnorisis* in the end.

---

[61] And their characteristic binary paradigms.

■ GLOSSARY

Actant The structural role performed by an individual character within the narrative; including key roles (sometimes paired) such as hero, opponent, donor, helper, etc.

Addressee *See* Audience.

Anachrony Narration in which events are presented out of a strictly linear chronological sequence in an artificial or emplotted order that disrupts the natural or story order of such events.

Anagnorisis Aristotle's term for recognition (literally, a re-cognition or knowing again), often attending *peripeteia*.

Analepsis Narrative flashback to an earlier point on the story timeline; a type of anachrony.

Anangke Aristotle's term describing one of the key conditions for a well-constructed plot in that its events and characters should be 'necessary' (often paired with *eikos*).

Athetisis The marking of sections of text that are 'not to be read' in the Greek scholia.

Audience The real or imagined addressees (or narratees) to whom a narrative communication is directed.

Autodiegetic narration First-person and typically homodiegetic storytelling by a narrator who is also a central character in the story; Odysseus telling of his own adventures in the *Odyssey* is an autodiegetic narrator.

Desis Aristotle's term to describe the 'tightening' of a plot towards its climax.

Dianoia Aristotle's term to describe character 'thought' or intention.

Diegesis Often paired in opposition to *mimesis*, *diegesis* is used to describe various narrative phenomena: (1) for Plato's Socrates it refers to the broad genus of narrative, of which there are three species: simple narration (*haple diegesis*), narration through imitation (*diegesis dia mimeseos*), and a mix of the two (*diegesis di' amphoteron*); (2) for Aristotle it refers to a type of *mimesis* in which the narrator's mediating role is overt, as in Homeric epic (which Aristotle describes as 'diegetic *mimesis*'); (3) for most modern narratologists it similarly refers to a type or level of narrative in which the narrator's mediating role is overt (e.g. in indirect discourse); often associated with (4) a mode of 'telling' as opposed to 'showing'.

Diegetic (*diégèse*) Genette's term (adopting the formula proposed by film theorists Metz and Souriau) to describe the story level or storyworld.

Diegesis di' amphoteron See Diegesis.

Diegesis dia mimeseos *See Diegesis.*

Direct discourse (DD) Often paired in contrast to (free) indirect discourse, a mode in which the narrator mimetically reproduces character speech, eschewing speech tags (s/he said, etc.) to create the effect of unmediated verbatim presentation of a character's words.

Discours Often paired in opposition to *histoire*, in structuralist narratology (adopting the term proposed by Benveniste) *discours* is distinguished as the level of story as discoursed or emplotted; broadly equivalent to the Russian formalist notion of *syuzhet*.

Dispositio In Roman rhetorical handbooks, the arrangement of individual words, sentences, and ideas in order to achieve optimal impact and affect upon an audience.

Eikos Often paired with *anangke, eikos* is Aristotle's term to describe one of the key conditions for a well-constructed plot in that its events should be 'probable'.

Emplotment The dynamic linking together of actions and events so as to produce a plot.

Epeisodion For Aristotle, a discrete episode or series of events that are tangential or inessential to the central plot.

Ethos Aristotle's term to describe 'character' and 'characterization'.

Extradiegetic Typically third-person or heterodiegetic storytelling by a narrator who is not a character in the story; refers to a narrative level deemed to exist outside of the storyworld; the Homeric narrator of the *Iliad* and *Odyssey* is therefore an extradiegetic narrator.

Fabula Shlovsky's term to describe the raw story material from which a plot or *syuzhet* is formed; for Petrovsky (reversing Shlovsky's terms), the emplotted or poetically handled *syuzhet*.

Focalization Genette's term to distinguish between those who see and those who speak in a story, refining the less precise concepts of perspective and point of view; external focalization offers a view from outside of the storyworld, internal focalization presents a view from within (which may include access to a character's thoughts or *dianoia*).

Focalizer Bal's term to describe the person or agent (which may be a narrator or a character) from whose point of view focalization is oriented.

Free direct discourse (FDD) *See* Direct discourse.

Free indirect discourse (FID) *See* Indirect discourse.

Haple diegesis *See Diegesis.*

Haplodiegetic *See Diegesis.*

Heterodiegetic Typically third-person or extradiegetic storytelling by a narrator who is not a character in the story; refers to a narrative level deemed to exist outside of the storyworld; the Homeric narrator of the *Iliad* and *Odyssey* is a heterodiegetic narrator.

Histoire In structuralist narratology (adopting a term first proposed as a mode of enunciation by Benveniste), *histoire* is distinguished from *discours* as the untreated and unmediated story; broadly equivalent to Aristotle's *logos* and the Russian formalists' *fabula*.

Homodiegetic Typically first-person or autodiegetic storytelling by a narrator who is also a character in the story; Odysseus telling of his own adventures in the *Odyssey* is a homodiegetic narrator.

Hupothesis See *Oikonomia*.

Hypodiegesis A story within a story; Odysseus telling of his own adventures in the *Odyssey* is hypodiegetic narrative.

Implied author Booth's term for the storytelling *persona* adopted by a flesh-and-blood author.

Implied reader Iser's term for the intended addressee or ideal audience to whom the implied author communicates a story.

In medias res Horace's term for beginning a story 'in the middle of things'.

Indirect discourse Often paired in contrast to direct discourse, a mode in which the narrator reports character speech, using speech tags (s/he said, etc.) in the overtly mediated and summary presentation of a character's words.

Intradiegetic The narrative of a character-narrator; in the hypodiegetic and homodiegetic telling of his own adventures in the *Odyssey*, Odysseus is an intradiegetic narrator.

Lexis In Plato and Socrates, the style or form of narrative discourse (as distinct from its subject or content).

Logos In Plato and Socrates, the subject or content of narrative discourse (as distinct from its style or form).

Lusis Aristotle's term to describe the 'loosening' of a plot towards its denouement.

Mediacy Stanzel's term for the hallmark of narrative discourse and storytelling, that is the necessary mediation (whether overt or covert) by the narrator in his or her representation of raw story material; the key characteristic of telling in contrast to showing.

Metalepsis Genette's term for the transgression of boundaries separating different narrative levels.

Mimesis Often paired in opposition to *diegesis*, (1) for Plato's Socrates it describes a species of *diegesis* or narration through imitation (*diegesis dia mimeseos*); (2) for Aristotle it refers to the broad genus of artistic—including dramatic and narrative—representation; (3) for most modern narratologists it refers to a type or level of narrative in which the narrator's mediating role is covert or minimal (e.g. in direct discourse); (4) a mode of 'showing' as opposed to 'telling'.

Muthos Aristotle's term for the rearrangement and synthesis of actions and events into a coherent plot; broadly equivalent to the Russian formalists' *syuzhet*, and the structuralists' *discours*.

Narratee The real or imagined addressees (or ideal audience) to whom a narrative communication is directed (as distinct from the real or implied reader); like narrators, narratees may be extradiegetic, intradiegetic, etc.

Narration The dynamic processes by which a narrative is communicated; for some structuralists, this represents a separate narrational level distinct from story (*histoire*) or plot (*discours*) levels.

Narrative situations Stanzel's term for three key modes of narration: first-person, third-person, or mixed (blending the voices of a third-person narrator and reflector character or characters).

Narrativity The (contested) properties that lend a story its 'storiness'.

Narrator The agent whose voice communicates a narrative; narrators may be autodiegetic, extradiegetic, heterodiegetic, homodiegetic, intradiegetic, etc.

Oikonomia In the Greek scholia, a term describing the arrangement of story material or *hupothesis*.

Paradiegesis In the Greek scholia, a term describing the 'para-narrative' digressions and incidental parts of a narrative which do not form part of the central plot.

Peripeteia Aristotle's term for a change or reversal, applied particularly to the pivotal moment at which a plot, appearing to develop in one direction, unexpectedly turns in another.

Perspective, point of view *See* Focalization.

Plot The rearrangement and synthesis of actions and events into a coherent and affective narrative; broadly equivalent to Aristotle's *muthos*, the Russian formalists' *syuzhet*, and the structuralists' *discours*.

Prolepsis Narrative flashforward to a later point on the story timeline; a type of anachrony.

Story The chronological series of actions and events deemed to precede emplotment that can be retrospectively reconstructed from the emplotted narrative; broadly equivalent to Aristotle's *logos*, the Russian formalists' *fabula*, and the structuralists' *histoire*.

Storyworld (or **story universe**) The mimetic world conjured by the story.

Syuzhet Shlovsky's term for the rearrangement and synthesis of actions and events into a coherent and affective narrative; equivalent to plot, Aristotle's *muthos*, and the structuralists' *discours*.

Taxis In rhetorical handbooks (and occasionally in the scholia) contrasted with *oikonomia* to differentiate between the 'natural' and 'unnatural' order of words; (2) what narratologists used before Uber.

■ BIBLIOGRAPHY

Abbott, H. Porter (ed.) (2002), *Cambridge Introduction to Narrative*, Cambridge: Cambridge University Press.

Abbott, H. Porter (2003), 'Unnarratable Knowledge: The Difficulty of Understanding Evolution by Natural Selection', in David Herman (ed.), *Narrative Theory and the Cognitive Sciences*, Chicago: Chicago University Press, pp. 143–62.

Adams, J.-K. (1989), 'Causality and Narrative', *Journal of Literary Semantics* 18: 149–62.

Alber, Jan (2002), 'The "Moreness" or "Lessness" of "Natural" Narratology: Samuel Beckett's "Lessness" Reconsidered', *Style* 36.1: 54–75.

Alber, Jan (2009), 'Impossible Storyworlds—and What to Do with Them', *Storyworlds* 1: 79–96.

Alber, Jan (2013), 'Unnatural Narratology: The Systematic Study of Anti-Mimeticism', *Literature Compass* 10: 449–60.

Alber, Jan (2014), 'Unnatural Narratives', in Peter Hühn et al., *Handbook of Narratology*, Berlin: De Gruyter, pp. 887–95.

Alber, Jan (2016), *Unnatural Narratives: Impossible Worlds in Fiction and Drama*, Lincoln: University of Nebraska Press.

Alber, Jan and Monika Fludernik (eds.) (2010), *Postclassical Narratology*, Columbus: Ohio State University Press.

Alber, Jan, Stefan Iversen, Henrik Skov Nielsen, and Brian Richardson (2010), 'Unnatural Narratives, Unnatural Narratology: Beyond Mimetic Models', *Narrative* 18.2: 113–36.

Alber, Jan, Stefan Iversen, Henrik Skov Nielsen, and Brian Richardson (2013), 'What Really Is Unnatural Narratology?', *Storyworlds: A Journal of Narrative Studies* 5: 101–18.

Alber, Jan and Heinze Rüdiger (eds.) (2011), *Unnatural Narratives—Unnatural Narratology*, Berlin: De Gruyter.

Appelrot, B. G. (ed.) (1893), *Aristotel: Ob iskusstve poezii*, Moscow: Goslitizdat.

Armstrong, David (1993), 'The Addressees of the *Ars Poetica*: Herculaneum, the Pisones and Epicurean Protreptic', *Materiali e discussioni* 31: 185–230.

Armstrong, David, Jeffrey Fish, Patricia A. Johnston, and Marilyn B. Skinner (eds.) (2003), *Vergil, Philodemus, and the Augustans*, Austin: University of Texas Press.

Auerbach, Erich (1974), *Mimesis: The Representation of Reality in Western Literature*, Princeton: Princeton University Press.

Aumüller, Matthias (2009), 'Russische kompositionstheorie', in W. Schmid (ed.), *Slavische erzähltheorie: russische und tschechische ansätze*. Berlin: De Gruyter, pp. 90–140.

Bakhtin, Mikhail (1981), 'Discourse in the Novel', in *The Dialogic Imagination: Four Essays*, Austin: University of Texas Press, pp. 259–422.

Bal, Mieke (1977), *Narratologie: essais sur la signification narrative dans quatre romans modernes*, Paris: Klincksieck.

Bal, Mieke (1981), 'Aristoteles Semioticus', *Spektator* 10: 490–5.

Bal, Mieke (1982), 'Mimesis and Genre Theory in Aristotle's *Poetics*', *Poetics Today* 3.1: 171–80.

Bal, Mieke (1985), *Narratology: Introduction to the Theory of Narrative*, Toronto: University of Toronto Press.

Bal, Mieke (1996), *Double Exposures: The Subject of Cultural Analysis*, New York; London: Routledge.

Bal, Mieke (1997), *Narratology: Introduction to the Theory of Narrative*, 2nd edition, Toronto: University of Toronto Press.

Banfield, Ann (1982), *Unspeakable Sentences: Narration and Representation in the Language of Fiction*, Boston: Routledge & Kegan Paul.

Barchiesi, Alessandro (1994), *Homeric Effects in Vergil's Narrative*, Princeton: Princeton University Press.

Barchiesi, Alessandro (2001), *Speaking Volumes: Narrative and Intertext in Ovid and Other Latin Poets*, London: Duckworth.

Barthes, Roland (1966), 'Introduction à l'analyse structurale des récits', *Communications* 8: 1–27.

Barthes, Roland (1974), *S/Z*, New York: Hill and Wang.

Barthes, Roland (1975a), 'An Introduction to the Structural Analysis of Narrative', *New Literary History* 6.2: 237–72.

Barthes, Roland (1975b), *The Pleasure of the Text*, New York: Hill and Wang.

Barthes, Roland (1989), *The Rustle of Language*, New York: Hill and Wang.

Bassino, P. (ed.) (2014), 'Pseudo-Plutarch, Life of Homer 1.1–5', https://livingpoets.dur.ac.uk/w/Draft:Pseudo-Plutarch,_Life_of_Homer_1.1-5.

Beardsley, Monroe C. (1984), 'La postura Aristotélica', in Monroe C. Beardsley and John Hospers (eds.), *Estética: historia y fundamentos*, Madrid: Cátedra, pp. 26–31.

Beecroft, A. (2010), *Authorship and Cultural Identity in Early Greece and China*, Cambridge: Cambridge University Press.

Belfiore, Elizabeth S. (1992), *Tragic Pleasures: Aristotle on Plot and Emotion*, Princeton: Princeton University Press.

Belfiore, Elizabeth S. (2000), 'Narratological Plots and Aristotle's Mythos', *Arethusa* 33.1: 37–70.

Belfiore, Elizabeth S. (2001), 'Dramatic and Epic Time: "Magnitude" and "Length" in Aristotle's Poetics', in Øivind Andersen and Jon Haarberg (eds.), *Making Sense of Aristotle: Essays in Poetics*, London: Duckworth, pp. 25–49.

Benveniste, Emile (1966), *Problème de linguistique générale*, Paris: Gallimard.

Block, E. (1982), 'The Narrator Speaks: Apostrophe in Homer and Vergil', *Transactions of the American Philological Association* 112: 7–22.

Blondell, Ruby (2002), *The Play of Character in Plato's Dialogues*, Cambridge: Cambridge University Press.

Bloom, H. (1973), *The Anxiety of Influence*, New York: Oxford University Press.

Boillat, Alain (2009), 'La diégèse dans son acception filmologique', *Cinemas* (Montreal), 19.2–3: 217–45.

Booth, Wayne C. (1961), *Rhetoric of Fiction*, Chicago; London: University of Chicago Press.

Booth, Wayne C. (1988), *The Company We Keep*, Berkeley: University of California Press.

Booth, Wayne C. (1992), 'The Poetics for a Practical Critic', in Amélie Rorty (ed.), *Essays on Aristotle's Poetics*, Berkeley: University of California Press, pp. 387–408.

Booth, Wayne C. (2004), 'My Life with Rhetoric: From Neglect to Obsession', in Walter Jost and Wendy Olmsted (eds.), *A Companion to Rhetoric and Rhetorical Criticism*, Oxford: Blackwell, pp. 494–504.

Bordwell, D., J. Staiger, and K. Thompson (1985), *Classical Hollywood Cinema*, New York: Columbia University Press.

Bortolussi, M. and P. Dixon (2003), *Psychonarratology*, Cambridge: Cambridge University Press.

Bouchard, E. (2010), 'The Meaning of βλαβερϙόν in the *Poetics*', *Greek, Roman, and Byzantine Studies* 50: 309–36.

Bowie, Angus (2004), 'Aristophanes', in Irene de Jong, René Nünlist, and Angus Bowie (eds.), *Narrators, Narratees, and Narratives in Ancient Greek Literature*, Leiden: Brill, pp. 281–96.

Boyd, Brian (2009), *On the Origin of Stories: Evolution, Cognition, and Fiction*, Harvard: Harvard University Press.

Branigan, Edward (1984), *Point of View in the Cinema: A Theory of Narration and Subjectivity in Classical Film*, Berlin: Mouton Publishers.

Branigan, Edward (1992), *Narrative Comprehension and Film*, London: Routledge.

Bremond, Claude (1966), 'La logique des possibles narratifs', *Communications* 8: 60–76.

Brewer, Mária Minich (1984), 'A Loosening of Tongues: From Narrative Economy to Women Writing', *Modern Language Notes* 99: 1141–61.

Brink, C. O. (1963), *Horace on Poetry: Prolegomena to the Literary Epistles*, Cambridge: Cambridge University Press.

Brink, C. O. (ed.) (1971), *Horace on Poetry: The 'Ars Poetica'*, Cambridge: Cambridge University Press.

Brisson, Luc (1998), *Plato the Myth Maker*, Chicago: University of Chicago Press.

Brooks, Peter (1977), 'Freud's Masterplot', *Yale French Studies* 55/56: 280–300.

Brooks, Peter (1984), *Reading for the Plot: Design and Intention in Narrative*, Cambridge, MA: Harvard University Press.

Brummer, J. (ed.) (1912), *Vitae Virgilanae*, Leipzig: Teubner.

Burke, Kenneth (1945), *A Grammar of Motives*, Berkeley: University of California Press.

Burke, Seán (ed.) (1995), *Authorship: From Plato to the Postmodern: Criticism and Subjectivity in Barthes, Foucault and Derrida*, Edinburgh: Edinburgh University Press.

Burnet, J. (ed.) (1903), *Platonis Opera*, Vol. 2. Oxford: Clarendon Press.

Butcher, S. H. (ed.) (1955), *Aristotle's Theory of Poetry and Fine Art*, London: Macmillan.

Butterworth, C. E. (ed.) (1977), *Averroes' Three Short Commentaries on Aristotle's Topics, Rhetoric and Poetics*, New York: State University of New York Press.

Byram, Katra (2015), *Ethics and the Dynamic Observer Narrator: Reckoning with Past and Present in German Literature*, Columbus: Ohio State University Press.

Bywater, Ingram (ed.) (1909), *Aristotle on the Art of Poetry*, Oxford: Clarendon Press.

Cambry, Émile (ed.) (1932), *Platon, Œuvres complètes*, Vol. 6: *La République Livres I–III, Platon, texte établi et traduit par Émile Chambry, avec introduction d'Auguste Diès*, Paris: Belles Lettres.

Carey, C. (1988), '"Philanthropy" in Aristotle's Poetics', *Eranos* 86: 131–9.

Caracciolo, Marco (2014), 'Experientiality', in Peter Hühn et al. (eds.), *Handbook of Narratology*, Berlin: De Gruyter, pp. 149–58.

Carroll, M. (2009), *Aristotle's Poetics, C. 25 in the Light of the Homeric Scholia*, La Vergne: Lighting Source Inc.

Casali, Sergio (2009), 'Ovidian Intertextuality', in Peter E. Knox (ed.), *A Companion to Ovid*, Malden: Wiley-Blackwell, pp. 341–54.

Casali, Sergio and F. Stok (eds.) (2008), *Servius: Exegetical Stratifications and Cultural Models*, Brussels: Éditions Latomus.

Chatman, Seymour (1978), *Story and Discourse: Narrative Structure in Fiction and Film*, New York; London: Cornell University Press.

Chatman, Seymour (1990), *Coming to Terms: The Rhetoric of Narrative in Fiction and Film*, New York; London: Cornell University Press.

Cobley, Paul (2012), 'Narratology', in Michael Groden, Martin Kreiswirth, and Imre Szeman (eds.), *Contemporary Literary and Cultural Theory*, Baltimore: Johns Hopkins University Press, pp. 348–54.

Cohn, Dorrit (1978), *Transparent Minds*, Princeton: Princeton University Press.

Communications (1966), *Recherches sémiologiques: l'analyse structurale du récit*, Paris: Le Seuil.

Conte, Gian Biagio (1986), *The Rhetoric of Imitation: Genre and Poetic Memory in Virgil and Other Latin Poets*, New York: Cornell University Press.

Cornils, Anja and Wilhelm Schernus (2003), 'On the Relationship between the Theory of the Novel, Narrative Theory, and Narratology', in T. Kindt and H.-H. Müller (eds.), *What Is Narratology? Questions and Answers Regarding the Status of a Theory*, Berlin: De Gruyter, 137–74.

Crane, Ronald, S. (1944), 'English Neo-Classical Criticism', in Joseph T. Shipley (ed.), *Dictionary of World Literature*, New York: The Philosophical Library, pp. 193–203.

Crane, Ronald, S. (1950), 'The Plot of Tom Jones', *Journal of General Education*, 4.2: 112–30.

Crane, Ronald, S. (ed.) (1952), *Critics and Criticism, Ancient and Modern*, Chicago: University of Chicago Press.

Crane, Ronald, S. (1953), *The Languages of Criticism and the Structure of Poetry*, Toronto: University of Toronto Press.

Cronk, Nicholas (1999), 'Aristotle, Horace, and Longinus: The Conception of Reader Response', in Glyn P. Norton (ed.), *The Cambridge History of Literary Criticism*, Vol. 3: *The Renaissance*, Cambridge: Cambridge University Press, pp. 199–204.

Culler, J. (1975), *Structuralist Poetics: Structuralism, Linguistics, and the Study of Literature*, Ithaca: Cornell University Press.

Currie, Mark (2007), *About Time: Narrative, Fiction and the Philosophy of Time*, Edinburgh: Edinburgh University Press.

Currie, Mark (2013), *The Unexpected: Narrative Temporality and the Philosophy of Surprise*, Edinburgh: Edinburgh University Press.

Darby, D. (2001), 'Form and Context: An Essay in the History of Narratology', *Poetics Today* 22.4: 829–52.

Day, G. (2007), 'Forster as Literary Critic', in D. Bradshaw (ed.), *The Cambridge Companion to E. M. Forster*, Cambridge: Cambridge University Press, pp. 223–34.

de Jong, Irene J. F. (1987), *Narrators and Focalizers: The Presentation of the Story in the Iliad*, Amsterdam: Grüner.

de Jong, Irene J. F. (1991), *Narrative in Drama: The Art of the Euripidean Messenger Speech*, Leiden: Brill.

de Jong, Irene J. F. (1997), 'Homer and Narratology', in Ian Morris and Barry B. Powell (eds.), *A New Companion to Homer*, Leiden; New York: Brill, pp. 305–25.

de Jong, Irene J. F. (2001a), 'The Anachronical Structure of Herodotus; *Histories*', in Stephen Harrison (ed.), *Texts, Ideas, and the Classics: Scholarship, Theory, and Classical Literature*, Oxford: Oxford University Press, pp. 93–116.

de Jong, Irene J. F. (2001b), *Narratological Commentary on the Odyssey*, Cambridge: Cambridge University Press.

de Jong, Irene J. F. (2005a), 'Ancient Theories of Narrative (Western)', in David Herman, Manfred Jahn, and Marie-Laure Ryan (eds.), *Routledge Encyclopedia of Narrative Theory*, London: Routledge, pp. 19–22.

de Jong, Irene J. F. (2005b), 'Aristotle on the Homeric Narrator', *Classical Quarterly* 55.2: 616–21.

de Jong, Irene J. F. (2005c), 'In medias res', in David Herman, Manfred Jahn, and Marie-Laure Ryan (eds.), *Routledge Encyclopedia of Narrative Theory*, London: Routledge, p. 242.

de Jong, Irene J. F. (2007), 'Introduction: Narratological Theory on Time', in I. de Jong and René Nünlist (eds.), *Time in Ancient Greek Literature*, Leiden: Brill, pp. 1–14.

de Jong, Irene J. F. (2009), 'Metalepsis in Ancient Greek Literature', in J. Grethlein and A. Rengakos (eds.), *Narratology and Interpretation: The Content of the Form in Ancient Texts*, Berlin: De Gruyter, pp. 87–116.

de Jong, Irene J. F. (2011), 'Homer and Narratology', in Ian Morris and Barry Powell (eds.), *A New Companion to Homer*, Leiden; New York: Brill, pp. 305–25.

de Jong, Irene J. F. (ed.) (2012), *Space in Ancient Greek Literature*, Leiden: Brill.

de Jong, Irene J. F. (2014), *Narratology and Classics*, Oxford: Oxford University Press.

de Jong, Irene J. F. and René Nünlist (eds.) (2007), *Time in Ancient Greek Literature*, Leiden: Brill.

de Jong, Irene J. F., René Nünlist, and Angus Bowie (eds.) (2004), *Narrators, Narratees, and Narratives in Ancient Greek Literature*, Leiden: Brill.

de Lauretis, T. (1984), *Alice Doesn't*, Bloomington: Indiana University Press.

de Ste. Croix, G. E. M. (1992), 'Aristotle on History and Poetry', in Amélie Rorty (ed.), *Essays on Aristotle's Poetics*, Berkeley: University of California Press, pp. 23–32.

Dickey, Eleanor (2007), *Ancient Greek Scholarship: A Guide to Finding, Reading, and Understanding Scholia, Commentaries, Lexica, and Grammatical Treatises, from their Beginnings to the Byzantine Period*, New York; Oxford: Oxford University Press.

Diengott, Nilli (1988), 'Narratology and Feminism', *Style* 22: 42–51.

Dietz, David B. (1995), '*Historia* in the Commentary of Servius', *Transactions of the American Philological Association* 125: 61–97.

Doherty, Lillian Eileen (1995), *Siren Songs: Gender, Audiences, and Narrators in the Odyssey*, Ann Arbor: University of Michigan Press.

Doherty, Lillian Eileen (2001), 'The Snares of the *Odyssey*: A Feminist Narratological Reading', in Stephen Harrison (ed.), *Texts, Ideas, and the Classics: Scholarship, Theory, and Classical Literature*, Oxford: Oxford University Press, pp. 117–34.

Doležel, Lubomír (1990), *Occidental Poetics*, Lincoln: University of Nebraska Press.

Doležel, Lubomír (1997), *Historia breve de la poética*, Madrid: Síntesis.

Doležel, Lubomír (1998), *Heterocosmica: Fiction and Possible Worlds*, Baltimore: Johns Hopkins University Press.

Doležel, Lubomír (2010), *Possible Worlds of Fiction and History*, Baltimore: Johns Hopkins University Press.

Downing, E. (1984), '*Hoion Psyche*: An Essay on Aristotle's *Muthos*', *Classical Antiquity* 3: 164–78.

Duckworth, G. E. (1931), '*Proanaphonesis* in the Scholia to Homer', *American Journal of Philology* 52: 320–38.

DuPlessis, Rachel Blau (1985), *Writing beyond the Ending: Narrative Strategies of Twentieth-Century Women Writers*, Bloomington: Indiana University Press.

Dupont-Roc, Roselyne and Jean Lallot (eds.) (1980), *Aristote: la poétique*, Paris: Seuil.

Eco, Umberto (1996), 'Thoughts on Aristotle's *Poetics*', in Calin Andrei Mihailescu and Walid Hamarneh (eds.), *Fiction Updated: Theories of Fictionality, Narratology, and Poetics*, Toronto: University of Toronto Press, pp. 229–43.

Eggs, E. (1984), *Die Rhetorik des Aristoteles: Ein Beitrag zur Theorie der Alltagsargumentation und zur Syntax von komplexen Sätzen (im Französischen)*, Frankfurt am Main: Lang.

Eichenbaum, Boris (1965), *Russian Formalist Criticism*, Lincoln: University of Nebraska Press.

Else, Gerald F. (ed.) (1957), *Aristotle's Poetics: The Argument*, Cambridge, MA: Harvard University Press.

Emmott, Catherine (1997), *Narrative Comprehension: A Discourse Perspective*, Oxford: Oxford University Press.

Enos, Richard L. and Lois P. Agnew (eds.) (1998), *Landmark Essays on Aristotelian Rhetoric*, Mahwah: Lawrence Erlbaum.

Erbse, Hartmut (ed.) (1969–88), *Scholia Graeca in Homeri Iliadem Scholia Vetera, Recensuit Hartmut Erbse*, Berolini: De Gruyter.

Erlich, Victor (1955), *Russian Formalism: History-Doctrine*, The Hague: Slavistic Printings and Reprintings.

Erlich, Victor, R. Jackson, and S. Rudy (1985), *Russian Formalism*, New Haven: Yale Center for International and Area Studies.

Falco, Raphael (2000), 'Satan and Servius: Milton's Use of the Helen Episode (*Aeneid* 2.567–88)', in Kristin A. Pruitt and Charles W. Durham (eds.), *Living Texts: Interpreting Milton*, Cranbury; London; Ontario: Associated University Presses, pp. 131–43.

Fantuzzi, Marco (1988), *Ricerche su Apollonio Rodio*, Rome: Edizioni dell'Ateneo.

Farwell, Marilyn (1996), *Heterosexual Plots and Lesbian Narratives*, New York: New York University Press.

Faulkner, A. and O. Hodkinson (eds.) (2015), *Hymnic Narrative and the Narratology of Greek Hymns*, Leiden: Brill.

Fehn, A., I. Hoesterey, and M. Tatat (eds.) (1992), *Neverending Stories: Toward a Critical Narratology*, Princeton: Princeton University Press.

Ferenczi, Attila and Philip Hardie (eds.) (2014), *New Approaches to Horace's 'Ars Poetica'*, Pisa: Serra.

Ferrari, G. R. F. (1989), 'Plato and Poetry', in George Kennedy (ed.), *Cambridge History of Literary Criticism*, Vol. 1: *Classical Criticism*, Cambridge: Cambridge University Press, pp. 92–148.

Fludernik, Monika (1993), *The Fictions of Language and the Languages of Fiction: The Linguistic Representation of Speech and Consciousness*, London: Routledge.

Fludernik, Monika (1996), *Towards a Natural Narratology*, London; New York: Routledge.

Fludernik, Monika (2001), 'New Wine in Old Bottles? Voice, Focalization and New Writing', *New Literary History* 23.3: 619–38.

Fludernik, Monika (2003), 'The Diachronization of Narratology', *Narrative* 11.3: 331–48.

Fludernik, Monika (2005a), 'Histories of Narrative Theory (II): From Structuralism to the Present', in James Phelan and Peter J. Rabinowitz (eds.), *A Companion to Narrative Theory*, Oxford: Blackwell Publishing, pp. 36–59.

Fludernik, Monika (2005b), 'Speech Representation', in David Herman, Manfred Jahn, and Marie-Laure Ryan (eds.), *Routledge Encyclopedia of Narrative Theory*, London: Routledge, pp. 558–63.

Fludernik, Monika (2006), *Einführung in die Erzähltheorie*, Darmstadt: Wissenschaftliche Buchgesellschaft.

Fludernik, Monika (2009), *An Introduction to Narratology*, London: Routledge.

Fludernik, Monika (2012), 'How Natural Is "Unnatural" Narratology; or, What Is Unnatural about Unnatural Narratology?', *Narrative* 20.3: 357–70.

Fludernik, Monika and Uri Margolin (2004), 'Introduction', *Style* 38: 148–87.

Ford, Andrew Laughlin (2004), *The Origins of Criticism: Literary Culture and Poetic Theory in Classical Greece*, Princeton: Princeton University Press.

Forster, E. M. (1927), *Aspects of the Novel*, New York: Harcourt, Brace & Company.

Fowler, Don (1997), 'The Virgil Commentary of Servius', in Charles Martindale (ed.), *The Cambridge Companion to Virgil*, Cambridge: Cambridge University Press, pp. 73–8.

Fowler, Don (2000), *Roman Constructions: Readings in Postmodern Latin*, Oxford: Oxford University Press.

Fowler, Don (2001), 'Introduction', in Stephen Harrison (ed.), *Texts, Ideas, and the Classics: Scholarship, Theory, and Classical Literature*, Oxford: Oxford University Press, pp. 65–9.

Freudenberg, Kirk (2002), *The Walking Muse: Horace on the Theory of Satire*, Princeton: Princeton University Press.

Friedman, Norman L. (1967), 'Forms of the Plot', in Philip Stevick (ed.), *The Theory of the Novel*, New York: The Free Press, pp. 145–66.

Friedman, Norman L. (1955), 'Point of View in Fiction: The Development of a Critical Concept', *Publications of the Modern Language Association of America* 70: 1160–84.

Frischer, B. (1991), *Shifting Paradigms*, Atlanta: Scholars Press.

Fusillo, Massimo (1985), *Il tempo delle Argonautiche: un'analisi del racconto in Apollonio Rodio*, Rome: Edizioni dell'Ateneo.

Fyfe, W. Hamilton (ed.) (1927), *Aristotle: The Poetics*, London.

Gale, Monica (2004), *Latin Epic and Didactic Poetry*, Swansea: Classical Press of Wales.

García Landa, José Ángel (1998), *Acción, relato, discurso: estructura de la ficción narrativa*, Salamanca: Ediciones Universidad de Salamanca.

Gaudreault, A. and T. Barnard (2009), *From Plato to Lumière*, Toronto: University of Toronto Press.

Genette, Gérard (1966), 'Frontières du récit', *Communications* 8: 152–63.

Genette, Gérard (1966–72), *Figures I–III*, Paris: Éditions du Seuil.

Genette, Gérard (1976), 'Boundaries of Narrative', *New Literary History* 8.1: 1–13.

Genette, Gérard (1980), *Narrative Discourse: An Essay in Method*, translated by Jane E. Lewin, New York: Cornell University Press.

Genette, Gérard (1988), *Narrative Discourse Revisited*, Ithaca: Cornell University Press.

Genette, Gérard (1993), *Fiction and Diction*, Ithaca: Cornell University Press.

Gerrig, Richard J. (1993), *Experiencing Narrative Worlds: On the Psychological Activities of Reading*, New Haven: Yale University Press.

Gibson, Andrew (1996), *Towards a Postmodern Theory of Narrative*, Edinburgh: Edinburgh University Press.

Gigante, Marcello (ed.) (1996), *Philodemus in Italy: The Books from Herculaneum*, Ann Arbor: University of Michigan Press.

Gill, Christopher (1986), 'The Question of Character and Personality in Greek Tragedy', *Poetics Today* 7.2: 251–73.

Gill, Christopher (1993), 'Plato on Falsehood—Not Fiction', in Christopher Gill and T. P. Wiseman (eds.), *Lies and Fiction in the Ancient World*, Exeter: University of Exeter Press, pp. 38–87.

Gill, Christopher (1996), 'Afterword: Dialectic and Dialogue Form in Late Plato', in C. Gill and M. M. McCabe (eds.), *Form and Argument in Late Plato*, Oxford: Clarendon Press, pp. 283–311.

Gill, Christopher (1998), *Personality in Greek Epic, Tragedy, and Philosophy: The Self in Dialogue*, Oxford: Oxford University Press.

Gill, Christopher (2002), 'Dialectic and the Dialogue Form', in J. Annas and C. Rowe (eds.), *Perspectives on Plato: Modern and Ancient*, Cambridge, MA: Harvard University Press, pp. 145–71.

Golden, Leon (1992), *Aristotle on Tragic and Comic Mimesis*, Atlanta: Scholars Press.

Golden, Leon (2010), 'Reception of Horace's *Ars Poetica*', in Gregson Davis (ed.), *A Companion to Horace*, London: Wiley-Blackwell, pp. 391–413.

Goldhill, Simon (1997), 'The Audience of Athenian Tragedy', in P. E. Easterling (ed.), *The Cambridge Companion to Greek Tragedy*, Cambridge: Cambridge University Press, pp. 54–68.

Goldhill, Simon (2010), 'Review of *Narratology and Interpretation: The Content of Narrative Form in Ancient Literature*', *Bryn Mawr Classical Review*: http://bmcr. brynmawr.edu/2010/2010-02-27.html.

Grabes, Herbert (2014), 'Sequentiality', in Peter Hühn et al. (eds.), *Handbook of Narratology*, Berlin: De Gruyter, pp. 765–76.

Graziosi, Barbara (2002), *Inventing Homer: The Early Reception of Epic*, Cambridge: Cambridge University Press.

Graziosi, Barbara (2013), 'The Poet in the *Iliad*,' in A. Marmodoro and J. Hill (eds.), *The Author's Voice in Classical and Late Antiquity*, Oxford: Oxford University Press, pp. 9–38.

Greimas, A. (1983), *Structural Semantics: An Attempt at a Method*, Lincoln: University of Nebraska Press.

Greimas, A. (1987), *On Meaning*, Minneapolis: University of Minnesota Press.

Grethlein, Jonas and Christopher B. Krebs (eds.) (2012), *Time and Narrative in Ancient Historiography: The 'Plupast' from Herodotus to Appian*, Cambridge; New York: Cambridge University Press.

Grethlein, Jonas and Antonio Rengakos (eds.) (2009), *Narratology and Interpretation: The Content of Narrative Form in Ancient Literature*, Berlin: De Gruyter.

Griffin, Jasper (1986), 'Greek Myth and Hesiod', *The Oxford History of the Classical World*, Oxford: Oxford University Press, pp. 82–106.

Grisolia, Raffaele (2001), *Oikonomia: struttura e tecnica drammatica negli scoli antichi ai testi drammatici*, Naples: Pubblicazioni del Dipartimento di Filologia Classica dell'Università degli Studi di Napoli.

Habib, M. A. R. (2005), *A History of Literary Criticism: From Plato to the Present*, Oxford: Blackwell.

Hagen, F. (2011), *Narratives of Egypt and the Ancient Near East*, Leuven: Peeters.

Hall, Vernon (1963), *A Short History of Literary Criticism*, New York: New York University Press.

Halliwell, Stephen (1989), 'Aristotle's *Poetics*', in George Kennedy (ed.), *Cambridge History of Literary Criticism*, Vol. 1: *Classical Criticism*, Cambridge: Cambridge University Press, pp. 149–83.

Halliwell, Stephen (ed.) (1998), *Aristotle's Poetics*, London: Duckworth.

Halliwell, Stephen (ed.) (1999), *Aristotle, Poetics (with Longinus on the Sublime and Demetrius On Style)*, Loeb Classical Library, Harvard: Harvard University Press.

Halliwell, Stephen (2002), *The Aesthetics of Mimesis: Ancient Texts and Modern Problems*, Princeton: Princeton University Press.

Halliwell, Stephen (2009), 'The Theory and Practice of Narrative in Plato', in J. Grethlein and A. Rengakos (eds.), *Narratology and Interpretation: The Content of the Form in Ancient Texts*, Berlin: De Gruyter, pp. 15–42.

Halliwell, Stephen (2011), *Between Ecstasy and Truth: Interpretations of Greek Poetics from Homer to Longinus*, Oxford: Oxford University Press.

Halliwell, Stephen (2012), 'Unity of Art without Unity of Life? A Question about Aristotle's Theory of Tragedy', *Atti Accademia Pontaniana, Napoli—Supplemento* 61: 25–40.

Halliwell, Stephen (2014), 'Diegesis—Mimesis', in Peter Hühn et al. (eds.), *Handbook of Narratology*, Berlin: De Gruyter, pp. 129–37.

Hamburger, Käte (1973), *The Logic of Literature*, Bloomington: Indiana University Press.

Hankinson, J. R. (1998), *Cause and Explanation in Ancient Greek Thought*, Oxford: Oxford University Press.

Hansen-Löve, A. (1978), *Der russische Formalismus*, Vienna: Verl. d. Österr. Akad. d. Wiss.

Hardie, Philip (2009), 'Fame's Narratives: Epic and Historiography', in Jonas Grethlein and Antonio Rengakos (eds.), *Narratology and Interpretation: The Content of Narrative Form in Ancient Literature*, Berlin: De Gruyter, pp. 555–72.

Hardison, O. B., Jr., and Leon Golden (eds.) (1968), *Aristotle's Poetics: A Translation and Commentary for Students of Literature*, Englewood Cliffs: Prentice-Hall.

Hardy, Joseph (ed.) (1932), *La poétique (Platon)*, Paris: Les Belles Lettres.

Harrison, S. J. (ed.) (1991), *Vergil, Aeneid 10: With Introduction, Translation, and Commentary*, Oxford; New York: Oxford University Press.

Harrison, S. J. (ed.) (2001), *Texts, Ideas and the Classics*, Oxford: Oxford University Press.

Hartman, G. (1980), *Criticism in the Wilderness*, New Haven: Yale University Press.

Haslam, Michael (1972), 'Plato, Sophron, and the Dramatic Dialogue', *Bulletin of the Institute of Classical Studies* 19: 17–38.

Heath, Malcolm (1989), *Unity in Greek Poetics*, Oxford: Clarendon Press.

Heath, Malcolm (1991), 'The Universality of Poetry in Aristotle's *Poetics*', *Classical Quarterly* 41: 389–402.

Heath, Malcolm (2009), 'Cognition in Aristotle's Poetics', *Mnemosyne* 62.1: 51–75.

Heath, Malcolm (ed.) (1996), *Aristotle, Poetics*, London: Penguin Books.

Herman, David (1997), 'Scripts, Sequences, and Stories: Elements of a Postclassical Narratology', *PMLA* 112.5: 1046–59.

Herman, David (ed.) (1999), *Narratologies*, Columbus: Ohio State University Press.

Herman, David (2002), *Story Logic: Problems and Possibilities of Narrative*, Lincoln: University of Nebraska Press.

Herman, David (2003) (ed.), *Narrative Theory and the Cognitive Sciences*, Stanford: CLSI.

Herman, David (2005), 'Histories of Narrative Theory (I): A Genealogy of Early Developments', in J. Phelan and P. J. Rabinowitz (eds.), *A Companion to Narrative Theory*, Malden: Blackwell, pp. 19–35.

Herman, David (ed.) (2007), *The Cambridge Companion to Narrative*, Cambridge; New York: Cambridge University Press.

Herman, David (2014a), 'Cognitive Narratology', in Peter Hühn et al. (eds.), *Handbook of Narratology*, Berlin: De Gruyter, pp. 46–64.

Herman, David (2014b), *Storytelling and the Sciences of Mind*, Cambridge, MA: MIT Press.

Herman, David (2018), *Narratology beyond the Human: Storytelling and Animal Life*, Oxford: Oxford University Press.

Herman, David, Manfred Jahn, and Marie-Laure Ryan (eds.) (2005), *Routledge Encyclopedia of Narrative Theory*, London: Routledge.

Herman, David, James Phelan, Peter J. Rabinowitz, Brian Richardson, and Robyn Warhol (2012), *Narrative Theory: Core Concepts and Critical Debates*, Columbus: Ohio State University Press.

Herman, Luc and Bart Vervaeck (2005), *Handbook of Narrative Analysis*, Lincoln: University of Nebraska Press.

Herrick, Marvin T. (1946), *The Fusion of Horatian and Aristotelian Literary Criticism, 1531–1555*, Urbana: Illinois University Press.

Hexter, Ralph (2010), 'On First Looking into Vergil's Homer', in Joseph Farrell and Michael C. J. Putnam (eds.), *A Companion to Vergil's Aeneid and its Tradition*, London: Wiley-Blackwell, pp. 26–36.

Hill, Kevin (1998), 'Genealogy', in E. Craig (ed.), *The Routledge Encyclopedia of Philosophy*, London: Routledge, pp. 1–5.

Hinds, Stephen (1987), *Metamorphoses of Persephone: Ovid and the Self-Conscious Muse*, Cambridge: Cambridge University Press.

Hinds, Stephen (1998), *Allusion and Intertext: Dynamics of Appropriation in Roman Poetry*, Cambridge: Cambridge University Press.

Hogan, Patrick Colm (2003a), *The Mind and Its Stories: Narrative Universals and Human Emotion*, Cambridge: Cambridge University Press.

Hogan, Patrick Colm (2003b), *Cognitive Science, Literature, and the Arts: A Guide for Humanists*, London: Routledge.

Hogan, Patrick Colm and Lalita Pandit (2005), 'Ancient Theories of Narrative (Non-Western)', in David Herman, Manfred Jahn, and Marie-Laure Ryan (eds.), *Routledge Encyclopedia of Narrative Theory*, London: Routledge, pp. 14–19.

Hornblower, Simon (1994), *Greek Historiography*, Oxford: Clarendon Press.

House, Humphrey (ed.) (1956), *Aristotle's Poetics*, London: Greenwood Press.

Hühn, Peter, Jan Christoph Meister, John Pier, and Wolf Schmid (eds.) (2014), *Handbook of Narratology*, Berlin: De Gruyter.

Huxley, G. (1979), 'Historical Criticism in Aristotle's "Homeric Questions"', *Proceedings of the Royal Irish Academy: Archaeology, Celtic Studies, History, Linguistics, Literature* 79: 73–81.

Hyde, Michael J. and Craig R. Smith (1993), 'Aristotle and Heidegger on Emotion and Rhetoric: Questions of Time and Space', in Ian Angus and Leonore Langsdorf (eds.), *The Critical Turn: Rhetoric and Philosophy in Postmodern Discourse*, Carbondale: Southern Illinois University Press, pp. 68–99.

Iser, W. (1972), *The Implied Reader*, Baltimore: Johns Hopkins University Press.

Jahn, Manfred (1996), 'Windows of Focalization: Deconstructing and Reconstructing a Narratological Concept', *Style* 30: 241–67.

Jahn, Manfred (1999), 'The Mechanics of Focalization: Extending the Narratological Toolbox', *Revue des Groupes de Recherches Anglo-Américaines de l'Université François Rabelais de Tours* 21: 85–110.

Jahn, Manfred (2007), 'Focalization', in David Herman (ed.), *The Cambridge Companion to Narrative*, Cambridge: Cambridge University Press, pp. 94–108.

James, Henry (1894), 'The Art of Fiction', in *Partial Portraits*, London: Macmillan, pp. 375–408.

James, Henry (1921), 'Review of Harriet Elizabeth Prescott, "Azarian: an Episode"', in Pierre de Chaignon la Rose (ed.), *Notes and Reviews*, Cambridge, MA: Harvard University Press, pp. 25–7.

James, Henry and R. Blackmur (1937), *The Art of the Novel*, New York: C. Scribner's Sons.

Janko, Richard (1984), *Aristotle on Comedy: Towards a Reconstruction of Poetics II*, London: Duckworth.

Janko, Richard (ed.) (1987), *Aristotle, Poetics*, Indianapolis: Hackett Publishing.

Janko, Richard (ed.) (2001), *Philodemus, On Poems, Book I*, Oxford: Oxford University Press.

Janko, Richard (ed.) (2011), *Philodemus, On Poems, Books 3–4*, Oxford: Oxford University Press.

Jannidis, Fotis (2014), 'Character', in Peter Hühn et al. (eds.), *Handbook of Narratology*, Berlin: De Gruyter, pp. 14–29.

Jannidis, Fotis, Matias Martínez, John Pier, and Wolf Schmid (eds.) (2014), *Narratologia: Contributions to Narrative Theory*, Berlin; New York: De Gruyter.

Jauss, Hans Robert (1982), *Aesthetic Experience and Literary Hermeneutics*, Minneapolis: University of Minnesota Press.

Johnson, Gary (2012), *The Vitality of Allegory: Figural Narrative in Modern and Contemporary Fiction*, Columbus: Ohio State University Press.

Kafalenos, Emma (2006), *Narrative Causalities*, Ohio: Ohio State University Press.

Kawashima, R. (2011), 'The Syntax of Narrative Forms', in Fredrik Hagen et al. (eds.), *Narratives of Egypt and the Ancient Near East*, Leuven: Peeters, pp. 341–69.

Keaney, J. J. and Robert Lamberton (eds.) (1996), *Essay on the Life and Poetry of Homer*, Atlanta: Scholars Press.

Kearns, Michael (2005), 'Genre Theory in Narrative Studies', in David Herman, Manfred Jahn, and Marie-Laure Ryan (eds.), *Routledge Encyclopedia of Narrative Theory*, London: Routledge, pp. 201–5.

Kennedy, George A. (ed.) (1989), *Cambridge History of Literary Criticism*, Vol. 1: *Classical Criticism*, Cambridge: Cambridge University Press.

Kermode, Frank (1967), *The Sense of an Ending*, New York: Oxford University Press.

Kindt, T. and H. Müller (2006), *The Implied Author*, Berlin: De Gruyter.

Kirby, John T. (1991), 'Mimesis and Diegesis: Foundations of Aesthetic Theory in Plato and Aristotle', *Helios* 18: 113–28.

Kitto, H. D. F. (1966), *Poiesis: Structure and Thought*, Berkeley and Los Angeles: University of California Press.

Klauk, Tobias and Tilmann Köppe (2013), 'Reassessing Unnatural Narratology: Problems and Prospects', *Storyworlds* 5: 77–100.

Knight, W. F. Jackson (1958), 'Vergil's Latin', *Acta Classica* 1: 31–44.

Kolodny, Annette (1975), 'Some Notes on Defining a "Feminist Literary Criticism"', *Critical Inquiry* 2.1: 75–92.

Kolodny, Annette (1985), 'Dancing through the Minefield: Some Observations on the Theory, Practice, and Politics of a Feminist Literary Criticism', in E. Showalter (ed.), *New Feminist Criticism*, New York: Pantheon, pp. 144–55.

Korthals-Altes, Liesbeth (2005), 'Ethical Turn', in D. Herman et al. (eds.), *Routledge Encyclopedia of Narrative Theory*, London: Routledge, pp. 142–6.

Laird, Andrew (1999), *Powers of Expression, Expressions of Power: Speech Presentation and Latin Literature*, Oxford: Oxford University Press.

Laird, Andrew (ed.) (2005), *Oxford Readings in Ancient Literary Criticism*, Oxford: Oxford University Press.

Laird, Andrew (2007), 'The Ars Poetica', in Stephen Harrison (ed.), *The Cambridge Companion to Horace*, Cambridge: Cambridge University Press, pp. 132–43.

Lämmert, Eberhard (1967), *Bauformen des Erzählens*, Stuttgart: Metzler.

Lanser, Susan (1981), *The Narrative Act: Point of View in Prose Fiction*, Princeton: Princeton University Press.

Lanser, Susan (1986), 'Toward a Feminist Narratology', *Style* 20: 341–63.

Lanser, Susan (1988), 'Shifting the Paradigm: Feminism and Narratology', *Style* 22: 52–60.

Lanser, Susan (1992), *Fictions of Authority: Women Writers and Narrative Voice*, Ithaca: Cornell University Press.

Lanser, Susan (1995), 'Sexing the Narrative: Propriety, Desire, and the Engendering of Narratology', *Narrative* 3: 85–94.

Lanser, Susan (2010), 'Are We There Yet? The Intersectional Future of Feminist Narratology', *Foreign Literature Studies* 32: 32–41.

Lanser, Susan (2014), 'Gender and Narrative', in Peter Hühn et al. (eds.), *Handbook of Narratology*, Berlin: De Gruyter, pp. 206–18.

Larkin, Philip (1983), *Required Writing: Miscellaneous Pieces 1955–1982*, London: Faber and Faber.

Laurenti, R. (1984), 'Critica alla mimesi e recupero del pathos: il *De Poetis* di Aristotele', *AION* 6: 51–63.

Lausberg, H. (1998), *Handbook of Literary Rhetoric*, Leiden: Brill.

Lazzarini, Caterina (1984), 'Historia / fabula: forme della costruzione poetica Virgiliana nel commento di Servio all' *Eneide*', *Materiali e Discussioni* 12: 117–44.

Lazzarini, Caterina (1989), 'Elementi di una poetica serviana', *Studi Italiani di Filologia Classica* 82: 56–109.

Ledbetter, Grace M. (2003), *Poetics before Plato: Interpretation and Authority in Early Greek Theories of Poetry*, Princeton: Princeton University Press.

Leitch, Thomas (1986), *What Stories Are: Narrative Theory and Interpretation*, University Park: Pennsylvania State University Press.

Lemon, L. and M. Reis (eds.) (1965), *Russian Formalist Criticism*, Lincoln: University of Nebraska Press.

Leonard, Miriam (2015), *Tragic Modernities*, Cambridge, MA: Harvard University Press.

Lessing, Gotthold Ephraim (1984), *Laocoon: An Essay on the Limits of Painting and Poetry*, translated by E. C. Beasley, London: Longman, Brown, Green and Longmans.

Lévi-Strauss, C. (1955), 'The Structural Study of Myth', *Journal of American Folklore* 68: 428–44.

Liotsakis, V. and S. Farrington (eds.) (2016), *The Art of History: Literary Perspectives on Greek and Roman Historiography*, Berlin; Boston: De Gruyter.

Lipking, L. (1983), 'Aristotle's Sister: A Poetics of Abandonment', *Critical Inquiry*, 10.1: 61–81.

Liveley, Genevieve (2011), 'Narratology', *The Classical Review* 61.2: 341–3.

Liveley, Genevieve and Patricia Salzman-Mitchell (eds.) (2008), *Latin Elegy and Narratology: Fragments of Story*, Columbus: Ohio State University Press.

Lloyd, G. (1984), *The Man of Reason*, Minneapolis: University of Minnesota Press.

Löschnigg, Martin (2005), 'Summary and Scene', in David Herman, Manfred Jahn, and Marie-Laure Ryan (eds.), *Routledge Encyclopedia of Narrative Theory*, London: Routledge, pp. 576–7.

Lowe, N. J. (2000), *The Classical Plot and the Invention of Western Narrative*, Cambridge: Cambridge University Press.

Lowrie, M. (1997), *Horace's Narrative Odes*, Oxford: Clarendon Press.

Lubbock, Percy (2014), *The Craft of Fiction*. London: Cape.

Lucas, D. W. (ed.) (1968), *Aristotle: Poetics*, Oxford: Clarendon Press.

Lucas, F. L. (1928), *Tragedy in Relation to Aristotle's Poetics*, New York: Harcourt.

Lyne, R. (1992), *Further Voices in Vergil's Aeneid*, Oxford: Clarendon Press.

Macleod, C. W. (1979), 'Horatian *Imitatio* and *Odes* 2.5', in David West and A. J. Woodman (eds.), *Creative Imitation and Latin Literature*, Cambridge: Cambridge University Press, pp. 89–102.

Margolin, Uri (2014), 'Narrator', in Peter Hühn et al. (eds.), *Handbook of Narratology*, Berlin: De Gruyter, pp. 646–66.

Martindale, Charles (1993), *Redeeming the Text: Latin Poetry and the Hermeneutics of Reception*, Cambridge: Cambridge University Press.

Martindale, Charles (ed.) (1997), *The Cambridge Companion to Virgil*, Cambridge: Cambridge University Press.

Mathieu-Colas, Michel (1986), 'Frontieres de la narratologie', *Poetique* 65: 91–110.

Matzner, Sebastian and Gail Trimble (eds.) (forthcoming), *Breaking and Entering: Metalepsis in Classical Literature*, Oxford: Oxford University Press.

McCabe, M. M. (1994), *Plato's Individuals*, Princeton. Princeton University Press.

McHale, Brian (1978), 'Free Indirect Discourse: A Survey of Recent Accounts', *Journal for Descriptive Poetics and Theory of Literature* 3: 249–78.

McHale, Brian (2001), 'Weak Narrativity: The Case of Avant-Garde Narrative Poetry', *Narrative* 9: 161–7.

McKeon, Richard (1965), 'Rhetoric and Poetic in the Philosophy of Aristotle', in Elder Olson (ed.), *Aristotle's Poetics and English Literature*, Chicago: University of Chicago Press, pp. 201–36.

McQuillan, M. (ed.) (2000), *The Narrative Reader*, London: Routledge.

Meijering, Roos (1987), *Literary and Rhetorical Theories in Greek Scholia*, Groningen: Egbert Forsten.

Meister, Christoph (2003), *Computing Action*, Berlin: De Gruyter.

Meister, Christoph (2014), 'Narratology', in Peter Hühn et al. (eds.), *Handbook of Narratology*, Berlin: De Gruyter, pp. 623–45.

Metz, Christian (1966), 'La grande syntagmatique du film narratif', *Communications* 8: 120–4.

Metz, Christian (1974), *Film Language: A Semiotics of the Cinema*, Chicago: Chicago University Press.

Mezei, Kathy (ed.) (1996), *Feminist Narratology and British Women Writers*, Chapel Hill: University of North Carolina Press.

Miller, D. A. (1992), *Bringing out Roland Barthes*, Berkeley: University of California Press.

Miller, J. Hillis (1998), *Reading Narrative*, Norman: University of Oklahoma Press.

Miller, J. Hillis (2002), *On Literature*, London; New York: Routledge.

Miller, Nancy K. (1981), 'Emphasis Added: Plots and Plausibilities in Women's Fiction', *Publications of the Modern Language Association of America* 96: 36–48.

Mittell, Jason (2015), *Complex TV: The Poetics of Contemporary Television Storytelling*, New York: New York University Press.

Morales, Helen (2004), *Vision and Narrative in Achilles Tatius' Leucippe and Clitophon*, Cambridge: Cambridge University Press.

Morgan, K. (2004), 'Plato', in Irene de Jong, René Nünlist, and Angus Bowie (eds.), *Narrators, Narratees, and Narratives in Ancient Greek Literature*, Leiden: Brill, pp. 357–76.

Morrison, Andrew D. (2007), *The Narrator in Archaic Greek and Hellenistic Poetry*, Cambridge: Cambridge University Press.

Morson, Gary Saul (1994), *Narrative and Freedom: The Shadows of Time*, New Haven; London: Yale University Press.

Morson, Gary Saul (1998), 'Sideshadowing and Tempics', *New Literary History* 29.4: 599–624.

Morson, Gary Saul (1999), 'Essential Narrative: Tempics and the Return of Process', in David Herman (ed.), *Narratologies*, Ohio: Ohio State University Press, pp. 277–314.

Mountford, J. F. and J. T. Schultz (eds.) (1930), *Index rerum et nominum in scholiis Servii et Aelii Donati tractatorum*, New York: Cornell University.

Müller, Günther (1968), 'Erzählzeit und erzählte Zeit', in *Morphologische Poetik: Gesammelte Aufsätze*, Darmstadt: WBG, pp. 269–86.

Mulvey, Laura (1975), 'Visual Pleasure and Narrative Cinema', *Screen* 16.3: 6–18.

Murgia, Charles E. (ed.) (2004), *Prolegomena to Servius, 5: The Manuscripts*, Berkeley: University of California Press.

Nagy, Gregory (2011), 'Homeric Scholia', in Ian Morris and Barry Powell (eds.), *A New Companion to Homer*, Leiden; New York: Brill, pp. 101–22.

Nash, Katherine (2014), *Feminist Narrative Ethics: Tacit Persuasion in Modernist Form*, Columbus: Ohio State University Press.

Niederhoff, Burkhard (2014), 'Perspective—Point of View', in Peter Hühn et al. (eds.), *Handbook of Narratology*, Berlin: De Gruyter, pp. 692–705.

Nielsen, Henrik Skov (2011), 'Unnatural Narratology, Impersonal Voices, Real Authors, and Non-Communicative Narration', in Jan Alber and Rüdiger Heinze (eds.), *Unnatural Narratives—Unnatural Narratology*, Berlin; Boston: De Gruyter, pp. 71–88.

Nikolopoulos, Anastasios D. (2004), *Ovidius Polytropos: Metanarrative in Ovid's Metamorphoses*, Zurich; New York: Georg Olms.

Novosadskiy, N. I. (ed.) (1927), *Aristotel: Poetika*, Leningrad: Academia.

Nünlist, René (2003), 'The Homeric Scholia on Focalization', *Mnemosyne* 56.1: 61–71.

Nünlist, René (2009a), 'Narratological Concepts in Greek Scholia', in Jonas Grethlein and Antonio Rengakos (eds.), *Narratology and Interpretation: The Content of Narrative Form in Ancient Literature*, Berlin: De Gruyter, pp. 63–83.

Nünlist, René (2009b), *The Ancient Critic at Work: Terms and Concepts of Literary Criticism in Greek Scholia*, Cambridge: Cambridge University Press.

Nünning, Ansgar (2003), 'Narratology or Narratologies?', in T. Kindt and H.-H. Müller (eds.), *What Is Narratology? Questions and Answers Regarding the Status of a Theory*, Berlin: De Gruyter, pp. 239–75.

Nünning, Ansgar (2005), 'Reliability', in David Herman, Manfred Jahn, and Marie-Laure Ryan (eds.), *Routledge Encyclopedia of Narrative Theory*, London: Routledge, pp. 495–7.

Nünning, Ansgar and Vera Nünning (2002), 'Von der strukturalistischen Narratologie zur "postklassischen" Erzähltheorie: Ein Überblick über neue Ansätze und Entwicklungstendenzen', in Ansgar Nünning and Vera Nünning (eds.), *Neue Ansätze in der Erzähltheorie*, Trier: WVT, pp. 1–33.

Obbink, Dirk (ed.) (1995), *Philodemus and Poetry: Poetic Theory and Practice in Lucretius, Philodemus and Horace*, Oxford: Oxford University Press.

Olson, Elder (1951), 'The Poetic Method of Aristotle: Its Powers and Limitations', in *English Institute Essays*, New York: Columbia University Press, pp. 70–94.

Olson, Elder (1965), *Aristotle's Poetics and English Literature*, Chicago: University of Chicago Press.

Onega, Susana and José Angel García Landa (eds.) (1996), *Narratology: An Introduction*, London: Longman.

O'Neill, Patrick (2005), 'Narrative Structure', in David Herman, Manfred Jahn, and Marie-Laure Ryan (eds.) *Routledge Encyclopedia of Narrative Theory*, London: Routledge, pp. 366–70.

Ooms, Stephen and Casper C. De Jonge (2013), 'The Semantics of ΕΝΑΓΩΝΙΟΣ in Greek Literary Criticism', *Classical Philology* 108: 95–110.

Pariker, K. Ayyanda (2003), *Indian Narratology*, New York: Sterling Publishing.

Partenie, C. (ed.) (2009), *Plato's Myths*, Cambridge: Cambridge University Press.

Pascal, Roy (1977), *The Dual Voice: Free Indirect Speech and its Functioning in the Nineteenth-Century European Novel*, Manchester: Manchester University Press.

Pausch, Dennis (2011), *Livius und der Leser: Narrative Strukturen in ab urbe condita*, Munich: C. H. Beck.

Peirce, C. S. (1977), *Semiotics and Significs*, Bloomington: Indiana University Press.

Peirce, C. S. (1998), *The Essential Peirce*, Vol. 2. Peirce Edition Project, Bloomington: Indiana University Press.

Pelling, Christopher (2009), 'Seeing through Caesar's Eyes: Focalisation and Interpretation', in Jonas Grethlein and Antonio Rengakos (eds.), *Narratology and Interpretation: The Content of Narrative Form in Ancient Literature*, Berlin: De Gruyter, pp. 507–26.

Petrovsky, Mikhail (1925), 'Morfologiya pushkinskogo "Vystrela"', in V. Ya. Bryusov (ed.), *Problemy poetiki*, Moscow: Zemlia i Fabrika, pp. 173–204.

Petrovsky, Mikhail (1987), 'Morphology in the Novella', in Philip Franz and Ray Parrott (eds.), *Essays in Poetics* 12.2: 22–50.

Petterson, Bo (2012), 'Beyond Anti-Mimetic Models: A Critique of Unnatural Narratology', in S. Isomaa et al. (eds.), *Rethinking Mimesis: Concepts and Practices of Literary Representation*, Cambridge: Cambridge Scholars Publishing, pp. 73–92.

Phelan, James (1989a), *Reading Narrative*, Columbus: Ohio State University Press.

Phelan, James (1989b), *Reading People, Reading Plots*, Chicago: University of Chicago Press.

Phelan, James (1996), *Narrative as Rhetoric*, Columbus: Ohio State University Press.

Phelan, James (2005), *Living to Tell about It*, Ithaca: Cornell University Press.

Phelan, James (2007a), *Experiencing Fiction: Judgments, Progressions, and the Rhetorical Theory of Narrative*, Columbus: Ohio State University Press.

Phelan, James (2007b), 'Rhetoric/Ethics', in David Herman (ed.), *The Cambridge Companion to Narrative*, Cambridge: Cambridge University Press, pp. 203–16.

Phelan, James (2014), 'Ethics', in Peter Hühn et al. (eds.), *Handbook of Narratology*, Berlin: De Gruyter, pp. 531–46.

Phelan, James (2015), 'The Chicago School', in Marina Grishakova and Silvi Salupere (eds.), *Theoretical Schools and Circles in the Twentieth-Century Humanities*, New York; London: Routledge, pp. 133–51.

Phelan, James (2017), *Somebody Telling Somebody Else: A Rhetorical Poetics of Narrative*, Columbus: Ohio State University Press.

Phelan, James and David H. Richter (2010), 'The Literary Theoretical Contribution of Ralph W. Rader', *Narrative* 18.1: 73–90.

Phelan, James and Peter Rabinowitz (eds.) (1994), *Understanding Narrative*, Columbus: Ohio State University Press.

Phelan, James and Peter Rabinowitz (eds.) (2005), *A Companion to Narrative Theory*, Malden: Blackwell.

Phelan, James and Peter Rabinowitz (2012), 'Narrative as Rhetoric', in D. Herman et al. (eds.),, *Narrative Theory: Core Concepts and Critical Debates*, Columbus: Ohio State University Press, pp. 3–8.

Phelan, James and David H. Richter (2011), 'Introduction', in Ralph Rader, *Fact, Fiction, and Form: Selected Essays*, edited by James Phelan and David H. Richter, Columbus: Ohio State University Press, pp. 1–30.

Pier, John (2003), 'On the Semiotic Parameters of Narrative: A Critique of Story and Discourse', in T. Kindt and H.-H. Müller (eds.), *What Is Narratology? Questions and Answers Regarding the Status of a Theory*, Berlin: De Gruyter, pp. 73–97.

Pier, John (2009), 'Diegesis', in T. A. Sebeok et al. (eds.), *Encyclopedic Dictionary of Semiotics*, Vol. 1, Berlin: De Gruyter, pp. 217–19.

Pirlet, Caroline (2011), 'Toward a Hybrid Approach to the Unnatural', in Jan Alber et al. (eds.), *Unnatural Narratives—Unnatural Narratology*, Berlin: De Gruyter, pp. 104–24.

Porter, James (1995), 'Content and Form in Philodemus', in Dirk Obbink et al. (eds.), *Philodemus and Poetry: Poetic Theory and Practice in Lucretius, Philodemus and Horace*, Oxford: Oxford University Press, pp. 97–147.

Poulheria, Kyriakou (1995), *Aristotle's Poetics: Its Theoretical Foundations and Its Reception in Hellenistic Literary Theory*, Columbus: Ohio State University.

Poulheria, Kyriakou (1997), *Aristotle's Poetics and Stoic Literary Theory*, Cologne: Universitäts und Stadtbibliothek Köln.

Pratt, Mary Louise (1977), *Toward a Speech Act Theory of Literature*, Bloomington: Indiana University Press.

Prince, Gerald (2003), *A Dictionary of Narratology*, Lincoln: University of Nebraska Press.

Prince, Gerald (1995), 'Narratology', in R. Selden (ed.), *The Cambridge History of Literary Criticism*, Vol. 7: *From Formalism to Poststructuralism*, Cambridge: Cambridge University Press, pp. 110–30.

Prince, Gerald (2008), 'Classical and/or Postclassical Narratology', *L'Esprit Créateur* 482: 115–23.

Prince, Gerald (2014), 'Reader', in Peter Hühn et al. (eds.), *Handbook of Narratology*, Berlin: De Gruyter, pp. 743–55.

Propp, Vladimir (1968), *Morphology of the Folktale*, Austin: University of Texas Press.

Propp, Vladimir (1984), *Theory and History of Folklore*, Minneapolis: University of Minnesota Press.

Pyrhönen, H. (2007), 'Genre', in David Herman (ed.), *The Cambridge Companion to Narrative*, Cambridge: Cambridge University Press, pp. 109–24.

Quint, David (1993), *Epic and Empire: Politics and Generic Form from Virgil to Milton*, Princeton: Princeton University Press.

Rabel, Robert J. (2007), *Plot and Point of View in the Iliad*, Michigan: University of Michigan Press.

Rabinowitz, Peter (1987), *Before Reading*, Ithaca: Cornell University Press.

Rabinowitz, Peter (2005), 'Audience', in David Herman, Manfred Jahn, and Marie-Laure Ryan (eds.), *Routledge Encyclopedia of Narrative Theory*, London: Routledge, pp. 29–31.

Rader, Ralph (1999), 'Tom Jones: The Form in History', in David. H. Richter (ed.), *Ideology and Form in Eighteenth-Century Literature*, Lubbock: Texas Tech University Press, pp. 47–74.

Rader, Ralph (2011), *Fact, Fiction, and Form: Selected Essays*, edited by James Phelan and David H. Richter, Columbus: Ohio State University Press.

Rajnath, A. (1996), 'Russian Formalism and its Relevance', *Journal of Literary Criticism* 8: 2–34.

Reed, Joseph D. (2009), *Virgil's Gaze: Nation and Poetry in the Aeneid*, Princeton: Princeton University Press.

Rees, B. R. (1981), 'Aristotle for the Structuralist', *Classical Review* 31: 178–9.

Reformatsky, Alexander (1973), 'An Essay on the Analysis of the Composition of the Novella', in Stephen Bann and J. E. Bowlt (eds.), *Russian Formalism: A Collection of Articles and Texts in Translation*, New York: Barnes & Noble, pp. 85–101.

Richardson, Brian (2002), 'Beyond Story and Discourse: Narrative Time in Postmodern and Nonmimetic Fiction', in Brian Richardson (ed.), *Narrative Dynamics: Essays on Time, Plot, Closure, and Frames*, Columbus: Ohio State University Press, pp. 47–63.

Richardson, Brian (2012), 'Unnatural Narratology: Basic Concepts and Recent Work', *DIEGESIS. Interdisziplinäres E-Journal für Erzählforschung/Interdisciplinary E-Journal for Narrative Research* 1.1: 95–103.

Richardson, Brian (2015), *Unnatural Narrative: Theory, History, and Practice*, Columbus: Ohio State University Press.

Richardson, N. J. (1980), 'Literary Criticism in the Exegetical Scholia to the *Iliad*: A Sketch', *Classical Quarterly* 30.2: 265–87.

Richardson, Scott (1990), *The Homeric Narrator*, Nashville: Vanderbilt University Press.

Richter, David (1974), *Fable's End*, Chicago: University of Chicago Press.

Richter, David (1982), 'The Second Flight of the Phoenix: Neo-Aristotelianism since Crane', *The Eighteenth Century: Theory and Interpretation* 23.1: 27–48.

Richter, David (1996), *The Progress of Romance*, Columbus: Ohio State University Press.

Richter, David (ed.) (1999), *Ideology and Form in Eighteenth-Century Literature*, Lubbock: Texas Tech University Press.

Richter, David (2005), 'The Chicago School', in David Herman, Manfred Jahn, and Marie-Laure Ryan (eds.), *Routledge Encyclopedia of Narrative Theory*, London: Routledge. pp. 57–9.

Ricoeur, Paul (1978), *The Rule of Metaphor: Multi-Disciplinary Studies of the Creation of Meaning in Language*, London: Routledge and Kegan Paul.

Ricoeur, Paul (1982), 'Mimesis and Representation', *Annals of Scholarship* 2.2: 15–32.

Ricoeur, Paul (1984–8), *Time and Narrative*, Vols. 1–3, Chicago: University of Chicago Press.

Ridgeway, W. (1912), 'Three Notes on the *Poetics* of Aristotle', *Classical Quarterly* 6: 235–45.

Rimmon-Kenan, Shlomith (1983), *Narrative Fiction: Contemporary Poetics*, London: Methuen.

Rood, Tim (1998), *Thucydides: Narrative and Explanation*, Oxford: Clarendon Press.

Roof, Judith (1996), *Come as You Are: Sexuality and Narrative*, New York: Columbia University Press.

Rorty, Amélie Oksenberg (ed.) (1996), *Essays on Aristotle's Rhetoric*, Berkeley: University of California Press.

Rorty, Richard (1980), *Philosophy and the Mirror of Nature*, Princeton: Princeton University Press.

Rosati, G. (1979), 'Punto di vista narrativo e antichi esegeti di Virgilio', *Annali della Scuola Normale Superione di Pisa, Classe di Lettere e Filosofia*, pp. 539–62.

Rosati, G. (2002),'Narrative Techniques and Narrative Structures in the *Metamorphoses*', in Barbara Boyd (ed.), *Brill's Companion to Ovid*, Leiden: Brill, pp. 271–304.

Rose, V. (ed.) (1886), *Aristotelis qui ferebantur librorum fragmenta*, Leipzig: Teubner.

Rostagni, A. (ed.) (1930), *L'Arte Poetica di Orazio*, Turin: Chiantore

Rostagni, A. (ed.) (1934), *La Poetica di Aristotele*, Turin: Chiantore.

Rostagni, A. (ed.) (1955), *Scritti Minori I: Aesthetica*, Turin: Erasmo.

Rudd, Niall (ed.) (1989), *Horace, Epistles, Book II; and Epistle to the Pisones (Ars Poetica)*, Cambridge: Cambridge University Press.

Ruelle, Charles-Émile (ed.) (1922), *Aristote, Poétique et Rhétorique*, Paris: Garnier Frères.

Russell, D. A. (ed.) (1964), *Longinus, On the Sublime*, Oxford: Clarendon Press.

Russell, D. A. (1973), '*Ars poetica*', in C. D. N. Costa (ed.), *Horace*, London: Routledge and Kegan Paul, pp. 113–34.

Russell, D. A. (1981), *Criticism in Antiquity*, London: Duckworth.

Ryan, Marie-Laure (1991), *Possible Worlds, Artificial Intelligence, and Narrative Theory*, Bloomington: Indiana University Press.

Ryan, Marie-Laure (1992), 'The Modes of Narrativity and Their Visual Metaphors', *Style* 26: 368–87.

Ryan, Marie-Laure (1999), 'Cyberage Narratology: Computers, Metaphor, and Narrative', in David Herman (ed.), *Narratologies*, Ohio: Ohio State University Press, pp. 113–41.

Ryan, Marie-Laure (2001), *Narrative as Virtual Reality: Immersion and Interactivity in Literature and Electronic Media*, Baltimore: Johns Hopkins University Press.

Ryan, Marie-Laure (2003), 'Cognitive Maps and the Construction of Narrative Space', in David Herman (ed.), *Narrative Theory and the Cognitive Sciences*, Stanford: CLSI, pp. 214–42.

Sacks, Sheldon (1964), *Fiction and the Shape of Belief*, Berkeley: University of California Press.

Sanford, Anthony and Catherine Emmott (2012), *Mind, Brain and Narrative*, Cambridge: Cambridge University Press.

Schaeffer, Jean-Marie and Ioana Vultur (2005), 'Mimesis', in David Herman, Manfred Jahn and Marie-Laure Ryan (eds.), *Routledge Encyclopedia of Narrative Theory*, London: Routledge, pp. 309–10.

Scheffel, Michael (2014), 'Narrative Constitution', in Peter Hühn et al. (eds.), *Handbook of Narratology*, Berlin: De Gruyter, pp. 507–20.

Schironi, Francesca (2009), 'Theory into Practice: Aristotelian Principles in Aristarchean Philology', *Classical Philology* 104.3: 279–316.

Schissel von Fleschenberg, Otmar (1910), *Novellenkomposition in E. T. A. Hoffmann Elixieren des Teufels*, Frankfurt am Main: Deutscher Klassiker Verlag.

Schmid, Wolf (ed.) (2009a), *Russische Proto-narratologie: Texte in kommentierten Übersetzungen*, Berlin: De Gruyter.

Schmid, Wolf (ed.) (2009b), *Slavische erzähltheorie: Russische und tschechische Ansätze*, Berlin; Boston: De Gruyter.

Schmid, Wolf (2010), *Narratology: An Introduction*, Berlin: De Gruyter.

Schmitz, Thomas (2007), *Modern Literary Theory and Ancient Texts: An Introduction*, Malden: Blackwell Publishing.

Schneider, Ralf (2005), 'Reader-Response Theory', in David Herman, Manfred Jahn, and Marie-Laure Ryan (eds.), *Routledge Encyclopedia of Narrative Theory*, London: Routledge, pp. 484–86.

Schofield, Malcolm (1991), 'Explanatory Projects in *Physics* 2.3 and 7', *Oxford Studies in Ancient Philosophy (Supplementary Volume)* 9: 29–40.

Scholes, Robert (1975), 'Preface', in T. Todorov, *The Fantastic*, Cleveland: Press of Case Western Reserve University.

Scholes, Robert (1979), *Fabulation and Metafiction*, Urbana: University of Illinois Press.

Scholes, Robert, James Phelan, and Robert Kellogg (2006), *The Nature of Narrative: Revised and Expanded*, New York; Oxford: Oxford University Press.

Schultz, Anne-Marie (2013), *Plato's Socrates as Narrator: A Philosophical Muse*, Plymouth: Lexington Books.

Schwindt, Jürgen Paul (2014), 'Ordo and Insanity: On the Pathogenesis of Horace's *Ars poetica*', *Materiali e discussioni* 72: 55–70.

Scodel, Ruth (2008), 'Zielinski's Law Reconsidered', in *Transactions of the American Philological Association* 138.1: 107–25.

Sedley, David (2014), 'Horace's Socraticae chartae (*Ars poetica* 295–322)', *Materiali e discussioni* 72: 97–120.

Shen, Dan (2014), *Style and Rhetoric of Short Narrative Fiction: Covert Progressions behind Overt Plots*, New York: Routledge.

Shklovsky, Victor (1965a), 'Art as a Technique', in L. T. Lemon and M. J. Reis (eds.), *Russian Formalist Criticism*, Lincoln: University of Nebraska Press, pp. 3–24.

Shklovsky, Victor (1965b), 'Sterne's Tristram Shandy: Stylistic Commentary', in L. T. Lemon and M. J. Reis (eds.), *Russian Formalist Criticism*, Lincoln: University of Nebraska Press, pp. 25–57.

Shklovsky, Victor (1990), *Theory of Prose*, Elmwood Park: Dalkey Archive Press.

Shklovsky, Victor (2002), *Third Factory*, Ann Arbor: Ardis.

Showalter, Elaine (1977), *A Literature of Their Own: British Women Novelists from Brontë to Lessing*, Princeton: Princeton University Press.

Showalter, Elaine (1985), *The New Feminist Criticism*, New York: Pantheon.

Slings, S. (ed.) (2003), *Platonis Republicam*, Oxford: Clarendon Press.

Smith, Barbara Herrnstein (1980), 'Narrative Versions, Narrative Theories', *Critical Inquiry* 71: 213–36.

Smith, Barbara Herrnstein (1981), 'Narrative Versions, Narrative Theories', in W. J. T. Mitchell (ed.), *On Narrative*, Chicago: University of Chicago Press, pp. 209–32.

Smith, R. Alden (1997), *Poetic Allusion and Poetic Embrace in Ovid and Virgil*, Ann Arbor: University of Michigan Press.

Society of Vertebrate Paleontology (2014), 'Prequel Outshines the Original: Exceptional Fossils of 160-Million-Year-Old Doahugou Biota', *Science Daily*, 4 March. Retrieved 4 May 2017 from www.sciencedaily.com/releases/2014/03/140304141728.htm.

Souriau, Étienne (1951), 'La structure de l'univers filmique et le vocabulaire de la filmologie', *Revue international de Filmologie* 7–8: 231–40.

Spentzou, Efrossini and Don Fowler (eds.) (2002), *Cultivating the Muse: Struggles for Power and Inspiration in Classical Literature*, Oxford: Oxford University Press.

Stanzel, F. (1955), *Narrative Situations in the Novel*, Bloomington: Indiana University Press.

Stanzel, F. (1984), *A Theory of Narrative*, Cambridge: Cambridge University Press.

Steiner, P. (2014), *Russian Formalism*, Ithaca: Cornell University Press.

Sternberg, Meir (1973), 'Elements of Tragedy and the Concept of Plot in Tragedy: On the Methodology of Constituting a Generic Whole', *Hasifrut* 4: 23–69.

Sternberg, Meir (1978), *Expositional Modes and Temporal Ordering in Fiction*, Baltimore: Johns Hopkins University Press.

Sternberg, Meir (1982), 'Proteus in Quotation-Land: Mimesis and the Forms of Reported Discourse', *Poetics Today* 3: 107–56.

Sterne, L. (1761), *The Life and Opinions of Tristram Shandy, Gentleman*, Champaign: Project Gutenberg.

Stewart, G. (2009), *Novel Violence*, Chicago: University of Chicago Press.

Sturgess, P. (1989), 'A Logic of Narrativity', *New Literary History* 20.3: 736–83.

Thilo, G. and H. Hagen (eds.) (2011), *In Vergilii carmina comentarii: Servii grammatici qui feruntur in Vergilii carmina commentarii*, Leipzig: Teubner.

Thomas, Richard F. (2001), *Virgil and the Augustan Reception*, Cambridge: Cambridge University Press.

Todorov, Tzvetan (1966), 'Les catégories du récit littéraire', *Communications* 8: 125–51.

Todorov, Tzvetan (1969), 'Structural Analysis of Narrative', *Novel* 3: 70–6.

Todorov, Tzvetan (1975), *The Fantastic*, Cleveland: Press of Case Western Reserve University.

Todorov, Tzvetan (1977), *The Poetics of Prose*, Ithaca: Cornell University Press.

Todorov, Tzvetan (1980), 'Introduction', in Dupont-Roc, Roselyne and Jean Lallot (eds.), *Aristote: La Poétique*, Paris: Seuil.

Todorov, Tzvetan (1981), *Introduction to Poetics*, Brighton: Harvester Press.

Tomashevsky, Boris (1965), 'Thematics', in L. T. Lemon and M. J. Reis (eds.), *Russian Formalist Criticism: Four Essays*, Lincoln: University of Nebraska Press, pp. 61–95.

Tomashevsky, Boris (1967), *Toeriya literatury: poetika*. Moscow: Gosizdat.

Tomashevsky, Boris (1978), 'Letter to Shklovsky of April 12, 1925', *Slavica Hierosolymitana* 3: 385–6.

Too, Yun Lee (1998), *The Idea of Ancient Literary Criticism*, Oxford: Clarendon Press.

Toolan, Michael J. (1988), *Narrative: A Critical Linguistic Introduction*, London; New York: Routledge.

Toporov, V. (1985), 'A Few Remarks on Propp's Morphology of the Folktale', in R. L. Jackson and S. Rudy (eds.), *Russian Formalism: A Retrospective Glance*, New Haven: Yale Center for International and Area Studies, pp. 252–71.

Trowbridge, Hoyt (1944), 'Aristotle and the "New Criticism"', *The Sewanee Review* 52.4: 537–55.

Tynyanov, Yury (1921), *Dostoevskii i Gogol*, Petrograd: Opoyaz.

Tynyanov, Yury (1981), 'On the Foundations of Cinema', in H. Eagle (ed.), *Russian Formalist Film Theory*, Ann Arbor: University of Michigan Press, pp. 81–100.

van Thiel, Helmut (ed.) (2000), *Scholia D in Iliadem*, Cologne: Universitäts und Stadtbibliothek Köln.

Veselovsky, A. N. (1876), *Belletristika u drevnykh grekov*, Moscow: Evropeisky vestnik.

Volek, Emil (1985), *Metaestructuralismo*, Madrid: Editorial Fundamentos.

von Contzen, Eva (2017), 'Unnatural Narratology and Premodern Narratives: Historicizing a form', *Journal of Literary Semantics* 46.1: 1–23.

Warhol, Robyn R. (1986), 'Toward a Theory of the Engaging Narrator: Earnest Interventions in Gaskell, Stowe, and Eliot', *Publications of the Modern Language Association of America* 101: 811–18.

Warhol, Robyn R. (1989), *Gendered Interventions: Narrative Discourse in the Victorian Novel*, New Brunswick: Rutgers University Press.

Warhol, Robyn R. (1999), 'Guilty Cravings: What Feminist Narratology Can Do for Cultural Studies', in David Herman (ed.), *Narratologies: New Perspectives on Narrative Analysis*, Columbus: Ohio State University Press, pp. 340–55.

Warhol, Robyn R. (2003), *Having a Good Cry: Effeminate Feelings and Pop-Culture Forms*, Columbus: Ohio State University Press.

Warhol, Robyn R. and Susan S. Lanser (2015), *Queer/Feminist Narrative Theory*, Columbus: Ohio State University Press.

Weinberg, Bernard (1961), *A History of Literary Criticism in the Italian Renaissance*, Vols. 1–2, Chicago: University of Chicago Press.

Westerink, L. G. and W. O'Neill (eds.) (2011), *Proclus' Commentary on the First Alcibiades*, Westbury: The Prometheus Trust.

Whalley, G., J. Baxter, and P. Atherton (eds.) (1997), *Aristotle's Poetics*, Montreal: McGill-Queen's University Press.

Wheeler, Stephen (1999), *A Discourse of Wonders*, Philadelphia: University of Pennsylvania Press.

Wheeler, Stephen (2000), *Narrative Dynamics in Ovid's Metamorphoses*, Tübingen: Narr.

Whitmarsh, Tim (2009), 'An I for an I: Reading Fictional Autobiography', in Anna Marmodoro and Jonathan Hill (eds.), *The Author's Voice in Classical and Late Antiquity*, Oxford: Oxford University Press, pp. 233–50.

Whitmarsh, Tim (2011), *Narrative and Identity in the Ancient Greek Novel: Returning Romance*, Cambridge: Cambridge University Press.

Whitmarsh, Tim (2013), 'Radical Cognition: Metalepsis in Classical Greek Drama', *Greece and Rome* 60.1: 4–16.

Williams, R. D. (1966–7), 'Servius, Commentator and Guide', *Proceedings of the Virgil Society* 6: 50–6.

Wimsatt, William K. and Cleanth Brooks (1957), *Literary Criticism: A Short History*, New York: Knopf.

Winkler, John J. (1985), *Auctor and Actor: A Narratological Reading of Apuleius's 'Golden Ass'*, Berkeley; Los Angeles: University of California Press.

Woodruff, P. (1992), 'Aristotle on Mimesis', in A. Rorty (ed.), *Essays on Aristotle's Poetics*, Princeton: Princeton University Press, pp. 73–95.

Wolf, Werner (2003), 'Narrative and Narrativity: A Narratological Reconceptualization and its Applicability to the Visual Arts', *Word & Image* 19: 180–97.

Wolf, Werner (2013), '"Unnatural" Metalepsis and Immersion: Necessarily Incompatible?', in Jan Alber, Henrik Skov Nielsen, and Brian Richardson (eds.), *A Poetics of Unnatural Narrative*, Columbus: Ohio State University Press, pp. 113–41.

Zetzel, James (1981), *Latin Textual Criticism in Antiquity*, New York: Arno Press.

Zielinsky, T. (1899–1901), 'Die Behandlung gleichzeitiger Ereignisse im antiken Epos', *Philologus Suppl.* 8: 405–49.

Zirminsky, Victor (1923), *Valerij Brjusov i nasledie Puškina: opyt sravnitel'no-stilističeskogo issledovanija*, Petrograd: El'zevir.

Zunshine, Lisa (2006), *Introduction to Cognitive Cultural Studies*, Baltimore: Johns Hopkins University Press.

■ INDEX